THE PRINCETON REVIEW

Cracking the GRE®

Paper & Pencil

THE PRINCETON REVIEW

Cracking the GRE®

Paper & Pencil

BY ADAM ROBINSON AND JOHN KATZMAN

1999 EDITION

RANDOM HOUSE, INC.
NEW YORK 1998
www.randomhouse.com

Princeton Review Publishing, L.L.C.
2315 Broadway
New York, NY 10024
E-mail: info@review.com

ISSN 1062-5534
ISBN 0-375-75161-0

GRE test directions are reprinted by permission of the Educational Testing Service, the copyright owner. However, the test questions and other testing information are provided in their entirety by The Princeton Review. No endorsement of this publication by Educational Testing Service should be inferred.
GRE is a registered trademark of Educational Testing Service.

Editor: Lesly Atlas
Production Editor: Amy Bryant
Designed by: Illeny Maaza
Illustrations by: The Production Department of The Princeton Review

Manufactured in the United States of America on partially recycled paper.

9 8 7 6 5 4 3 2 1

1999 Edition

ACKNOWLEDGMENTS

A successful GRE program is a collaborative effort. We'd especially like to thank our teachers John Sheehan, Mark Sawula, Jim Reynolds, Dave Schaller, Adam Frank, and Adam Landis for their suggestions and contributions.

We'd like to thank our agent, Julia Coopersmith, for her tireless help and editorial suggestions. To our editor Diane Reverand, our deep appreciation for her patience with our perfectionist delays and for her sponsorship of the entire project. And many thanks to Emily Bestler and Martha Schueneman—we realize authors aren't always easy to deal with.

Finally we'd like to thank all those who have taught us everything we know about taking tests—our students.

CONTENTS

Foreword

So you're thinking about graduate school, eh? Maybe you're still in college planning ahead, or maybe you've been out of school for a few years figuring now's a good time to return to get that advanced degree. Anyway, you're going to have to take the GRE, the "SAT" for graduate school.

A lot of people think that because the GRE is so similar to the SAT they don't need to do much preparation. After all, they took the SAT already. How different can the GRE be?

Very different.

While there are many similarities between the two tests, there are also many important differences. As you might have expected, the GRE verbal sections require more advanced vocabulary than the SAT verbal. But perhaps you didn't know that GRE math is actually easier than SAT math. Paradoxically, that makes the math harder! How long ago did you add two fractions, or use the Pythagorean theorem? Did you know that while the SAT penalizes errors, the GRE doesn't? And of course you know that the GRE has two logic sections. Or did you?

Don't kid yourself. While you are older and wiser than you were when you took the SAT, the test is correspondingly more difficult. And you're probably rusty; it's been a while since you had to fill in ovals with a No. 2 pencil.

How is The Princeton Review different from other GRE courses? Well, the bottom line is that Princeton Review students improve more than other students. Much more.

How do we do it? Some coaches require you to memorize dozens of math theorems and thousands of words. In short, they get you to learn every little fact that could possibly show up on the GRE, without providing any focus.

The Princeton Review, on the other hand, knows how busy you are. We realize that in a month or two there is simply no way you could master every word and every theorem and every game that could possibly show up on your GRE.

So instead we focus on the concepts that appear the most frequently on the GRE. This information is surprisingly limited. These key concepts can be mastered in a month or two.

And we go a step further. After teaching you the most important material, we teach you how to attack questions when you don't know all the information. For example, Princeton Review students know how to attack an analogy when they don't know all the words. Do you? Princeton Review students know how to attack a geometry question when they can't remember all of their theorems. Do you?

Reading this book is not enough. You'll have to practice our techniques on actual GREs. An indispensable companion to this book is *Practicing to Take the GRE*, published by the same folks who write the actual test, the Educational Testing Service (ETS). This book is available in some of the larger bookstores, or can be ordered directly from ETS. We'll give you order information in the Orientation chapter.

We use actual GREs in our course. It is very important that you practice our techniques on real GRE questions to convince yourself that they actually work.

When *Cracking the System: The SAT* first appeared in 1986, many people asked us when we'd be coming out with books on other tests and subjects. Since then we've published the book you are reading and dozens of other titles, including *Word Smart* and *Word Smart II* (vocabulary books that will help you prepare for the GRE, by the way), and guides to the GMAT, LSAT, MCAT, and ACT.

If you have any questions about our course, or about academic matters in general, give us a call at 1-800-REVIEW-6.

Good luck on your GRE!

John Katzman
President and Co-founder

PART I

Orientation

1
About the GRE Paper & Pencil

WHAT IS THE GRADUATE RECORD EXAMINATION?

The Graduate Record Examination (GRE) is a standardized, multiple-choice admissions test intended for applicants to graduate schools. This book is designed to prepare you for the paper and pencil version, not the computer adaptative version (CAT). The paper and pencil version is only offered twice a year, in April and November. The paper and pencil GRE is a three-and-a-half-hour "aptitude" test that is divided into seven sections, not necessarily in this order:

Start preparing to take the GRE early.

1. Two thirty-eight-question "verbal ability" (vocabulary and reading) sections

2. Two thirty-question "quantitative ability" (math) sections

3. Two twenty-five-question "analytical ability" (logic games and arguments) sections

4. One experimental section

Each of these sections lasts thirty minutes. You will receive separate verbal, quantitative, and analytical scores. The experimental section, which will look like a verbal, a quantitative, or an analytical section, won't count toward your score. It is used by the test's publisher to try out new GRE questions and to establish how difficult your GRE is in comparison with GREs given in the past.

The verbal sections of the GRE paper and pencil Test contain four types of questions:

1. Sentence completions

2. Analogies

3. Reading comprehension

4. Antonyms

The quantitative sections of the GRE paper and pencil Test contain three types of questions:

1. Quantitative comparisons

2. Discrete quantitatives (word problems)

3. Data interpretations (charts)

The analytical sections of the GRE paper and pencil Test contain two types of questions:

1. Analytical reasoning (games)

2. Logical reasoning (arguments)

Each of these question types will be dealt with in detail later in the book.

WHERE DOES THE GRE COME FROM?

Like most standardized tests in this country, the GRE is published by the Educational Testing Service (ETS), a big, tax-exempt private company in New Jersey. We'll tell you more about ETS in chapter 2. ETS publishes the GRE under the sponsorship of the Graduate Record Examinations Board, which is an organization affiliated with the Association of Graduate Schools and the Council of Graduate Schools in the United States.

HOW IS THE GRE SCORED?

Scores on the GRE paper and pencil Test are reported on a scale that runs from 200 to 800. For reasons known only to ETS, the scale for some subject tests runs from 200 to 990. You will receive only one score for each of the three sections of the General Test and for each Subject Test you take. Do nothing but fill out your name correctly and you will receive anywhere from 200 to 300 points, depending on the section or the subject. For every question you answer (or guess) correctly, you will receive about ten points. (Although virtually all GRE questions are worth ten points, the actual value ranges from zero to twenty points; the number of points is determined *not* by the difficulty of the question but by the number of other questions you have answered correctly.) GRE scores can rise or fall only by multiples of ten. The third digit in a GRE score is thus always a zero. You can't receive a score of 409 or 715 on the GRE.

Your score on each part of the GRE will first be calculated as a "raw score," which is simply the number of questions you answered correctly. (**There is no deduction for incorrect answers on the GRE General Test**. We'll tell you more about this very important fact later in the book.) Raw scores are then converted to the 200–800 scale, according to a formula that takes into account the relative difficulty of your test.

Your score report will also contain your "percentile score" for each section of the test. Your percentile score tells you (and graduate school admissions officers) what percentage of people did worse than you did on the test. If your scaled score on the test places you in the 70th percentile, you know that 70 percent of the people who took the test scored lower than you did. So cheer up!

WHAT IS THE PRINCETON REVIEW?

The Princeton Review is the nation's fastest-growing test-preparation service. We have branches in dozens of cities all across the country, and our list of locations is constantly expanding. We prepare more students for the SAT than any other coaching school, and our programs for the GRE, LSAT, MCAT, and GMAT are growing rapidly. The Princeton Review has the highest average score improvements in the country.

Our teaching methods for the GRE were developed through exhaustive analysis of all available GREs and careful research into the methods by which standardized tests are constructed. Our focus is on the basic concepts that will

Find out if the programs you are applying to require a Subject Test in addition to the General GRE.

The Princeton Review spends over a million dollars a year on research into cracking the GRE and standardized tests like it.

enable you to attack any problem, strip it down to its essential components, and solve it in as little time as possible. Our approach has been widely imitated, but no one else achieves our results.

A NOTE ABOUT SCORE IMPROVEMENTS

We have found in our courses that students' scores don't improve gradually; instead, they tend to go up in spurts, from one plateau to another. Our students typically achieve score gains of 100 points or more after mastering the initial concepts of the course. Their scores then level off, only to take another jump a few weeks later when more course material has been assimilated.

If you work steadily through this book, you, too, will feel yourself moving from plateau to plateau. But you will have to work. You won't have one of our teachers standing over you, reminding you to review what you have learned.

A WARNING

Many of our test-taking techniques at first seem to violate common sense. In order to take full advantage of our methods, you will have to trust them enough to make them automatic. **The best way to do this is to practice them on real GREs.**

By "real GREs," we *don't* mean the practice tests in coaching books. The questions on such tests often bear only a superficial resemblance to the questions actually used on the test. Even the questions in our book are not actual GRE questions, although we have designed our questions using the same methods as those used in designing real GREs. **The only source of real GREs is the publisher of the test. We strongly recommend, therefore, that you purchase at least the most recent edition of** *Practicing to Take the GRE General Test,* **which is published by the Educational Testing Service for the Graduate Record Examinations Board.** This book contains real GRE General Tests (minus their experimental sections) that were actually administered to test-takers. If you don't find it in your local bookstore, you can order it directly from ETS. To order, contact ETS at:

> Graduate Record Examinations
> Educational Testing Service
> Order Services Dept.
> CN 6785
> Princeton, NJ 08541-6785

If you're in a hurry, you can call the GRE publications office at (609) 771-7243, or visit their web site at http://www.gre.org.

WHAT ABOUT THE CAT?

For more than a decade, researchers at the ETS have discussed the use of computers to administer the GRE. ETS uses computers to score the exam, so why not use computers to administer them, too? That's the theory, anyway.

In 1991, ETS began offering a computerized GRE. This computer-based test (CBT) was exactly the same as the paper-and-pencil GRE except that it was given on a computer. Well, the CBT is no longer used, and in its place, ETS is offering a different computerized exam: the computer-adaptive GRE (also known as the CAT).

ETS has been phasing out the paper-based version of the GRE throughout the 1990s. It is now only offered twice a year, in April and November, whereas the CAT is offered most days. For more CAT information, check out *The Princeton Review Cracking the GRE CAT*.

Be aware that prepping for the paper and pencil GRE is not the same as prepping for the GRE CAT (and vice versa). The content of the tests is the same, but there are important differences you need to take into account. If you don't have one already, get a copy of the GRE Information and Registration bulletin, or visit the web site.

2
How to Think About the GRE Paper & Pencil

WHY DOES THE GRE SEEM SO FAMILIAR?

You've already taken the GRE paper and pencil General Test. You took it back in high school, when you took the SAT. The SAT and the GRE are published by the same company. Although there are important differences in levels of difficulty, questions on the two tests are very similar. In many cases, questions for the two tests are written by the same people.

Not all GRE question types are the same as SAT question types. For example, questions in the GRE's analytical sections are instead similar to question types used on the Law School Admission Test (LSAT).

We'll tell you much more about the differences and similarities between the GRE and the SAT and LSAT later in the book.

The reason for the 200–800 scale is that the College Board didn't want a scale that looked like the 0–100 scale used in schools.

WHADJAGET?

Because the GRE and the SAT are so much alike, your old SAT scores can give you some indication of how well you would do on the GRE if you took the test tomorrow, without any help from us. In fact, the correlation between SAT scores and GRE scores is so strong that graduate schools would make virtually the same admissions decisions if they used old SAT scores instead of new GRE scores.

That they don't do this is good news for you. It gives you a chance to push up your scores between now and the time you apply.

MORE ABOUT WHERE THE GRE COMES FROM

The publishers of the GRE, the Educational Testing Service (ETS), are the people who publish the SAT, the Graduate Management Admissions Test (GMAT), the Secondary School Admissions Test (SSAT), Advanced Placement tests (AP), the National Teacher Examination (NTE), the National Assessment of Educational Progress (NAEP), and licensing and certification exams in dozens of fields, including hairstyling, plumbing, and golf.

ETS uses Princeton, New Jersey, as its return address, implying a connection with the university. But ETS is actually located outside Princeton, in Lawrence Township. It is a private company, not a government agency. Although it pays no taxes, it does earn a lot of money from its testing monopoly.

You've probably taken many ETS tests in your life. Unless you're planning to become a teacher (in which case you'll have to take the NTE) or an investment banker (in which case you'll have to take the GMAT), the GRE may be the last ETS test you'll ever have to take.

WHAT DOES THE GRE MEASURE?

The GRE General Test used to be known as the GRE Aptitude Test. Changing the name was an effort by ETS to distance the GRE from the numerous controversies that have arisen concerning "aptitude" and "intelligence" testing. Even so, admissions officers tend to view GRE scores as measurements of raw mental power. They will use your GRE scores as an "objective" standard against which to judge your college grades. That is, if your grades are high and your scores are low, they'll believe your scores and refer to you as an "overachiever" (rather than an "undertester"). If your scores are below a certain level, an admissions officer may reject you before even looking at your grades.

> Despite what ETS says or admissions officers think, the GRE is less a measure of your intelligence than it is a measure of your ability to take ETS tests.

THIS IS *VERY* GOOD NEWS FOR YOU

Fortunately, your ability to take ETS tests can be improved dramatically in a matter of weeks. With proper instruction and sufficient practice, virtually all test-takers can raise their scores, often substantially. You don't need to make yourself smarter in order to do this. You just need to make yourself better at taking ETS tests.

| You CAN improve your scores.

ISN'T THE GRE COACHING-PROOF?

ETS has long claimed that its tests, including the GRE, are virtually impervious to special preparation. Indeed, this is supposed to be the chief attraction of such tests in the minds of admissions officers. However, this has been proven otherwise. The good news is that all ETS tests can be prepared for.

The first step in doing better on the GRE is developing the proper attitude about aptitude. Before you can raise your score, you must accept the idea that your so-called verbal, quantitative, and analytical abilities can be improved. These abilities are not innate.

You have no trouble accepting this in your ordinary classes. If a professor gives you a disappointing grade on a test, you probably tell yourself, "I need to study more," or "I need to pay more attention in class."

The same is true on the GRE. A low test score doesn't mean you're stupid; it just means you have to work harder at learning to take the test.

Keep in mind that dramatic improvements are possible. Some students actually raise their scores hundreds of points after brief, albeit rigorous, preparation.

YOU MUST LEARN TO THINK LIKE ETS

Despite what many people believe, the GRE isn't written by distinguished professors, renowned scholars, or graduate-school admissions officers. For the most part, it's written by ordinary ETS employees, sometimes with freelance help from local graduate students. You don't need to feel intimidated by these people. Indeed, once you learn to view the GRE in the proper light, you will begin to find examples in the test of sloppy writing and confused thinking.

As you become more familiar with the test, you will also develop a sense of what we call "the ETS mentality." This is a predictable kind of institutional thinking that influences nearly every part of nearly every ETS exam. By learning to recognize the ETS mentality, you will enable yourself to earn points even when you aren't certain why an answer is correct. You will do better on the test by learning to think like the people who wrote it.

The Only "Correct" Answer Is the One that Earns You Points

As is true on all ETS multiple-choice tests, the instructions on the GRE tell you to select the "best" answer to each question. ETS talks about "best" answers instead of "correct" answers to protect itself from the complaints of test-takers who might be tempted to quarrel with ETS's judgment or who realize that ETS often gives credit for answers that aren't entirely correct. Your job is not to find the correct answer, therefore, but rather to find the one answer for which ETS gives credit.

To remind you of this, we will speak in this book not of "correct" answers or of "best" answers but of "ETS's answers." ETS's answer to a question is the answer that is worth points.

Cracking the System

Our emphasis on earning points rather than on finding the "correct" answer may strike you as somewhat cynical, but it is a key to doing well on the GRE. Like all ETS multiple-choice tests, the GRE leaves you no room to make explanations or justifications for your responses. Your test will be graded by a machine that recognizes one kind of pencil mark. If the space you darken on your answer sheet is different from the one darkened by the question writers at ETS, you'll be out of luck.

We teach our students to do better on the GRE and other tests by teaching them to put aside their feelings about *real* education and to surrender themselves to the strange logic of standardized tests. "Cracking the system" is our term for getting inside the minds of the people who write the tests and who, in so doing, help determine where—or whether—you'll attend graduate school. Learning to crack the system puts you on an equal footing with people in a position to decide your educational fate.

Onward and Upward

In chapter 3, we'll teach you the basic principles behind our method for scoring higher on the GRE. Then, in chapter 4, we'll elaborate on these basic principles and teach you how an imaginary student named Joe Bloggs can help you push your GRE paper and pencil score out of sight.

3

Cracking the System: Basic Principles

TEST YOUR ETHICS

Shortly before he took the GRE, a student we'll call Johnny X was approached by a stranger who offered to give him a document containing ETS's answer to every single question on the test he was about to take. Johnny X accepted the document.

What would you have done? Would you have told the proctor what had happened? Or would you have taken the document?

Of course you would have taken it. The stranger *was* the proctor and the document was the GRE test booklet. As is true of every multiple-choice test in the world, the answer to every single GRE question is printed right there beneath the question in the test booklet. All you have to do is learn to recognize it.

You have all the answers at your fingertips: in your test booklet.

WHAT'S PI?

Recognizing the answer to a question is vastly simpler than trying to come up with the answer off the top of your head. Here are two math questions that will demonstrate what we mean. Try them both, and see which one is easier to answer:

1. Calculate π to 10 decimal places and write your answer here: _____

2. π calculated to 10 decimal places is
   (A) 5.1828765678
   (B) 4.9387222567
   (C) 3.1415926535
   (D) 2.1760023644
   (E) 1.2099837657

Even if you're a math whiz, you probably found the second question easier than the first. The correct answer to both questions is 3.1415926535, but to answer the first question correctly you would have needed to have all eleven digits memorized and on the tip of your tongue. (Of course, you could also get the correct answer to question 1 by looking ahead to question 2.) All you needed to know to answer the second question correctly, in contrast, was that π is about 3.

THE AMAZING POWER OF POE— PROCESS OF ELIMINATION

In tackling the second question above, you didn't need to know the exact answer ahead of time in order to find it among the choices. Instead, you found it by examining the five possible answers and eliminating the four that you knew to be incorrect. In other words, you used the Process of Elimination.

The Process of Elimination is an extremely powerful tool on the GRE. We refer to it so often in our courses that we call it simply "POE."

The Importance of Wrong Answers

By using POE, you will be able to improve your score on the GRE by looking for *wrong* answers instead of for *right* ones on difficult questions. Why would anyone want to look for wrong answers on a test? Simple. On hard questions, wrong answers are usually easier to find. And once you've found the wrong ones, picking the right one can be a piece of cake.

Incorrect choices on standardized multiple-choice tests are known in the testing industry as "distractors." Their purpose is to distract less knowledgeable students away from correct choices on questions they don't understand. This keeps them from earning points accidentally, by picking the right answer for the wrong reasons.

This simple fact can be an enormous help to you. By learning to recognize these distractors, you can greatly improve your score.

Not surprisingly, some distractors are harder to spot than others. Some are quite obvious, once you know what to look for. By first eliminating the *most obviously incorrect* choices on difficult questions, you can more effectively focus your energies on the smaller number of truly tempting choices.

Improving Your Odds *Indirectly*

Every time you are able to eliminate an incorrect choice on a GRE question, you improve your odds of finding ETS's answer. The more incorrect choices you eliminate, the better your odds.

For this reason, most of our test-taking strategies are aimed at helping you to arrive at ETS's answer *indirectly*. Doing this will make you much more successful at avoiding the traps laid in your path by the people who write the questions. This is because most of the traps are designed to catch unwary test takers who approach the problems *directly*.

Approaching a problem indirectly is like sneaking into a house through the back door. If you sneak in through the back door, you won't be drenched by the water bucket perched on top of the front door.

POE and Guessing

On questions where POE and the techniques based on it don't lead you all the way to ETS's answer, POE will help you substantially improve your chances of earning points by guessing.

GUESS, GUESS, GUESS!

If you guessed blindly on a five-choice GRE problem, you would have one chance in five of picking ETS's answer. Eliminate one incorrect choice, and your chances improve to one in four. Eliminate three, and you have a fifty-fifty chance of earning points by guessing.

But Isn't Guessing Discouraged on the GRE?

No. Guessing is an absolute necessity on the GRE. There is no "guessing penalty" on the test. Your score will be based solely on the number of questions you answer correctly, with no deduction or penalty for incorrect answers. *This wasn't true when you took the SAT, but it's true on the GRE.*

Guessing on standardized tests is an issue that produces an enormous amount of confusion among test-takers. Should you or shouldn't you? As it happens, guessing *always* works to the advantage of savvy test-takers, even on tests that, like the SAT, deduct points for incorrect answers.

With the GRE, there is no confusion. If you don't mark a choice for *every* question, you will earn fewer points than you should. This is so important that we will state it in the form of a rule:

> You should mark a choice for every question on the GRE, even if you have to mark some of your choices blindly in the final seconds of the testing period.

WHAT GUESSING CAN DO FOR YOUR SCORE

To see how important guessing can be, look at the case of a hypothetical student working on the verbal sections of his GRE.

The two thirty-eight-question sections that make up a student's GRE verbal score are timed separately, and you can't move between them. For the sake of this example, though, we'll lump them together.

Let's assume, then, that our student is able to attempt fifty-six of the seventy-six questions and that he selects ETS's answer on forty-two of these. If he stops right now, his forty-two correct choices will translate into a scaled score of about 470, which is roughly the national average.

But let's suppose that instead of leaving twenty questions blank, our hypothetical student guesses blindly on them. The laws of probability say that on average he'll guess correctly on four of the twenty questions. These four additional correct choices will raise his score from 470 to 510, or from the 50th percentile to the 60th.

Now let's assume further that instead of guessing blindly, our student is able to eliminate one obviously incorrect choice from each of the twenty questions before making his guess. We can now expect him to make five correct guesses, raising his scaled score to 520. If he is able to eliminate two obviously incorrect choices on each question—which is quite possible—his expected score rises again to about 540, or close to the 70th percentile.

Intelligent guessing, in other words, can transform a run-of-the-mill student into one who is far above average.

HOW TO MAKE FOUR MISTAKES AND STILL EARN A PERFECT SCORE

You must be absolutely certain to mark an answer for every question on the test. **But you probably should not *read* every question on the test.** Because of the way the GRE is scored, it is sometimes possible to miss as many as four questions and still earn a perfect score of 800. **Most students would *score higher* if they saved time by ignoring some questions on the test. And we really mean ignoring—that is, spending no time whatsoever on the questions, except the time it takes to mark an answer.**

We'll tell you more about which questions to consider skipping as we go along in the book.

Don't Listen to What They Tell You

You should tackle the GRE the same way you put together your new stereo: without reading the instructions. Students who read the instructions during the test are wasting very, very valuable time and costing themselves points.

Memorize the instructions beforehand. Don't even glance at them when you take the test.

You Take the Test, Don't Let the Test Take You!

There's no rule that says that you always have to start with the first question in each section and do the questions in numerical order. You can use your time for the test section more efficiently by jumping around a bit within the section. We'll give you explicit strategies for each of the verbal, math, and analytical sections.

Do the questions in the order you choose, not the order ETS chooses for you.

Using Your Test Booklet

Many test-takers are reluctant to write in their test booklets. Such nice fresh paper—why mess it up?

But you *must* mess up your test booklet. By the end of the exam period, your booklet should be filled with pencil marks. Your quantitative and analytical sections should be covered with scratch work and diagrams. Your verbal sections should be filled with notes and cross-outs.

Students who write in their test booklets sometimes feel ambivalent about doing it. So they make the tiniest, faintest pencil marks they can. When they're finished, they erase what they have written.

This is ridiculous.

Your Test Booklet Is Just Going to Be Thrown Away

ETS will hang on to your booklet for a while in case anyone accuses you of using it to send messages to the person sitting next to you. After that, your booklet will be thrown away. There is no GRE score for "booklet neatness." No one will know that you couldn't figure out what 2 + 2 equaled without writing it down. You won't get extra credit for solving problems in your head.

The Importance of Being a Slob

Imagine that you're halfway through the math section on a standardized test. Suddenly, the proctor announces, "Five more minutes!" You look at the sea of questions you haven't answered yet, and you lose your train of thought. You jump ahead to the next question. First one choice seems correct. Then another. You start again. Then you panic and jump ahead to another question without marking a choice.

This is five-minute meltdown.

A student who panics on a test can't remember which choices he has eliminated. He runs through the same choices over and over again, making the same calculations and weighing the same considerations. His mind is spinning. He desperately selects choices that two seconds earlier he had decided were incorrect. Before he knows it, the exam period is over and the entire five minutes was wasted.

One of the best ways to prevent five-minute meltdown is to leave your mind uncluttered by doing as much of your work as possible in your test booklet. If you use your test booklet properly, you'll be much less likely to spin out of control in the final minutes of the test. You'll also work much more efficiently in the early part of the exam, before you can think of nothing but the clock.

A FEW RULES

Here are some simple rules that you should follow not only when you take the GRE but also as you work through this book and when you practice on published GREs:

1. When you eliminate an incorrect choice on a question, cross it out in your test booklet.

2. If you are uncertain about a choice, don't eliminate that choice, try to eliminate other choices.

3. When you believe you have found ETS's answer on a question, circle it and write its letter clearly in the margin beside the question. Transfer your answers in blocks at the end of each subsection or the end of each page.

WHY YOU SHOULD CROSS OUT INCORRECT CHOICES

By crossing out a clearly incorrect choice, you permanently eliminate it from consideration. If you don't cross it out, you'll keep reading and rereading it as you make your deliberations. Crossing out incorrect choices can make it significantly easier to find ETS's answer, because there will be fewer places where it can hide. Sometimes, crossing out one or two incorrect choices will make ETS's answer seem to leap right off the page.

Always cross off wrong answer choices in your test booklet.

WHY YOU SHOULD MAKE GUESSES AS YOU GO ALONG INSTEAD OF LEAVING BLANKS TO FILL IN LATER

Often on the GRE you will feel that you are tantalizingly close to ETS's answer, but that you need more time to work on it than you can afford to spend. Many students in this situation will leave the answer space blank in the hope of coming back to work on the question later.

This is a bad idea.

When you've gone as far as you can go on a question, circle the entire question and *make your best guess then*, even if you plan to come back. (We'll tell you how to mark your best guess later.) By circling the question, you'll make sure you know where to find it later if you do end up with time on your hands. And by making a guess in the meantime, you'll make sure that you don't inadvertently leave the space blank in your hurry to beat the clock.

Why You Should Mark Your Choices in Your Test Booklet and Transfer Them in Blocks

Most students mark their answer choices on their answer sheets immediately after answering each question. They read the question, select an answer, and mark it on the sheet.

This is a bad idea.

Constantly moving your eyes and pencil back and forth between a test booklet and an answer sheet is a waste of time. It's also an invitation to disaster. If your concentration falters for a moment, you may mismark an answer or even an entire column of answers. If you mark your answer for question 11 in the space for question 12, you may inadvertently keep mismarking answers until the end of the exam. This happens more often than you might think.

The best way to prevent this sort of careless error is to transfer your answers from your booklet to your answer sheet in blocks. If you are working on the eleven questions in an antonym subsection, for example, wait until you have tackled all eleven before transferring any of your choices to your answer sheet. When working on subsections that extend over more than one page, you can transfer your answers when you reach the end of each page.

Marking your choices in your booklet and transferring them in blocks has at least three other advantages:

1. Keeping your eyes focused on your test booklet will improve your concentration and make it easier for you to develop a good question-answering rhythm.

2. On certain kinds of GRE questions, such as reading comprehension, you may find that your feelings about your answer choice on one question are altered by your choice on another. If you haven't transferred your answers yet, you can make the change without making an erasure on your answer sheet. This is important, because erasures and stray marks can trip up ETS's scoring computers and hurt your score.

3. Marking your answer choices in your test booklet gives you a second record of your answers, in addition to the one on your answer sheet. If you do inadvertently mismark your answer sheet by shifting your answers up or down by one place, it will be much easier to correct your bubble sheet.

> Transferring your answers to your answer sheet in blocks will help you avoid mismarking your answers.

SUMMARY

1. The Process of Elimination—POE—is an extremely powerful tool on the GRE. It is the foundation on which we build our techniques. When you eliminate an incorrect choice on a question, cross it out in your test booklet.

2. Most students would score higher if they skipped some questions on the test. There is no penalty for guessing on the GRE. You should mark a choice for every question on the test, even if you have to mark some of your choices blindly at the end of the testing period.

3. Your test booklet should be filled with notes and scratch work by the time you finish the test. When you believe you have found ETS's choice on a question, circle it and write its letter clearly in the margin beside the question. Transfer your answers in groups at the end of each subsection or the end of each page.

4

Cracking the System:
Advanced Principles

PUTTING THE BASIC PRINCIPLES TO WORK

As we told you in chapter 3, POE is a very powerful tool. If you use it to focus on eliminating incorrect choices rather than on finding correct ones, you'll improve your odds of earning a good score on the GRE.

There is, however, more to cracking the system than simply understanding the Process of Elimination. To put our techniques fully to work, you'll need to understand something about how the GRE is composed and how you can turn its predictability to your advantage.

ORDER OF DIFFICULTY

One of the single most important facts to know about the GRE is that the questions on it are arranged in order of increasing difficulty. In a nine-item analogy subsection, for example, the first few items are relatively easy, the next few items are somewhat more difficult, and the last few items are quite hard. In fact, the last couple of items in the subsection will be so hard that very few of the people taking the test will be able to answer them correctly. (Questions on the computer-adaptive version of the GRE are not arranged in order of difficulty; see chapter 25.)

With some important exceptions that we'll explain later in the book, this is true of other subsections as well. Questions in each group or subsection on the GRE—as on the SAT and other standardized tests—are presented in order of increasing difficulty: first easy, then medium, then hard. If you're a veteran test-taker, you've probably noticed this yourself.

Is This Always True?

Yes. If the hardest questions were given first, or if the order of difficulty were jumbled, many students would become discouraged and drop out of the test before finding most of the questions they were able to answer. Scores from one administration of the test would be wildly inconsistent with scores from another. Since tests like the GRE are used to compare students who take the test in different versions in different places at different times, consistency is crucial. Maintaining a consistent order of difficulty is a statistical necessity.

Because of this statistical necessity, it is possible to divide every group of questions on the GRE into thirds:

1. *The easy third:* Questions in the first third of each group are easy.

2. *The medium third:* Questions in the second third of each group are medium.

3. *The difficult third:* Questions in the last third of each group are difficult.

Always note the difficulty of the question you're working on.

How Does ETS Know How Difficult the Questions Are?

ETS tries out all its GRE questions ahead of time, in pretests. This is the main purpose of the experimental section. Each new question is assigned a difficulty rating, called its *delta*, based on how many students answer it correctly on the pretest. If very few students answer a question correctly, it is judged to be a difficult question and is assigned a high delta; if many students answer it correctly, it is judged to be an easy question and is given a low delta. ETS constructs new GREs according to an explicit blueprint that dictates where questions of different deltas should be placed.

ETS uses pretests to calculate another statistic, called the *biserial correlation*, for each new question. The biserial correlation is a comparison of how students do on particular questions with how they do on the entire test. On hard questions, for example, ETS wants to be sure that the small number of students selecting ETS's answer are high-scorers, not low-scorers. The biserial correlation tells them if this is so. Questions on which low-scorers do better than high-scorers are eliminated.

Knowing the Order of Difficulty Can Help You Improve Your Score

Knowing the order of difficulty helps you in several ways. Most obviously, it enables you to make the best possible use of the limited time you are given in which to take the test. Hard questions aren't worth more points than easy ones. Your score will be based solely on your number of correct answers. Ten correct answers on ten easy questions are worth exactly the same number of points as ten correct answers on ten hard questions. To make the most efficient use of your time, answer the easy questions first. If puzzling over a difficult question prevents you from answering an easy question, you're throwing away points.

Here's the Rule

The rule concerning order of difficulty is simple: **Answer easy and medium questions first; save hard questions for last.** In fact, most students could improve their scores by working on *fewer* questions; they waste so much time struggling with items that are too hard for them that they overlook items they could answer with relative ease.

As we go along, we'll give you specific information about how the order of difficulty should affect your approach to each item type on the test.

Spend more time getting the easy and medium questions correct. Don't worry about the difficult ones.

Knowing the Order of Difficulty Can Also Help You Find ETS's Answers!

In addition to helping you make the most efficient use of your time, knowing the order of difficulty can actually help you find ETS's answers on questions that you don't understand.

To show you why this is true, we need to tell you something about how most people take standardized tests.

CHOICES THAT "SEEM" RIGHT

What do most people do when they take a multiple-choice test? They work through a problem as far as they can and then select the answer choice that *seems right*, all things considered. On easier questions, they may be completely certain of their choices; on harder questions, they may simply have to trust their hunches.

There's nothing strange or mysterious about this. It's what almost everybody does. Whether they do well or poorly, people select the choices that, for whatever reason, seem right to them. Even *you* select choices that seem right.

WHICH CHOICES *SEEM* RIGHT?

That depends on who the students are and how hard the questions are. Specifically, here's what happens:

1. On easy questions, ETS's answer seems right to almost everyone: high-scorers, average-scorers, and low-scorers.

2. On medium questions, ETS's answer seems *wrong* to low-scoring students, right to high-scoring students, and sometimes right and sometimes wrong to average-scoring students.

3. On hard questions, ETS's answer seems *right* to high-scoring students and *wrong* to everyone else.

There's nothing tricky about what we've just told you. It's really just common sense. Here's another way to think of it: If ETS's answer on a difficult question *seemed right* to almost everyone, the question wouldn't be difficult, would it? If ETS's answer seemed right to everyone, everyone would pick it, and the question would be an easy one. It would be located in the first third rather than the last third of the group of questions.

To help you remember this important concept, we can state it as a simple rule:

> Easy questions have easy answers; hard questions have hard answers.

COULD IT WORK THE OTHER WAY?

Could there ever be a question on the GRE in which ETS's answer seemed right to low-scoring students and seemed wrong to high-scoring students?

No. ETS uses its biserial correlations to eliminate any such flawed questions from its pool of GRE items. For the average student, an "easy" solution to a hard question will always be wrong.

JOE BLOGGS, THE AVERAGE TEST TAKER

There isn't much to say about the test-taking behavior of very high-scoring students or very low-scoring students. High-scorers are right almost all the time; low-scorers are wrong almost all the time. But we can say a great deal about, and learn a great deal from, the test-taking behavior of the average-scoring student.

In fact, the average-scoring student is so important that we have a special name for him at The Princeton Review. We call him Joe Bloggs.

Joe Bloggs is exactly average. He's Mr. Fiftieth Percentile. Half the people who take the GRE do better than he does; half the people do worse. He isn't stupid. He isn't brilliant. He's right in the middle.

How can Joe Bloggs help you on the GRE? He can help you by showing you how to recognize the traps that ETS sets for him and for other average students on hard questions on the GRE. Since Joe Bloggs *always* falls into these traps, you can learn to avoid them simply by learning what it is about them that makes them irresistible to Joe.

Learning how Joe Bloggs thinks isn't difficult, because all of us think at least a little like Joe at least some of the time. By honing your sense of Joe's thought processes, you can improve your score on the GRE.

HOW DOES JOE BLOGGS DO ON THE GRE?

Joe Bloggs's performance on the GRE is exactly average, of course. Specifically, here's how he performs:

1. On easy questions, the answers that seem right to Joe really are right.

2. On medium questions, the answers that seem right to Joe are sometimes right and sometimes wrong.

3. On difficult questions, the answers that seem right to Joe are always wrong.

JOE BLOGGS AND YOU

Let's assume you want to earn a high score on the GRE. Could Joe Bloggs, whose scores are just average, be of any help to you?

You may not think so. But you'd be wrong. Joe Bloggs can be an enormous help to you. How? By showing you what *not* to do on difficult questions.

Remember, Joe is always wrong on difficult questions. If you can figure out which choices would appeal to Joe on these questions, you can improve your score simply by doing something else.

Specifically, here's what you're going to do:

1. On the easy third of each group of questions, you're going to do what Joe would do.

2. On the medium third, you're going to be suspicious of what Joe would do.

3. On the difficult third, you're going to figure out what Joe would do and then *do something else*.

WHAT *DOES* JOE DO?

To give you a better idea of how Joe Bloggs thinks on the GRE, let's take a look at a hard math question and see how Joe handles it. Here's the question:

Eliminate Joe Bloggs's answers on difficult questions.

30. What is the greatest number of nonoverlapping regions into which a square can be divided with exactly three lines?

    (A) 4
    (B) 5
    (C) 6
    (D) 7
    (E) 8

This is a hard question, and Joe never gets the hard ones right. Why? Because the answer that seems right to him always turns out to be wrong.

Remember, hard questions have hard answers. But Joe doesn't like hard answers. He looks for easy solutions—answers that *seem right to him*. And the answers that seem right to Joe on hard questions are always wrong. If this weren't true, the question would never have survived its pretest.

Which answer choice seems right to Joe on this problem? To find out, we merely have to look for an easy, obvious solution. What's the easiest, most obvious way to fulfill the requirements of the problem? Think of the drawing as a pizza with one cut down the middle.

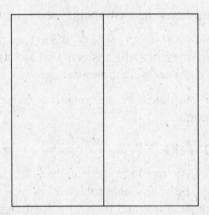

What would be the easiest way to make two more cuts? Just like this:

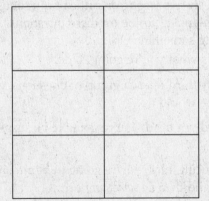

Now we have six pieces of pizza or, in the terms of the problem, six non-overlapping regions. Finding our answer was easy, wasn't it?

It certainly was. In fact, it was *too* easy. If doing what we did were all that was necessary to find ETS's answer, then Joe Bloggs and everyone else would answer this question correctly, and it would be an easy problem instead of a hard one. (Remember, we know it's a hard problem because of its location in the test; its number, 30, shows that it's from the difficult end of a math section.)

Because we were able to produce six regions so easily, we know that answer choice C can't possibly be correct. So we can eliminate it, and cross it out.

We refer to such easy, tempting choices as *Joe Bloggs attractors*.

Do we know anything else? Yes. Because we have been able to divide the figure into *six* regions, we know that neither five nor four could be the *greatest* number of regions into which the figure can be divided. So we can eliminate choices A and B as well.

Now we're down to two possibilities, D and E. Guessing blindly would give us a 50 percent chance of being right. On a real test, only about 10 percent of the test-takers will answer a question like this correctly. *Twice as many would answer it correctly if they simply guessed wildly from among all five choices.* But with Joe Bloggs's help, we've turned it into a coin toss.

We can do even better than that. As you will learn later in the book, the wording of some GRE questions irresistibly leads some students to select certain incorrect choices. This question contains an example of such irresistible wording—the phrase "greatest number." There are a significant number of low-scoring students who when they see the words "greatest number" invariably select the *greatest number* among the possible choices. The greatest number in this case is 8, choice E. We can eliminate it, because these low-scoring students are correct even less often than Joe Bloggs is. *A difficult greatest-number question in which the greatest number was ETS's answer would be highly unlikely to survive a pretest, because its biserial correlation would be much too low.*

ETS's answer has to be D, the only choice left. Incidentally, the correctly completed diagram would look something like this:

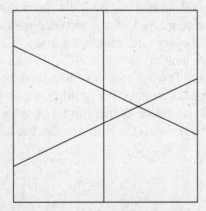

Don't bother trying to figure out this problem mathematically. It isn't really a math question at all. The only way to find ETS's answer (except for our way) is to use sophisticated intuition or time-consuming trial and error.

Knowing how ETS writes its tests will help you score more.

Notice that on this problem our knowledge of Joe Bloggs enabled us to:

1. Sidestep all of ETS's traps
2. Spend less time on this problem than the high-scoring students who found ETS's answer without Joe's help
3. Avoid careless mistakes
4. Earn ten points we would have lost otherwise

WHY NOT SIMPLY ELIMINATE *ANY* CHOICE THAT SEEMS CORRECT?

That would be a disaster. Remember, the choices that seem correct to Joe *really are correct* on all of the easy questions and some of the medium questions. That means that on easy questions you want to *pick* the choices that Joe would pick. (On medium questions, you need to be suspicious of Joe's hunches, but they won't always get you into trouble.) It's only on the hard questions that you can safely eliminate any choice that would appeal to Joe.

We'll teach you much more about Joe Bloggs as we go along. As unimpressive as his own score is, he can help you make big gains on the GRE.

COULDN'T ETS GET RID OF THIS PROBLEM BY CHANGING THE GRE?

There really isn't very much that ETS could do. ETS could make the GRE difficult or impossible to crack if it entirely abandoned the multiple-choice format, but there is no chance that this will happen. ETS and the College Board have recently added a limited number of open-ended, or fill-in-the-blank, questions on the math SAT, but this change was mostly cosmetic. The open-ended questions still require students to darken spaces on their answer sheets with No. 2 pencils. Doing this is very time-consuming. Converting the entire math SAT to this format would not be practical, since such a test would take several hours to complete. And ETS's open-ended format cannot be used on verbal questions.

A test that consists substantially of multiple-choice questions is the only kind of test that can be administered in a reasonable period of time and graded quickly and cheaply. If every GRE required a living, breathing grader, the test would be so expensive that no one could afford to take it.

As long as ETS doesn't switch to a true fill-in-the-blank format, we'll be able to crack the test with relative ease. The multiple-choice format is built around predictable statistical requirements that can all be turned on their heads. The statistical rules by which the test is built are also the keys to cracking it wide open.

SUMMARY

1. Questions on the GRE are arranged in order of increasing difficulty. Groups of questions begin easy, become medium, then turn difficult. All GRE questions are worth the same number of points. You should thus tackle easy and medium questions first and save the hard questions for last.

2. Easy questions have easy answers; hard questions have hard answers.

3. Here's how Joe Bloggs does on the GRE:

    ◆ On easy questions, the answers that seem right to Joe Bloggs really are right.

    ◆ On medium questions, the answers that seem right to Joe Bloggs are sometimes right and sometimes wrong.

    ◆ On difficult questions, the answers that seem right to Joe Bloggs are always wrong.

PART ◆ II

How to Crack the Verbal Sections

5

What Do the Verbal
Sections Test?

GEOGRAPHY OF THE VERBAL SECTIONS

Every GRE contains two scored "verbal ability" sections. Your test could also contain a third verbal section, as an experimental section. This experimental verbal section would look like the other two verbal sections but would not count toward your score.

Each verbal section on your test will last thirty minutes and contain thirty-eight items, as follows:

1. Seven sentence completions (items 1–7)

2. Nine analogies (items 8–16)

3. Eleven reading comprehension questions divided between two reading passages (items 17–27)

4. Eleven antonyms (items 28–38)

The items are arranged this way in each verbal section. Since there are two scored sections, your verbal score will be based on your performance on fourteen sentence completions, eighteen analogies, twenty-two reading comprehension questions, and twenty-two antonyms.

With the exception of the reading comprehension items (as we'll explain in chapter 10), each group of items is arranged in order of increasing difficulty, as follows:

Item Type	Item Number	Difficulty
Sentence Completions	1–2 3–5 6–7	Easy Medium Difficult
Analogies	8–10 11–13 14–16	Easy Medium Difficult
Reading Passage 1 Reading Passage 2	Varies Varies	Varies Varies
Antonyms	28–30 31–35 36–38	Easy Medium Difficult

You Take the Test, Don't Let the Test Take You!

Take charge of the verbal section by doing the problems in the following order:

1. Analogies
2. Sentence completion
3. Antonyms
4. Reading comprehension

What Difference Does It Make?

After learning our problem-solving techniques for each type of verbal question, analogies and sentence completions should be your strongest areas of the verbal test. **You should *not* skip any analogies or sentence completion questions.** Spending more time on these problems is worth the investment, since you'll learn Process of Elimination techniques that will improve your performance on even the most difficult questions.

Do reading comprehension last. The danger is that you could get bogged down on the passages and run out of time for antonym problems that you could have answered correctly! The only questions to skip altogether are the most difficult antonyms and some reading comprehension questions. But don't forget to fill in answers for these on your bubble sheet!

> Don't skip any analogies or sentence completions.

HAVE YOU EVER SEEN A VERBAL ABILITY?

ETS says that the seventy-six items in the verbal section test "one's ability to reason with words in solving problems." In truth, they mostly test your vocabulary. Even the reading comprehension items are largely a vocabulary quiz.

You need to get to work on your vocabulary right away, because of the heavy emphasis on vocabulary on the GRE. Most people seem to find that increasing a verbal score is more difficult than increasing a math score. The reason for this is that vocabulary places something of a ceiling on scores. The better the vocabulary, the higher the ceiling and the higher the possible scores.

The best way to build a good vocabulary is to read a wide variety of good books over the course of a lifetime. Since you don't have a lifetime to prepare for the GRE, you should see chapter 6, Vocabulary for the GRE. It contains a relatively short vocabulary list that consists of the words that are most frequently tested on the GRE. It also contains some solid vocabulary-building advice. Skim through chapter 6 right now and sketch out a vocabulary-building program for yourself. You should work on your vocabulary a little bit every day while you work through the rest of the book. This will give each new word plenty of time to soak in.

Using your newly strengthened vocabulary as a foundation, you will be able to take full advantage of the powerful techniques we describe in the next four chapters. Our techniques will enable you to get as much mileage as possible from the words you do know.

> Improving your vocabulary is one of the most important actions you can take to improve your score.

THREE KINDS OF WORDS

You may think that you either know the definition of a word or you don't know it. But actually, if you think about it a bit, there are really three kinds of words. Always approach a vocabulary word on the GRE by identifying which type of word it is for you:

Do you know the **DICTIONARY DEFINITION** of the word?

- ◆ **Words you know.** These are words you can define accurately. If you can't give a definition of a word that's pretty close to what a dictionary would say, then it's not a word you know.

- ◆ **Words you "sort of know."** These are words you've seen before, or heard, but you can't define accurately. You may have a sense of how these words are used, but beware! Day-to-day usage is often different from the dictionary meanings of words, and the only meanings that count on the GRE are those given in the dictionary. You have to treat these words very differently from the words you can define. After you encounter a word you sort of know, be sure to look it up in the dictionary and make it a word you know from then on.

If you only "sort of know" the meaning of a word, **DON'T ELIMINATE IT!**

- ◆ **Words you've never seen before.** On every GRE you can expect to see some words you've never seen before. They'll probably show up in the hardest verbal problems. After you encounter a word like this, go to the dictionary and look it up! If it's been on one GRE, there's a good bet it will show up again. If you've never seen one of the words in an answer choice, *don't eliminate that choice*. Focus on the answer choices for which you can define the words.

PRACTICE, PRACTICE

Beyond vocabulary, your score will improve as you learn our techniques for attacking questions with partial knowledge and increasing problem-solving speed. Mastering these techniques is a critical step toward achieving your maximum score on the GRE.

As you work along through this book, be sure to practice on real GREs. Work slowly at first, then increase your speed as you gain confidence in our techniques. Practice will rapidly sharpen your test-taking skills. Unless you trust our techniques, you may be reluctant to use them fully and automatically on a real administration of the GRE. The best way to develop that trust is to practice.

GRE vs. SAT

The verbal GRE is a lot like the verbal SAT, but with harder vocabulary and more tempting distractors. That doesn't mean you'll necessarily find it harder than you found the SAT back in high school. After all, your vocabulary has grown substantially since high school. But the test isn't easy. The GRE's pool of test-takers consists of students who did well enough on the SAT to get into college, and then did well enough in college to make it at least most of the way to graduation. You'll have to stay on your toes.

6

Vocabulary for the GRE

THE VERBAL GRE IS A VOCABULARY TEST

Your GRE verbal score will be a close reflection of the size and strength of your vocabulary. If you're an avid reader of good books and publications, your vocabulary is probably in good shape. If your idea of cultural enrichment is watching MTV, you may be in trouble.

Start working on your vocabulary now!

Our techniques for cracking the verbal GRE are very powerful, but how helpful they are to you will depend in large measure on the quality of your vocabulary. Our techniques can help you get maximum possible mileage out of the words you do know. The more words you know, the more help we can be.

GET TO WORK

The best way to build a good vocabulary is to absorb it slowly over an entire lifetime. Unfortunately, you don't have an entire lifetime to prepare for the GRE. Since you don't, you need to be as efficient as possible in learning new words. We can help you do just that.

The most efficient way to learn new words for the GRE would be to learn only those words tested on the edition of the test that you take. Obviously, you won't be able to do exactly that. But you *can* do the next best thing. The Princeton Review has compiled a vocabulary list that contains the most frequently tested words on the GRE. We compiled this list, which we call the *Hit Parade*, by analyzing released GREs with our computers. The words are listed in order of their importance on the GRE. Words that appear in ETS's answers to questions are weighted more heavily than words that don't.

THE HIT PARADE

Learning the GRE Hit Parade may be the single most important thing you do in preparation for the exam. Learning these words will give you a solid background in the vocabulary most likely to appear on your test. It will also give you a better idea of the kinds of words that crop up again and again on the GRE. Learning the Hit Parade will give you a feel for the level of vocabulary that ETS likes to test. This in turn will make it easier to spot other possible GRE words in your reading.

Each entry on the Hit Parade is followed by a brief definition. Most of the words on the list have other meanings as well, but the definitions we have given are the ones you are most likely to encounter on the GRE. As you'll note, we've organized the list into five weeks' worth of learning.

THE PRINCETON REVIEW'S GRE HIT PARADE

Week One

eulogy	an oration praising someone or something
pedagogy	the art, science, or profession of teaching
miser	a covetous, grasping person, esp. one who hoards money
relevant	applying to the case at hand; to the point
amorphous	without definite form or shape
laud	to praise highly
volatile	changeable; fickle; explosive
erudite	very learned; scholarly
hypothesis	a tentative theory or explanation
profound	far-reaching; deep
redundant	exceeding what is natural or necessary; superfluous
plummet	to plunge or drop straight down
intractable	not easily managed or directed; stubborn; obstinate
qualify	to limit or restrict; to modify the meaning of (a word or phrase)
disabuse	to set right
censure	to criticize severely; an official rebuke
fastidious	careful in all details; meticulous; very difficult to please
misanthrope	one who hates mankind
placate	to appease; to pacify
articulate	to speak distinctly and carefully
discrete	separate; individually distinct; composed of distinct parts
elegy	a mournful poem, esp. one lamenting the dead
sanction	authoritative permission or approval; a penalty intended to enforce compliance
foil	to defeat; to render an effort in vain
plastic	capable of being shaped or formed; pliable
proximity	nearness; closeness
didactic	intended to teach or instruct
recluse	a person who leads a secluded or solitary life
stem	to hold back or stop by or as if by damming
subside	to sink to a lower level; to fall into a state of quiet; abate
temper	to soften or moderate; to tune or adjust
tirade	a long, angry, and often abusive speech

ARCANE: known or knowable only to one having the key; secret

veneer	a layer of valuable material overlaying an inferior one; superficial show; gloss
lucid	clear; easily understood
whim	a sudden or capricious idea; passing fancy
assuage	to ease or lessen; to appease or pacify
egregious	outstandingly bad; flagrant; outrageous
flattery	insincere praise
iconoclast	one who attacks and seeks to overthrow traditional or popular ideas or institutions
obdurate	unyielding; hardhearted; intractable
qualm	a doubt or misgiving; uneasiness; a pang of conscience
rarefy	to make or become thin, less dense; to refine
resolve	to make a firm decision about; to separate (something) into constituent parts; firmness of purpose; resolution
synthesis	the combination of parts to make a whole
deliberate	to consider or discuss (a matter) carefully
insipid	without taste or savor; lacking in spirit; dull
indifferent	having no interest or concern; apathetic; showing no bias or preference; impartial
allude	to make an indirect reference to
gregarious	seeking and enjoying the company of others; sociable
ephemeral	lasting for a brief time; short-lived
waver	to move to and fro; sway; to be unsettled in opinion
abscond	to depart clandestinely; to steal off and secrete oneself
diatribe	a bitter or abusive speech; a prolonged discussion
abstruse	difficult to understand
garrulous	pointlessly talkative; talking too much
gullible	easily deceived or cheated
presumptuous	overstepping due bounds (as of propriety or courtesy); taking liberties
repudiate	to refuse to have anything to do with; disown
sap	to exhaust gradually
heresy	a controversial or unorthodox opinion, esp. as in religion; at variance with established beliefs

Week Two

allocate	to allot; to assign
utopian	one who believes in the perfectibility of human society; impossibly ideal; visionary

zeal	eagerness or ardent interest in pursuit of something; fervor
implicit	involved though not shown; understood though not expressed; not explicit
incoherent	incapable of being understood; incomprehensible
lethargy	drowsy or sluggish indifference; apathy
malevolent	having or showing often vicious ill will, spite, or hatred
plaintive	expressive of sorrow or melancholy
tout	to praise or publicize loudly or extravagantly
vituperate	to use harsh condemnatory language; to abuse or censure severely or abusively; berate
imminent	about to happen; impending
appease	to pacify, often by satisfying; conciliate; calm; soothe
color	to give a distinctive character to; influence; to misrepresent, distort
corroborate	to make more certain; to confirm
deter	to prevent or discourage (someone) from acting by means of fear or doubt
equivocate	to use ambiguous language with a deceptive intent
conventional	following accepted practice; customary
impetuous	hastily or rashly energetic; impulsive and vehement
mercurial	characterized by rapid and unpredictable change in mood
anarchy	absence of any form of government or law; disorder and confusion
placid	undisturbed; peaceful; quiet
capricious	inclined to change one's mind impulsively; erratic; unpredictable
quiescence	quality of being at rest; motionless
harangue	a long pompous speech; tirade
taciturn	habitually silent or uncommunicative
polemical	controversial; argumentative
specious	having deceptive attraction or allure
squelch	to suppress; to silence
affable	friendly; good-natured; amiable
subpoena	a writ commanding a person to appear in court; to serve such a writ
superfluous	exceeding what is sufficient or necessary
sycophant	a person who gains another's favor with insincere flattery; a brownnoser

BURNISH: to make shiny or lustrous, especially by rubbing; polish

unfeigned	genuine; not false or hypocritical
mitigate	to make or become less severe or intense; moderate
antipathy	opposition in feeling; aversion or dislike
partisan	a strong supporter of a party, cause, faction, or person
elaborate	to work out with care and detail; develop thoroughly
catalyst	a substance that modifies and increases the rate of a chemical reaction without itself changing; a person or thing that causes a change
enigmatic	mysterious; obscure; difficult to understand
adulterate	to make impure or inferior by adding unnecessary or improper ingredients
incipient	beginning to come into being or to become apparent
candor	frankness of expression; sincerity; straightforwardness
obsequious	exhibiting a fawning attentiveness
obtuse	lacking sharpness of intellect; not clear or precise in thought or expression
penury	extreme poverty; destitution
pine	to yearn intensely; to languish; to lose vigor
anomaly	deviation from the normal order, form, or rule; abnormality
plethora	superabundance; excess
pragmatic	practical, as opposed to idealistic
quaff	to drink deeply
eclectic	composed of elements drawn from various sources
cacophony	harsh, jarring, discordant sound; dissonance
malleable	capable of being shaped or formed; tractable; pliable
transitory	tending to pass away; not persistent
vapid	lacking liveliness, briskness, or force
viable	capable of living or developing under normal conditions
viscid	having an adhesive quality or glutinous consistency; sticky
provincial	limited in perspective; narrow and self-centered
conviction	a strong opinion or belief

Week Three

hamper	to interfere with the operation of; to restrain; to disrupt
apathy	lack of emotion or feeling; indifference
latency	the state of being present but undeveloped; dormant
martial	relating to army or military life
pedestrian	commonplace; ordinary; unimaginative
convalesce	to recuperate from an illness or injury

pluck	a ready courage to fight against the odds
probity	adherence to highest principles; uprightness
hyperbole	an exaggerated statement, often used as a figure of speech
prolific	producing abundant works or results; productive
propensity	a natural inclination or tendency; penchant
static	not moving, active, or in motion; at rest
prune	to reduce by removing superfluous matter
resilience	the ability to recover from or adjust easily to stresses
saccharine	overly sweet; overly sentimental
shard	a piece or fragment of a brittle substance
esoteric	intended for or understood by only a small group
stanch	to check or stop the flow of
subliminal	existing or functioning below the level of conscious awareness
taunt	a sarcastic challenge or insult; to challenge in a mocking way
tenuous	having little substance or strength; flimsy; weak
treacherous	likely to betray trust; marked by hidden dangers; perfidious
erratic	not consistent or uniform; irregular
dilettante	one with an amateurish or superficial interest in the arts or a branch of knowledge
quotidian	occurring or recurring daily; commonplace
beneficent	doing or producing good; performing acts of kindness
equivocal	subject to different interpretations; intentionally misleading
hackneyed	rendered trite or commonplace by frequent usage
imperturbable	marked by extreme calm, impassivity, and steadiness
implacable	not capable of being appeased or significantly changed
laconic	using few words; terse
menace	to show an intent to harm
nostalgia	a wistful or sentimental yearning to return to the past; homesickness
paean	a song or hymn of praise and thanksgiving
stymie	to block; thwart
profuse	given or coming forth abundantly; extravagant
preen	to dress up; to primp; to congratulate oneself for achievement
contrite	feeling regret for (what one has done or failed to do); repentant; penitent

CASTIGATE: to subject to severe punishment, reproof, or criticism; punish

caustic	burning; corrosive; marked by sharp and bitter wit; cutting
protean	readily taking on different shapes or forms
supplant	to take the place of; supersede
taut	having no give or slack; high-strung; tense; in proper order
abstain	to keep oneself from doing something
ascetic	one who practices rigid self-denial, esp. as an act of religious devotion
dearth	smallness of quantity or number; scarcity; paucity
scrupulous	having moral integrity; acting in strict regard to what is considered right or proper
vagrant	one who has no established residence and wanders from place to place without visible means of support
disinterested	free of bias and self-interest; impartial
vigilant	alertly watchful
aberrant	deviating from the normal, usual, or expected
writ	a formal written document; a written order
adversity	great hardship; misfortune; a calamitous event
furtive	marked by stealth; covert; surreptitious
bolster	to support; to reinforce; to give a boost
cogent	appealing forcibly to the mind or reason; convincing
commensurate	corresponding in size, degree, extent, or duration; proportionate
condone	to pardon or overlook voluntarily; to treat as if trivial
cajole	to coax; wheedle
cynical	contemptuously distrustful of human nature and motives
discretion	cautious reserve in speech; ability to make responsible decisions

Week Four

exonerate	to free from blame
foment	to promote the growth of; rouse; incite
credulous	tending to believe too readily; gullible
spendthrift	one who spends money wastefully
inured	accustomed to accepting something undesirable
vacillate	to waver indecisively between one course of action or opinion and another
paradox	a statement that appears to contradict itself or be contrary to common sense, but that may be true
perspicacious	acutely perceptive; having keen discernment

genre	type or class; a particular type or category of literary work
pithy	having the essential part or core; precise and meaningful
connoisseur	an informed and astute judge in matters of taste; expert
precedent	an earlier occurrence that may serve as an example or rule
proscribe	to condemn or forbid as harmful and unlawful; prohibit
recalcitrant	obstinately defiant of authority; difficult to manage
recondite	hidden; concealed; difficult to understand; obscure
discern	to detect or perceive with the eye or mind; to perceive the distinctions of; discriminate
fallacy	a false idea or notion; a belief or argument deceptive in appearance or meaning
spurious	lacking authenticity or validity; false; counterfeit
subtle	not obvious; difficult to understand; obscure; elusive
supercilious	characterized by haughty scorn; disdainful
tangential	making a sudden digression or change of course; incidental; peripheral
quell	to put down forcibly; suppress; to pacify
tenacity	the quality of adherence or persistence to something valued
predilection	a disposition in favor of something; preference
whet	to sharpen; to make keen or more acute
aesthetic	dealing with, appreciative of, or responsive to the beautiful
banal	lacking originality, freshness, or novelty
florid	flushed or ruddy in appearance; heavily embellished; flowery
distend	to enlarge from internal pressure; swell; expand
squalid	having a dirty or wretched appearance; morally repulsive; sordid
ebullience	the quality of lively or enthusiastic expression of thoughts and feelings
facilitate	to make easier
prodigal	recklessly wasteful; extravagant; profuse; lavish
indolent	disinclined to work; habitually lazy
glib	marked by ease or informality; nonchalant; lacking in depth; superficial
inchoate	in an initial stage; not fully formed
pedantic	the parading of learning; excessive attention to minutiae
pigment	a substance that imparts color
abet	to encourage; incite

DISINGENUOUS: lacking in candor; giving a false appearance of simple frankness; calculating

pristine	not corrupted; fresh and clean; innocent
prologue	an introductory or preceding speech or event
quixotic	foolishly impractical; marked by lofty, romantic ideals
austere	without adornment; bare; severely simple; ascetic
torque	a force that causes rotation
ubiquitous	existing everywhere at the same time; constantly encountered; widespread
wrought	worked into shape by artistry or effort; fashioned; formed
adhere	to give support; to hold fast to; to bind oneself to
boor	a rude or insensitive person
solvent	able to pay all legal debts
fickle	marked by lack of constancy; erratically changeable
stoic	not affected by or showing passion or feeling, esp. firmly restraining in response to pain or distress
immutable	not capable of change
inert	unable to move or act; moving or acting slowly; sluggish
maverick	an independent individual who does not go along with a group or party
metaphor	a figure of speech in which a word or phrase denoting one kind of object or idea is used in place of another to suggest a likeness or analogy between them
mettlesome	full of vigor and stamina; spirited
pervasive	diffused through every part of
platitude	a banal, polite, or stale remark
precursor	one that precedes and indicates or announces another; forerunner
ameliorate	to make better or more tolerable
prescience	foreknowledge of events; foresight

Week Five

pretense	false appearance or action intended to deceive; ostentation
travesty	a debased, distorted, or grossly inferior imitation
provocation	the act of inciting; something that excites or evokes
trenchant	vigorously effective and articulate; sharply perceptive; keen; penetrating
redemptive	something that frees or extricates from harm
refute	to prove wrong by argument or evidence; to show to be false

ineluctable	impossible to avoid or overcome; inevitable
rift	a clear space or interval; fissure; breach; divide
salubrious	promoting health or well-being
intrepid	characterized by fearlessness and endurance
satirize	to expose human vices and follies to ridicule and scorn
sear	to burn or scorch; to make dry or withered; parch
sporadic	occurring only occasionally, or in scattered instances
hone	to sharpen
ingenuous	lacking sophistication; naive; artless
tact	a keen sense of what to do and say in order to avoid offense
troupe	a group of theatrical performers; company; to travel in such a company
anachronism	mistake of placing something in the wrong historical period
turpitude	inherent baseness; depravity
vindictive	disposed to seek revenge; vengeful; intended to cause harm
wither	to shrivel from loss of moisture; to lose vitality or freshness
fervor	intensity of emotion; ardor; intense heat
bombast	pretentious and inflated speech or writing
dupe	one who is easily deceived or used; to deceive or trick
complaisant	inclined to please or oblige; amiable
convoke	to call together for a meeting
despotic	the exercise of absolute power in an oppressive fashion; tyrannical
hedonism	pursuit of or devotion to pleasure
devoid	being without an expected attribute or quality; empty
neophyte	a recent convert; a beginner; novice
dissemble	to hide under a false appearance; to conceal facts, feelings, or intentions under some pretense; to disguise
dogmatic	stubbornly opinionated
efficacy	the power to produce an effect
spartan	marked by strict self-discipline or self-denial, esp. by simplicity, frugality, or avoidance of luxury and comfort
embellish	to make beautiful with ornamentation; decorate; enhance
emollient	something that softens or soothes
mosaic	a picture or decorative design made by setting small, colored pieces of glass or tile in cement
emulate	to strive to equal or excel; to imitate; to follow as example
guile	deceitful cunning; craftiness

EXHAUSTIVE: testing all possibilities or considering all elements; thorough

astringent	tending to draw together or tighten living tissue; harsh; severe
succinct	marked by briefness and clarity of expression; concise
mundane	of the world; typical of or concerned with the ordinary
euphemism	the substitution of an agreeable phrase for one that may offend or be unpleasant; the phrase itself
exacerbate	to make more violent or severe
prosaic	lacking in imagination or interest; dull
diffident	lacking self-confidence; timid; shy
impassive	revealing no emotion; expressionless; stolid
pirate	to reproduce without authorization
inimitable	not capable of being imitated
alchemy	a medieval chemical philosophy concerned primarily with the conversion of base metals into gold; any seemingly magical power
inundate	overwhelm; to cover with a flood
inveigle	to obtain by deceit or flattery
labyrinthine	resembling a labyrinth or maze; intricate or involved
levee	an embankment to prevent flooding; a pier or dike
soporific	causing sleep or drowsiness
maladroit	lacking in dexterity; clumsy
respite	a short interval of rest or relief
prodigy	a person, esp. a child, with exceptional talent
precipitate	to cause to happen before anticipated or required; acting with excessive haste or impulse
phlegmatic	having or showing a calm, stolid temperament; unemotional

THE PRINCETON REVIEW APPROACH TO LEARNING NEW WORDS

Helping students learn new words is one of the most important things we do at The Princeton Review. Students with big vocabularies simply do better on standardized tests than students with small vocabularies. Since most of our students have little time in which to learn new words, we've given a lot of thought to fast, efficient methods of memorization and retention. That's why we wrote *Word Smart* and *Word Smart II*, our vocabulary guides. (Look for them at your local bookstore.)

To build your vocabulary for the GRE in a hurry, you need to do two things. You need to learn to spot GRE words—the kind of words that ETS tests on the

GRE—and you need to find an effective memorization routine that you feel comfortable with. We describe several solid ones in *Word Smart* and *Word Smart II*.

Learning the words on the Hit Parade is an ideal way not only to learn the most important GRE words, but also to get a solid feel for the level of vocabulary on the test. Once you've nailed down the Hit Parade, you'll have no trouble spotting other GRE words in your daily reading.

How will you remember all these words? You'll do it by developing a standard routine for learning new words. We suggest that you begin with our method and then tailor it to suit your own preferences. Here's our method:

Learn new words little by little. Don't try to learn 200 words at once.

STEP 1: When you encounter a new word in your reading, try to deduce its meaning from context. That is, treat the unknown word as though it were a blank in a GRE sentence completion and attempt to anticipate what it must mean. You may not be able to tell, and the context may lead you astray, but the mental effort you make will help register the new word in your mind.

STEP 2: Look it up. If you don't have a dictionary handy, write down the new word and look it up later. We tell our students to "look it up" so often that we simply say "LIU." If you have somehow managed to make it through college without owning a dictionary, the time has come for you to make the plunge. Go buy one right now.

STEP 3: When you look up the word, say it out loud, being careful to pronounce it correctly. Saying the word to yourself isn't enough. You'll remember it better if you make a little noise.

STEP 4: When you look up your word in the dictionary, don't assume that the first definition is the one that applies in your case. The first definition may be an archaic one, or one that applies only in a particular context. Scan through all the definitions, looking for the one that fits the context in which you found your word.

STEP 5: If you have time, compare the definition of your new word with the definitions of its synonyms, assuming that it has some. A thesaurus can be helpful for this. Checking the meanings of synonyms can help you nail down the nuances of meaning that distinguish one word from others closely related to it.

STEP 6: Now that you've learned the dictionary's definition of your new word, restate it in your own words. You'll find it much easier to remember a word's meaning if you make it your own. You'll have to be certain, of course, that your definition is consistent with the one in the dictionary.

STEP 7: Use a memory aid, such as a mnemonic or a mental image, to fix the new word in your mind. For example, you might try to help yourself remember the word *conventional* by picturing a "customary" convention of word memorizers. Or you might remind yourself that *enfranchise* means "to give the right to vote" by picturing people lined up to vote in a McDonald's franchise. The crazier the image, the better. Even if you can't think of a good one, the mental effort you go through in trying to think of one will help etch the word's meaning in your brain.

STEP 8:   Keep a vocabulary notebook and use flash cards. We tell our students to carry spiral notebooks in which they can jot down new words and make notes about definitions. Simply having a notebook with you will remind you to be on the lookout for new words. And using it will help you remember the ones you encounter.

The best way to use a vocabulary notebook is to devote an entire page to each new word. Jot down the word when you find it, note its pronunciation and definition (in your own words) when you LIU, and jot down your mnemonic or mental image. You might also copy the sentence in which you originally found the word, to remind yourself of how the word looks in context.

To nail down the meanings of your new words, you should also make flash cards. Our students usually make theirs out of three-by-five index cards. They write the word on one side and the pronunciation, meaning, and perhaps a mental image on the other. They can then quiz each other or themselves in idle moments through the day. By sticking five or six of your flash cards in your pocket every morning and using them when you can, you'll make surprisingly rapid progress. You can also use your flash cards for review.

STEP 9:   Write the new word on your brain. Many students find that writing something down makes it easier to memorize. Use your notebook to write down sentences incorporating your new words.

STEP 10:   Use your new word every chance you get. Bore your friends! Infuriate your family! The only sure way to master a word is to make it part of your life. When you're learning a new word, bend over backward to find reasons to use it. Insert it into your speech at every opportunity. A powerful vocabulary requires lots of exercise.

JUST KNOWING THEY'RE THERE

The Hit Parade can help you in more ways than one. Hit Parade words have a marked tendency to turn up in ETS's answers on the GRE. That means that Hit Parade words make very good guesses on items where you have no other reason for preferring one choice to another.

7 Analogies

ABOUT ANALOGIES

Each verbal section of your GRE will contain nine analogy items, numbered 8–16. Items 8–10 will be easy, items 11–13 will be medium, and items 14–16 will be difficult.

In this chapter, analogies will be numbered 8–16 exactly as they are on the GRE. Always pay attention to the item position when answering GRE questions. The item number will help determine which technique or combination of techniques you will use to crack the problem.

LEARN THESE DIRECTIONS

Before we begin, take a moment to read and memorize the following set of directions. These are the directions exactly as they will appear on your GRE. You shouldn't even glance at them when you take the test. If you do, you will waste time and lose points. Here are the directions:

> Directions: In each of the following questions, a re-
> lated pair of words or phrases is followed by five
> lettered pairs of words or phrases. Select the let-
> tered pair that best expresses a relationship similar
> to that expressed in the original pair.

OUR ANALOGIES TECHNIQUES

The Princeton Review's techniques for cracking analogies are very powerful. All are based on POE. Sometimes you will be able to use POE to eliminate all four incorrect choices; you should always be able to eliminate at least one. Eliminating even one incorrect choice will improve your odds of earning points.

Our techniques for cracking analogies will enable you to:

1. Eliminate incorrect choices

2. Improve your guessing odds

3. Find ETS's answer even if you don't know the meaning of the words in the original pair

4. Find ETS's answer even if you don't know one or more words among the choices

JUST WHAT IS AN ANALOGY, ANYWAY?

ETS isn't terribly clear about what it means by an analogy, so it should be no surprise if you aren't either. Some of the graduate schools to which you are applying may require you to take a peculiar standardized test called the Miller Analogy Test (MAT). Miller analogies are based on a broad factual knowledge of the world, whereas GRE analogies are based almost entirely on vocabulary. Also, Miller analogies are in a format different from GRE analogies, and the kinds of relationships between the words are different. Do not apply our GRE analogy techniques to Miller analogies!

There is only one kind of relationship in GRE analogies. We call this kind of relationship a *clear and necessary* relationship. A clear and necessary relationship is just what it sounds like. It's a tight, solid, logical relationship that is based on the meanings of the words. **A clear and necessary relationship is the kind of relationship that exists between a word and its dictionary definition.** Here's an example:

SHIP : OCEAN

Is there a clear and necessary relationship between these two words? Yes, there is. A ship travels in an ocean. There is a tight, logical link between the meanings of the words. You don't have to stretch your imagination or suspend your disbelief to see the connection between the words. The connection exists because of what the words mean.

Now here's an unclear and unnecessary relationship:

SHIP : MAGAZINE

How are *ship* and *magazine* related? Well, we once saw a picture of a ship in a magazine.

Clear and necessary?

No. The words are unrelated, except in the strained context we've created. The relationship is neither clear nor necessary, and it has nothing to do with the definitions of the words.

Here's another unclear and unnecessary relationship:

SHIP : SNIP

The two words rhyme and have three of four letters in common. You might find such a pair on the Miller Analogy Test, but you won't find one on the GRE. Don't look for this sort of tricky item on the GRE. ETS plays tricks on the GRE, but not like this.

WHAT YOU HAVE TO DO

On the GRE, your job is to determine the clear and necessary relationship between a given pair of words (printed in capital letters and called the *stem* in ETS lingo) and then select another pair of words, from among the five choices, that has exactly the same relationship. If SHIP : OCEAN were the stem, ETS's answer might be "rocket : space." A rocket travels in space, just as a ship travels in an ocean. That's a GRE analogy.

WHEN YOU CAN DEFINE BOTH OF THE STEM WORDS:

MAKE A SENTENCE THAT DEFINES THE RELATIONSHIP

Your first step in solving a GRE analogy problem is to find the relationship between the stem words. To do this, you will form a simple sentence that links the two words and illustrates their meaning. That's exactly what we did in the SHIP : OCEAN example above. "A ship travels in an ocean" is a simple sentence that links the two words through their definitions. It states the relationship between the two words.

Remember: There must be a clear and necessary relationship between the words.

Let's try this approach on an easy question:

8. STONE : SCULPTOR ::

    (A) brick : house
    (B) words : poet
    (C) bust : portrait
    (D) scalpel : surgeon
    (E) mine : ore

Here's how to crack it

First we form a sentence. How about this one: "Stone is the medium in which a sculptor creates his art."

That's the relationship, all right, but the sentence is too wordy. It's important to be as succinct as possible. Here's another try: "Stone is shaped by a sculptor." That's pretty economical. We may have to tinker with it as we go along, but it's good enough for now.

Now that we have our sentence, we plug in the choices:

    (A) Is brick shaped by a house? No. Bricks are used to build a house. Eliminate (and cross out).

    (B) Are words shaped by a poet? Yes, figuratively speaking. A possibility. Let's check the other choices.

    (C) Is a bust shaped by a portrait? No. A bust could be a portrait and made of stone by a sculptor, but the relationship between *bust* and *portrait* is not the same as the relationship between *stone* and *sculptor*. Eliminate.

    (D) Is a scalpel shaped by a surgeon? No. A surgeon might wield a scalpel in something like the same way a sculptor wields a chisel, but there's no *chisel* in the stem. Eliminate.

    (E) Is a mine shaped by ore? Don't get too clever here. You might stretch matters and say that a mine takes its shape from the removal of ore, but that's not what ETS is looking for. *ETS doesn't get cute with analogies.* Eliminate. ETS's answer must be B, the only choice we haven't eliminated. And it is.

MAKING GOOD SENTENCES

In looking at this item, there seem to be many possible ways to state the relationship between the stem words. We could have said, "Stone is a sculptor's medium," or "A sculptor makes art from stone," or something similar. It doesn't matter which we choose, and you should never waste time on the GRE by trying to find the *perfect* sentence. **All that matters is that you find a sentence that expresses the clear and necessary relationship.**

DO WE HAVE TO MAKE A SENTENCE FROM LEFT TO RIGHT?

No. Sometimes it's easier to define the second word in terms of the first. Do it! Just be sure to plug in the answer choices in the same order that you used to make your sentence.

WRITE IT DOWN!

If you try to make your sentence "in your head," you might forget it after you try a few answer choices. Then you would have to go back to the stem words and start all over. Even worse, if you try to "remember" your sentence, you might change it to agree with one of the answer choices. That defeats the whole purpose of POE! You lose the power to eliminate choices that making a sentence for the original relationship provides.

Always write your sentence in the test booklet, right on top of the question. But, of course, you don't have to start your sentence with a capital letter and end it with a period. By all means, keep it simple. If you make your sentence from right to left, draw an arrow for that question to remind you to plug in the answer choices from right to left.

USING PROCESS OF ELIMINATION

Let's go back to our example. Notice that even though choice B looked good immediately, and even though this is an easy question, we still went ahead and evaluated all the choices. **You should always check out all the choices on GRE analogies.** Even though one choice may look good immediately, you may very well find a better choice farther down the list. When Joe Bloggs makes mistakes on easy analogies, it's out of carelessness.

There is no excuse for careless mistakes on the GRE.

As the questions increase in difficulty, you will start to encounter more words that you can't define in the answer choices. **Never eliminate an answer choice if you can't define both of the words in that choice.** We will discuss below what to do when you are left with several answer choices.

> If you can't define a word, don't eliminate it.

WHAT IF MORE THAN ONE ANSWER CHOICE FITS YOUR ORIGINAL SENTENCE?

You will sometimes find two or more choices that seem to fit your sentence when you plug in an analogy. When this happens, you'll have to go back and **make your sentence more specific.** Here's an example:

> 14. AVIARY : BIRDS ::
>   (A) sanitarium : nurses
>   (B) gallery : paintings
>   (C) library : books
>   (D) penitentiary : inmates
>   (E) dictionary : words

Here's how to crack it

A possible sentence might be, "An aviary is a place where birds are found." Now plug in the choices:

(A) Is a sanitarium a place where nurses are found? Yes.
    A possibility.

(B) Is a gallery a place where paintings are found? Yes.
    A possibility.

(C) Is a library a place where books are found? Yes.
A possibility.

(D) Is a penitentiary a place where inmates are found? Yes.
A possibility.

(E) Is a dictionary a place where words are found? Yes.
A possibility.

We've checked all the choices and eliminated none. What did we do wrong?

We didn't make our sentence specific enough. We now need to go back and fiddle with it. A better sentence would be "An aviary is where birds are confined," or "An aviary is a man-made (or artificial) place to keep birds." Birds aren't just found in an aviary. Try to *define* one of the stem words in terms of the other. What's ETS's answer? Choice D.

MAKING BETTER SENTENCES: PARTS OF SPEECH

If both words in the stem are nouns, both words in each choice will be nouns. If the first stem word is a verb and the second is an adjective, the first word in each choice will be a verb and the second will be an adjective. ETS never violates this principle.

You may sometimes have trouble determining the part of speech in one of the words in the stem. If this happens, look at the answer choices. ETS uses the choices to "establish the part of speech" when the stem is ambiguous. In other words, if you aren't sure about the words in the stem, check the words in the choices. The parts of speech should be clear from at least one of the choices.

Always determine the parts of speech before you make your sentence for the stem words.

COMMON GRE RELATIONSHIPS

Many types of relationships are possible in GRE analogies. Some of the most common relationships of the GRE are:

1. Degree (ADMIRE : IDOLIZE)

2. Cause and effect (DRUG : CURE)

3. Type of (FRUIT : ORANGE)

4. Part of (CHAPTER : BOOK)

5. Function of (BRAIN : THINKING)

6. Characterized by (ZEALOT : FERVOR)

7. "To be . . . is not to have . . ." (POOR : MONEY)

You'll notice other types as you practice on real GREs. Being familiar with the sorts of relationships that crop up again and again can make it easier for you to form sentences quickly. And the faster you form your sentence, the faster you'll find ETS's answer.

Still, there's no need to memorize these or other specific types. Identifying relationship types is not an end in itself. Much more important than any particular type of relationship you might find is the one general type of relationship you must always find: the *clear and necessary* relationship based on *the meanings of the words*.

ELIMINATE UNRELATED ANSWER CHOICES

You will sometimes find answer choices containing two words that seem to be related to each other but that are, in fact, related only to a third word. Here are four examples:

> lemon : orange
>
> irrigation : fertilizer
>
> salt : pepper
>
> weight : age

None of these pairs contains a clear and necessary relationship. Lemons and oranges are related in the sense that they are both fruits, but there is no relationship *between* them. You can't make a good GRE sentence using them: "A lemon is a slightly smaller and yellower orange, sort of," is not a definitive sentence.

All these pairs sound good together, but not one contains a clear and necessary relationship. The relationships are triangular. *Irrigation* and *fertilizer* are both related to crops, but not to each other. *Salt* and *pepper* are both related to seasoning, but not to each other. *Weight* and *age* are both related to measurement, but not to each other.

Choices containing such triangular nonrelationships can always be eliminated.

DON'T TELL STORIES

GRE analogies are not a test of how clever you are at thinking of bizarre relationships between words. Such a test of creativity might be more interesting than the boring old GRE, but you're stuck with the boring old GRE. Any two words can be twisted and bent into some sort of relationship. That's not the point. This isn't creative writing. It's a vocabulary test. Remember the dictionary and dictionary definitions.

Beware of triangular relationships between words.

DRILL 1

Here's a drill that will help you get the hang of creating sentences for GRE analogies. Determine the relationship (if any) between the two words and then write a sentence that expresses it in the space at the side. If a pair of words is not related, write "unrelated" in the space. If you don't know the meaning of one of the two words, you'll have to play it safe with a "?" Be sure to look up any words you don't know, after you finish this drill. (You can check your answers on page 294.)

1. needle : thread _____
2. vernal : spring _____
3. breach : dam _____
4. dog : cat _____
5. vacillate : steadfast _____
6. scintilla : minuscule _____
7. calumniate : reputation _____
8. sedulous : piquancy _____
9. witty : mordant _____
10. mendacity : truth _____
11. apposite : impertinent _____
12. infraction : felony _____
13. door : wall _____
14. door : roof _____
15. sanctuary : protection _____
16. flustered : composure _____
17. malinger : work _____
18. timorousness : intrepid _____
19. plagiarize : murder _____
20. snobbishness : sycophant _____
21. metal : filings _____
22. inexperience : neophyte _____
23. gaggle : geese _____
24. evangelism : serenity _____
25. fervor : emotion _____
26. stultify : stupid _____
27. layer : stratification _____
28. ineluctable : avoid _____

29. lethargic : stimulate _____

30. legal : system _____

31. fuel : log _____

32. carapace : turtle _____

33. stealth : detection _____

34. promiscuous : chaos _____

35. fortuitous : planning _____

36. ruminate : meditation _____

37. vindictive : revenge _____

38. coltish : discipline _____

39. vernacular : language _____

40. ventral : conclusion _____

41. arsenal : weapon _____

42. obscurity : light _____

43. venal : money _____

44. tortuous : curves _____

45. illicit : legality _____

46. histrionic : dramatic _____

47. glaze : window _____

48. voter : election _____

49. manacle : freedom _____

50. empirical : observation _____

WHEN YOU CAN'T DEFINE BOTH OF THE STEM WORDS

You should now have a good understanding of the sort of relationship that must exist between stem words and correct answer choices in ETS analogy problems. You've already used this understanding to make sentences linking various stem words. Now we're going to show you how to use the same concept to eliminate incorrect answer choices *even if you don't know the meaning of either of the words in the stem.*

HUH?

How can it be possible to eliminate choices if you don't know the words in the stem? Easy.

You already know two facts about GRE analogies:

1. The words in the stem must be related to each other in a clear and necessary way.

2. The words in ETS's answer must be linked by exactly the same relationship as the words in the stem.

Don't give up if you don't know the stem words!

From these two rules, we can easily deduce a third:

3. The words in ETS's answer must be related to each other in a clear and necessary way.

That is, since the relationship in ETS's answer must be identical to the relationship in the stem, the relationship in ETS's answer must also be clear and necessary.

Where does this get us? Everywhere. We can now deduce a fourth rule:

4. Any answer choice containing words that are *not* related to each other in a clear and necessary way could not possibly be ETS's answer and therefore can be eliminated.

That's right. Since you know that the stem and ETS's answer must both be based on a clear and necessary relationship, you also know that any choice *not* based on a clear and necessary relationship *must be wrong*.

ELIMINATE UNRELATED PAIRS

Keeping in mind the fourth rule above, try your hand at the following analogy. Notice that we've left out the words in the stem:

16. _____ : _____ ::
    (A) speculation : factions
    (B) forestation : grass
    (C) theorizing : rumors
    (D) replication : duplicates
    (E) animation : characters

Here's how to crack it

Give up? Don't! You already have enough information to find ETS's answer.

As usual, the first thing to do is to try to form a sentence. We need to do it with each of the choices. The point in trying to form a sentence is to see if each pair of words is related in a clear and necessary way. Start with the first pair:

(A) Is there a clear and necessary relationship between speculation and factions? No. You might try to get tricky and say something like, "Speculation among the delegates led to the formation of factions at the political convention," but this is an unclear and unnecessary relationship. We can eliminate this choice.

(B) There might be grass in a forest, but there's nothing clear or necessary about the relationship between these two words. This is not an ETS relationship. We can eliminate this choice.

(C) Can you think of a clear, succinct sentence linking *theorizing* and *rumors* through their meanings? We can't. We can eliminate this choice.

Eliminate unrelated pairs.

(D) Replication is the creation of duplicates. This is a clear and necessary relationship based on the meanings of the words. A possibility.

(E) Cartoon characters are sometimes animated, but be careful: There is no other relationship between these words. To animate something is to give life to it. There is no clear and necessary relationship here. Many GRE analogy choices will contain pairs of words that sort of sound right together, even though they are unrelated. These are traps for Joe Bloggs. We can eliminate this choice.

ETS's answer must be choice D, the only choice we couldn't eliminate. It is. (The missing stem is RAMIFICATION : BRANCHES. Ramification is the process of forming branches, just as *replication* is the process of forming *duplicates*.)

Here's another example of how eliminating unrelated pairs can enable you to zero in on ETS's answer:

13. _____ : _____ ::
    (A) captious : criticism
    (B) kind : admiration
    (C) questionable : response
    (D) reprehensible : censure
    (E) incredible : ecstasy

Here's how to crack it

Once again, look for unrelated pairs.

(A) A captious person is a carping or critical person. Therefore, our sentence might be "To be captious is to make criticism." This sentence expresses a clear and necessary relationship. A possibility.

(B) Kind people or kind acts often inspire admiration, but there is *not* a clear and necessary relationship between these two words. The words are not linked through their definitions. We can eliminate this choice.

(C) *Questionable* and *response* sort of seem as though they ought to go together. But they don't really. *Question* and *response* would be clearly and necessarily related, but these two words aren't. We can eliminate this choice.

(D) *Reprehensible* means "worthy of rebuke or censure," according to the dictionary. These two words are clearly and necessarily related. Our sentence might be, "To be reprehensible is to deserve censure." A possibility.

(E) *Incredible* means unbelievable. *Ecstasy* is intense delight or emotion. The two words are not related in a clear and necessary way. We can eliminate this choice.

We've eliminated all choices but A and D. If we guess now, we'll have a fifty-fifty chance of being right—a coin toss. Not bad, considering we still don't know anything about the stem words. (The missing stem is MERITORIOUS : PRAISE. Meritorious means deserving of praise. ETS's answer is choice D.)

In the next section, we'll show you techniques that will often enable you to determine which of the remaining choices is most likely to be ETS's answer.

You Can't Eliminate Words You "Sort of Know"

Never initially eliminate a choice if you can't absolutely, positively define the meanings of both words in it. You can't be certain that two words are unrelated if you are not really sure what one of them means. We'll discuss guessing shortly. But there's more that you can do before you have to guess.

Working Backward from the Choices

Working backward is especially useful when the meaning of one of the words in the stem is unknown or only "sort of" known. It is a method of testing a choice by determining its relationship and then assessing whether the words in the stem could possibly be related in the same way.

Working backward is effective because it takes advantage of our favorite immutable fact about relationships between paired words in GRE analogies: The relationship between the stem words must be exactly the same relationship as the one between the words in ETS's answer.

Let's look at an example. Suppose that we don't know the meaning of the first word in the stem but that by identifying unrelated pairs we have been able to eliminate three choices. Here's what's left:

10. _____ : KNIFE ::
    (A) tune : piano
    (B) [eliminated]
    (C) baste : dryness
    (D) [eliminated]
    (E) [eliminated]

Here's how to crack it

We will look for ETS's answer by forming a sentence for each of the remaining choices and applying it backward to the stem.

Our sentence for choice A is "To tune a piano means to improve its quality." Could _____ mean to improve the quality of a knife? Sure. It's easy to imagine that there could be a word for that, like *sharpen*. We don't have to think of the exact word to feel certain that such a word could exist.

Now choice C. Our sentence is "To baste [something] reduces its dryness."
Could _____ing something reduce its knife? No. This sentence is nonsense.
ETS's answer is A. (The missing word in the stem is HONE.)
Here's another example:

14. _____ : INSIGHT ::
   (A) authoritative : despotism
   (B) audacious : hearing
   (C) torpid : activity
   (D) avaricious : generosity
   (E) zealous : enthusiasm

Beware of Joe Bloggs's answer choices on questions 13–16.

Here's how to crack it

Once again, we're assuming that we don't know the meaning of the first word in
the stem. What can we do without it? First we can eliminate unrelated pairs.

(A) Are *authoritative* and *despotism* related in a clear and necessary
    way? Well, a despot could be authoritative, or one could
    believe that being authoritative might possibly lead to despo-
    tism, but the relationship between these two words is not
    necessary. You won't find either word in the dictionary defini-
    tion of the other. Eliminate.

(B) *Audacious* means recklessly bold or having audacity. It has nothing
    to do with hearing. (The similarity in sound between the word
    audacious and the root *audio-* is a trap for Joe Bloggs.) Eliminate.

(C) Are *torpid* and *activity* related? Maybe you're not totally sure of
    the meaning of *torpid*. Keep this choice! If you're not sure, it has
    to remain a possibility. (To be torpid is to be inactive, or to
    display no activity. So it is a clear and necessary relationship.)

(D) Are *avaricious* and *generosity* related? Maybe. *Avaricious* means
    "greedy." To be avaricious is to display no generosity. A
    possibility.

(E) Are *zealous* and *enthusiasm* related? Yes. To be *zealous* is to
    exhibit great enthusiasm. A possibility.

Our search for unrelated pairs has enabled us to eliminate two choices.
Here's what we're left with:

14. _____ : INSIGHT ::
   (C) torpid : activity
   (D) avaricious : generosity
   (E) zealous : enthusiasm

Now we can work backward from the relationships in the choices we have
not eliminated. Here's what we know:

1. If choice C is ETS's answer, the missing word must mean
   "displaying no insight."

2. If choice D is ETS's answer, we know that the missing word must mean "displaying no insight."

3. If choice E is ETS's answer, we know that the missing word must mean "displaying great insight."

The first thing to notice is that, at least as we have formed our sentences, the words in choice C are related in exactly the same way as the words in choice D. What does this mean? It means that neither can be ETS's answer, because if one of them were ETS's answer then the other would have to be as well, and GRE questions have only one credited answer. We need to be careful, though, because we may have overlooked a nuance.

Even so, we can tell from our remaining choices that the missing stem word must mean either something like "displaying no insight" or "displaying great insight." With this in mind, let's look at the complete stem:

14. PERSPICACIOUS : INSIGHT

Selecting an answer choice is now merely a matter of deciding whether PERSPICACIOUS seems more likely to mean "displaying no insight" or "displaying great insight." This is a vastly simpler task than attempting to guess the definition of a word out of context. Indeed, if you've heard or seen the unknown stem word before, narrowing your possibilities in this way may jog your memory and enable you to select ETS's answer, which is E. You don't need to know the exact definition of a word in order to deduce that definition by working backward.

THE TICKING CLOCK

Won't it take hours to apply all these techniques? No. With a little practice, you'll make them an automatic part of your thought process on GRE analogies. In fact, they'll save you time by making you much more efficient in your approach to difficult items. You'll spend less time on these items because you'll spend less time spinning your wheels.

WHEN YOU DON'T KNOW WORDS IN THE ANSWER CHOICES

Assuming you know both words in the stem, you can still ask yourself whether *any* word could create a relationship in the choice identical to the relationship in the stem. If not, you can eliminate the choice.

14. INVARIABLE : CHANGE ::
    (A) incurable : disease
    (B) unfathomable : depth
    (C) extraneous : proposition
    (D) ineffable : expression
    (E) variegated : appearance

Your sentence for the relationship between the stem words would be something like "Something *invariable* is without change." Notice that *change* is a noun, not a verb.

(A) Is something *incurable* without disease? No. Eliminate this choice.

(B) Is something *unfathomable* without depth? Nope. Eliminate this choice too.

(C) Is something *extraneous* without proposition? Do you know the dictionary definition of *extraneous*? Keep this choice and check out the other choices.

(D) Is something *ineffable* without expression? If you don't know the definition of *ineffable*, you'd better keep this choice.

(E) Is something *variegated* without appearance? Now, we may not know the exact definition of *variegated*, but from what we sort of know, it wouldn't fit our sentence. It has something to do with appearance, but it doesn't mean *without appearance*.

Now we're guessing between choices C and D. Do you think it's more likely that some word means "without proposition" or that some word means "without expression"? If you guessed choice D, you found the ETS answer even though you didn't know all of the words in the answer choices.

JOE BLOGGS AND GRE ANALOGIES

Whether a question is easy, medium, or difficult, Joe Bloggs finds some answer choices much more appealing than others. Most of all, Joe is attracted to choices containing words that:

1. Remind him of words in the stem

2. "Just seem to go with" the words in the stem

3. Are easy to understand

Here's an example:

8. WELD : METAL ::

    (A) cater : gala
    (B) tweak : skin
    (C) catheterize : fluid
    (D) nail : wood
    (E) lash : whip

> Don't always eliminate Joe Bloggs's choices.

Here's how to crack it

Which choice "just seems to go with" the stem? Choice D. Welding metal, nailing wood. Joe Bloggs is definitely attracted to this choice. Should we eliminate it? No!

Don't forget: On the easy third of a subsection, Joe Bloggs's hunches are correct. This question is a number 8, the easiest in the group. Choice D is ETS's answer.

Now let's look at a hard analogy:

16. APOSTATE : FAITH ::
    (A) apostle : leader
    (B) altruist : literature
    (C) defector : allegiance
    (D) potentate : religion
    (E) patriot : principle

Here's how to crack it

First, eliminate unrelated pairs:

(A) Is there a clear and necessary relationship between *apostle* and *leader*? Maybe. Do you know the dictionary definition of *apostle*? A possibility.

(B) How about *altruist* and *literature*? No. An altruist is a generous or selfless person. This has nothing to do with literature. Eliminate.

(C) A defector is someone who forsakes an allegiance, such as to a country. Clear and necessary? Yes. A possibility.

(D) *Potentate* and *religion*? Are you sure you know the definition of *potentate*? If not, you can't eliminate this choice.

(E) Is there a clear and necessary relationship between *patriot* and *principle*? Be careful. A patriot might have principles, but there is nothing clear or necessary about the relationship between these two words. You would not find either word in the dictionary definition of the other. Eliminate.

We're left with choices A, C, and D. We've already improved our odds on this difficult item to one in three. What do we do now? It's time to guess, but don't guess blindly. Look for Joe Bloggs attractors.

Which choices "just seem to go with" the stem? Choices A and D. *Apostle* is a religious word. And what could be more attractive than choice D? These choices are Joe Bloggs attractors—so you can eliminate them. Remember, if finding ETS's answer were as easy as Joe thinks it is, this would be an easy question, not a hard one. Before you guess on a difficult question, be sure you don't guess a Joe Bloggs answer choice.

ETS's answer is choice C. An *apostate* is one who *forsakes* his faith.

HARD QUESTIONS, HARD ANSWERS

Joe Bloggs is lazy. As a result, he has a powerful tendency to select choices that he understands. That is, he's unlikely to select a choice if it contains words he's never heard of (unless there's something else about the choice that attracts him, such as an easy word that reminds him of the stem). When Joe takes a stab at a question, he tends to pick something familiar.

What does this mean? It means that one of the best places to look for ETS's answer on a hard question is in a hard answer—a choice that Joe doesn't get. When all else fails on a hard question, the best strategy is to eliminate what you can and then simply select the remaining choice with the hardest words. That is, in guessing on harder questions, you want to look for the choice that is *least likely to seem correct to Joe*.

SUMMARY

When You Can Define Both of the Stem Words

1. Make a sentence that defines one of the stem words in terms of the other. Write it down.

2. Eliminate answer choices that don't fit in your sentence.

3. If you're not sure of the definition of a word in an answer choice, don't eliminate that choice.

4. If more than one answer choice seems to fit your original sentence for the stem words, make your sentence more specific.

5. If you have more than one answer choice left, pay attention to the order of difficulty. Easy questions have easy answers. Hard questions have hard answers.

When You Can't Define Both of the Stem Words

1. Go right to the answer choices and eliminate answer choices that do not have clear and necessary relationships.

2. If you're not sure of the definition of a word in an answer choice, don't eliminate that choice.

3. Work backward from the answer choices that do have clear and necessary relationships. Eliminate answer choices that have relationships that would be impossible for the stem words to have, given what you "sort of know" about the stem words.

When You Can't Define Both in the Answer Choices

1. Pay attention to the order of difficulty! Easy questions have easy answers. Hard questions have hard answers. On questions 13–16, eliminate Joe Bloggs's choices before you guess, and try to choose the hardest choice.

8

Sentence Completions

ABOUT SENTENCE COMPLETIONS

Each verbal section of your GRE will contain seven sentence completion items, numbered 1–7. Items 1 and 2 will be easy, items 3–5 will be medium, and items 6 and 7 will be difficult.

In this chapter, sentence completions will also be numbered 1–7. Always pay attention to the item position in answering GRE questions. The item number will help determine the technique or combination of techniques you will use to crack it.

LEARN THESE DIRECTIONS

Before we begin, take a moment to read and learn the following set of directions. These are the directions exactly as they will appear on your GRE. You shouldn't even glance at them when you take the test. If you do, you will waste time and lose points. Here are the directions:

> Directions: Each sentence below has one or two blanks, each blank indicating that something has been omitted. Beneath the sentence are five lettered words or sets of words. Choose the word or set of words for each blank that best fits the meaning of the sentence as a whole.

OUR APPROACH TO SENTENCE COMPLETIONS

The Princeton Review's techniques for cracking sentence completions are very powerful. All are based on POE. Sometimes you will be able to use POE to eliminate all four incorrect choices. In any event, you should always be able to eliminate at least one. **Eliminating even one incorrect choice will improve your odds of earning points**.

Our techniques for sentence completions will enable you to:

1. Zero in on ETS's answer by understanding how the items were written.

2. Use contextual clues to anticipate ETS's answer.

3. Use structural clues.

4. Eliminate Joe Bloggs attractors.

LEARNING TO LOVE SENTENCE COMPLETIONS

Sentence completions—which you've known since kindergarten under the less ominous title of "fill in the blanks"—are among the most crackable items on the entire test. You'll soon be wishing there were more than seven of them in each verbal section.

Remember fill-in-the-blanks from grade school? Here they are, but now they're called sentence completions.

FINDING THE CLUE IN GRE SENTENCE COMPLETIONS

The ETS answer for a sentence completion question is always based on information that is stated explicitly in the sentence. We call this information the "clue." Never base your answer on outside knowledge of the topic discussed in the sentence! Rely only on the clue.

Look for the clue.

To find the clue in the sentence, ask yourself:

◆ What is the blank talking about?

◆ What other part of the sentence talks about this?

That's probably the clue for the blank!

How ETS Writes Sentence Completion Items

Let's pretend that we just started work at ETS, writing sentence completions. We've got a rough idea for our first question:

> Museums are good resources for students of
> -------.
>
> (A) art
> (B) science
> (C) religion
> (D) dichotomy
> (E) philanthropy

As we've written it, this question is unanswerable. Almost any choice could be defended. We couldn't use this question on a real test, because students would justly complain that none of the choices is much better than any of the others.

To make this into a real GRE question, we'll have to change the sentence in such a way that only one of the answer choices can be defended. Here's another try:

> 1. Museums, which house many paintings and sculptures, are good resources for students of
> -------.
>
> (A) art
> (B) science
> (C) religion
> (D) dichotomy
> (E) philanthropy

Here's how to crack it

Now there's only one solid answer: choice A. The clause we added to our original sentence makes this obvious. This clause—containing the words *paintings and sculptures*—is the clue. Our finished question is very easy. Joe Bloggs will have no problem with it. That's why it's number 1.

But suppose that the verbal section we're writing already has a number 1 sentence completion. Suppose that what we really need is a number 4—a medium.

How could we turn our item into a medium? We'll do it by inserting a harder clue—by throwing in some moderately difficult vocabulary words:

4. Museums, which often house elaborate reliquaries, talismans, and altarpieces, are good resources for students of -------.

   (A) art
   (B) science
   (C) religion
   (D) dichotomy
   (E) philanthropy

Here's how to crack it

ETS's answer is choice C. To find it, you need to know that reliquaries, talismans, and altarpieces are religious articles.

We might also have created a medium question by complicating the sentence structure:

4. Because the paintings in their collections sometimes illustrate changing perceptions of the workings of the physical world, museums can be good resources for students of the history of -------.

   (A) art
   (B) science
   (C) religion
   (D) dichotomy
   (E) philanthropy

Here's how to crack it

Here, ETS's answer is choice B. Choice A, *art*, would be too simple an answer for a medium question that mentioned both paintings and museums. Choices D and E are simply too peculiar to be ETS's answer on a medium.

On a hard question, ETS's answer will be *peculiar*, and Joe Bloggs won't be able to find it, even by accident. Let's rewrite our item once again to make it a number 7:

7. Because the paintings and sculptures in their collections tend to reflect the shifting tastes of that class of privileged individuals capable of turning private means to public ends, museums are interesting resources for students of trends in -------.

   (A) art
   (B) science
   (C) religion
   (D) dichotomy
   (E) philanthropy

Here's how to crack it

Here ETS's answer is choice E. Joe Bloggs doesn't pick it, because *philanthropy* is a hard word and he doesn't associate it with museums. Also, the sentence is long and impossible for Joe to decipher. Joe Bloggs has heard of art museums and science museums, and as a result he's strongly attracted to both those choices. ETS's answer has to be something that doesn't occur to him.

LOOK BEFORE YOU LEAP

Knowing how the sentence completions are constructed, we can do the same thing in reverse to take them apart. By finding the clue, we can tune in to ETS's wavelength. Doing this will enable us to anticipate ETS's answer, even before we look at the choices.

Many students read sentence completions quickly, then go immediately to the choices and begin trying the answers in the sentence. This approach may work on easy items, but it will only confuse you on difficult ones. If you take the time to understand what ETS is up to, you'll have a much easier time selecting the best answer from among the choices.

COVER THE ANSWER CHOICES

Physically cover the answer choices, read the sentence, find the clue, and write down your own words for the blank(s) *before* you look at the answer choices. Here's an example of what we mean:

1. Wilson worked ------- on his first novel, cloistering himself in his study for days on end without food or sleep.

Here's how to crack it

Where's the clue in the sentence that will tell us how Wilson worked? It's the phrase *days on end*. Without it, any number of different words could plausibly fill in the blank. Finding the clue, now let's anticipate ETS's answer. You don't have to think of a difficult word, since this is an easy question. How about *hard*? The ETS answer has to mean something like "hard," since we know Wilson worked "for days on end." Now take a look at the complete item:

1. Wilson worked ------- on his first novel, cloistering himself in his study for days on end without food or sleep.

   (A) carelessly
   (B) creatively
   (C) tirelessly
   (D) intermittently
   (E) voluntarily

Here's how to crack it

(A) Does *carelessly* mean *hard*? No. Eliminate.

(B) Does *creatively* mean *hard*? No. Get rid of this choice.

(C) Does *tirelessly* mean *hard*? Maybe, since we know that Wilson worked "for days on end without food or sleep." Let's keep this and consider the rest of the choices.

Trigger words help you to find the relationship between the blanks and the clue.

(D) Does *intermittently* mean *hard*? Be careful! Are you sure you know the dictionary definition of the word? If not, keep this choice and keep going.

(E) Does *voluntarily* mean *hard*? Definitely not. Eliminate.

Now that we're down to two choices, how difficult is question 1? Easy. Easy questions have easy answers. So if we don't know the definition of *intermittently*, it's too difficult to be the right answer to an easy question. Also, we know that *tirelessly* fits, because we know that Wilson worked "for days on end without food or sleep." So the ETS answer must be choice C.

DRILL 1

In each of the following sentences, find the clue and underline it. Then see if you can anticipate ETS's answer. Write a word or phrase near the blank. It doesn't matter if your guesses are awkward or wordy. All you need to do is capture the general idea. (You can check your answers on page 295.)

2. Despite the apparent ------- of the demands, the negotiations dragged on for over a year.

4. Most students found Dr. Schwartz's lecture on art excessively detailed and academic; some thought his display of ------- exasperating.

DRILL 2

Now that you've anticipated ETS's answers, look at the same two questions again, this time with the choices provided. See if you can use your notes above to find ETS's answer. (You can check your answers on page 295.)

2. Despite the apparent ------- of the demands, the negotiations dragged on for over a year.

   (A) hastiness
   (B) intolerance
   (C) publicity
   (D) modesty
   (E) desirability

4. Most students found Dr. Schwartz's lecture on art excessively detailed and academic; some thought his display of ------- exasperating.

   (A) pedantry
   (B) logic
   (C) aesthetics
   (D) erudition
   (E) literalism

TRIGGER WORDS

Certain words signal changes in the meaning of sentence completions. We call them *trigger words*. They provide important clues about the meaning of the sentence, and—because they confuse Joe Bloggs—they are often the key to finding ETS's answer.

Here are the most important sentence completion trigger words:

In two-blank sentences, concentrate on the easier blank.

but	while
although (though, even though)	however
unless	unfortunately
rather	in contrast
yet	similarly
despite	heretofore
thus	previously

Trigger words go a long way toward determining the meaning of the sentence. To see how these words can provide clues to ETS's answer, fill in the blanks in the following pair of simple sentences:

A fair *and* ------- judge.
A fair *but* ------- judge.

Now here's an example of a full sentence completion in which finding ETS's answer turns on understanding the function of a trigger word:

1. Although originally created for ------- use, the colorful, stamped tin kitchen boxes of the early twentieth century are now prized primarily for their ornamental qualities.

   (A) traditional
   (B) practical
   (C) occasional
   (D) annual
   (E) commercial

Here's how to crack it

What's the clue in the sentence that will tell us what the boxes were originally created for? Well, we know that they "are now prized primarily for their ornamental qualities." Does this mean that they were originally created for "ornamental" use? No. The trigger word *although* indicates that the word for the blank will mean the opposite of *ornamental*. What would be a good word that means the opposite of *ornamental*? *Useful* would be a good word, even though it may sound strange to say "useful use." Don't worry about how your words sound; it's what they mean that's important.

(A) Does *traditional* mean *useful*? No. Eliminate.

(B) Does *practical* mean *useful*? Yes. But don't just stop here; be sure to consider the remaining choices.

(C) Does *occasional* mean *useful*? No. Get rid of it.

(D) Does *annual* mean *useful*? Nope.

(E) Does *commercial* mean *useful*? Only if you tell some long story. The ETS answer is based on the dictionary definitions of the words in the choices. There is no clue in the sentence about commerce. Eliminate this choice. The ETS choice is B.

THE GOOD, THE BAD, AND THE INDIFFERENT

On the easy and medium problems you should try your best to come up with your own word(s) for the blank(s). But in some cases, you may think of *several* words that could go in the blanks. Rather than spend a lot of time trying to find the "perfect" word, look at the blank and ask yourself whether the missing word will be a "good" word (one with positive connotations) or a "bad" word (one with negative connotations). Then write a + or a – symbol in the blank itself.

Here's an example:

3. Trembling with anger, the belligerent colonel ordered his men to ------- the civilians.

Here's how to crack it

Is the missing word a "good" word or a "bad" word? It's a "bad" word, isn't it? The colonel is clearly going to do something nasty to the civilians. You don't have to anticipate exactly which nasty thing the colonel ordered. Just go to the answer choices and eliminate any choices that are positive and therefore couldn't be correct:

(A) congratulate
(B) promote
(C) reward
(D) attack
(E) worship

Here's how to crack it

Choices A, B, C, and E are all positive words. All, therefore, can be eliminated. ETS's answer is choice D, the only negative word among the choices.

TWO BLANKS

ELIMINATE CHOICES ONE BLANK AT A TIME

Many sentence completions will have two blanks instead of one. Does this mean that two-blank sentence completions are harder than one-blank sentence completions? Many students feel this way, but they shouldn't. *Two-blank sentence completions are harder than one-blank sentence completions only if you insist on trying to fill in both blanks at the same time.*

You'll do much better if you concentrate on just one of the blanks at a time. Remember, a two-blank answer choice can be ETS's answer only if it works for *both* blanks; if you can determine that one of the words in the choice doesn't work in its blank, you can eliminate the choice without testing the other word.

Which blank should you concentrate on? The easier one, of course. Usually, this will be the second blank.

Once you've decided which blank is easier, anticipate what sort of word should fit into it, then go to the answer choices and look only at the ones provided for that blank. Then *eliminate* any choice that doesn't work for that blank.

Here's an example of how you can crack a hard two-blank sentence completion by tackling it one blank at a time:

Are you learning GRE vocabulary?

6. A growing number of heretical scientists are claiming the once ------- theory of evolution must be -------, if not actually shelved.

Here's how to crack it

Ignoring the first blank, which looks more difficult, we reduce the sentence to this: "The theory of evolution must be -------, if not actually shelved." You ought to be able to anticipate roughly what this blank must mean. It must mean something like "*almost* shelved," or "changed in some basically negative way." Now look at the choices, paying attention only to the second word in each:

(A) ------- . . postulated
(B) ------- . . popularized
(C) ------- . . reexamined
(D) ------- . . modified
(E) ------- . . promulgated

Here's how to crack it

Do any of these words fit the rough restriction we've anticipated for the second blank? How about choices C and D? To *reexamine* or *modify* a theory is to do something negative to it that falls short of actually throwing it out. Now look at the first word in each of these choices:

(C) sacrosanct . . reexamined
(D) modern . . modified

Here's how to crack it

There's no clue for the word *modern,* so ETS's answer must be choice C. It is. *Sacrosanct* means "inviolably sacred." Joe Bloggs would never think of a theory of evolution as "sacred," so he would be attracted to the wrong choice. This is a number 6 question, so we want the answer Joe Bloggs *wouldn't* choose.

TRIGGER WORDS AND TWO-BLANK QUESTIONS

Trigger words and punctuation can be especially important on questions with two blanks. For some two-blank sentence completions, the most efficient way to eliminate answer choices is to consider the relationship between the two blanks.

To find the relationship between the two blanks in the sentence, pay special attention to trigger words. Sometimes a trigger word tells you that the two blanks are opposites of each other. Or trigger words can show you that the two blanks are similar to each other, but both have connotations opposite from the clue in the sentence. If you know that the words for the two blanks have to be opposites, eliminate answer choices in which the two words have similar connotations. Likewise, if the words for the two blanks should be similar, eliminate answer choices in which the two words have different connotations.

This is a useful POE technique even when you have your own words for the blanks. Crossing out choices that don't fit the pattern will make you less likely to make a careless error.

Here's an example:

> 7. Although he was usually ------- and -------, his illness blunted both his appetite and his temper.
>
> (A) gluttonous . . contentious
> (B) sated . . belligerent
> (C) avaricious . . responsive
> (D) eloquent . . reflective
> (E) ravenous . . reticent

Here's how to crack it

From the trigger word *although*, we can say, roughly, that his illness blunted both his appetite and his temper, which would usually be unblunted or extreme:

> Although he was usually [*un*blunted in his appetite] and [*un*blunted in his temper], his illness blunted both his appetite and his temper.

So both of the words in the blanks will be negative words. Now we can eliminate any choice that has a positive word in it.

> (A) gluttonous . . contentious
> (B) sated . . belligerent
> (C) avaricious . . responsive
> (D) eloquent . . reflective
> (E) ravenous . . reticent

Immediately eliminate choices C and D. If you "sort of know" that *sated* is a positive word, eliminate choice B, too. Since either *gluttonous* or *ravenous* would work in the first blank, you have to ask yourself whether *contentious* or *reticent* could mean "unblunted in temper." The ETS answer is choice A. Look up any vocabulary words that you didn't know in this difficult question.

GUESSING: MR. BLOGGS, I PRESUME?

As usual, Joe Bloggs is attracted to easy answer choices that remind him of the question. Having read the word *poison* in a sentence, his eye falls quickly on the choice that contains the word *antidote*. On difficult questions, this choice will be wrong. When you're down to two or three choices, on questions 5–7, eliminate Joe Bloggs's choices.

Here's an example of what we mean:

7. Although bound to impose the law, a judge is free
    to use her discretion to ------- the anachronistic
    ------- of some criminal penalties.

    (A) enforce . . judiciousness
    (B) impose . . legality
    (C) exacerbate . . severity
    (D) mitigate . . barbarity
    (E) restore . . impartiality

Here's how to crack it

This is a number 7—a difficult item. In this sentence, from the trigger word *although,* you know that the words in the two blanks will be opposites. The word for the first blank will be positive since the judge is "free to use her discretion" to do it. The word for the second blank will be negative, since the word *anachronistic* is the clue for this blank.

You can eliminate choices A, B, and C, since the first words in these choices are negative. You can eliminate choice E because *impartiality* isn't negative (it's a positive word to ETS). So the ETS answer is choice D.

But if you had to guess, which choices would Joe Bloggs find attractive? His top guesses are choices A and B, because *judiciousness* and *legality* make him think of judges and the law. If you had to guess between choices D and E, Joe Bloggs chooses E, because *impartiality* reminds Joe of judges.

EASY QUESTIONS HAVE EASY ANSWERS; HARD QUESTIONS HAVE HARD ANSWERS

The general rule on the GRE is that easy questions have easy answers and hard questions have hard answers. This is because Joe Bloggs has a strong preference for easy answers that remind him of the question. The only exception to this rule is with antonyms, which we'll discuss in the next chapter, where hard questions often could have easy answers (easy words with obscure secondary meanings).

On sentence completions, the general rule again applies. On easy questions, ETS's answer will consist of easy words that Joe Bloggs understands and that remind him of the question; on hard questions, ETS's answer will usually consist of hard words that Joe has never heard of.

Take another look at an item we've already discussed:

7. Although bound to impose the law, a judge is free
    to use her discretion to ------- the anachronistic
    ------- of some criminal penalties.

    (A) enforce . . judiciousness
    (B) impose . . legality
    (C) exacerbate . . severity
    (D) mitigate . . barbarity
    (E) restore . . impartiality

Remember fill-in-the-blanks from grade school? Here they are, but now they're called sentence completions. Look for the clue. Trigger words help you to find the relationship between the blanks and the clue.

Here's how to crack it

Note that ETS's answer, choice D, contains the hardest of the ten words among the answer choices. Joe Bloggs has no idea what *mitigate* means (and isn't at all certain what *barbarity* means). This means he won't pick this choice, which makes it a strong candidate for being ETS's answer.

Here's another example:

> 6. While many people enjoy observing rituals and customs not ------- their culture, they ------- participating in them.
>
> (A) sanctioned by . . discourage
> (B) endemic to . . eschew
> (C) upheld in . . condone
> (D) central to . . relish
> (E) relevant to . . avoid

Here's how to crack it

You can use the trigger word *while* to determine that the two blanks must be opposites. Since the clue is "enjoy observing rituals," you can tell that the word for the second blank has to be something like *don't enjoy* or *avoid*. So you can eliminate choices C and D. You might get rid of choice A, upon closer examination, because there is no clue in the sentence that indicates that people "discourage" others from participating. Since this is a hard question, what are the hardest words among the remaining answer choices? *Endemic* and *eschew*. What is ETS's answer? Choice B.

BAILING OUT

When all else fails on the difficult third, simply select the answer choice containing the hardest words. Don't waste a lot of time on the most difficult questions. Spend more time answering the easy and medium questions correctly, and less time puzzling over the hardest problems.

SUMMARY

1. Cover the answer choices.

2. Read the entire sentence.

3. Find the clue(s) for the blank(s).

4. Find the trigger words in the sentence.

5. Write your own word(s) in the blank(s).

6. If you can't come up with exact words, write positive or negative in the blank(s).

7. On two-blank sentence completions, find the relationship between the two blanks. Are they the same or opposites?

8. Use POE. On two-blank sentences, eliminate entire answer choices using one blank at a time.

9. When guessing, remember:

   ◆ Easy questions have easy answers. Hard questions have hard answers.

   ◆ Eliminate Joe Bloggs's choices on questions 5–7.

9
Antonyms

ABOUT ANTONYMS

Each verbal section of your GRE will contain eleven antonym items, numbered 28–38. Items 28–30 will be easy, items 31–35 will be medium, and items 36–38 will be difficult.

In this chapter, antonyms will be numbered 28–38. Always pay attention to the item number in answering GRE questions. The item number will help determine which technique or combination of techniques you will use to crack the problem.

LEARN THESE DIRECTIONS

Before we begin, take a moment to read and learn the following set of directions. These are the directions exactly as they will appear on your GRE. You shouldn't even glance at them when you take the test. If you do, you will waste time and lose points. Here are the directions:

> Directions: Each question below consists of a word printed in capital letters, followed by five lettered words or phrases. Choose the lettered word or phrase that is most nearly opposite in meaning to the word in capital letters.
>
> Since some of the questions require you to distinguish fine shades of meaning, be sure to consider all the choices before deciding which one is best.

ARE THERE REALLY ANY TECHNIQUES?

It may seem that if you have a big vocabulary, you'll do well. If you have a tiny vocabulary, you'll have trouble. And of course, the best way to improve your antonym score is to improve your GRE vocabulary. Can you give a solid, dictionary definition for *corpulent* and *opprobrium*? Try, then look them up. And if you haven't begun studying our GRE Hit Parade (see chapter 6), do so now.

Even though antonyms are hard to crack, we do have techniques that can enable you to squeeze the maximum number of points out of your vocabulary. These techniques are based on POE. *They are also closely geared to the difficulty of the items*. So pay careful attention to item numbers.

POE ON ANTONYMS

In the antonyms section, there are a variety of techniques that you can use to eliminate bad answer choices. Certain techniques will work well for you on some examples but not on others. Use these techniques as the questions merit.

APPROACHING ANTONYMS

Remember that there are three types of words on the GRE:

- ◆ Words you know
- ◆ Words you sort of know
- ◆ Words you have never seen

Your approach to antonyms will vary depending on the type of word that you are dealing with, as well as the position of the question in the order of difficulty. Since you are learning the Hit Parade, you may find that you can now define some of the words that appear in very difficult problems.

But be extremely honest with yourself! It's better to be conservative, and to admit that you only "sort of" know a word, than to think you can define a word when you really can't.

APPROACHING ANSWER CHOICES

Start by eliminating answer choices with words that you can really define. If you only "sort of know" the definition of a word in an answer choice, don't eliminate that choice on the first round!

WHEN YOU CAN DEFINE THE STEM WORD

You may have noticed that ETS specifically warns you in the directions to check all of the answer choices. When you can define the stem word, rather than grabbing at the first choice that looks right, avoid careless errors by using the following steps.

- Cover the answer choices.

- Think of a simple definition for the stem word.

- Think of a simple opposite for the stem word.

- Use Process of Elimination.

At first, eliminate the answer choices that are nowhere near your own opposite for the stem word. Then **make opposites for the choices** that remain and work backward to the stem word.

Try this example:

| Work backward!

29. DISINCLINED
    (A) notable
    (B) gentle
    (C) willing
    (D) versatile
    (E) robust

Here's how to crack it

Let's assume we can define *disinclined*. It means something like "not liking." So our own word for the opposite would be something like *liking*.

Does *notable* mean "liking"? Not really, but to be safe, let's look at the rest of the choices.

Does *gentle* mean "liking"? No. Get rid of it.

Does *willing* mean "liking"? Maybe. Let's keep it for now.

Does *versatile* mean "liking"? No. Eliminate.

Does *robust* mean "liking"? No.

Just to be sure, let's make opposites for choices A and C. Does *disinclined* mean "not notable" or "not willing"? It's closer to "not willing." So the best answer is choice C.

29. DUBIOUS
    (A) unclear
    (B) boring
    (C) assured
    (D) fanciful
    (E) unofficial

Here's how to crack it

Let's assume we can define *dubious*. It means something like "not certain." So our own word for the opposite would be something like *certain*.

(A) Watch out! This choice is close to a synonym of *dubious*. ETS sometimes puts synonyms in the answer choices to induce careless mistakes. Cross off this wrong answer.

(B) Does *boring* mean "certain"? No. Eliminate.

(C) Does *assured* mean "certain"? Yes. But don't stop. Check all of the answer choices.

(D) Does *fanciful* mean "certain"? No. Eliminate.

(E) Does *unofficial* mean "certain"? No.

The ETS answer is choice C.

EASY QUESTIONS HAVE EASY ANSWERS

Don't be alarmed if you don't know the meaning of one or more of the *choices* on an antonym item in the easy third. As always, easy questions have easy answers. So, on easy antonyms you can eliminate answer choices that are too difficult.

WHEN YOU "SORT OF KNOW" THE STEM WORD

POSITIVE/NEGATIVE

Sometimes you can't define a stem word but you can determine whether it has a positive or negative connotation. If the stem word has a positive connotation, its antonym has to be negative, so eliminate positive answer choices. If the stem word is negative, eliminate negative choices. Write a + sign on top of positive stem words, and a – sign on top of negative stem words. Don't forget that you're looking for the *opposite* of the stem.

Try using positive/negative on this example.

30. DIGRESS: + / –
    (A) belittle   _____
    (B) confuse   _____
    (C) facilitate _____
    (D) convince   _____
    (E) focus   _____

Here's how to crack it

Since *digress* is negative, the antonym must be positive, so you can eliminate negative answer choices. Eliminate choices A and B. Next, make opposites for the remaining choices. *Facilitate* means to make easier. Could *digress* mean to "make harder"? Maybe. Could *digress* mean to "fail to convince"? Could *digress* mean to "lose focus"? That's what it means. The ETS answer is choice E.

WORKING BACKWARD FROM THE ANSWER CHOICES

Even in the easy third, you may occasionally find that you aren't entirely certain of the meaning of the word in capital letters. In such cases, you can often spur your memory, or at least improve your odds, by working backward from the choices. You can do this by taking each choice, turning it into its opposite, and comparing it with the word in capital letters. Here's an example:

30. GARISH:

    (A) adaptable
    (B) understated
    (C) explicable
    (D) generous
    (E) nonchalant

Here's how to crack it

Let's assume you aren't sure what *garish* means, but that you "sort of know" that it's a negative word so the answer must be positive. That eliminates choice E because "nonchalant" is a neutral word. But be careful! *Understated* is not a negative word! Now turn each choice into its opposite and see what you have:

    (A) not adaptable
    (B) overstated
    (C) inexplicable
    (D) stingy

As you turn each word into its opposite, compare it to the capitalized word and determine whether it could mean the same thing.

Could *garish* mean "not adaptable"?

Could *garish* mean "overstated"?

Could *garish* mean "inexplicable"?

Could *garish* mean "stingy"?

If no choice presents itself yet, eliminate the least likely choices, one at a time, and try to zero in on ETS's answer. On the easy third, you'll probably find it. Simply spending a few extra seconds on the item often makes something click in your mind, showing you what ETS is up to. (ETS's answer on this item is choice B. Look it up.)

Working backward is also a powerful method to use on the medium and difficult questions. ETS's answers on these items are seldom exactly what you would think of at first. You'll often have to turn the words over in your mind for a while to find ETS's wavelength.

ELIMINATE ANSWER CHOICES THAT HAVE NO OPPOSITES

What's the opposite of *cake*? What's the opposite of *baritone*? What's the opposite of *calligraphy*?

These words have no clear opposites. If they were choices on an antonym item on the GRE, you could eliminate them automatically, even if you didn't know the meaning of the word in capital letters. Why? Because if a choice has no opposite, the capitalized word can't possibly *be* its opposite.

Here's an example:

> 36. EXHUME:
>
> (A) breathe
> (B) inter
> (C) approve
> (D) assess
> (E) facilitate

Here's how to crack it

Let's assume we don't know the meaning of *exhume*. Work through the choices, turning each into its opposite:

(A) not breathe? Is there really a word for this? There's probably not a direct opposite. Eliminate.

(B) If you don't know this word, *don't* eliminate it!

(C) disapprove

(D) There's no clear opposite. Eliminate.

(E) make difficult

Doing this improves our guessing odds to one in three.

Our chances of finding ETS's answer now depend on whether narrowing down our choices has made anything click in our minds. ETS's answer is B; *inter* means "bury," *exhume* means "dig up."

WORD ASSOCIATION

Sometimes you don't know what the stem word means, but you've heard it used with another word or phrase. Use that knowledge to help you eliminate incorrect answer choices. Taking the time to do this may jog your memory of a word's meaning.

33. DEPLOY:

  (A) relinquish
  (B) convert
  (C) insulate
  (D) concentrate
  (E) deceive

You're not exactly sure what *deploy* means. However, you've probably heard it used in the phrases "deploy missiles," and "deploy troops."

Make opposites for the answer choices and plug them into your phrase.

Does "keep troops" make any sense?

Does "remain unchanged troops" make any sense?

Does "expose troops" make any sense?

Does "spread out troops" make any sense?

Does "remain truthful to troops" make any sense?

This technique usually won't eliminate all of the incorrect answer choices, but it can help you narrow them down. The ETS answer is D; *deploy* means to "spread out," *concentrate* means to "gather in."

Try this technique on the following question:

Use phrases you know to help you understand words you aren't sure about.

34. HEDGE:

  (A) attack repeatedly
  (B) risk commitment
  (C) seek advantage
  (D) lose pressure
  (E) become interested

Here's how to crack it

You've probably heard the phrase "to hedge your bets."

(A) There is no direct opposite for "attack repeatedly." Eliminate.

(B) Does "not risk commitment (with) your bets" make sense?
     Sure. Keep this choice.

(C) Does "not seek advantage (with) your bets" make sense?
     Maybe.

(D) Does "gain pressure (with) your bets" make sense? Huh?
     Eliminate.

(E) Does "become uninterested (in) your bets" make sense? Probably not.

Now that we're down to two choices, do you think it's more likely that "to hedge your bets" means to not take risks, or to not seek advantage? The ETS choice is B. To *hedge a bet* is to counterbalance it with other transactions so as to limit risk.

Sometimes you can eliminate a couple of choices by using positive/negative, then use word association on the choices that remain. Don't forget to work backward when you are down to two choices.

SECONDARY MEANINGS

On medium and difficult antonym questions, you may notice some "easy" words, and you wonder what makes them so medium or difficult. Did ETS suddenly abandon order of difficulty? Absolutely not! These "easy" words have secondary meanings that Joe Bloggs would never recognize.

When you see a "simple" word on the last two-thirds of the antonyms section, go beyond the first meaning that comes to mind. Think of alternative meanings for the word.

Try this example.

35. FLUSH:

    (A) meager
    (B) undeveloped
    (C) lacking motion
    (D) quick to agree
    (E) accurately portrayed

Here's how to crack it

What's the first meaning you think of? "To flush a toilet." That's what Joe Bloggs would think, too. Then why is this a number 35? Which answer choice looks very attractive? Yep, choice C is the trap answer choice. There must be an alternative meaning.

PAY ATTENTION TO PARTS OF SPEECH

You can determine the parts of speech in antonym questions the same way you can on analogy questions. To figure out whether the stem word is a noun, a verb, or an adjective check the answer choices. At least one of the answer choices will be unambiguous. You can see from choice A in the example above that the stem word *flush* is an adjective, since *meager* is an adjective. What does *something flush* mean? Perhaps you've heard of someone or some company "flush with cash." Let's make opposites from the answer choices.

(A) Could someone be "abundant" with cash? Sure.

(B) Could someone be "developed" with cash? Not likely.

(C) Could someone be "moving" with cash? Nope. This was the trap choice anyway. Eliminate.

(D) Could someone be "quick to disagree" with cash? Probably not. After all, people listen when money talks.

(E) Could someone be "inaccurately portrayed" with cash? Not likely.

The ETS answer is choice A. One of the meanings of *flush* as an adjective is "abundant" or "plentiful."

A Last Resort: Choose Extremes

If, after using all of the other techniques, you are still left with a few answer choices, use the following guessing technique to further eliminate incorrect choices.

Extreme words are more likely to be correct than moderate words. Look at the following examples. What are the most extreme answer choices? What are the most extreme answers in the examples below? Are they correct?

37. PRECOCIOUS:

(A) stunted
(B) insensitive
(C) capricious
(D) destructive
(E) ignorant

Here's how to crack it

You may have heard of a "precocious child." However, in this question, using word association doesn't really help you eliminate anything right off the bat. Since all the answer choices are negative, you can't really use positive/negative to eliminate anything. Since this is one of the two most difficult antonym problems, let's not waste too much time puzzling over it. The most extreme answer choices are *stunted* and *destructive*. Just guess one of these two choices! The ETS answer is A. *Precocious* means characterized by unusually early development or maturity, especially in mental abilities.

Try another difficult antonym.

38. PERFIDY:

(A) flippancy
(B) optimism
(C) aptitude
(D) loyalty
(E) humility

Here's how to crack it

Did you "sort of know" that *perfidy* is a negative word? Since *perfidy* is negative, eliminate choice A. What are the most extreme choices left? *Optimism* and *loyalty* are the most extreme. Do you think *perfidy* means "pessimism" or "treachery"? Which is more extreme? *Perfidy* means "treachery," so the ETS answer is choice D.

Be Careful: Hard Questions Often Have Easy Answers, Too

Back in the chapter on analogies, we told you that hard items tend to have hard answers. That was true for analogies. It's also true on sentence completions. It's often *not* true on antonyms. Simply picking the hardest choice on a difficult antonym is *not* a dependable strategy. On difficult antonym questions, "easy" words often have weird secondary meanings.

WHEN YOU'VE NEVER SEEN THE WORD BEFORE

KNOW WHEN TO BAG IT

Don't spend too much time on any one question.

Hard antonym items can be *really* hard. Quickly make an opposite for each answer choice. Eliminate any answer choice that doesn't have a clear, direct opposite. Guess the most extreme answer choice you have left. Then move on! It's better to use the time you have left to attack Reading Comprehension.

SUMMARY

When You Can Define the Stem Word

1. Make your own opposite for the stem word. Write it down.

2. Use POE.

3. Down to two choices? Make opposites for each choice and work backward.

4. Easy questions have easy answers.

When You "Sort of Know" the Stem Word

1. Use positive/negative. If the stem word is positive, eliminate positive answer choices. If the stem word is negative, eliminate negative answer choices.

2. If you've heard the word used with another word or phrase, use word association.

3. Make opposites for whatever answer choices remain and work backward to the Stem Word. Eliminate choices that don't have direct opposites.

4. To guess, choose the most extreme answer choice you have left.

When You've Never Seen the Stem Word

1. Make opposites for the answer choices. Eliminate answer choices that don't have direct opposites.

2. Don't waste a lot of time on these. Eliminate whatever you can and guess.

3. Choose the most extreme remaining answer choice.

P. S.: Learn the Hit Parade!

10
Reading Comprehension

ABOUT READING COMPREHENSION

Each verbal section of your GRE will contain two reading passages. Each passage will be followed by three to eight questions. The questions from the two passages will be numbered 17–27. **Reading comprehension questions are the only ones on the verbal GRE that do not appear in order of difficulty.** We'll explain more about this later in the chapter.

MEMORIZE THESE DIRECTIONS

Before we begin, take a moment to read and learn the following set of directions. These are the directions exactly as they will appear on your GRE. You shouldn't even glance at them when you take the test. If you do, you will waste time and lose points. Here are the directions:

> Directions: Each passage in this group is followed by questions based on its content. After reading a passage, choose the best answer to each question. Answer all questions following a passage on the basis of what is stated or implied in that passage.

OUR APPROACH TO READING COMP

Nobody likes reading comp. The passages are boring and hard to understand, the questions are either difficult or infuriating, and the whole thing takes too much time. Fortunately, we have solutions to these problems.

Our techniques for cracking reading comp will enable you to:

1. Learn more by doing less

2. Read quickly and efficiently

3. Improve your guessing odds by eliminating choices that could not possibly be correct

4. Find ETS's answers without reading the passages in some cases

SAVE READING COMP FOR LAST

Partly because the passages and questions are so poorly written, reading comprehension is incredibly time-consuming. In fact, answering the eleven reading comp questions in one of your verbal sections could easily take you more time than answering all twenty-seven other questions in the section. And yet those eleven reading comp questions aren't worth any more points than any other eleven questions. Three hard reading comp questions, which might take you five or more minutes to answer, are worth exactly the same number of points as three easy antonym questions, which you might be able to answer in a few seconds.

For this reason, you must **always save reading comp for last**. Don't even peek at a reading comp passage until you've finished every other item in the verbal section you're working on. When you come to the reading comp pages in each verbal section, skip over them immediately and answer the eleven antonym questions hidden behind them. Don't sacrifice 110 points in the hope of earning thirty.

In Fact, It Would Probably Make Sense for You to Skip One Reading Passage Entirely

The vast majority of students could score higher on the GRE if they skipped at least one reading comp passage in each verbal section. Skipping a passage gives you a big chunk of time that you can invest much more profitably in other parts of the test.

Lengths of Passages

Each of the two verbal sections on your GRE will typically contain one long passage and one short one. The short passage may look more appealing, but it will often be denser and harder to understand than the long one. In a short passage, you may have to read every sentence carefully to figure out what is being said.

What to Skip

Unless you are scoring above 700, skip the short passage. *But be sure you mark answers on your bubble sheet, of course.* Spend your time on the long passage. It has more questions—and more points.

Reading the Passages: Forget About Comprehension

There are many different reasons for reading. Sometimes you read for pleasure; sometimes you read for general knowledge; sometimes you read in order to discover a particular piece of information.

On the GRE, you read for one reason only: *to earn points.*

Your first step is to forget about "reading comprehension." If you actually sat down and tried to *comprehend* a passage on the GRE—by reading and rereading it until you understood it thoroughly and were able to discuss it intelligently— you would have no time for the rest of the test.

Read to get the answers; don't read for full comprehension.

Good News

Fortunately, reading to earn points is much easier than reading for comprehension. The questions test only a tiny fraction of the boring, hard-to-remember details that are crammed into each passage. All you have to do to maximize your score is learn to identify the important 10 to 20 percent of the passage that is being tested. That's what our techniques are designed to do.

SAMPLE PASSAGE AND QUESTIONS

In the discussion that follows, we will refer again and again to the sample passage and questions printed on pages 98–101.

It is well known that termites are blind, but little has been discovered about the other sense organs of these insects or their reactions to various stimuli. Body

Line odors, as well as odors related to sex and to colony,

(5) certainly play a part in the activities of the termite colony. When specimens of eastern subterranean termites are placed in a jar containing a colony of rotten wood termites from the Pacific Coast, the host termites recognize these foreign insects by differences

(10) in odor and eventually kill the invaders. The progress of the chase and kill is very slow, and the larger host termites appear awkward in their efforts to bite and kill their smaller but quicker-moving cousins. Finally, more or less by sheer numbers and by accident, they

(15) corner and exterminate the enemy.

Eastern dealated (wingless) termites that manage to survive in the rotten wood termite colony for more than a week, however, are no longer molested. This is noteworthy, since eastern termites of this variety had

(20) previously been pursued and killed. Fresh eastern wingless specimens placed in the colony alongside the week-old visitors are immediately attacked, thus indicating that the rotten wood termites have in no way lost their capacity for belligerence.

(25) What else besides odor helps termites interpret the world around them? The insects have sense or "chorodontal" organs located on the antennae, on the bristles, on the base of the mandibles, and on the legs. These organs apparently enable termites to receive

(30) vibrations sent through the air, or, more precisely, aid in the reception of stimuli sent through the nest material or through air pockets within the nest material. When alarmed, soldier termites exhibit synchronous, convulsive movements that appear to be a

(35) method of communication adapted to the chorodontal organ system, although no sound that is audible to man is produced by these movements. Termite soldiers also strike their heads against wood and other nest materials, producing noises that, after passing through the

(40) sounding board formed by the nest material, become rustling and crackling sounds plainly audible to man's duller and possibly differently attuned perceptions. In fact, soldiers of one termite species, found in the arid regions of California, strike their heads against the dry,

(45) dead flower stalks of Spanish bayonets and agave plants with such force that the sound produced can be heard several feet away. Other types of soldier termites found in the tropics make audible clicking noises with their jaws.

(50) There is a clear correlation between the functioning of the chorodontal system and termite settlement patterns. Seldom are termites found infesting railroad ties over which there is frequent heavy traffic, or on the woodwork of mill or factory buildings where heavy

(55) machinery in motion would cause vibrations. Small-scale tests with a radio speaker and vibrator yielded interesting results when termites were placed in the speaker and exposed to various frequency vibrations. When the vibrations ranged from 50–100 per second,

(60) the termites were thrown about; at vibrations of 100–500, termites set their feet and mandibles and held on with all their power; at 2,000–5,000 vibrations per second, the termites crawled about undisturbed.

21. The author's primary concern in the passage is to

   (A) show how little is known of certain organ systems in insects
   (B) describe the termite's method of overcoming blindness
   (C) provide an overview of some termite sensory organs
   (D) relate the termite's sensory perceptions to man's
   (E) describe the termite's aggressive behavior

22. It can be inferred from the passage that dealated eastern termites that have survived a week in a rotten wood termite colony are no longer attacked because they

   (A) have come to resemble the rotten wood termites in most ways
   (B) no longer have an odor provocative to the rotten wood termites
   (C) no longer pose a threat to the host colony
   (D) have learned to resonate at the same frequency as the host group
   (E) have changed the pattern in which they use their mandibles

23. The passage provides support for which of the following?

      I. Termites vary in speed and agility.
      II. Soldier termites frighten intruders by striking their heads against wood and other nest materials.
      III. Termites are found both in North America and outside its boundaries.

(A) I only
(B) II only
(C) I and II only
(D) I and III only
(E) I, II, and III

24. According to the passage, the struggle by rotten wood termites against invading wingless termites is

(A) a brutal fight until one of the two colonies is completely destroyed
(B) a lengthy matter with an element of uncertainty
(C) carried out by shaking the invaders from the host nest
(D) usually a short affair since the rotten wood termites are so much larger
(E) successful if the invading termites are not too large a group

25. It can be inferred from the passage that an insecticide designed to confuse soldier termites would be most effective if it deprived the insect of its

(A) eyes
(B) ears
(C) bristles
(D) wings
(E) odor

26. According to the passage, a termite's jaw can be important in all of the following EXCEPT

(A) aggression against intruders of other termite species
(B) the reception of vibrations sent by other termites
(C) stabilization of the insect against physical disturbances
(D) the production of sound made by striking wood or plants
(E) sounding an alert to notify other termites of danger

27. The passage would most likely be followed by
    (A) a discussion of the reasons for the blindness of termites
    (B) a discussion of how to use the characteristics of the termites' sensory organs to exterminate termites
    (C) a discussion of the effects of termites' vibrations on man
    (D) a discussion of the differences between termites found in temperate climates and those found in tropical ones
    (E) a list of various structures classified by the government as safe from termite attack

OUR STEP-BY-STEP APPROACH TO THE GRE READING COMP

Most students read much too slowly and carefully on reading comps. Trembling with the importance of what they're doing, they circle every other word, underline entire sentences, look for hidden meanings, and generally become completely lost. When they reach the end of the passage, they often gulp and realize they have no idea what they have just read.

Our years of experience with ETS reading comps have enabled us to develop a simple and effective approach to reading passages and answering the questions that follow them. We'll outline our approach first, then discuss each step in detail. Here's the outline:

STEP 1: **Find the main idea of the passage.** Don't read the passage. Just spend a minute or two getting a sense of its main idea or theme. We'll tell you exactly how to do this in a moment. When you have a sense of the main idea, jot it down in the margin of your booklet.

Concentrate on the main idea of the passage, not the details.

STEP 2: **Find and answer the general questions.** General questions are ones that ask about the theme of the passage, or the tone of the passage, or the main idea of the passage, and so on. A general question is broader than a specific question, which might ask you about a single fact. Very often, the very first question will be a general one. In fact, the very first question may well concern the "main idea" that you just spent one or two minutes discovering. General questions are usually the easiest. Answering them will also help you solidify your sense of what the passage is about, making it easier for you to find the answers to specific questions later on.

STEP 3: **Find and answer the specific questions.** Specific questions are ones that concern specific facts in the passage. Before looking at the passage, see if you can eliminate any of the answer choices ahead of time. If you can eliminate a choice, cross it out in your test booklet so that it won't confuse you. Then go to the passage and find ETS's answer. If you don't find it immediately, skim quickly until you locate it.

Don't try to keep more than one question in your mind at a time. Read one question, eliminate any obviously impossible choices, go to the passage, find ETS's answer, then move to the next. Don't do what many students do and read all the questions before trying to answer any. Reading comp is much easier if you attack it one step at a time. Students who try to do too much at once often end up feeling overwhelmed.

STEP 1: FIND THE MAIN IDEA OF THE PASSAGE

Most GRE reading passages (and most paragraphs within them) have a similar structure: An idea is expressed, then the idea is supported. That's all there is to it. Support for an idea may take the form of details, examples, counterexamples, or secondary ideas. Some reading comp questions—the general ones—are about the main idea or ideas; other questions—the specific ones—are about the details.

The main idea of the passage is what the passage is *about*. A question that asks you to choose the best title for a passage is really asking you to find its main idea. The main idea may be presented immediately, in the very first sentence—in effect, introducing the details that follow. Or the main idea may be presented gradually, in the first sentences of the paragraphs. Or the main idea may come last, as a conclusion to, or summary of, the details or arguments that have been presented.

You may find it helpful to think of a reading passage as a house. The main idea of the passage is like the overall plan of the house. Finding the main idea of the passage is like walking quickly through the house. As you walk, you want to develop a sense of the overall plan of the house: two floors, no basement, big family room, bedrooms upstairs. You don't want to get bogged down in upholstery patterns, the contents of bureau drawers, or other tiny details. Later, if you are asked what is sitting on the kitchen counter, you won't know the answer off the top of your head, but you'll have a pretty good idea of where to find it. And your mind won't be cluttered with a lot of extraneous information—most of which you will have forgotten anyway.

Finding the main idea of a passage is usually pretty easy. Here's all you have to do:

- Read the first sentence of each paragraph.
- Read the last sentence of the passage.
- In the margin of your booklet, jot down three simple words that express the main idea you've found.

If a paragraph is very short, you may find that it makes sense to read more than just the first sentence. But don't spend a lot of time doing this. And don't try to memorize what you are reading, or to learn any of the supporting details.

Don't even try to "skim" the entire passage—your eyes will slide over the words, and you'll end up remembering nothing. All you should be doing is looking for a general sense of the overall passage that can be reduced to a few simple words.

Main Ideas and Passage Types

There are two basic types of GRE reading passages: science and nonscience. The science passages may be either specific or general. Knowing a little about the types will help you anticipate the main ideas.

Knowing the types of passages will help point you toward the main ideas.

Specific science passages deal with the "hard facts" of science. They are almost always objective or neutral (and often boring) in tone. The sample passage, about "termite senses," is an example of a specific science passage. Other typical themes: how an organism adapts to its environment; a description of an experiment; a discussion of a phenomenon we don't understand; a popular misconception. When dealing with one of these passages, you should avoid looking for a complex theme or a strong point of view. The terminology may be complex (words like *isotopic* or *racemization*), but the main idea or theme won't be. Don't be thrown into confusion by big words. You can almost always read around them. If you focus on the main idea, you won't have to worry about the jargon.

General science passages deal with the history of a scientific discovery, the development of a scientific procedure or method, why science fails or succeeds in explaining certain phenomena, and similar "soft" themes. The authors of these passages have a more definite point of view than do the authors of the specific science passages; that is, the tone may not be neutral or objective, and the author may be expressing an opinion. For example, the author may take a side in a disagreement about types of contemporary research, or warn about the possible dangers of a certain avenue of inquiry. The main theme will be whatever point or argument the author is trying to make.

Nonscience passages deal with topics in the humanities (art, literature, philosophy, music, folklore) or social science (history, law, economics). **Humanities passages** typically take a specific point of view, or compare several views. Typical themes: a particular author's weaknesses and strengths; differences between competing trends, such as abstract and realist painting; pioneering techniques in an art form; a forgotten craft. The language may be abstract and dense.

Social science passages usually introduce an era or event by focusing on a specific problem, topic, person, or group of persons. The key is usually the relationship between the focus and some larger context. Typical themes: a revisionist interpretation of an era that arose from the discovery of new evidence; the adaptation of a certain social class to changing conditions; new contributions to a field of study. The tone is likely to be partisan and opinionated, although some social-science passages take the form of a neutral discussion of facts.

Finding the Main Idea: A Test Drive

Let's try this technique on the sample passage that begins on page 98. Remember, all you want to read at this point are the first sentences of the paragraphs and the last sentence of the passage. Here's the first sentence:

> It is well known that termites are blind, but little has been discovered about the other sense organs of these insects or their reactions to various stimuli.

Having read just this much, what would you say is the main idea? Something to do with "termite senses"? Most likely. (The very first sentence of a passage is the most common hiding place for main ideas.) Let's check the first sentences of the other paragraphs, and the last sentence of the passage, just to make sure.

First sentence, second paragraph:

> Eastern dealated (wingless) termites that manage to survive in the rotten wood termite colony for more than a week, however, are no longer molested.

First sentence, third paragraph:

> What else besides odor helps termites interpret the world around them?

First sentence, fourth paragraph:

> There is a clear correlation between the functioning of the chorodontal system and termite settlement patterns.

Last sentence, passage:

> When the vibrations ranged from 50–100 per second, etc.

There's nothing in these sentences to change our initial impression of the main idea, and some of the sentences directly support it. Good. That means we're on the right track. We scrawl a quick note—"termite senses"—in the margin of our test booklet, and head for the first general question. Total elapsed time: about a minute.

STEP 2: FIND AND ANSWER THE GENERAL QUESTIONS

Now that you've found the main idea of the passage, you are ready to attack the general questions. There are two main types of general questions: *main idea* and *tone*. We'll cover them one at a time.

Main Idea Questions

A main idea question asks you to find the main idea of the passage. Since you have just done that, a question like this should be a piece of cake. Main idea questions usually come either first or last. They can be phrased in several different ways:

> "The author's main purpose is . . ."

> "The main idea of the passage is . . ."

"Which of the following is the best title for the passage?"

"Which of the following questions does the passage answer?"

All of these are *general* questions; therefore, they will almost always have general answers. That means that you can eliminate any choice that is too specific. (The main idea of a passage will not be "to describe the rate of vibration that causes termites to be thrown about.")

Do the main idea questions first.

At the same time, ETS's answer won't be a statement that is *so* general that it could be true of virtually any passage. (The main idea will not be "to explain the author's point of view.")

Nor will the main idea of a passage ever be something that could not possibly be accomplished in a few short paragraphs. (The author's purpose in writing a 250-word essay could never be "to explain the meaning of life.")

ETS's answer to one of these questions will be like Baby Bear's porridge: not too hot, not too cold—*just right*. Practicing with real GRE reading passages will help you develop a good sense of the kind of answer ETS invariably looks for.

The incorrect choices on a question like this will likely be statements that are partly true, or are true of part of the passage but not of the whole thing. Or they may be choices that sound almost exactly right, but with one or two teeny differences. That's why you need to use POE and cross out incorrect choices as you eliminate them.

Main Idea Questions: A Test Drive

The first question following a GRE reading comp passage is usually a general question and often a main-idea question. That's the case with our sample passage on pages 98–99. Take another look at the first question:

21. The author's primary concern in the passage is to

   (A) show how little is known of certain organ systems in insects

   (B) describe the termite's method of overcoming blindness

   (C) provide an overview of some termite sensory organs

   (D) relate the termite's sensory perceptions to man's

   (E) describe the termite's aggressive behavior

Here's how to crack it

A "primary concern" is the same thing as a main idea or main theme or author's purpose. Check out each choice without looking back at the passage. (If possible, you should always answer a main-idea question without referring back to the passage. Why? Because the details in the passage may lead you astray. The main idea you found should be enough to lead you to ETS's answer.)

(A) Termites are insects, but the passage is not about insects; it is about termites. This choice can be eliminated for that reason alone. If the main purpose of a passage is to describe a particular person or thing, then that particular person or thing will definitely be mentioned specifically in ETS's answer. If you have a passage about Charles Dickens, its main purpose will not be to "discuss the works of English novelists." Similarly, if the main purpose of a passage is to describe termites, then on a main idea question you can eliminate any choice that contains no mention of termites. So eliminate this choice.

(B) Common sense alone tells you that termites have no methods of "overcoming blindness" (tiny Seeing Eye dogs?). Eliminate.

(C) This corresponds closely with the main idea we discovered. Hang on to this choice. It's a possibility.

(D) We can tell from our quick search for the main idea that the author's primary concern is not a comparison between termites and humans. A quick glance back at the passage confirms this. Eliminate.

(E) Sort of possible, although this choice makes no mention of senses. The passage touches on fighting, but not as the main idea. Probably not ETS's answer.

The best choice? Undoubtedly C—ETS's answer.

Because you've only read a tiny portion of the passage, you shouldn't always expect ETS's answer to seem obvious to you on your first pass through the questions. But you should be able to eliminate some obviously incorrect choices right off the bat. You must be absolutely certain to cross out these incorrect choices as you eliminate them. The key to doing well on reading comp is to narrow the field as rapidly as possible. With five choices swimming in your head, you'll keep covering the same ground over and over again. Small differences are easier to see once you've swept away the clutter. After eliminating two or three choices, you can look back at the passage quickly to help you zero in. When you look back at the passage, though, keep in mind that you are looking only for enough information to enable you to find ETS's answer and earn points. This is not the time to brush up on your knowledge of termites.

Questions About Tone, Attitude, or Style

This is the second main type of general question. These questions ask you to identify the author's tone, style, or overall point of view. Is the author being critical, neutral, or sympathetic? Is the passage subjective or objective? Like main idea questions, these questions can be phrased in several ways:

"The author's tone is best described as . . ."

"The author views his subject with . . ."

"The author's presentation is best characterized as . . ."

"The passage is most likely from . . ."

"The author most likely thinks the reader is . . ."

These questions are usually easy to spot, because they seldom contain many words. In fact, each choice may be just a single word. Almost every GRE will have at least one of these questions.

These questions are also usually easy to answer, because ETS writes them in very predictable ways. Knowing a little about the "ETS mentality"—the very predictable point of view of ETS's test-question writers—will help you find ETS's answer. Here are the main things for you to remember:

Knowing how ETS thinks will help you choose the correct answers.

- ◆ ETS uses only passages and authors that it feels good about. The passages are meant to be thoughtfully conceived, carefully written, and uncontroversial. ETS doesn't use crackpot diatribes, bitter invectives, or scathing harangues. The authors of GRE reading passages are almost always thoughtful, optimistic, reflective, instructive, or something similarly positive. They are never cynical, desperate, hateful, vengeful, or apathetic. As a result, you can eliminate any choice that is too negative or too extreme. The tone of a science passage will be objective, neutral, unbiased, analytical, or something similar. It will not be careless, dogmatic, ambivalent, or contradictory.

- ◆ ETS has great respect for artists, writers, intellectuals, professors, doctors, lawyers, scientists, scholars, and professionals of all kinds. It does not use passages that reflect badly on these people. You will not find a reading passage about dishonest lawyers. Nor will you find one about untalented novelists. If an answer choice says that the purpose of a passage is "to demonstrate the intellectual dishonesty of college professors," you can safely eliminate it without so much as glancing at the passage.

- ◆ ETS has no strong emotions; its reading passages have no strong emotions, either. ETS is middle-of-the-road, conservative, responsible, establishment, boring. The tone of a passage would never be scathing. An author's style would never be violent. An author would never be irrational.

- ◆ ETS is politically correct. Most GREs contain one reading passage concerning a minority group or its members. Such passages are almost always positive or inspirational in tone. Any negative or politically *incorrect* choices can quickly be eliminated.

STEP 3: FIND AND ANSWER THE SPECIFIC QUESTIONS

Always attack the specific questions in order, one at a time. If you try to keep two or more questions in your mind at once, you'll become confused and waste time. Remember that the order of the questions follows the structure of the passage. After reading a question, look back to the passage and skim quickly till you find

Put your finger on the place in the passage where you found the answer to the question. Answer the question in your own words before you go to the answer choices.

the information you are looking for. Use POE to eliminate two or three choices quickly, then zero in on ETS's answer.

Don't waste time. If you find yourself in a rut, eliminate what you can, mark an answer, and move on. You can circle the question if you think you'll have time to return to it for another look, but coming back to reading comp questions is usually a waste of time. (You won't remember what the passage was about or where to look for ETS's answer; any remaining time at the end of the section would probably be better spent on other item types.)

The following techniques will help you use POE to eliminate incorrect answer choices and zero in on ETS's answer.

Use Common Sense

ETS takes its reading passages from textbooks, collections of essays, works of scholarship, and other sources of serious reading matter. You won't find a passage arguing that literature is stupid, or that history doesn't matter, or that the moon is made of green cheese. As a result, you will often be able to eliminate answer choices simply because the facts or opinions they represent couldn't possibly be found in ETS reading passages.

Here's an example. You don't need to see the reading passage it refers to. Which choices can you eliminate?

25. The author argues that poetry

(A) has no place in a modern curriculum, because it is irrelevant to most students' lives

(B) is often slighted at the secondary level, because teachers are not trained to overcome the resistance of their pupils

(C) will become more important as modern life becomes more complex

(D) is the cornerstone of a classical education

(E) should not be taught because it is more difficult for most students to understand than prose

Here's how to crack it

Even without the passage, you should be able to see that some of these choices couldn't possibly be ETS's answer. Let's look at each one:

(A) Would any reputable essayist or scholar—the likely sources of the reading passage—argue that poetry has no place in a curriculum? No. Eliminate.

(B) This isn't as off-the-wall as choice A, but it's a bit dumb. Unlikely.

(C) Nothing screwy here. This could be ETS's answer.

(D) A possibility.

(E) Easy to eliminate, for the same reason we eliminated choice A.

Here's another example:

27. The author's attitude toward scientists who first test
    experimental vaccines by injecting them into
    themselves can best be described as one of

    (A) apathy
    (B) skepticism
    (C) admiration
    (D) confusion
    (E) consternation

Here's how to crack it

Any scientist who injected an experimental vaccine into himself before trying it
on other people would have to be pretty brave, right? So what would the
author's attitude in all likelihood be? It would be admiration, choice C. The other
choices just don't make sense.

Use Outside Knowledge

ETS says to answer questions based only on "what is *stated or implied*" in the
passage. In other words, don't use outside knowledge. But this is bad advice.
Outside knowledge can be very helpful in answering reading comp questions. It
can enable you to eliminate incorrect answer choices and even to find ETS's
answer. Although ETS does not use reading comp to test your knowledge of
biology, history, or other topics, its answers will not contradict established fact.
This means that you can be quite confident in eliminating choices that *do* contradict established fact. Here's an example:

ETS's answers will not
contradict established fact.

18. In the passage, a "true vacuum" is

    (A) empty space with ether in it
    (B) an indivisible unit of matter
    (C) empty space with nothing in it
    (D) empty space filled only by air
    (E) the space between planets

Here's how to crack it

If you were even half awake in sixth-grade science, you should be able to find
ETS's answer to this question without reading the passage. It has to be choice C.
None of the other choices describes a vacuum.

Attack Extreme Statements

ETS doesn't want to spend all its time defending its answer choices to grumpy
test-takers. If even one percent of the people taking the GRE decided to quibble
with an answer, ETS would be deluged with angry phone calls. To keep this
from happening, ETS tries very hard to construct correct answer choices that
cannot be disputed.

What makes a choice indisputable? Take a look at the following example:

    (A) Picasso had many admirers.
    (B) Everyone loved Picasso.

Analysis

Which choice is indisputable? Choice A. Choice B contains the highly disputable word *everyone*. Did *everyone* really love Picasso? Wasn't there even one person somewhere who didn't think all that much of him? Of course there was. Choice A is complaint-proof (who can say how many *many* is?). Choice B could never be ETS's answer.

Avoid extreme words.

Since ETS will always prefer an indisputable answer to a disputable one, you should focus your attention on the *most extreme* choice that you have not yet eliminated. If you can find any reason to doubt the choice, you should eliminate it. In the example above, you only need to find one person who didn't like Picasso to prove choice B false; to prove choice A wrong, you'd have to poll everybody in the world.

What makes a choice disputable? It's too extreme and absolute. **The more extreme a choice is, the less likely it is to be ETS's answer.**

Certain words make choices highly extreme and therefore easy to dispute. Here are a few of these extreme words:

must	the best
the first	only
each	totally
every	always
all	no

You don't want to automatically eliminate a choice containing one of these words, but you want to turn your attention to it immediately and attack it vigorously. If you can find even one exception, you can eliminate that choice.

Other words make choices moderate, more qualified, and therefore hard to dispute. Here are a few of these general words:

may	many
can	sometimes
some	often

Now look at a complete example:

18. The author implies that the founding fathers
    - (A) could resolve contemporary questions were they alive
    - (B) were completely unaware of the ethical implications of slavery
    - (C) avoided the issue of slavery as it pertained to human rights
    - (D) had no understanding of social problems
    - (E) originally thought slavery was a just institution

Here's how to crack it

Which choices are easiest to dispute? Choices B and D. What makes them extreme? The words *completely* and *no*. ETS's answer will most likely be found among the other three choices.

Where Disputable Choices Come From

Very often on the GRE, the words that make a choice extreme (*totally, never,* etc.) were inserted into the choices *specifically in order to make those choices incorrect.* All GRE questions undergo reviews at ETS. If a reviewer finds a distractor for which he thinks a test-taker could make a case, he or the test's assembler will edit it in an effort to make it indisputably wrong. If you make yourself familiar with these words, they'll jump off the page at you when you take the test.

Avoid Direct Repetitions

Joe Bloggs's favorite guesses on reading comps are choices that repeat significant portions of the passage. The more a choice sounds like the passage, the more that choice will seem right to Joe Bloggs.

This means that you should be very wary of choices that exactly reproduce the wording of the passage. **ETS's answer will almost always be a paraphrase, not a direct repetition.**

Here's an example of what we mean:

> The Molniya orbit looks peculiar on a map. Its perigee, or lowest point, is just 600 kilometers above a spot in the Southern Hemisphere, and its apogee, or highest point, is more than 40,000 kilometers above Hudson Bay. Because each Molniya satellite takes twelve hours to travel around the earth—half the time it takes the earth to turn on its axis—it actually makes two loops each day. Twelve hours after the Hudson Bay apogee it reaches another one, over central Siberia. Only the Hudson Bay apogee is used for television transmission; the Soviets use the Siberian one for voice and data transmission.

> The author of the passage implies that which of the following is the primary reason for the peculiar appearance of the Molniya orbit?

> (A) Its apogee is more than 40,000 kilometers above Hudson Bay.
> (B) The satellite is required to be used for voice and data transmission.
> (C) The difference in altitude between the high and low points of the orbit is so dramatic.
> (D) The satellite requires only twelve hours to travel around the earth.
> (E) The Soviets are incapable of placing a satellite in a normal orbit.

Here's how to crack it

Three of the choices contain verbatim repetitions of significant chunks of the passage: A, B, and D. These are, therefore, Joe Bloggs attractors and highly unlikely to be ETS's answer. (Also notice that outside knowledge tells us that choice E is factually incorrect and can be eliminated, even though we haven't been shown the part of the passage to which it refers.) ETS's answer is choice C.

Of course, ETS will often have to use *some* words from the passage in its answer. But the general rule is a good one:

> The more closely a choice resembles a substantial part of the passage, the less likely the choice is to be ETS's answer.

Line-Number Questions

These questions ask you to interpret the meaning of a certain word or phrase in the context of the passage. You will usually be referred to a specific line number in the text. These questions can be phrased in a number of ways:

> The "great conversation" (line 29) is used as a metaphor for . . .
>
> Which of the following words would be the best substitute for the word "adopted" (line 11) . . .
>
> The author uses the term "indigenous labor" (line 40) to mean . . .
>
> The author quotes Richard Hofstadter in the last paragraph in order to . . .

Joe Bloggs loves these questions, because he thinks they tell him exactly where to find ETS's answer. Therefore, you will generally *not* find ETS's answer in the exact line referred to. **Read at least the five lines before it and the five lines after it as well.**

Make certain you understand exactly what the question is asking for.

Down to two choices? Go back to the place in the passage where you found the answer to the question.

Inference Questions

Questions that use words like *inferred* or *implied* aren't really any different from other general or specific questions. If the question refers to the passage as a whole, treat it as a general question and do it right away. If the question deals with a specific detail, approach it as a specific question.

Least/Except/Not Questions

Lots of careless errors are made on these questions. To keep from making them yourself, you need to keep reminding yourself that ETS's answer will be the choice that is *wrong*. Here are some of the ways these questions are phrased:

With which of the following statements
would the author be LEAST likely to agree?

According to the passage, all of the following
are true EXCEPT:

Which of the following does NOT support
the author's argument that the best offense is
a good defense?

One effective approach is to write a Y for "yes" next to the answers that are found in the passage, and an N for "no" next to the choice that isn't—ETS's answer.

Do these weird format questions after you've answered all the "normal" questions. Circle the word LEAST, EXCEPT, or NOT. That way you'll be less likely to forget it's there.

ETS's answer will be the dumb choice, the wrong choice, the crazy choice.

Look for "correct" answers—and eliminate them. That is, refer back to the passage with each remaining choice and see if the passage supports it. If it does, cross it out. You're looking for the one choice that doesn't make sense.

I, II, III Questions

These time-consuming questions—in which you are asked to analyze three statements identified with Roman numerals—really contain three true-false questions. Unfortunately, you may have to get all three right to receive credit.

These questions are a good place to use POE: Start with the shortest of the Roman-numeral statements. Go back to the passage to find out if it's true or false.

When you find a false statement, be sure to eliminate all appropriate answer choices that include the Roman numeral for that statement. When you find a true statement, eliminate any answer choice that does not include its Roman numeral. See our analysis on page 117 of question 23 from the sample passage on pages 98–99.

Don't do more work than you have to.

Do I, II, III questions last.

NOW BACK TO THE QUESTIONS

Now you can gather up all your techniques and strategies and throw them at the specific questions following the sample passage back on pages 98–99.

Here is the first specific question:

22. It can be inferred from the passage that dealated
eastern termites that have survived a week in a
rotten wood termite colony are no longer attacked
because they

(A) have come to resemble the rotten wood termites in most ways
(B) no longer have an odor provocative to the
rotten wood termites
(C) no longer pose a threat to the host colony
(D) have learned to resonate at the same frequency
as the host group
(E) have changed the pattern in which they use
their mandibles

Here's how to crack it

This is just the second question, and the first specific one, so it probably refers back to a very early part of the passage. It does. "Dealated" termites are first mentioned in the first sentence of the second paragraph; by skimming that paragraph, and a few sentences in the previous one, you can zero in on ETS's answer. As you do, eliminate as many choices as you can. Here are the choices:

(A) This is an absurd statement that is nowhere supported in the passage. While it may be true that the alien termites have come to resemble the hosts in *one* way, there is nothing in the passage to suggest that they have come to resemble them in *most* ways. Eliminate.

(B) This sounds like just what we're looking for. A good possibility.

(C) The annihilated termites didn't pose a threat in the first place; all they really did was smell funny. Eliminate.

(D) Making sounds has not yet been mentioned in the passage. Eliminate.

(E) A nutty choice, unsupported by the passage. Eliminate.

ETS's answer is choice B.

The next question, number 23, is a I, II, III question, so we'll leave it for now and move on to 24:

> 24. According to the passage, the struggle by rotten wood termites against invading wingless termites is
>
>   (A) a brutal fight until one of the two colonies is completely destroyed
>   (B) a lengthy matter with an element of uncertainty
>   (C) carried out by shaking the invaders from the host nest
>   (D) usually a short affair since the rotten wood termites are so much larger
>   (E) successful if the invading termites are not too large a group

Here's how to crack it

Since we had to read the sentences about the termite attack to answer question 22, answering this question should be easy.

(A) The big termites invariably win, so the phrase "one of the two colonies" doesn't make any sense. Eliminate.

(B) This moderate, indisputable sentence neatly describes what the passage says happens. A good possibility.

(C) No mention of shaking in the passage. Eliminate.

(D) The rotten wood termites are larger, but the passage says that killing off the little termites takes a long time. Eliminate.

(E) This seems plausible, but saying it would require us to go beyond the information in the passage. Eliminate.

ETS's answer is B.
The next question is nice and short. Here it is:

25. It can be inferred from the passage that an insecticide designed to confuse soldier termites would be most effective if it deprived the insect of its

(A) eyes
(B) ears
(C) bristles
(D) wings
(E) odor

Here's how to crack it

Another inference question. Go back and look for the answer. Soldier termites are mentioned in the third paragraph. Then check the choices:

(A) Termites are blind. Eliminate.

(B) There's no mention of ears in the passage. For all we know, termites don't have them. Eliminate.

(C) Bristles are part of a termite's chorodontal system. A possibility.

(D) No mention of wings, which have nothing to do with senses. Eliminate.

(E) We've just been talking about odor. Could this be ETS's answer? Odorless termites might confuse soldier termites. But why would depriving a soldier termite of its own odor confuse it? Choice C seems a better choice. Eliminate E.

> Check all the choices.

ETS's answer is C.
The next question is an EXCEPT question. Let's save it for later. The question after that is an inference question. It requires us to make a judgment about what sort of paragraph might follow the last paragraph in the passage. Here's the question:

27. The passage would most likely be followed by

(A) a discussion of the reasons for the blindness of termites
(B) a discussion of how to use the characteristics of the termites' sensory organs to exterminate termites
(C) a discussion of the effects of termites' vibrations on man
(D) a discussion of the differences between termites found in temperate climates and those found in tropical ones
(E) a list of various structures classified by the government as safe from termite attack

Here's how to crack it

We have to be careful, since inference questions require us to use judgment. Check each choice carefully:

(A) The blindness of termites is mentioned in the first sentence of the passage and then never discussed again. There's nothing in the passage to indicate that the author is about to return to this subject. Eliminate.

(B) Termites are pests. The final paragraph discusses the aversion of termites to certain kinds of vibrations. A paragraph discussing how this knowledge might be used to keep termites away from other structures could logically follow this paragraph. A possibility.

(C) This is a dumb choice. Termite vibrations have no effect on man. Eliminate.

(D) There undoubtedly are differences, but there is nothing in the final paragraph or in the rest of the passage to indicate that such a discussion is coming. Eliminate.

(E) Why would the author suddenly append such a list to this essay? The final paragraph does mention some structures that are seldom infested with termites, but we have no reason to believe that a list of other such structures is coming. Eliminate.

ETS's answer is B.

Now let's go back to that EXCEPT question. Remember that ETS's answer will be the one *incorrect* statement among the choices. Here's the question:

26. According to the passage, a termite's jaw can be important in all of the following EXCEPT

(A) aggression against intruders of other termite species
(B) the reception of vibrations sent by other termites
(C) stabilization of the insect against physical disturbances
(D) the production of sound made by striking wood or plants
(E) sounding an alert to notify other termites of danger

Be careful of extreme wording, especially in EXCEPT questions.

Here's how to crack it

Check each choice, eliminating those that hold up.

(A) The first paragraph says that termites kill intruders by biting them. This statement is correct. Eliminate.

(B) The second sentence in the third paragraph says that some of a termite's chorodontal organs are located on its mandibles, or jaws. This statement is correct. Eliminate.

(C) The final sentence of the passage says that termites "set their
     . . . mandibles" when subjected to certain physical disturbances.
     This statement is correct. Eliminate.

(D) Termites strike wood and plants with their heads, not their
     jaws. This statement appears to be incorrect. It is therefore a
     possibility.

(E) The final sentence of the third paragraph describes termites
     making a sound with their jaws. This sentence is part of a
     discussion of how termites communicate with other termites
     "when alarmed." This statement is correct. Eliminate.

ETS's answer is D.
Now we're ready for the I, II, III question we skipped earlier. Here it is:

23. The passage provides support for which of the
     following?
           I.   Termites vary in speed and agility.
           II. Soldier termites frighten intruders by
                striking their heads against wood and
                other nest materials.
           III. Termites are found both in North
                America and outside its boundaries.

     (A) I only
     (B) II only
     (C) I and II only
     (D) I and III only
     (E) I, II, and III

Here's how to crack it

The main question here is an inference question ("supported by the passage").
Our strategy, remember, is to start with the shortest of the three Roman-numeral
statements. That's statement I. Is it true or false that such an inference could be
drawn from the passage? Clearly, it's true. The next-to-last sentence of the first
paragraph mentions "smaller but quicker-moving cousins."

Statement I, therefore, is true. This means we can eliminate choice B.

The next shortest statement is statement III. Does the passage suggest that
termites are found both in North America and outside its borders? Yes. The last
sentence of the third paragraph mentions termites in the tropics.

Statement III is true. Knowing this, can we eliminate any other choices? Yes.
We can eliminate choices A and C.

Now we have to deal with statement II. Is there anything in the passage to
suggest that termites strike their heads in order to *frighten intruders*, rather than
to communicate with other termites in their colonies? There is not. This statement is not supported by the passage. Eliminate choice E.

ETS's answer is D.

SUMMARY

The Passages

1. Do the long passage first. Skip the short passage unless you're already scoring over 700 in verbal.

2. Just read the topic sentences of each paragraph to get the main idea of the passage. Write down the main idea.

The Questions

3. General questions are about the passage as a whole. Find the general questions and do them first. Focus on the main idea of the passage, not on the details.

   - Use POE to eliminate choices that:
     - Mention something you didn't read about in the topic sentences
     - Are too detailed and specific
     - Use extreme language
     - Go against common sense

4. Do specific questions next.

   - Go back to the passage to find the details.

   - Put your finger on the place in the passage where you find the detail. Look for a paraphrase of that information.

   - Use POE to eliminate choices that:
     - Misrepresent the information in the passage
     - Use extreme language
     - Go against common sense

5. Do EXCEPT and I, II, III questions last.

   - Use POE efficiently

PART III

How to Crack the Math Sections

11

What Do the Math Sections Test?

GEOGRAPHY OF THE MATH SECTIONS

Every GRE contains two scored "quantitative ability," or math, sections. Your test could also contain a third math section as an experimental section. This experimental math section would look like the other two math sections but would not count toward your score.

Each math section on your test will last thirty minutes and contain thirty items, as follows:

- Fifteen quantitative comparisons (items 1–15)
- Ten regular math questions (items 16–20 and 26–30)
- Five chart questions (items 21–25, based on a single chart)

As the item numbers indicate, the quantitative comparisons come first. They are followed by five regular math questions, five chart questions, and five more regular math questions. Each math section will be arranged this way. Since there are two scored sections, your math score will be based on your performance on thirty quantitative comparisons, twenty regular math questions, and ten chart questions.

Each group of items will be arranged in order of increasing difficulty, as follows:

Item Type	Item Number	Difficulty
Quant Comp	1–5	Easy
	6–10	Medium
	11–15	Difficult
Regular Math	16–18	Easy
	19, 20	Medium
Chart	21, 22	Easy
	23	Medium
	24, 25	Difficult
Regular Math	26, 27	Medium
	28–30	Difficult

A TRIP DOWN MEMORY LANE

ETS says that the math sections test "ability to reason quantitatively and to solve problems in a quantitative setting." In truth, they mostly test how much you remember from the math courses you took in junior high and high school. Why is a passing knowledge of eighth grade algebra important for a future Ph.D. in English literature? Don't ask us. All that matters is that ETS thinks there's a connection.

In the previous section, we told you that the verbal GRE is really just a harder version of the verbal SAT—same questions, harder words. What about the math GRE? Brace yourself: It's an *easier* version of the math SAT.

Why is it easier?

Because most students study little or no math in college. If the GRE tested "college-level" math, everyone but math majors would bomb.

If you're willing to do a little work, this is good news for you. By brushing up on the modest amount of math you need to know for the test, you can make a big difference in your score.

> Practice doing simple math with your pencil. Don't use a calculator as you normally would. Balance your checkbook, check the arithmetic on your bills, figure out the exact percentage tip to leave at a restaurant.

A WORD OF CAUTION

In constructing the math GRE, ETS is limited to the math that nearly everyone has studied: arithmetic, basic algebra, and basic geometry. There's no calculus (or even precalculus), no trigonometry, and no high-tech algebra or geometry.

Because of these limitations, ETS has to resort to sleight of hand in order to create hard problems. Even the most difficult GRE math problems are typically based on relatively simple principles. What makes the problems difficult is that these simple principles are disguised.

To do well on the math GRE, you need to sharpen two sets of skills: your basic math skills and your skill at thinking like ETS. The following chapters will help you do both.

A MATTER OF TIME

Since no points are deducted for incorrect answers on the GRE, you must not fail to mark an answer for every problem. Should you try to *solve* every problem? No. Each GRE math section gives you just thirty minutes to solve thirty problems, some of them quite difficult.

You will enjoy yourself more, and score higher, if you spend your time working on the questions that are designed to be easier, and ignore the ones that are designed for almost everyone to get wrong. **Unless you're getting all the easy and medium questions correct, don't even attempt difficult questions. Spend more time on the easy and medium questions.**

Students should worry less about finishing problems than about being more careful on the ones they attempt to solve. The major cause of poor math scores is carelessness, not ignorance.

If you make more than five mistakes on the math part of the GRE, not including items on which you merely guess, then you are working too quickly. You will raise your score by working out fewer questions.

You Take the Test, Don't Let the Test Take You

You should do the easy and medium problems first. Work slowly and carefully so that you get these completely right. Take the math section in the following order.

1–10 (easy and medium quant comp)

16–20 (easy and medium word problems)

26, 27 (medium word problems)

21–23 (easy and medium charts)

If you correctly answer all easy and medium questions, and simply fill in one letter on the answer sheet for all of the difficult questions, what do you think your score would be? Your math score would be about 600, without ever doing the difficult problems.

If you are getting all of the easy and medium questions correct, then start to pick and choose among the difficult problems. After you learn some of our powerful techniques, you should look for opportunities to use them on the difficult problems. Start by going back to the difficult quantitative comparison questions.

11–15 (difficult quant comp)

28–30 (difficult word problems)

24, 25 (difficult charts—major time wasters)

HOW WE'VE ORGANIZED THIS SECTION

If you're really interested in reviewing math for the fun of it, take an adult education course. Our only interest is in improving your score on the math sections of the GRE. To get a higher score, you need to review math concepts that you haven't thought about since high school, *and* you need to develop the best test-taking techniques for math problems—as they appear on the GRE.

Since we care only about your performance on the GRE, we won't cover math topics if they aren't tested on the GRE. Our approaches to some of the topics may be different from those that your math teachers taught you many years ago. Your math teachers may have been great, but we hope they were teaching you math not coaching you to take the GRE. We're going to show you the ways of doing math problems that work best for taking the GRE, based on our years of experience preparing thousands of students for this test.

So we've put together *both* the rules of math and the best techniques for solving GRE problems in a way that builds cumulatively from the most basic level to the most advanced. We've purposely made the chapters very short and focused on only a few topics. The chapters are arranged in the order of importance of the contents of the GRE.

HOW TO STUDY

Make sure you learn the content of each chapter cold before you go on to the next one. Don't try to cram everything in all at once. It's much better to do a small amount of studying each day over a longer period. You will master both the math concepts and the techniques if you focus on a little bit at a time.

PRACTICE, PRACTICE, PRACTICE

As you work through this book, be sure to practice on real GREs. Practice will rapidly sharpen your test-taking skills. Unless you trust our techniques, you may be reluctant to use them fully and automatically on a real administration of the GRE. The best way to develop that trust is to practice.

GRE Mathematics

THE BASICS ABOUT THE BASICS

Even though all of the math concepts we will review are conceptually very simple, that doesn't mean they're not important. Every GRE math question uses these simple rules and definitions. You need to be rock solid on this math "vocabulary." Many students find that making flash cards is as important in helping you memorize math definitions and rules as it is in learning vocabulary words for the verbal section.

GRE MATH DEFINITIONS

Learn this math vocabulary!

Quick—what's an integer? Is 0 positive or negative? How many even prime numbers are there? Read on.

INTEGERS

Integers are numbers that can be written without decimals or fractions:

–6, –5, –4, –3, –2, –1, 0, 1, 2, 3, 4, 5, 6.

Fractions, such as $\frac{1}{2}$, are not integers.

Remember that 0 is an integer! Positive integers get bigger as they move away from 0 (6 is bigger than 5); negative integers get smaller as they move away from 0 (–6 is smaller than –5).

CONSECUTIVE INTEGERS

Consecutive integers are integers listed in order of increasing value without any integers missing in between. Here are some groups of consecutive integers:

0, 1, 2, 3, 4, 5

–6, –5, –4, –3, –2, –1, 0

–3, –2, –1, 0, 1, 2, 3

Here is a group of consecutive even integers:

2, 4, 6, 8, 10

No numbers other than integers can be consecutive.

ZERO

Zero is an integer, but it is neither positive nor negative. It's just nothing.
Zero is even (see below).
The sum of 0 and any other number is that other number.
The product of 0 and any other number is 0.

DIGITS

There are ten digits: 0, 1, 2, 3, 4, 5, 6, 7, 8, and 9. All integers are made up of digits. The integer 10,897 has five digits: 1, 0, 8, 9, 7. It is therefore called a five-digit integer. Each of its digits has its own name. In the number 10,897:

7 is the units digit.

9 is the tens digit.

8 is the hundreds digit.

0 is the thousands digit.

1 is the ten-thousands digit.

Knowing these basic facts will help you score more.

POSITIVE OR NEGATIVE

A positive number is greater than zero. A negative number is less than zero. To arrange positive and negative numbers in order, draw a number line. Always remember what happens when you multiply positive and negative numbers:

$$pos \times pos = pos \qquad 2 \times 2 = 4$$
$$neg \times neg = pos \qquad -2 \times -2 = 4$$
$$pos \times neg = neg \qquad 2 \times -2 = -4$$

Try this real GRE problem.

16. What is the distance between –4 and 6 on a number line?

(A) 2 (B) 4 (C) 6 (D) 8 (E) 10

Here's how to crack it

Draw a number line and plot –4 and +6. Then count how far it is.

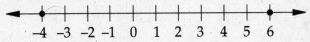

When you draw the number line, you can see that it's a distance of 10. So the ETS answer is choice E.

ODD OR EVEN

An even number is any integer that can be divided evenly by 2; an odd number is any integer that can't.

Here are some even integers: –4, –2, 0, 2, 4, 6, 8, 10.

Here are some odd integers: –3, –1, 1, 3, 5, 7, 9, 11.

0 is even.

Fractions are neither even nor odd.

Any integer is even if its units digit is even; any integer is odd if its units digit is odd.

Always remember what happens when you add and multiply odd and even integers:

$$even + even = even \qquad even \times even = even$$

$$odd + odd = even \qquad odd \times odd = odd$$

$$even + odd = odd \qquad even \times odd = even$$

Don't confuse odd and even with positive and negative—a major Joe Bloggs error.

Let's try a real GRE problem.

29. If p is an even negative integer and q is an odd positive integer, then pq must be which of the following?

(A) Even and positive
(B) Even and negative
(C) Odd and positive
(D) Odd and negative
(E) It cannot be determined from the information given.

Here's how to crack it

Why is this number 29? Because the average person (Joe Bloggs) gets it wrong. What would Joe choose? He'd say "Who knows? It could be anything." So Joe would choose choice E on this question. That choice must be wrong, because if Joe got it right that easily, it wouldn't be number 29. We know that an even number times an odd number must be even. Eliminate choices C and D. A negative number multiplied by a positive number must be negative. Eliminate choice A. So the ETS answer must be B.

DIVISIBILITY

An integer is divisible by 2 if its units digit is divisible by 2. For example, we know just by glancing that 598,467,896 is divisible by 2, because we know that 6 is divisible evenly by 2.

An integer is divisible by 3 if the sum of its digits is divisible by 3. We know that 2,145 is divisible by 3, for instance, because $2 + 1 + 4 + 5 = 12$, and 12 is divisible by 3.

An integer is divisible by 4 if its last two digits form a number divisible by 4. For example, 712 is divisible by 4 because 12 is divisible by 4.

An integer is divisible by 5 if its units digit is either 0 or 5.

An integer is divisible by 6 if it is divisible by *both* 2 *and* 3.

An integer is divisible by 9 if the sum of its digits is divisible by 9.

An integer is divisible by 10 if its units digit is 0.

REMAINDERS

The remainder is the number left over when one integer cannot be divided evenly by another. The remainder is always an integer.

- ◆ 4 divided by 2 is 2; there is nothing left over, so there's no remainder (4 is divisible by 2). You could also say that the remainder is 0.
- ◆ 5 divided by 2 is 2 with 1 left over; 1 is the remainder.
- ◆ 6 divided by 7 is 0 with 6 left over; 6 is the remainder.

PRIME NUMBERS

A prime number is a number that can be divided evenly *only* by itself and 1. Here are *all* the prime numbers less than 30:

2, 3, 5, 7, 11, 13, 17, 19, 23, 29.

0 is not a prime number.

1 is not a prime number.

2 is the only even prime number.

FACTORS

x is a factor of y if y can be divided by x without leaving a remainder. 1, 2, 3, 4, 6, and 12 are all factors of 12. Write the factors down systematically in pairs:

1 and 12,

2 and 6,

3 and 4.

If you always start with 1 and the number itself, then you won't forget that pair of factors.

MULTIPLES

A multiple of a number is that number multiplied by an integer other than 0. For example, –20, –10, 10, 20, 30, 40, 50, and 60 are all multiples of 10 (10×-2, 10×-1, 10×1, 10×2, 10×3, 10×4, 10×5, and 10×6).

STANDARD SYMBOLS

Here are some standard symbols you can expect to see on the GRE:

Symbol	Meaning
$=$	is equal to
$\neq$	is not equal to
$<$	is less than
$>$	is greater than
$\leq$	is less than or equal to
$\geq$	is greater than or equal to
$|x|$	absolute value of x

STANDARD TERMS

Here are some more standard terms.

Term	Meaning
sum	the result of addition
difference	the result of subtraction
product	the result of multiplication
quotient	the result of division
absolute value	the distance on the number line of the number from zero i.e., the positive value of a number

Now try a GRE problem that uses this terminology.

18. Which of the following is the product of two positive integers whose sum is 6?

(A) 2
(B) 3
(C) 5
(D) 7
(E) 12

Here's how to crack it

There aren't really too many integers that add up to 6. Just list them. 1 and 5, 2 and 4, 3 and 3. Now, since product means multiplication, just multiply. 5×1 is 5, so the ETS answer must be choice C. Let's just check the other choices. 2 times 4 is 8, and 3 times 3 is 9. Although 8 and 9 also answer the question, they are not choices.

GRE ARITHMETIC

ORDER OF OPERATIONS

Many problems require you to perform more than one operation to find ETS's answer. In these cases, it is absolutely necessary that you perform these operations in *exactly* the right order. In many cases, the correct order will be apparent from the way the problem is written. In cases when the correct order is not apparent, you need only remember the following mnemonic:

Please Excuse My Dear Aunt Sally

PEMDAS stands for Parentheses, Exponents, Multiplication, Division, Addition, Subtraction. This is the order in which the operations are to be performed. (Exponents are numbers raised to a power; don't worry, we'll review them soon.) Multiplication and division are inverses of the same operation, so you don't have to do multiplication before division, you just work left to right. The same is true for addition and subtraction; just work left to right.

Here's an example:

$$10 - (6 - 5) - (3 + 3) - 3 =$$

Here's how to crack it

Start with the parentheses. The expression inside the first pair of parentheses, $6 - 5$, equals 1. The expression inside the second pair equals 6. We can now rewrite the problem as follows:

$$10 - 1 - 6 - 3 =$$
$$9 - 6 - 3 =$$
$$3 - 3 =$$
$$= 0$$

Try this one:

$$6 \div 2 \times 25 \div 5 =$$

Here's how to crack it

Since it's only multiplication and division, just work from left to right: 6 divided by 2 is 3; 3 times 25 is 75; 75 divided by 5 equals 15.

Try one more.

$$3(2 + 1)^2 - 2(2^2 + 1) =$$

Here's how to crack it

Do the parentheses first: $2 + 1 = 3$. Then square it: 3 squared is 9. Then multiply $3(9) = 27$. Then go to the second set of parentheses. Here the exponent is inside the parentheses, so do that first: 2 squared is 4; $4 + 1 = 5$. So the expression inside the parentheses is 5. Now multiply 5 by 2, which equals 10. So what we've got is:

$$27 - 10 = 17$$

DRILL 1

Check your answers on page 295.

1. List three consecutive negative integers.

2. List three consecutive odd integers.

3. What is the least prime number greater than 8?

4. What is the least integer greater than –5.8?

5. What is the greatest integer less than 3.6?

6. If you interchange the first and last digits of 7,845, what is the resulting number?

7. Name a three-digit number whose digits add up to 14.

8. If set A consists of {4, 5, 6, 7}, how many members of set A are odd?

9. What is the remainder when 99 is divided by 5? (Find your answer *without* performing division.)

10. What is the remainder when 12,345,671 is divided by 10? (Find your answer *without* performing division.)

11. A multiple of both 3 and 7 is also a multiple of what other number?

12. If 34,569 is multiplied by 227, will the result be odd or even?

13. If two even numbers are multiplied together and then the product is multiplied by an odd number, will the result be odd or even?

14. Express 36 as the product of prime numbers.

15. If –2 is multiplied by –345, will the result be positive or negative?

16. $7 + (-8) + 9 + (-10) =$

17. $2(7 + 3)^2 + 27 - 13 + 1 =$

18. $2^2(3^2) + 4^2 =$

19. $\left(\dfrac{3(8 + 2)^2}{6} \right) =$

20. $(-2)\left[\dfrac{10 + 2}{3} + 2(-4) - 4 \right] =$

13

Fractions and Decimals

"I HATE FRACTIONS"

Let's face it, most of us don't use fractions very much in our day-to-day lives. If we do any math at all, we usually use a calculator or computer, and decimals rather than fractions. ETS knows this, and uses this knowledge to create the GRE. ETS knows that fractions look like they're going to be complicated, and most people are lazy. So you'll see lots of fractions on the GRE. That's something you can't change.

The only thing you *can* change is your attitude toward fractions. In fact, the easiest way to improve your GRE math score is to *learn to love fractions*, and use them as much as you can. Once you get used to using fractions again, you'll see that they're not very complicated—after all, you mastered them in the fourth grade.

FRACTIONS

FRACTIONS ARE SHORTHAND FOR DIVISION

The fraction $\frac{2}{3}$ is just another way of writing the division problem 2 ÷ 3.

REDUCING FRACTIONS

To reduce a fraction, simply express the numerator and denominator as the products of their factors. Then cross out, or "cancel," factors that are common to both. Here's an example:

$$\frac{16}{20} = \frac{2 \times 2 \times 2 \times 2}{2 \times 2 \times 5} = \frac{\cancel{2} \times \cancel{2} \times 2 \times 2}{\cancel{2} \times \cancel{2} \times 5} = \frac{2 \times 2}{5} = \frac{4}{5}$$

You can achieve the same result by dividing numerator and denominator by the factors that are common to both. In the example you just worked, 4 is a factor of both the numerator and the denominator. That is, both the numerator and the denominator can be divided evenly (without remainder) by 4. Doing this yields the much more manageable fraction $\frac{4}{5}$.

When you confront GRE math problems involving big fractions, always reduce them before doing anything else. Sometimes reduction alone will lead you to ETS's answer.

Remember: You *cannot* reduce across an equal sign (=), a plus sign (+), or a minus sign (–).

ADDING AND SUBTRACTING FRACTIONS: THE BOWTIE

Adding fractions that have the same denominators is easy: Just add up the numerators and put the sum over the shared denominator. Here's an example:

$$\frac{1}{9} + \frac{2}{9} + \frac{4}{9} = \frac{1+2+4}{9} = \frac{7}{9}$$

Handle subtraction the same way:

$$\frac{7}{9} - \frac{4}{9} - \frac{2}{9} = \frac{7-4-2}{9} = \frac{1}{9}$$

THE BOWTIE

When you're asked to add or subtract fractions with different denominators, you have to fiddle around with them so that they end up with the same denominator. To do this, all you need to do is multiply the denominators of the two fractions. Then multiply from each denominator up to the numerator of the other fraction, like this:

$$\frac{1}{3} + \frac{1}{4} = \frac{1 \quad 1}{3 \quad 4} = \frac{4+3}{12} = \frac{7}{12}$$

We call this technique the "Bowtie" because of its shape.

> To add, subtract, or compare fractions, use the BOWTIE.

Analysis

Using the Bowtie on these fractions doesn't change the values of the terms, but it does put them in a form that allows you to add or subtract them. Don't forget to reduce the result if necessary.

$$\frac{5}{6} - \frac{3}{4} = \frac{5 \quad 3}{6 \quad 4} = \frac{20-18}{24} = \frac{2}{24} = \frac{1}{12}$$

USING THE BOWTIE TO COMPARE FRACTIONS

ETS loves problems in which you are asked to compare two fractions and decide which is larger. These problems are a snap if you know what to do. Use the Bowtie!

Simply find which fraction would have a larger numerator if they had a common denominator. Just multiply the denominator of each fraction by the numerator of the other. Then you compare your two products.

Which of the following fractions is larger?

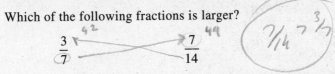

Analysis

Multiplying the first denominator by the second numerator gives us 49; multiplying the second denominator by the first numerator gives us 42. Forty-nine is bigger than 42, so the second fraction, $\frac{7}{14}$, is bigger than the first, $\frac{3}{7}$.

Here's the problem solved with the Bowtie:

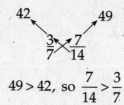

$$49 > 42, \text{ so } \frac{7}{14} > \frac{3}{7}$$

Using the Bowtie, always work from bottom to top, in the direction of the arrows in the problem we just solved. Working in the other direction will give you the wrong answer.

COMPARING MORE THAN TWO FRACTIONS

ETS loves to compare fractions, especially in quantitative comparisons.

You will sometimes be asked to compare more than two fractions. On such problems, don't waste time trying to find a common denominator for all of them. Simply use the Bowtie to compare two of the fractions at a time. Here's an example:

Which of the following fractions is smallest?

$$\frac{4}{7} \qquad \frac{5}{8} \qquad \frac{8}{11}$$

Here's how to crack it

Compare the first two fractions and eliminate the larger one (read the question carefully!); compare the remaining fraction with the next in line and eliminate the larger one; compare the remaining fraction with the next in line and eliminate the larger, and so on, until you're left with ETS's answer.

In this case, the smallest of the three fractions is $\frac{4}{7}$.

Let's see how this would appear on the GRE.

27. Which of the following is most nearly equal to $\frac{3}{4}$?

(A) $\frac{1}{2}$

(B) $\frac{3}{5}$

(C) $\frac{5}{7}$

(D) $\frac{9}{13}$

(E) $\frac{13}{15}$

Here's how to crack it
Use the Bowtie!

$$
\begin{array}{ccccc}
6 \quad 4 & 15 \quad 12 & 21 \quad 20 & 39 \quad 36 & 45 \quad 52 \\
\text{(A) } \frac{3}{4} \times \frac{1}{2} & \text{(B) } \frac{3}{4} \times \frac{3}{5} & \text{(C) } \frac{3}{4} \times \frac{5}{7} & \text{(D) } \frac{3}{4} \times \frac{9}{13} & \text{(E) } \frac{3}{4} \times \frac{13}{15}
\end{array}
$$

Since the answer choice in which the resulting bowtie numbers are closest is choice C, that must be the ETS answer.

MULTIPLYING FRACTIONS

There's nothing tricky about multiplying fractions. Just work straight across. All you have to do is place the product of the numerators over the product of the denominators. But see whether you can reduce before you multiply. Then you'll be multiplying smaller numbers. Here's an example:

$$\frac{21}{26} \times \frac{13}{14} = \frac{\overset{3}{\cancel{21}} \times \overset{1}{\cancel{13}}}{\underset{2}{\cancel{26}} \times \underset{2}{\cancel{14}}} = \frac{3 \times 1}{2 \times 2} = \frac{3}{4}$$

When one fraction is multiplied by another fraction, the product is smaller than either of the original fractions. Here's an example:

$$\frac{1}{2} \times \frac{1}{4} = \frac{1}{8}$$

DIVIDING FRACTIONS

Division of fractions is just like multiplication of fractions, with one crucial difference: Turn the second fraction upside down (that is, put its denominator over its numerator), then reduce before you multiply. Here's an example:

$$\frac{4}{5} \div \frac{2}{3} = \frac{4}{5} \times \frac{3}{2} = \frac{12}{10} = \frac{6}{5} = 1\frac{1}{5}$$

ETS will sometimes give you problems involving fractions whose numerators or denominators are themselves fractions. These problems look intimidating, but if you're careful you won't have any trouble with them. All you have to do is remember what we said about a fraction being shorthand for division. Always rewrite the expression horizontally. Here's an example:

A fraction is shorthand for division.

$$\frac{\frac{6}{1}}{\frac{1}{3}} = \frac{\frac{6}{1}}{\frac{1}{3}} = \frac{6}{1} \div \frac{1}{3} = \frac{6}{1} \times \frac{3}{1} = \frac{18}{1} = 18$$

CONVERTING MIXED NUMBERS INTO FRACTIONS

A mixed number is a number that is represented as an integer and a fraction, like this: $2\frac{3}{4}$. In most cases on the GRE, you should get rid of mixed fractions by converting them to fractions. How do you do this? By converting the integer to a fraction with the same denominator as the original fraction and then adding the two fractions. To convert $2\frac{3}{4}$, we rewrite 2 as $\frac{8}{4}$, a fraction that equals 2 and has the same denominator as $\frac{3}{4}$. Then we simply add, as follows:

$$\frac{8}{4} + \frac{3}{4} = \frac{11}{4}$$

Our result, $\frac{11}{4}$, is the same number as $2\frac{3}{4}$. The only difference is that $\frac{11}{4}$ is easier to work with in math problems.

BE CAREFUL

The most common source of errors on GRE fraction problems is carelessness. You'll see problems in which finding ETS's answer will require you to perform several of the steps or operations we've described. Keep your wits about you and remember that the goal of all these steps and operations is to simplify the fractions. **Always write down every step!**

Try this one:

Are fractions integers?

$$\frac{\frac{1}{5}-\frac{1}{6}}{\frac{1}{5}+\frac{1}{6}}=$$

(A) 0 (B) $\frac{1}{30}$ (C) $\frac{1}{11}$ (D) 1 (E) 11

Here's how to crack it

Use the Bowtie to determine the numerator and the denominator.

$$\frac{\overset{6-5}{\overbrace{\frac{1}{5}\searrow\nearrow\frac{1}{6}}}=30}{\underset{6+5}{\underbrace{\frac{1}{5}\searrow\nearrow\frac{1}{6}}}=30}=\frac{\frac{1}{30}}{\frac{11}{30}}$$

Then rewrite the division problem.

$$\frac{\frac{1}{30}}{\frac{11}{30}}=\frac{1}{30}\div\frac{11}{30}=\frac{1}{\cancel{30}}\times\frac{\cancel{30}}{11}=\frac{1}{11}$$

So the ETS answer is choice C. Yes, you should write all that down! Every careless mistake lowers your math score by ten points.

DRILL 1

Check your answers on page 296.

1. Reduce the following fractions:

   a. $\dfrac{5}{20}$

   b. $\dfrac{18}{24}$

   c. $\dfrac{12}{36}$

   d. $\dfrac{45}{30}$

   e. $\dfrac{78}{48}$

   f. $\dfrac{4}{9}$

> No, fractions are not integers. If you couldn't answer that question, review chapter 12.

2. Solve the following problems:

   a. $\dfrac{1}{6} + \dfrac{3}{10} =$

   b. $\dfrac{5}{8} - \dfrac{3}{4} =$

   c. $\dfrac{4}{5} \times \dfrac{5}{8} =$

   d. $\dfrac{1}{3} + \dfrac{6}{8} =$

   e. $\dfrac{\frac{1}{4}}{3}$

   f. $\dfrac{\frac{1}{5}}{\frac{2}{15}}$

3. Which fraction is larger: $\dfrac{8}{9}$ or $\dfrac{7}{8}$?

4. Convert $7\dfrac{1}{3}$ to an unmixed fraction.

5. How many halves are there in the number 6?

DECIMALS

DECIMALS ARE JUST FRACTIONS

Decimals and fractions are two different ways of expressing the same thing. Every decimal can be written as a fraction; every fraction can be written as a decimal. For example, the decimal .35 can be written as the fraction $\frac{35}{100}$. These two expressions, .35 and $\frac{35}{100}$, have exactly the same value.

To turn a fraction into its decimal equivalent, all you have to do is divide the numerator by the denominator. Here, for example, is how you would find the decimal equivalent of $\frac{3}{4}$:

$$\frac{3}{4} = 3 \div 4 = 4\overline{)3.00} = 0.75$$

$$\begin{array}{r} 0.75 \\ \hline 3.00 \\ 2.8 \\ \hline 20 \\ 20 \\ \hline 0 \end{array}$$

WHAT DO THOSE DECIMAL PLACES MEAN, ANYWAY?

Digits after the decimal point signify the tenths, hundredths, thousandths, ten thousandths, etc. places.

For example, in the number 3.1415 (which should be familiar):

3 is the units digit.

1 is the tenths digit.

4 is the hundredths digit.

1 is the thousandths digit.

5 is the ten-thousandths digit.

$$3.1415 = 3(1) + 1\left(\frac{1}{10}\right) + 4\left(\frac{1}{100}\right) + 1\left(\frac{1}{1,000}\right) + 5\left(\frac{1}{10,000}\right)$$

YOU DON'T NEED A DECIMAL POINT TO HAVE A DECIMAL

All the following numbers are decimals:

.5, 12, 0.8, –3, –32.908.

You may be unaccustomed to thinking of some of these numbers as decimals, but all of them could be written with decimal points. For example, 12 could be written as 12.0; 12 and 12.0 have exactly the same value.

You don't usually need to think about the missing decimal point with a number like 12. But when you add and subtract decimals, you will need to remember where it would go if it were there.

ADDING AND SUBTRACTING DECIMALS

No problem. Simply line up the decimal points and proceed as you would if the decimal points weren't there. If the decimal points are missing from the numbers you need to add or subtract, put them in. You can make all your numbers line up evenly by adding zeros to the right of the ones that need them. Here, for example, is how you would add the decimals 34.5, 87, 123.456, and 0.98:

$$
\begin{array}{r}
34.500 \\
87.000 \\
123.456 \\
+\ 0.980 \\
\hline
245.936
\end{array}
$$

Subtraction works the same way:

$$
\begin{array}{r}
17.66 \\
-\ 3.20 \\
\hline
14.46
\end{array}
$$

MULTIPLYING DECIMALS

The only tricky part is remembering where to put the decimal point. Handle the multiplication as you would with integers. Then position the decimal point according to this simple two-step rule:

1. Count the total number of digits to the right of the decimal points in the numbers you are multiplying. If you are multiplying 3.451 and 8.9, for example, you have a total of four digits to the right of the decimal points.

2. Place the decimal point in your solution so that you have the same number of digits to the right of it. Here's what you get when you multiply the numbers above:

> Don't forget about the decimal points when adding, subtracting, multiplying, or dividing decimals.

$$
\begin{array}{r}
3.451 \\
\times\ \ 8.9 \\
\hline
30.7139
\end{array}
$$

Except for placing the decimal point, we did exactly what we would have done if we had been multiplying 3,451 and 89:

$$
\begin{array}{r}
3,451 \\
\times\ \ \ \ 89 \\
\hline
307,139
\end{array}
$$

DIVIDING DECIMALS

Before you can divide decimals, you have to convert the divisor into an integer. (In the division problem 10 ÷ 2 = 5, the 10 is the dividend, the 2 is the divisor, and the 5 is the quotient.) This is easy to do. Set up the division as a fraction. All you have to do is move the decimal point all the way to the right. You must then move the decimal point in the dividend the same number of spaces to the right. Here's an example:

Divide 24 by 1.25.

Here's how to crack it

First, set up the division problem as a fraction:

$$\frac{24}{1.25}$$

Now start moving decimal points. The divisor, 1.25, has two digits to the right of the decimal point. To turn 1.25 into an integer, therefore, we need to move the decimal point two spaces to the right. Doing so turns 1.25 into 125.

Because we've moved the decimal point in the divisor two places, we also need to move the decimal point in the dividend two places. This turns 24 into 2,400. Here's what we're left with:

$$\frac{2,400}{125}$$

Now all we have to do to find our answer is reduce the fraction and complete the division problem.

$$\frac{2,400}{125} = \frac{480}{25} = \frac{96}{5} = 19.2$$

The answer is 19.2. During the test, don't forget to keep your eye on the answer choices as you calculate. Once you saw that the result was "a little less than 20," you had probably calculated enough to answer the question.

COMPARING DECIMALS

Which is larger, 0.00099 or 0.001? ETS loves this sort of problem. You'll never go wrong, though, if you do what we teach our students to do:

1. Line up the numbers on their decimal points.

2. Fill in the missing zeros.

Here's how to answer the question we just asked. First, line up the two numbers on their decimal points:

0.00099

0.001

Now fill in the missing zeros:

0.00099

0.00100

Can you tell which number is larger? Of course you can; 0.00100 is larger than 0.00099, just as 100 is larger than 99.

CONVERT DECIMALS TO FRACTIONS

Fractions are safer and easier to work with than decimals are. When you're stumped on a decimal problem, ask yourself whether finding ETS's answer would be easier if you converted the decimals to fractions. Wouldn't you rather find the square of $\frac{1}{4}$ than the square of 0.25? (If the answer choices are decimals, convert back to decimals when you finish your computation.)

Decimals are dangerous.
Fractions are safer.

DECIMALS AND MONEY

Money is based on the decimal system. For example, $5.98 is a decimal meaning five dollars plus $\frac{98}{100}$ of a dollar. What's $0.25? It's a quarter of a dollar, just as 0.25 equals $\frac{1}{4}$. When you find yourself stuck on a decimal problem, reminding yourself of the money connection may help you regain your bearings.

DRILL 2

Check your answers on page 296.

1. Add 1.045 to 5.12.

2. Subtract 10.54 from 15.82.

3. Multiply 22.65 by 0.5.

4. Divide 22.65 by 0.5.

5. Reduce $\frac{5.76}{3}$.

6. What is four one-thousandths plus three tenths?

7. Which is larger, .002 or .0015?

8. Convert $\frac{13}{2}$ to a decimal.

9. Convert .125 to a fraction.

10. Approximate $\frac{2.00465}{3.98136}$. (Don't use your pencil.)

14

Variables

WHAT'S A VARIABLE?

A variable, such as x, represents an unknown quantity in a math expression. The variable stands for the same number everywhere in that expression. If you have one equation with just one variable, you can solve for the variable—i.e., determine its value.

SOLVING FOR ONE VARIABLE

Try to get the variable on one side of the equation, and the numbers on the other side. To do this, you can add, subtract, multiply, or divide both sides of the equation by the same number. Be sure to write down every step. Let's look at a very simple example.

$$2x - 3 = 3$$

Here's how to crack it

You must always do the same thing to both sides of the equation.

It's always a good idea to try to get rid of negatives by adding something to both sides of the equation.

$$\begin{aligned} 2x - 3 &= 3 \\ +3 &= +3 \\ \hline 2x &= 6 \end{aligned}$$

You may already see that $x = 3$. But don't forget to write down that last step. Divide both sides of the equation by 2.

$$2x \div 2 = 6 \div 2$$
$$x = 3$$

Now try this real GRE problem.

18. If $27 \div x + 3 = 12$, then $x =$
   (A) −9
   (B) −3
   (C) 3
   (D) 9
   (E) 15

Here's how to crack it

First subtract 3 from both sides of the equation.

$$\frac{27}{x} = 9$$

Eliminate choices. Since we're not finished, eliminate choice D right now! You may see the answer already, but take the time to write each step. Multiply both sides by x.

$$27 = 9x$$

Now divide both sides by 9.

$$\frac{27}{9} = x$$

$$3 = x$$

So the ETS answer is choice C.
Try another GRE problem.

18. If $7x - 2 = 19$, then $3x + 1 =$

(A) $\frac{17}{7}$

(B) 3

(C) 9

(D) 10

(E) 21

Here's how to crack it

First add 2 to both sides of the equation.

$$7x = 21$$

Divide both sides by 7.

$$\frac{7x}{7} = \frac{21}{7}$$

$$x = 3$$

But we're not done! Eliminate choice B. Now what's the question asking exactly? What is $3x + 1$? Since $x = 3$, substitute 3 for x in the question: $3x + 1 = 3(3) + 1 = 10$. So the ETS answer must be choice D.

Don't forget to do all the steps in the problem!

INEQUALITIES

In an equation, one expression equals another. In an inequality, one expression does not equal another. The symbol for an equation is an equal sign. Remember the standard symbols we showed you in chapter 12? Most of them are symbols for inequalities:

≠   is not equal to

>   is greater than

<   is less than

≥   is greater than or equal to

≤   is less than or equal to

You can manipulate any inequality in the same way you can an equation, with one important difference. **When you multiply or divide both sides of an inequality by a negative number, the direction of the inequality symbol changes.** That is, if $x > y$, then $-x < -y$.

It's easy to understand the rationale for this. To see what we mean, take a look at a simple inequality:

$$10 - 5x > 0$$

Here's how to crack it

You could manipulate this inequality without ever multiplying or dividing by a negative number. Just add $5x$ to both sides. The sign stays the same. Then divide both sides by positive 5. Again, the sign stays the same.

Write everything down! Use your test booklet.

$$10 - 5x > 0$$

$$10 - 5x + 5x > 0 + 5x$$

$$10 > 5x$$

$$\frac{10}{5} > \frac{5x}{5}$$

$$2 > x$$

But suppose you subtract 10 from both sides at first.

$$10 - 5x > 0$$

$$10 - 5x - 10 > 0 - 10$$

$$-5x > -10$$

$$\frac{-5x}{-5} < \frac{-10}{-5}$$

$$x < 2$$

Since you changed the direction of the inequality symbol, the answer is the same.

ASSOCIATIVE LAW

There are actually two associative laws, one for addition and one for multiplication. For the sake of simplicity, we've lumped them together. You don't need to remember the name.

The Princeton Review associative law says: *When you are adding a series of numbers or multiplying a series of numbers, you can regroup the numbers in any way you'd like.* Here are some examples:

$$4 + (5 + 8) = (4 + 5) + 8 = (4 + 8) + 5$$

$$(a + b) + (c + d) = a + (b + c + d)$$

$$4 \times (5 \times 8) = (4 \times 5) \times 8 = (4 \times 8) \times 5$$

$$(ab)(cd) = a(bcd)$$

DISTRIBUTIVE LAW

This is one of the most important principles tested on the GRE. You must know it cold. Here's what it looks like:

$$a(b + c) = ab + ac$$

$$a(b - c) = ab - ac$$

This law is so important that you should apply it every chance you get. Here's an example:

$$13(67) + 13(33) =$$

Here's how to crack it

This is really just $ab + ac$. Using the distributive law, this must equal $13(67 + 33)$, or $13(100) = 1,300$.

The Distributive Law and Dear Aunt Sally

Earlier in this chapter we said that you should remember PEMDAS and always perform the operations in parentheses first. The distributive law provides something of an exception to this rule, because it gives you a better way of achieving the same result (better because ETS uses it so often). Here's an example:

Distributive: $7(5 + 4) = 7(5) + 7(4) = 35 + 28 = 63$

PEMDAS: $7(5 + 4) = 7(9) = 63$

ETS *loves* the distributive law.

FACTORING AND UNFACTORING

When you use the distributive law to rewrite the expression $xy + xz$ in the form $x(y + z)$, you are said to be *factoring* the original expression. That is, you take the factor common to both terms of the original expression (x), and "pull it out." This gives you a new, "factored" version of the expression you began with.

When you use the distributive law to rewrite the expression $x(y + z)$ in the form $xy + xz$, we like to say that you are *unfactoring* the original expression.

DRILL 1

Solve for the variable in the following equations. Check your answers on page 296.

1. $15 - 8x = -1$

2. $5x - 13 = 12 - 20x$

3. $22 = 11(2x - 2)$

4. $\dfrac{2x}{5} = \dfrac{1}{5}$

5. $x + \dfrac{1}{2}x + \dfrac{1}{4}x = 28$

6. $\dfrac{3x}{2} = \dfrac{4}{6}$

7. $\dfrac{5x + 3}{2} = 7x$

Use the distributive law to rewrite the following expressions. Check your answers on page 304.

8. $2(4 + 20) =$

9. $17(46) - 17(12) - 17(99) =$

10. $x(y - z) =$

11. $ab + ac + ad =$

12. $xyz - vwx =$

15

Quantitative Comparisons

WHAT IS QUANTITATIVE COMPARISON?

Now that you've mastered some basic math, let's look at a special problem format for half of the math questions on the GRE. To do well on the GRE Math sections you have to get used to this weird format—and apply techniques that will help you to *take advantage* of it!

Each math section of your GRE will contain fifteen quantitative comparison items, numbered 1–15. Items 1–5 will be easy, items 6–10 will be medium, and items 11–15 will be hard. Always pay attention to the item number in answering GRE questions. The item number will help determine which technique or combination of techniques you will use to crack the problem.

Here are the directions for quant comps as they will appear on your GRE:

> Directions: Each of the <u>Questions 1–15</u> consists of two quantities, one in Column A and one in Column B. You are to compare the two quantities and choose
>
> A if the quantity in Column A is greater;
> B if the quantity in Column B is greater;
> C if the two quantities are equal;
> D if the relationship cannot be determined from the information given.
>
> <u>Note</u>: Since there are only four choices, NEVER MARK (E).
>
> <u>Common Information</u>: In a question, information concerning one or both of the quantities to be compared is centered above the two columns. A symbol that appears in both columns represents the same thing in Column A as it does in Column B.

OUR OWN DIRECTIONS

Usually we tell you to learn ETS's directions. This time we're going to tell you to learn our own directions instead. Why? Because our directions are better than ETS's. They'll keep you out of trouble. Here they are:

> Directions: Each of the <u>Questions 1–15</u> consists of two quantities, one in Column A and one in Column B. You are to compare the two quantities and choose
>
> A if the quantity in Column A is *always* greater
>
> B if the quantity in Column B is *always* greater
>
> C if the quantities are *always* equal
>
> D if *different* numbers would result in *different* answers

WHAT'S THE DIFFERENCE?

It's not enough to determine that the quantity in Column A is *sometimes* greater than the quantity in Column B. You have to be certain that it *always* is. If you remember this key fact, you'll score more.

Never Mark "E"

Quant comps have only four answer choices. That's great: A blind guess has one chance in four of being correct. Unfortunately, each line on your answer sheet will have five spaces. If you accidentally mark choice E—which is easy to do if you're distracted—your answer will be counted as incorrect. Be careful.

Where Are the Answer Choices?

Always write ABCD next to every quant comp question. Then use Process of Elimination in the same way you would on questions that provide the answer choices. Cross off wrong answers as you work on each problem. When you decide on your choice, circle it and write it next to the question number. Fill in the bubbles on your answer sheet page by page.

Always write down the answer choices for quant comp. Use POE!

What About the Math?

Quant comps are drawn from the basic arithmetic, algebra, and geometry concepts that constitute GRE mathematics. In general, then, you'll apply the same techniques that you use on other types of math questions. Still, quant comps do require a few special techniques of their own.

If a Quant Comp Question Contains Only Numbers, Choice D Can't Be Correct

Any problem containing only numbers must have an exact solution. Therefore, choice D can be eliminated immediately on all such problems. Here's an example:

Column A	Column B
1. $\frac{2}{7} - 1$	$\frac{1}{3} - 1$

Here's how to crack it

Because this problem contains only numbers, you can calculate an exact value for the expression in each column. This means that choice D cannot possibly be ETS's answer. Eliminate it.

What *is* ETS's answer on this easy problem? It's choice B. Since −1 appears in both expressions, we can ignore it. That means all we have to decide is whether $\frac{2}{7}$ is bigger than, smaller than, or the same as $\frac{1}{3}$. Use the Bowtie to compare fractions! You don't want to make a careless mistake at this point.

Multiply the denominator of each fraction by the numerator of the other: 3 times 2 is 6. Write 6 in Column A. Seven times 1 is 7. Write 7 in Column B. So Column B is greater, and the ETS answer is B.

It's Not What It Is, But Which Is Bigger

You don't have to figure out what the exact values would be in both columns before you compare them. The prime directive is to compare the two columns!

Here's an example:

	Column A	Column B
3.	$9(3 + 24)$	$(9 \times 3) + (9 \times 24)$

Here's how to crack it

First of all, you should notice that choice D can't be ETS's answer: There's nothing here but numbers.

Now what? Should you multiply out those numbers? No. ETS isn't testing your ability to multiply. Finding ETS's answer simply depends on your noticing that the expressions in Column A and Column B are the factored and unfactored forms of the same number. ETS's answer is choice C.

TREAT THE TWO COLUMNS AS THOUGH THEY WERE THE TWO SIDES OF AN EQUATION

Anything you can do to both sides of an equation, you can also do to the expressions in both columns on a quant comp. You can add the same number to both sides; you can multiply both sides by the same number; you can simplify a single side by multiplying it by some form of 1.

DON'T MULTIPLY OR DIVIDE BOTH SIDES BY A NEGATIVE NUMBER

Remember what happens to an inequality if you multiply both sides by a negative number? When you multiply or divide both sides of an inequality by a negative number, the direction of the inequality symbol changes. If the quantity in Column A is greater than the quantity in Column B, multiplying or dividing through by a negative number will make Column B greater than Column A. So don't do it.

ALWAYS SIMPLIFY

If you *can* simplify the terms in a quant comp, you should *always* do so. As is so often true on the GRE, finding ETS's answer is frequently merely a matter of simplifying, reducing, factoring, or unfactoring. Here's an example:

	Column A	Column B
4.	25×7.39	$\dfrac{739}{4}$

Here's how to crack it

First of all, you should notice that choice D can't be ETS's answer: There's nothing here but numbers.

What should you do next? Whatever you do, *don't* do the multiplication in the first column and the division in the second. You'd find the answer that way, but it would take forever. Instead, get rid of the fraction in Column B by multiplying *both sides* by 4. Here's what you end up with:

	Column A	Column B
4.	100×7.39	739

Notice anything? You get 739 in both columns. That means ETS's answer is choice C.

Here's another example:

	Column A	Column B
6.	$\dfrac{1}{17} + \dfrac{1}{8} + \dfrac{1}{5}$	$\dfrac{1}{5} + \dfrac{1}{17} + \dfrac{1}{7}$

Here's how to crack it

Remember, you don't have to solve each column, just figure out which is bigger. Of course, first eliminate choice D. Then subtract the numbers that are common to both columns—just cross them off. What's left? In Column A you have $\dfrac{1}{8}$, in Column B $\dfrac{1}{7}$. How do you know which is greater? Use the Bowtie! The ETS answer is choice B.

JOE LOVES QUANT COMP

Joe Bloggs fairly sails through quant comps—no sweat! This means, of course, that you need to be extra careful.

On medium problems, especially 9 and 10, start to look for the Joe Bloggs choices and be very skeptical! On every difficult quant comp problem (11–15), eliminate the Joe Bloggs choices before you actually attempt to solve the problem.

On the problems below, identify the Joe Bloggs choices and cross them out.

Eliminate Joe Bloggs's choices on medium and difficult quant comp problems.

	Column A	Column B
9.	$(.89)(.89)$	$(.89)(.89)(.89)$

A B C D

Joe Bloggs's choice: _____

Analysis

Did you remember to cross off choice D? Joe picks Column B, because he thinks that the more you multiply a number the bigger it gets. But, as we've seen, when you multiply by a number between 0 and 1 the result is smaller than your original number. The ETS choice is A.

	Column A	Column B
11.	$-y$	$2y$

A B C D

Joe Bloggs's choice: _____

Analysis

Joe picks choice B, because he thinks that the number in Column A is negative and the one in Column B is positive. But is that *always* true? If y is a negative number, then Column A would be positive and Column B would be negative. Different numbers give you different answers. The ETS choice is D.

	Column A	Column B
10.	$n + 27p$	$27n + p$

A B C D

Joe Bloggs's choice: _____

Analysis

Joe thinks the two columns are equal, because you've got 27, and n and p, in both. So eliminate choice C. But, once again, if you plug in different numbers for p and n, you get different answers. The ETS choice is D.

A discount of 30 percent followed by a discount of 25 percent would equal a single discount of p percent.

13.	p	47.5

A B C D

Joe Bloggs's choice: _____

Analysis

Joe picks choice A, because he thinks that the two discounts add up to 55 percent. So eliminate choice A, and also eliminate choice D since there's no variable. In fact the two discounts are equal to a single discount of 47.5 percent. (We'll cover percentages in the chapter 17.) The ETS choice is C.

SUMMARY

Quantitative Comparisons

◆ Always write ABCD next to each problem.

◆ If a problem has all numbers and no variables, eliminate choice D!

◆ YOU DON'T HAVE TO SOLVE THE COLUMNS, JUST COMPARE THEM.

◆ Always simplify before you calculate.

◆ If you do difficult quant comp problems (11–15), eliminate Joe Bloggs's answer choices *before* you actually start to solve the problem.

16
Plugging In

THE MOST POWERFUL GRE MATH TECHNIQUE

Now that you've seen the questions on which half of your GRE math score depends, it's time to introduce you to the most powerful problem-solving technique you'll need for the GRE math sections.

Many GRE math problems have variables in the answer choices. ETS knows that most people try to do them algebraically. ETS also knows which algebraic mistakes most people will make, and what answers would result from those mistakes. That's how they design the *wrong* answers to these problems. To avoid frustration and trap answers on these problems, the fastest and easiest way to find ETS's answer is by making up numbers and plugging them in. Plugging in makes word problems much less abstract and much easier to solve.

Here's what you do:

1. Pick a number for each variable in the problem and write it next to the variable in all the answer choices.

2. Solve the problem using your numbers; write your numerical answer and circle it.

3. Do the arithmetic for the answer choices to see which one of them equals the solution you found in step 2.

When a problem has variables in the answer choices, **PLUG IN!**

Here's an example:

20. If $x + y = z$ and $x = y$, then all of the following are true EXCEPT:

(A) $2x + 2y = 2z$

(B) $x - y = 0$

(C) $x - z = y - z$

(D) $x = \dfrac{z}{2}$

(E) $x - y = 2z$

Here's how to crack it

All you have to do is pick simple values for x, y, and z that are consistent with the two given equations. Let's say that x and y (which we have been told are equal) are both 2. That means that z is 4. Be sure to write down these values in your test booklet, so you don't forget them.

Now we plug these values into the answer choices. Here's what we get:

(A) $2(2) + 2(2) = 2(4)$, or $4 + 4 = 8$. Yes, that's correct. Eliminate. (We're looking for the wrong choice, remember? This is an EXCEPT problem.)

(B) $2 - 2 = 0$. Correct again. Eliminate.

(C) $2 - 4 = 2 - 4$. Correct again. Eliminate.

(D) $2 = 2$. Correct again. Eliminate.

(E) $2 - 2 = 2(4)$. This is not correct. It must be ETS's answer.

WHICH NUMBERS SHOULD YOU PLUG IN?

You can plug in any numbers you like, as long as they're consistent with any restrictions stated in the problem. But you'll find ETS's answer faster if you use easy numbers.

What makes a number easy? That depends on the problem. In most cases, smaller numbers are easier to work with than larger numbers. Usually it's best to start small, with 2 or 3, for example. (Avoid 0 and 1 in these situations. Zero and 1 have special properties, about which we'll tell you more later.)

Plug in numbers that will make the arithmetic simple.

Do not plug in 0, 1, or numbers that show up a lot in the question or answer choices. Plug in numbers that make the arithmetic easy.

Try this one. Read through the whole question before you start to plug in numbers.

20. Celeste gave Dave n dollars. She gave Karen two dollars more than she gave Dave and she gave Amber three dollars less than she gave Karen. In terms of n, how many dollars did Celeste give Karen, Dave, and Amber altogether?

    (A) $\dfrac{n}{3}$

    (B) $n-1$

    (C) $3n$

    (D) $3n-1$

    (E) $3n+1$

Here's how to crack it

Plug in a number for n. Let's say 5. Write 5 in place of n in all the answer choices. Don't try to do this "in your head." Now let's solve the problem. If Celeste gave Dave 5 dollars, and she gave Karen 2 dollars more than she gave Dave, then she gave Karen 7. Write 7 for Karen. Since Celeste gave Amber three dollars less than she gave Karen, Amber got 4 dollars. Write that down. Now add up the amounts. $5 + 7 + 4 = 16$. Write down 16 and circle it. That's our target answer. Now let's go to the choices.

    (A) $\dfrac{5}{3}$ does not equal 16. Eliminate.

    (B) $5-1$ does not equal 16. Eliminate.

    (C) $3(5)$ does not equal 16. Gone.

    (D) $3(5)-1$ does not equal 16. Out.

    (E) $3(5)+1$ equals 16. Bingo.

GOOD NUMBERS MAKE LIFE EASIER

Small numbers aren't always best. In a problem involving percentages, for example, 10 and 100 are good numbers to use. In a problem involving minutes or seconds, 60 may be the easiest number. You should look for clues in the problem itself. Here's an example:

26. A street vendor has just purchased a carton containing 250 hot dogs. If the carton cost x dollars, what is the cost in dollars of 10 of the hot dogs?

(A) $\dfrac{x}{25}$

(B) $\dfrac{x}{10}$

(C) $10x$

(D) $\dfrac{10}{x}$

(E) $\dfrac{25}{x}$

Here's how to crack it

We could plug in anything at all for x (how about 199.99?) and still find ETS's answer. But let's pick an easy number. What's easy? How about 250? That means that the hot dogs cost $1 each. In your test booklet write "$x = 250$."

What is the cost of 10 of the hot dogs, given that 250 of them cost $250? That's easy. The cost of 10 hot dogs is $10. That's what ETS wants to know—the cost of 10 hot dogs. Write "10" in your test booklet and circle it. We're now looking for the answer choice that yields 10 when we plug in 250 for x. Now try the choices:

(A) Plugging in 250 for x, we get $\dfrac{250}{25}$, or 10. This is the number we're looking for. KEEP CHECKING all the the choices.

(B) $\dfrac{250}{10} = 25$. We're looking for 10, so eliminate this choice.

(C) 10 times 250 is way too big. We're looking for 10. Eliminate.

(D) $\dfrac{10}{250}$ is way too small. Eliminate.

(E) $\dfrac{25}{250}$ is also way too small. Eliminate.

Checking all the choices is worth doing. It's easy and fast. If more than one answer choice works with the first numbers you plugged in, eliminate the choices that don't work, and plug in new numbers. Get a new arithmetic answer and plug in your new numbers for the remaining answer choices. Then eliminate the answer choices that don't work with your new arithmetic answer.

ALWAYS ACCEPT A GIFT

ETS will sometimes give you a value for one of the variables or terms in an expression and then ask you for the value of the entire expression. Nothing could be easier. Simply plug in the value that ETS gives you and see what you come up with. Here's an example:

26. If $3x = -2$, then $(3x - 3)^2 =$

    (A) -9
    (B) -6
    (C) -1
    (D) 25
    (E) 36

Here's how to crack it

Forget about algebra; don't solve for x. Simply plug in -2 for $3x$ in the question. This gives you the following:

$$(3x - 3)^2 = (-2 - 3)^2$$
$$= (-5)^2$$
$$= 25$$

So the ETS answer is D. You should never, never, never try to solve problems like these by "solving for x" or "solving for y." Plugging in is much easier and faster, and you'll be less likely to make dumb mistakes.

PLUG IN MORE THAN ONCE FOR "MUST BE" PROBLEMS

These "algebraic reasoning" problems are much easier to solve by plugging in than by "reasoning." On these, you will have to plug in more than once in order to find ETS's answer. Here's an example:

17. If x and y are integers and xy is an even integer, which of the following must be an odd integer?

    (A) $xy + 5$

    (B) $x + y$

    (C) $\dfrac{x}{y}$

    (D) $4x$

    (E) $7xy$

> Try to disprove answer choices on MUST BE problems. Plug in numbers, eliminate answer choices with those numbers, then plug in different numbers to eliminate any remaining choices.

Here's how to crack it

Let's plug in 2 for x and 3 for y. Using these numbers, we can eliminate choices C, D, and E. But these numbers make both A and B odd. Did we make a mistake? No, this is standard operating procedure on a "must be" question. At first we made x even and y odd. Let's make them both even and just change y to 4. Is xy even, using these numbers? Yes. Now let's go back to the two remaining choices. Now when you add x and y you get 6, so eliminate choice B. ETS's answer is A.

We love plugging in so much that you should make these the first difficult problems you try to do, after you've finished all of the easy and medium questions in the section.

Try this difficult problem:

29. The positive difference between the squares of any two consecutive integers is always:

   (A) the square of an integer
   (B) a multiple of 5
   (C) an even integer
   (D) an odd number
   (E) a prime number

Here's how to crack it

The word *always* in the question tells us that all we need to find in order to eliminate a choice is a single instance in which it doesn't work. So let's start by picking two consecutive integers and squaring them. It doesn't matter which consecutive integers we choose. How about 2 and 3? Squaring 2 and 3 gives us 4 and 9. The positive difference between them (9 – 4, as opposed to 4 – 9) is 5. Now look at the choices:

   (A) Is 5 the square of an integer? No. Eliminate.

   (B) Is 5 a multiple of 5? Yes. A possibility.

   (C) Is 5 an even integer? No. Eliminate.

   (D) Is 5 an odd integer? Yes. A possibility.

   (E) Is 5 a prime number? Yes. A possibility.

We've eliminated choices A and C. That's good. It means that with very little effort we've boosted our guessing odds to 1 in 3 on this very difficult problem. But we can do better than that. Let's pick two more consecutive integers. How about 0 and 1? The squares of 0 and 1 are 0 and 1. The positive difference between them is 1. Now look at the remaining choices:

   (B) Is 1 a multiple of 5? No. Eliminate.

   (D) Is 1 an odd integer? Yes. A possibility.

   (E) Is 1 a prime number? No. Eliminate.

ETS's answer is choice D.

Notice that on the "second round" of elimination we plugged in "weird" numbers that we usually avoid. That's how we found what would always be true. Hmm. Doesn't that sound familiar?

PLUGGING IN ON QUANT COMPS

The easiest way to solve most quant comps involving variables is to plug in, just as you do on word problems. Here's an example:

	Column A	Column B
1.	$x + 1$	$1 - x$

Here's how to crack it

Plug in an easy number. How about 2? That gives us 3 as the quantity in Column A and –1 as the quantity in Column B. We know that 3 is greater than –1, so ETS's answer must be choice A, right?

Wrong. Because this isn't always true. To see this, try plugging in 0. That gives us 1 in Column A and 1 in Column B—now the two columns are equal.

In other words, if you plug in different numbers, you get different answers. Therefore ETS's answer is choice D.

Always Plug in at Least Twice in Quant Comp

Plugging in on quant comps is just like it is on "must be" problems. The reason for this is choice D. On quant comps, it's not enough to determine whether one quantity is sometimes greater than, less than, or equal to the other; you have to determine whether it always is. If different numbers lead to different answers, then ETS's answer is choice D.

Practice using this step-by-step procedure:

STEP 1: Write A B C D next to the question.

STEP 2: Plug in "normal" numbers like 2, 3, and 5.

STEP 3: Which column is bigger? Cross out the two choices that you've proved are wrong. Suppose the numbers you plugged in at first made Column A bigger; which answer choices cannot be correct? B and C. Cross them out! A and D are still possible choices.

STEP 4: Now try to get a different answer! Plug in weird numbers such as 0, 1, negatives, fractions, or really big numbers.

> On quant comp, plug in "normal numbers," and eliminate two choices. Then plug in "weird" numbers (zero, one, negatives, fractions, or big numbers) to try to disprove your first answer. If different numbers give you different answers, you've proved that the answer is D.

What makes these numbers weird? They behave in unexpected ways when added, multiplied, and raised to powers. For example:

0 times any number is 0.

0^2 is 0.

1^2 is 1.

$\left(\dfrac{1}{2}\right)^2$ is less than $\dfrac{1}{2}$.

$(-2)(-2)$ is 4.

A negative number squared is positive.

Really big numbers (100, 1,000) can make a really big difference in your answer.

Try this example:

Column A	Column B

$$x > y$$

	Column A	Column B
10.	x^2	y^2

Here's how to crack it

This is clearly a plug-in problem. Let's say we plug in 3 for x and 2 for y. That satisfies the condition, and it gives us 9 for Column A and 4 for Column B. Column A is bigger, so ETS's answer is A, right?

Not so fast. We know that Column A *can* be bigger, but we haven't proved that it *has* to be bigger. Eliminate B and C. We still have to "test for always." To do this, we need to plug in something different. How about –2 for x and –3 for y? This satisfies the condition, and it gives us 4 for Column A and 9 for Column B. Now Column B is bigger. ETS's answer is choice D.

JOE BLOGGS CAN HELP

On items 11–15, you should almost always be able to eliminate at least one Joe Bloggs trap. Remember, on these items, any answer that jumps out at you immediately has to be wrong. Joe never thinks of the weird numbers. Here's an example:

Column A	Column B
12. xy	$x\sqrt{y}$

Here's how to crack it

First, plug in a pair of easy numbers. Let's try 3 for x and 4 for y. (Four is a good plug-in for y, because $\sqrt{4}$ is an integer.) This gives us 12 for Column A and 6 for Column B. With these plug-ins, choice A looks like ETS's answer. It sure looks great to Joe. He would choose A and rush along to the next question.

What does this tell us? *Everything.* Plugging in the easiest numbers we could think of quickly made A look like ETS's answer. Because this is a difficult item, choice A *can't possibly be correct.* If choice A were correct, Joe would get this problem right and it would be an easy, not a difficult problem. So we can eliminate choice A.

Is that all we can do? No. We can also eliminate choices B and C. If the expression in Column A is at least sometimes greater than the expression in Column B, then the expression in Column B can't always be greater than the expression in Column A. That rules out choice B. Nor can the two always be the same. That rules out choice C.

Very quickly, then, we realize that ETS's answer has to be choice D. Now let's prove it by plugging in weird numbers. Let's get really weird. How about 0 for x and 0 for y? (There's no rule that says x and y have to be different.) That gives us 0 for Column A and 0 for Column B. Since these numbers make the two columns equal, this proves that A is not always the answer, and the ETS choice is D.

Here's another example:

Column A	Column B
	$y = x^2 + 1$
13. xy	x^3

Here's how to crack it

What are easy (Joe Bloggs) plug-ins? If we plug in 2 for x, we get $y = 4 + 1$, which means that if $x = 2$, $y = 5$. That gives us 10 for Column A and 8 for Column B. That was fast! So, just as fast, we eliminate choices A, B, and C and mark choice D.

To see why this is true, let's plug in a weird number for x. How about –1? That gives us $y = 1 + 1$, which means that if $x = -1$, $y = 2$. This gives us –2 for Column A and –1 for Column B. Once again, ETS's answer must be choice D.

FUNCTIONS AND FUNNY-LOOKING SYMBOLS

You may remember the phrase "f of x" from high school algebra. Usually written "$f(x)$," this phrase had to do with functions.

With funny symbols, follow the directions. Just do it.

The GRE contains function problems, but you probably won't recognize them. Instead of presenting them in "$f(x)$" form, it disguises them by using funny-looking symbols, such as $\oplus$, *, and #. These symbols represent arithmetic operations or series of arithmetic operations. If you remember how functions work, you can solve these problems simply by thinking of functions whenever you see the funny-looking symbols.

If you don't remember much about functions, don't worry. Just do what we tell you to do, and you shouldn't have much trouble.

In funny-looking symbol problems, the funny-looking symbol can be thought of as representing a set of operations or instructions. Here's an example:

$$\text{If } x \text{ @ } y = \frac{x - y}{2}, \text{ what is the value of } \frac{1}{3} \text{ @ } \frac{1}{5} \text{ ?}$$

Here's how to crack it

The symbol @ represents a series of operations. The problem tells us that x funny symbol y equals the difference of x and y divided by 2. What do we do to find ETS's answer? Easy: Plug in $\frac{1}{3}$ and $\frac{1}{5}$ for x and y. This means we have to subtract $\frac{1}{5}$ from $\frac{1}{3}$. To do this, we can use the Bowtie (remember the Bowtie?). Here's how we work it out:

$$\frac{1}{3} \text{ @ } \frac{1}{5} = \frac{\frac{1}{3} \times \frac{1}{5}}{2} = \frac{\frac{5-3}{15}}{2} = \frac{\frac{2}{15}}{2} = \frac{2}{15} \times \frac{1}{2} = \frac{2}{30} = \frac{1}{15}$$

For funny symbol problems, just follow the directions.

SUMMARY

Plugging In

1. Always plug in numbers when there are variables in the answer choices!

2. Plug in a number anytime there is an unknown in the question.

3. On "must be" problems, plug in more than once to disprove choices.

Plugging in on Quant Comp

1. Always plug in at least twice.

2. First plug in "normal" numbers and get an answer for the first round.

3. Eliminate two choices.

4. You'll have your first answer and choice D left.

5. Then plug in "weird" numbers (0, 1, negative numbers, fractions, or really big numbers) to try to disprove your first answer.

Funny Symbol Problems

1. Follow the directions. Just plug the numbers into the operation you're given in the directions.

17

Percentages, Ratios, and Averages

PERCENTAGES, RATIOS, AND AVERAGES ON THE GRE

Now let's review some topics that you'll see quite often on the GRE math sections. Again, as you've seen in chapter 16 on plugging in, the ways in which we approach these topics may be different from your approach in your high school math classes, or from what you might do in everyday life. But remember that you can't use a calculator on this test. Your focus must be on the best ways to do the problems as they appear on the GRE. It's worth changing some of your old habits.

PERCENTAGES

So far we've said that a fraction is another way of representing division and that a decimal is the same thing as a fraction. Well, a percentage is also another way of representing division and is also the same thing as a fraction and a decimal. A percentage is just a handy way of expressing a fraction whose denominator is 100.

Percent means "per 100" or "out of 100" or "divided by 100." If your best friend finds a dollar and gives you 50 cents, your friend has given you 50 cents out of 100, or $\frac{50}{100}$ of a dollar, or 50 percent of a dollar.

PERCENTAGES, FRACTIONS, AND DECIMALS

You should memorize these percentage–decimal–fraction equivalents. Use these "friendly" fractions and percentages to eliminate answer choices that are way outside the ballpark:

Memorizing these percentage–decimal–fraction equivalents will help you score more.

$$0.01 = \frac{1}{100} = 1 \text{ percent}$$

$$0.1 = \frac{1}{10} = 10 \text{ percent}$$

$$0.2 = \frac{1}{5} = 20 \text{ percent}$$

$$0.25 = \frac{1}{4} = 25 \text{ percent}$$

$$0.33 = \frac{1}{3} = 33\frac{1}{3} \text{ percent}$$

$$0.4 = \frac{2}{5} = 40 \text{ percent}$$

$$0.5 = \frac{1}{2} = 50 \text{ percent}$$

$$0.6 = \frac{3}{5} = 60 \text{ percent}$$

$$0.6\overline{6} = \frac{2}{3} = 66\frac{2}{3} \text{ percent}$$

$$0.75 = \frac{3}{4} = 75 \text{ percent}$$

$$0.8 = \frac{4}{5} = 80 \text{ percent}$$

$$1.0 = \frac{1}{1} = 100 \text{ percent}$$

$$2.0 = \frac{2}{1} = 200 \text{ percent}$$

16. Which of the following is 26 percent of 200?

    (A) .26
    (B) .52
    (C) 5.2
    (D) 52
    (E) 520

Here's how to crack it

The choices are so far apart that all you need to do is get the "ballpark answer." Twenty-six percent is very close to 25 percent, or $\frac{1}{4}$. What is $\frac{1}{4}$ of 200? It's 50. So the answer has to be slightly bigger than 50. The only possibility is choice D.

TRANSLATE WORD PROBLEMS INTO MATH EQUATIONS

When you have to find exact percentages it's much easier if you know how to translate word problems. Translating a problem lets you express it as an equation, which is easier to manipulate. Here's a word-problem "dictionary" that will help with your translations:

Word	Equivalent Symbol
percent	$\overline{100}$
is	=
of, times, product	×
what (or any unknown value)	any variable (x, k, b)
what percent	$\dfrac{x}{100}$

Translate percentage word problems into math equations.

Here's an example:
What is 30 percent of 200?

Here's how to crack it
First translate literally, term by term, then reduce and solve for the variable:

$$x = \frac{30}{100} \times 200$$

$$x = 30 \times 2$$

$$x = 60$$

That's the answer. Thirty percent of 200 is 60.
Now try a real GRE question.

Column A	Column B

x percent of 36 is 27

   3.   x   75

Here's how to crack it
Translate the common information, like this:

$$\frac{x}{100} \times \frac{36}{1} = 27$$

Putting the integer over 1 helps you keep your places straight.
So you get:

$$\frac{36x}{100} = 27$$

Then multiply both sides by 100——but keep things factored; don't get the total yet.

$$36x = 27 \times 100$$

Then divide both sides by 36 and reduce.

$$x = \frac{27}{36} \times 100$$

$$x = \frac{3}{4} \times 100$$

$$x = 75$$

So the ETS answer must be C.
Let's try another GRE question.

19. If the price of a certain item is $200 after a discount of 20 percent, what was the original price of the item before the discount?

(A) $160
(B) $180
(C) $240
(D) $250
(E) $1,000

Here's how to crack it

Let's ballpark to start with, since we know the answer has to be more than $200. That eliminates choices A and B right off the bat. Now, if you take away 20 percent of something, what's the rest? It's 80 percent. So the question is really asking, "Two hundred is 80 percent of what number?" Translated into an equation, it would be:

$$200 = \frac{80}{100} \times \frac{x}{1}$$

Now reduce and solve for x.

$$200 = \frac{4}{5} \times \frac{x}{1}$$

$$200 = \frac{4x}{5}$$

Multiply both sides by 5 and divide both by 4.

$$\frac{5}{4} \times 200 = x$$

$$5 \times 50 = x$$

$$250 = x$$

So the ETS answer is D.

CONVERTING FRACTIONS TO PERCENTAGES

Just translate the problem. Then solve for the variable. Here's an example:

Express $\frac{4}{5}$ as a percentage.

Here's how to crack it

"$\frac{4}{5}$ is what percent?"

$$\frac{4}{5} = \frac{x}{100}$$

(Multiply both sides by 100.)

$$\frac{400}{5} = x$$

$$80 = x$$

So $\frac{4}{5}$ is the same as 80 percent.

CONVERTING DECIMALS TO PERCENTAGES

Just move the decimal point two places to the *right*. This turns 0.8 into 80 percent, and 0.25 into 25 percent, and 0.5 into 50 percent, and 1 into 100 percent.

PERCENTAGE INCREASE/DECREASE

To find a percentage increase or decrease, first find the *amount* of increase or decrease, then ask yourself, "The amount of change is what percent of the original amount?"

$$\text{Amount change} = \frac{x}{100} \times \text{original number (starting point)}$$

DRILL 1

You can check your answers on page 297.

1. What is 20 percent of 300?

2. 2 is what percent of 4?

3. 2.2 is 20 percent of what number?

4. 10 percent of 24 equals 20 percent of what?

5. 20 percent of 25 percent of x is 10. What is x?

RATIOS

Ratios, like fractions, percentages, and decimals, are just another way of representing division. Ratios can be expressed in many different ways.

Ratios, fractions, percentages, and decimals are different ways of representing division.

The ratio of 1 to 4

1 : 4

1 is to 4

$$\frac{1}{4}$$

All of these expressions are equal.

Ratios and fractions look and act like fractions, and for some of the problems on the GRE, it's best to write ratios as fractions. Where in the GRE math section do you think that might be a good idea? Right. Quant comp. Why? Because you can use the Bowtie to compare fractions!

But there's an important difference between a ratio and a fraction.

Fraction

$$\frac{2}{5} = \frac{\text{part}}{\text{whole}}$$

Ratio

$$\frac{2}{3} = \frac{\text{part}}{\text{part}}$$

So if you are told there's a ratio of 2 of something to 3 of something, then there are 5 parts in the whole.

To find the whole, you have to add up the parts of the ratio.

THE RATIO BOX

If you have 3 coins in your pocket and the ratio of pennies to nickels is 2:1, how many pennies and nickels are there? That's easy. There are 2 pennies and 1 nickel.

If you have 24 coins in your pocket and the ratio of pennies to nickels is 2:1, how many pennies and nickels are there? Making a ratio box will help you visualize the problem. At the top put the labels for the things you have and for the whole. Make one row for the ratio (in this case 2:1), make another row (which we'll discuss shortly), and a third row for the actual numbers (we know that there are 24 coins in the whole).

	Pennies	Nickels	Whole
Ratio	2 +	1 =	3
Actual Numbers			24

Now we have to multiply everything in the top row by some number to get the actual numbers in the bottom row. What do you have to multiply 3 by to get 24? By 8. So multiply everything in the top row by 8 to get the actual numbers of pennies and nickels.

	Pennies	Nickels	Whole
Ratio	2 +	1 =	3
Multiply by	× 8	× 8	× 8
Actual Numbers	16	8	24

So, you have 16 pennies and 8 nickels.

> Draw ratio boxes in your test booklet.

Here's another example:

18. At a camp for boys and girls, the ratio of the girls to boys is 5:3. If the camp's enrollment is 160, how many of the children are boys?

(A) 20
(B) 36
(C) 45
(D) 60
(E) 100

Here's how to crack it

Make a ratio box. Don't be careless. ETS often makes subtle changes in wording; the question at the end of a word problem may change the order of the elements that were introduced earlier.

A ratio of 5:3 means the whole is 8 parts. Be sure to put 5 under the "Girls" and 3 under the "Boys." Put in the actual number of campers in the whole column.

	Girls		Boys		Whole
Ratio	5	+	3	=	8
Multiply by					
Actual Numbers					160

What do you multiply 8 by to get 160? By 20. Just go to the "Boys" column.

	Girls		Boys		Whole
Ratio	5	+	3	=	8
Multiply by			× 20		20
Actual Numbers			60		160

So the ETS answer is choice D.

Treat ratios and proportions like you would fractions.

PROPORTIONS

The GRE often has problems in which you are given two proportional, or equal, ratios from which one piece of information is missing. These questions take a given relationship, or ratio, and project it onto a larger or smaller scale. Here's an example:

8. If 10 baskets contain a total of 50 eggs, how many eggs would 7 baskets contain?

    (A) 10
    (B) 17
    (C) 35
    (D) 40
    (E) 50

Here's how to crack it

In this problem, you are given two equal ratios, one of which is missing one piece of information. To find ETS's answer, make a quick diagram:

$$10 \ (baskets) \qquad 7 \ (baskets)$$
$$50 \ (eggs) \qquad x \ (eggs)$$

Because you can treat ratios exactly like fractions, you can find the missing element by cross multiplying:

$$10x \qquad\qquad 350$$

$$\frac{10}{50} \times \frac{7}{x}$$

$$10x = 350$$

$$x = 35$$

ETS's answer is 35. (Note that we could have made our job simpler by reducing $\frac{10}{50}$ to $\frac{1}{5}$ before cross multiplying.)

AVERAGES

The average (arithmetic mean) of a set of numbers is the sum of all the numbers divided by the number of numbers in the set. The average of the set $\{1, 2, 3, 4, 5, 6, 7\}$ is the total of the numbers ($1 + 2 + 3 + 4 + 5 + 6 + 7$, or 28) divided by the number of numbers in the set (which is 7). Dividing 28 by 7 gives us 4. Thus 4 is the average of the set.

ETS always refers to an average as an "average (arithmetic mean)." This confusing parenthetical remark is meant to keep you from being confused by other kinds of averages, such as medians and modes. You'll be less confused if you simply ignore the parenthetical remark. Medians and modes are occasionally tested on the GRE. If you run into a median or mode question, all you need to know is that the median is the middle number in a set, and the mode is the number that shows up most frequently.

WHAT'S THE TOTAL?

Don't try to solve average problems all at once. Do them piece by piece. The critical formula to keep in mind is this:

$$\text{Average} = \frac{\text{the sum of the numbers being averaged}}{\text{the number of elements}}$$

For average problems, think TOTAL.

You are always going to need the sum of the numbers being averaged: the *total* amount, the *total* height, the *total* weight, the *total* number of petals, the *total* of the scores, the *total* distance. Average questions are always really about *totals*. In fact, an average is just another way of expressing a total; an average is the total divided by the number of elements.

In average problems, you should always find the total first, before you do anything else.

Try this one.

17. Lisa and Maria together weigh 240 pounds, and Peter weighs 198 pounds. What is the average (arithmetic mean) of their three weights?

   (A) 120
   (B) 146
   (C) 159
   (D) 219
   (E) 438

Here's how to crack it

First find the total of all three weights. 240 + 198 = 438. Now divide by 3.

$$\frac{438}{3} = 146.$$

Notice that you could have eliminated answer choices that are out of the ballpark. Pretend that Lisa and Maria each weigh 120 pounds (the average of their two weights). Peter weighs more, so the average of the three has to be somewhere between 120 and 198 pounds. Eliminate choices A, D, and E.

WATCH OUT FOR MISSING INFORMATION

ETS often turns an easy averaging problem into a medium averaging problem by leaving out certain information. Here's an example:

20. The average test score earned by a group of students is 80. If 40 percent of the students have an average score of 70, what is the average score of the remaining 60 percent?

   (A) $70 \frac{1}{3}$
   (B) 80
   (C) $86 \frac{2}{3}$
   (D) 90
   (E) 95

Here's how to crack it

There's a seemingly important piece of information missing from this problem: the number of students in the "group." Since this value is unknown, many students try to solve the problem by setting up a complex algebraic equation: $80 = (x + y + \ldots)$. That's about how far they get before giving up.

What should you do to solve the problem? Easy: Plug in! Simply plug in a number for how many students are in the group. Because we're dealing with percentages, 10 or 100 are easy numbers to work with. So we'll assume that our group contains 10 students. Four of those 10 (40 percent of 10) students have an average score of 70; we're supposed to determine the average score of the remaining 6.

The first thing we need to do (now that we've turned it back into an easy average problem) is to find the total. If the average score of 10 students is 80, what's their total score? It's 800. Four of the students have an average score of 70, which means that their total score is 280. What's the total score of the remaining 6 students? It's 800 − 280, or 520. What's their average score (which is what we're looking for)? It's 520 ÷ 6, or $86\frac{2}{3}$. ETS's answer is C.

UP OR DOWN

Averages are very predictable. You should make sure you know automatically what happens to them in certain situations. For example, suppose that you take three tests and earn an average score of 90. Now you take a fourth test. What do you know? The following:

1. If the average goes up as a result of the fourth score, then you know that the fourth score was higher than 90.

2. If the average stays the same as a result of the fourth score, then you know that the fourth score was exactly 90.

3. If the average goes down as a result of the fourth score, then you know that the fourth score was less than 90.

DRILL 2

Check your answers on page 297.

1. What is the average (arithmetic mean) of the numbers 24, 24, 26, 28, and 40?

2. If the average of 5 numbers is 20, what is their total?

3. If the average of 5 positive integers is 20, what is the largest that any of the numbers could be?

4. If the average of 11, 17, 15, 28, and x is 19.6, what is the value of x?

5. Sam's average score for four math tests was 80 out of a possible 100. If his scores on two of the tests were 65 and 70, what is the lowest that either of his other scores could have been?

You probably already have a lot of experience with averaging numbers: baseball statistics, test scores, GPAs (grade point *averages*).

SUMMARY

Percentages

1. Percentages are just fractions with 100 in the denominator.

2. **Translate** percentage word problems into math equations.

3. Use "friendly" percentages and their fraction equivalents to ballpark answer choices.

4. For percent increase or decrease, ask the question, "The change is what percent of the original number?"

Ratios

1. A fraction is a ratio of $\dfrac{\text{Part}}{\text{Whole}}$.

2. A ratio is $\dfrac{\text{Part}}{\text{Part}}$.

3. Add up the parts to get the whole.

4. Use the ratio box.

Proportions

1. Find the missing piece of information.

Averages

1. Think TOTAL. That's usually the first step.

2. $\text{Average} = \dfrac{\text{the sum of the numbers being averaged}}{\text{the number of elements}}$.

18
Charts

WHAT ARE CHARTS?

Buried in the middle of every GRE math section is a set of five questions based on a chart or graph (or on a group of charts or graphs). These questions are numbered 21–25. Question 21 and 22 are easy, question 23 is medium, and questions 24 and 25 are difficult.

Do It Last and Do It Fast

That's our approach to charts. These questions don't count any more in your score than any other math questions. But they take more time per question to answer correctly. That's why we skipped charts and did questions 26 and 27 before even looking at the chart problems. Since these questions are designed to waste your time, just work out the answers to questions 21–23, and skip 24 and 25 unless you've answered every other math question correctly.

What Do They Test?

ETS claims that the GRE's chart questions test your ability to read charts and graphs. Why ETS thinks this skill has anything to do with your fitness for graduate school is a great mystery.

But in fact, the most important thing that chart questions test is your ability to remember the difference between real life charts and ETS charts.

> On charts, look for information ETS is trying to hide.

Friends give you charts to display the information they want you to see, and to make that information easier to understand. ETS constructs charts to hide the information you need to know, and to make that information hard to understand.

Why Not Just Blow It Off Altogether?

Everyone should do at least questions 21 and 22, because easy questions have easy answers. Often you can use the information you gleaned for the first two questions to help you answer number 23. But then get out! Don't get sucked into doing questions 24 and 25.

ARE THERE ANY TECHNIQUES?

The chart problems just recycle the basic arithmetic concepts we've already covered: fractions, percentages, averages, ratios, and so on. Use the techniques we've discussed for each type of question.

But there are two techniques that are especially important to use when doing chart questions.

First Look Over the Charts to Find What ETS Is Trying to Hide

Don't start with the questions; start with the charts. Take a minute to look for and circle:

- **Information in titles:** If one chart is about Country X and the other is about Country Y, write a big "X" next to the Country X chart and a big "Y" next to Country Y's chart.

- **Asterisks, footnotes, parentheses, smaller type fonts:** Make sure you read these carefully and circle them—they're almost always added to hide crucial information.

- **Funny units:** Pay special attention when a title says "in thousands" or "in millions." You can usually ignore that to do the calculations, but you have to remember it to get the right answer.

Approximate, Estimate, and Ballpark

You probably don't estimate enough! As when using some of our other techniques, you've got to train yourself to do so. You should estimate, not calculate exactly, whenever:

- you see the word *approximately* in a question

- the answer choices are far apart in value

- you start to answer a question and you justifiably say to yourself, "This is going to take a lot of calculation!"

Review those "friendly" percentages and their fractions to use as reference points. For example, 34 percent is a little more than $\frac{1}{3}$.

Try this:

What is approximately 9.2 percent of 5.4?

Here's how to crack it

Use 10 percent as a friendlier percentage and 5 as a friendlier number: $\frac{1}{10}$ of 5 is $\frac{5}{10}$ or 1/2 or .5. That's all you need to do to answer most chart questions.

Don't forget to ESTIMATE answers.

A SAMPLE SECTION

Here's a sample chart section. It consists of two pie charts and five questions. We'll tackle the questions one at a time:

Questions 21–25 refer to the following graphs:

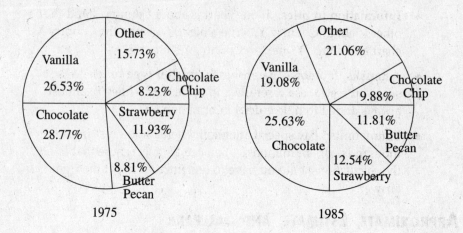

21. To the nearest one percent, what percentage decrease in popularity occurred for chocolate from 1975 to 1985?

    (A) 9%
    (B) 10%
    (C) 11%
    (D) 89%
    (E) 90%

22. What is the ratio of categories that increased in popularity to those that decreased?

    (A) 1:2 (B) 1:1 (C) 3:2 (D) 2:1 (E) 5:1

23. In 1985, if 20 percent of the "Other" category is lemon flavor, and 4,212 people surveyed preferred lemon, then how many people were surveyed?

    (A)   1,000
    (B)   10,000
    (C)   42,120
    (D)   100,000
    (E)   1,000,000

24. If a percentage-point shift results in annual additional sales of $50,000, how much, in dollars, did combined annual butter pecan and chocolate chip sales increase between 1975 and 1985?

    (A) $2,325
    (B) $4,650
    (C) $232,500
    (D) $465,000
    (E) $23,250,000

25. Which of the following statements can be deduced from the pie graphs?

    I. Both the butter pecan and vanilla percentages increased by more than 33 percent between 1975 and 1985.

    II. A higher percentage of people chose butter pecan and strawberry in 1975 than chose butter pecan and chocolate chip in 1985.

    III. The total share of vanilla, chocolate, and strawberry decreased by less than 20 percent from 1975 to 1985.

(A) I only
(B) II only
(C) III only
(D) II and III
(E) I, II, and III

ATTACKING THE QUESTIONS

That's what it looks like. Now let's go back and take another look at the first question:

21. To the nearest one percent, what percentage decrease in popularity occurred for chocolate from 1975 to 1985?

(A)   9%
(B) 10%
(C) 11%
(D) 89%
(E) 90%

Here's how to crack it

Looking over these charts, we notice that they are for 1975 and 1985, and that all we know are percentages. There are no total numbers for the survey, and since the percentages are pretty "ugly," we can anticipate doing a lot of estimating to answer the questions.

The first question is the easiest. It's asking you to do something very simple: to find the difference between 28.77 and 25.63 and then determine what percentage of 28.77 that difference is.

First, we need to find the difference between 28.77 (the 1975 figure) and 25.63 (the 1985 figure). The difference is 3.14.

Second, keeping in mind that ETS has asked for an *approximate* answer ("to the nearest one percent"), you should notice that 3.14 is in the neighborhood of 10 percent of 28.77. Eliminate choices D and E. Is it exactly 10 percent? No. That means choice B is out. Is it more or less than 10 percent? It's more—exactly 10 percent would be 2.877, and 3.14 is more than 2.877. That means ETS's answer is choice C.

22. What is the ratio of categories that increased in popularity to those that decreased?

(A) 1:2
(B) 1:1
(C) 3:2
(D) 2:1
(E) 5:1

Here's how to crack it

In ratio problems, the first step is always to "count the parts." How many parts are there? The same as the number of categories, which is the same as the number of pie slices in one of the charts. That's six. Now we need the number of categories that increased between 1975 and 1985, and the number that decreased. Vanilla went down; "other" went up; chocolate chip went up; butter pecan went up; strawberry went up; chocolate went down. That is, four of the six parts increased, and two of the six parts decreased. The ratio of increases to decreases, therefore, is 4:2 (not 4:6—be careful). The ratio 4:2 can be simplified to 2:1. That means ETS's answer is choice D.

23. In 1985, if 20 percent of the "Other" category is lemon flavor, and 4,212 people surveyed preferred lemon, then how many people were surveyed?

    (A)   1,000
    (B)   10,000
    (C)   42,120
    (D)   100,000
    (E)   1,000,000

Here's how to crack it

The questions are getting tougher, so we have to be careful. First, let's make sure we understand what ETS is looking for.

The first piece of information ETS has given us is a percentage of a percentage. The percentage of people who preferred lemon in 1985 is equal to 20 percent of 21.06 percent. Make certain you see that before we go on.

Now you should notice that the numbers in ETS's answer choices are very widely separated—they aren't consecutive integers. If we can just get in the ballpark, ETS's answer will be obvious.

Rather than try to use 21.06 percent, we'll call it 20 percent. And rather than use 4,212, we'll use 4,000. So the question is: "20 percent of 20 percent of what is 4,000?" So your equation would look like this:

$$\frac{20}{100} \times \frac{20}{100} \times x = 4,000$$

Do a little reducing.

$$\frac{4}{100} \times x = 4,000$$

That should do it. Four percent of 100 is 4, so 4 percent of 100,000 is 4,000. The ETS choice is D.

24. If a percentage-point shift results in annual additional sales of $50,000, how much, in dollars, did combined annual butter pecan and chocolate chip sales increase between 1975 and 1985?

    (A) $2,325
    (B) $4,650
    (C) $232,500
    (D) $465,000
    (E) $23,250,000

> Don't waste time on problems that require too much work; remember, each problem is worth the same amount of points no matter how much time it takes.

Here's how to crack it

The question number tells us that this is a hard problem, so if this were the real test, we would skip it. But this isn't the real test, so let's try it.

The first thing to keep in mind is that you find a percentage-*point* difference simply by subtracting percentages. The percentage-*point* decrease between 120 percent and 100 percent is 20; the *percentage* decrease between 120 percent and 100 percent is $16\frac{2}{3}$ percent.

Let's take one thing at a time. What happened to butter pecan between 1975 and 1985? It went from 8.81 percent to 11.81 percent. That's a 3 percentage-point increase.

What happened to chocolate chip between 1975 and 1985? It went from 8.23 percent to 9.88 percent. That's a 1.65 percentage-point increase.

Once again, the numbers in the answer choices are widely separated, so we can ballpark the answer. The exact combined percentage-point increase between 1975 and 1985 is 4.65, but you could just as easily use 4, 4.5, or 5. Simply multiply one of these numbers by 50,000. You get something between 200,000 and 250,000. What's ETS's answer? Choice C.

> 25. Which of the following statements can be deduced from the pie graphs?
>
> I. Both the butter pecan and vanilla percentages increased by more than 33 percent between 1975 and 1985.
>
> II. A higher percentage of people chose butter pecan and strawberry in 1975 than chose butter pecan and chocolate chip in 1985.
>
> III. The total share of vanilla, chocolate, and strawberry decreased by less than 20 percent from 1975 to 1985.
>
> (A) I only
> (B) II only
> (C) III only
> (D) II and III
> (E) I, II, and III

Here's how to crack it

This is an enormously time-consuming problem: It's difficult and a triple true–false. This question is saying, "Skip me!" But here's how to solve it.

To begin, check out the first statement. Did the butter pecan percentage increase by more than 33 percent (about one-third)? It increased from 8.81 to 11.81. That's a 3-point increase. Is 3 more than one-third of 8.81? Yes. Okay so far. Now check vanilla. Vanilla went from 26.53 to 19.08. That's a decrease, not an increase. Statement I isn't true. We can eliminate A and E.

Now there are three choices left, B, C, and D. Let's try Statement II. What's the combined percentage for butter pecan and strawberry in 1975? It's 8.81 plus 11.93, or 20.74. What's the combined percentage for butter pecan and chocolate chip in 1985? It's 11.81 plus 9.88, or 21.69. Statement II is false. We can eliminate choices B and D. ETS's answer is choice C.

SUMMARY

Charts

1. Do the charts after you've finished all the other easy and medium questions in the math section. Do questions 21–23. Skip 24 and 25.

2. First look over the charts to find the places where ETS is trying to hide information.

3. While doing the questions, approximate!

19

Backsolving

WHAT IS BACKSOLVING?

Backsolving is one of the most powerful techniques you can bring to bear on the GRE math sections. The idea is simple: Instead of setting up an equation—which can take forever—you simply try a choice and see if it works. If it works, you have ETS's answer. If it doesn't work, you try another. There are only five choices on regular math problems. One of these choices has to be ETS's answer. You will often find this answer by trying just one or two of the choices. You will never have to try all five.

In backsolving from the choices, it's usually a good idea to start in the middle and work your way out, beginning with choice C. Why work from the middle? Because GRE answer choices are almost always arranged in the order of size. When backsolving, you may be able to tell not only that a particular choice is incorrect, but also that it is larger or smaller than ETS's answer. Starting from the middle will save you time in such situations by enabling you to eliminate choices that are clearly too large or too small.

You will be able to use the backsolving technique on math questions in which all five choices are numbers.

Are you tempted to do algebra? Are there numbers in the answer choices? BACKSOLVE!

Backsolve:

- ◆ when there are numbers in the answer choices
- ◆ when the question tells a little story
- ◆ when the story involves finding some fraction, ratio, or percentage of some unspecified number or amount
- ◆ when the question asks you for a specific amount

Here's an example:

> 20. Which of the following values of a does not satisfy
> $5a - 3 < 3a + 5$?
>   (A) -2
>   (B) 0
>   (C) 2
>   (D) 3
>   (E) 4

Here's how to crack it

You have been given an inequality with one variable and five possible values for the variable. You're looking for the one that doesn't work. Should you attempt to rewrite the inequality—say, by putting all the as on one side? No. Simply try each choice. One of them will be correct.

(C) Plugging in 2 for a gives us $10 - 3 < 6 + 5$, or $7 < 11$. Is this True? Yes. Eliminate.

(B) $0 - 3 < 0 + 5$, or $-3 < 5$. True? Yes. Eliminate.

(D) $15 - 3 < 9 + 5$, or $12 < 14$. True? Yes. Eliminate.

(A) $-10 - 3 < -6 + 5$, or $-13 < -1$. True? Yes. Eliminate.

We now know that ETS's answer must be choice E. Here's how it works out:

(E)   20 − 3 < 12 + 5, or 17 < 17. True? No. This is ETS's answer.

Of course, if you realized after trying the first choice that ETS's answer would have to be a number larger than 2—as you might have—then you could have tried choice E, or choice D, immediately. But we found ETS's answer anyway, and we didn't even work up a sweat.

Here's another example:

> 19. The units digit of a 2-digit number is 3 times the tens digit. If the digits are reversed, the resulting number is 36 more than the original number. What is the original number?
>
> (A) 13
> (B) 26
> (C) 36
> (D) 62
> (E) 93

Here's how to crack it

The problem places two conditions on the answer. First, its second digit must be 3 times the first digit. Second, the reversed form of the number must be 36 more than the original number. Since ETS's answer must satisfy both conditions, we can eliminate any choice that fails to satisfy either of them. Therefore, we tackle one condition at a time.

Here's how:

(C)   Is 6 three times 3? No. Eliminate.

(B)   Is 6 three times 2? Yes. A possibility.

(D)   Is 2 three times 6? No. Eliminate.

(A)   Is 3 three times 1? Yes. A possibility.

(E)   Is 3 three times 9? No. Eliminate.

When you're backsolving, start with choice C (or the middle value).

We've narrowed it down to two possibilities, A and B. Now we apply the second condition:

(A)   Is 31 equal to 36 more than 13? No. Eliminate.

ETS's answer must be B. It is. 62 is exactly 36 more than 26.

Backsolving is fabulous for word problems.
Try this one.

> 17. Mike bought a used car and had it repainted. If the cost of the paint job was one-fifth of the purchase price of the car, and if the cost of the car and the paint job combined was $4,800, then what was the purchase price of the car?
>
> (A) $800
> (B) $960
> (C) $3,840
> (D) $4,000
> (E) $4,250

Here's how to crack it

Which costs more, the car or the paint job? The car. What do the answer choices represent? The cost of the car. Let's "ballpark" first. If the combined cost was $4,800, and the biggest chunk of that is the cost of the car, choices A and B are ridiculously low. A $4,000 paint job for an $800 car? No way. Eliminate those choices.

What's left? Start backsolving with the remaining choices: C, D, and E. D's the middle number, and the easiest number to work with. The story told us that the cost of the paint job was $\frac{1}{5}$ the cost of the car. One-fifth of $4,000 is $800 (now we see where that trap answer choice came from). Is $4,000 plus $800 equal to $4,800? We're done. The ETS answer is D.

WHAT'S THE CATCH?

ETS will sometimes make a straightforward problem harder by introducing information for the sole purpose of causing you to make a careless mistake. You may have to deal with this information before you can backsolve. Here's an example:

26. A restaurant owner sold two dishes to each of his customers at $4 per dish. At the end of the day, he had taken in $180, which included $20 in tips. How many customers did he serve?

   (A) 18
   (B) 20
   (C) 22
   (D) 40
   (E) 44

Here's how to crack it

The information about tips is the catch. Its only purpose is to cause careless errors. Before solving this problem, you should confront this trap. Simply reduce the day's total by $20—to $160—and pay no more attention to the tips.

What we're left with is a very straightforward problem. If each customer bought two dishes at $4 each, then each customer spent $8 on food. Now you can backsolve or just divide $160 by $8. Which answer times $8 equals $160? ETS's answer is choice B.

SUMMARY

Backsolve When:

- you're tempted to set up an algebraic equation
- there are *numbers* in the answer choices
- the question tells a little story
- the story involves finding some fraction, ratio, or percentage of some number
- the question asks you for a specific amount

To Backsolve:

- start with answer choice C, or the easiest number in the answer choices that's close to the middle value.
- try that number as the answer to the question. If it works with the rest of the information in the "little story," that's the answer!
- if the first answer choice you try is too large, eliminate that choice and all the choices that are larger.
- if the first answer choice you try is too small, eliminate that choice and all the smaller choices.

20

Exponents, Square Roots, and Factoring

WHAT ARE EXPONENTS?

Many numbers can be expressed as the product of one factor multiplied by itself a number of times. For example, 16 can be expressed as $2 \times 2 \times 2 \times 2$. We can also express the same thing using a sort of mathematical shorthand called *exponents*. Instead of writing $2 \times 2 \times 2 \times 2$, we can write 2^4. The little 4 is called an *exponent* and the big 2 is called a *base*.

MULTIPLICATION WITH EXPONENTS

There's nothing easier than multiplying two or more numbers with the same base. All you have to do is add up the exponents. For example:

$$2^2 \times 2^4 = 2^{2+4} = 2^6$$

You can see this when you expand it out.

$$2^2 \times 2^4 =$$

$$2 \times 2 \times 2 \times 2 \times 2 \times 2 = 2^6$$

Be careful, though.

Joe Bloggs erroneously thinks that this rule also applies to addition. It does not: $2^2 + 2^4$ *does not equal* 2^6. There's no quick and easy method of adding numbers with exponents.

If you EXPAND IT OUT, you'll never be in doubt.

DIVISION WITH EXPONENTS

Since division is just multiplication in reverse, dividing two or more numbers with the same base is easy, too. All you have to do is subtract the exponents. For example: $2^6 \div 2^2 = 2^{6-2} = 2^4$.

You can see this easily when you expand it out.

$$\frac{2 \times 2 \times 2 \times 2 \times 2 \times 2}{2 \times 2} = 2 \times 2 \times 2 \times 2 = 2^4$$

Once again, don't assume this same shortcut applies to subtraction of numbers with exponents. It doesn't.

PLEASE EXCUSE...

Pay close attention when there are exponents inside and outside the parentheses. You can simply multiply the exponents. Here's an example:

$$\left(4^5\right)^2 =$$

$$4^{5 \times 2} =$$

$$4^{10}$$

But don't be shy about expanding these out. It doesn't take too much time, and it's better to be correct than to be fast.

$$\left(4^5\right)^2 =$$

$$(4 \times 4 \times 4 \times 4 \times 4)(4 \times 4 \times 4 \times 4 \times 4) = 4^{10}$$

If You Always Expand It Out, You'll Never Be in Doubt

In solving problems involving exponents, it's extremely important to pay careful attention to terms within parentheses. When an exponent appears on the outside of a parenthetical expression, expanding it out is the safest way to ensure that you don't make a careless mistake. For example, $(3x)^2 = (3x)(3x) = 9x^2$, not $3x^2$.

The same is true of fractions within parentheses. $\left(\frac{3}{2}\right)^2 = \left(\frac{3}{2}\right)\left(\frac{3}{2}\right) = \frac{9}{4}$. No doubt. No complicated rules to remember.

When in doubt, expand it out!

The Peculiar Behavior of Exponents

1. Raising a number greater than 1 to a power greater than 1 results in a *bigger* number. For example, $2^2 = 4$.

2. Raising a number between 0 and 1 to a power greater than 1 results in a *smaller* number. For example, $\left(\frac{1}{2}\right)^2 = \frac{1}{4}$.

3. A negative number raised to an even power becomes *positive*. For example, $(-2)^2 = 4$.

4. A negative number raised to an odd power remains *negative*. For example, $(-2)^3 = -8$.

What, Me Worry?

Don't worry about negative exponents (for example, 10^{-2}). You won't see them on the GRE.

SQUARE ROOTS

The sign $\sqrt{}$ indicates the square root of a number. For example, $\sqrt{2}$. This is known as a *radical*. This means that something squared equals 2.

If $x^2 = 16$, then $x = \pm 4$. You must be especially careful to remember this on quantitative comparison questions. But when ETS asks you for the value $\sqrt{16}$, or the square root of any number, you are being asked for the *positive* root only. Although squaring -5 will yield 25, just as squaring 5 will, when ETS asks for $\sqrt{25}$, the only answer ETS is looking for is positive 5.

> You can multiply and divide any square roots, but you can only add or subtract roots when they are the same.

Know These Two Rules

There are only two rules concerning radicals that you need to know for the GRE:

1. $\sqrt{x}\sqrt{y} = \sqrt{xy}$. For example, $\sqrt{2}\sqrt{3} = \sqrt{6}$.

2. $\sqrt{\dfrac{x}{y}} = \dfrac{\sqrt{x}}{\sqrt{y}}$. For example, $\sqrt{\dfrac{5}{16}} = \dfrac{\sqrt{5}}{\sqrt{16}} = \dfrac{\sqrt{5}}{4}$.

Rule 1 also works in reverse. That is, a large radical can be broken down into its factors, which may be easier to manipulate. For example, $\sqrt{32} = \sqrt{16}\sqrt{2}$. You can add or subtract radicals *only* when they are the same.

So $\sqrt{2} + \sqrt{2} = 2\sqrt{2}$.

But $\sqrt{2} + \sqrt{3}$ does NOT equal $\sqrt{5}$!

KNOW THESE FIVE VALUES

To use our techniques, you'll need to have memorized the following values. You should be able to recite them without hesitation:

1. $\sqrt{1} = 1$

2. $\sqrt{2} \cong 1.4$

3. $\sqrt{3} \cong 1.7$

4. $\sqrt{4} = 2$

5. $\sqrt{5} \cong 2.2$

OTHER RADICALS

There are only four numbers under 100 with integer cube roots : 1, 8, 27, 64.

The sign $\sqrt[3]{}$ indicates the cube root of a number. For example, $\sqrt[3]{8}$. This means that something cubed equals 8. Since $2^3 = 8$, 2 is the cube root of 8. All the rules for square roots apply to other radicals. You can multiply, divide, and factor them, but you can't add or subtract any radicals unless they have the same root.

Don't worry, you probably won't see radicals besides square roots and cube roots on the GRE.

DRILL 1

Check your answers on page 297.

1. $3^4 \times 3^2 =$

2. If $x = 3$, what is $(2x)^3$?

3. If $x = 4$, what is $(x^2)^3$?

4. If $4^2 + 3^2 = x^2$, what is x?

5. Approximate $\sqrt[3]{26}$

SIMPLIFYING EXPRESSIONS, OR FACTORING

ETS is very predictable. **Because of this, we can tell you that on any problem that contains an expression that can be factored, you should always factor that expression.** If, for example, you encounter a problem containing the expression $4x + 4y$, you should immediately factor it, yielding the expression $4(x + y)$.

Similarly, whenever you find an expression that has been factored, you should immediately *un*factor it, by multiplying it out according to the distributive law. In other words, if a problem contains the expression $4(x + y)$, you should unfactor it, yielding the expression $4x + 4y$.

Why this game of musical factors? Because the key to finding ETS's answer on such problems is usually nothing trickier than factoring or unfactoring various expressions. As we have said, ETS isn't up to anything very complicated. And it asks essentially the same questions over and over again, on test after test.

FOIL

All you have to do is remember to multiply every term in the first expression by every term in the second. (Are you beginning to hear the long-forgotten voice of your ninth-grade algebra teacher?) Use "FOIL" to remember the method. FOIL stands for First, Outer, Inner, Last—the four steps of multiplication.

Here's an example:

$$(x + 4)(x + 3) = (x + 4)(x + 3)$$
$$= (x \cdot x) + (x \cdot 3) + (4 \cdot x) + (4 \cdot 3)$$
$$= x^2 + 3x + 4x + 12$$
$$= x^2 + 7x + 12$$

KNOW THESE THREE EXPRESSIONS

There are three expressions that appear over and over again on the GRE. You should know them cold, in both their factored and unfactored forms. Here they are:

Expression 1:

Factored form: $(x + y)(x - y)$

Unfactored form: $x^2 - y^2$ (the difference between two squares)

Expression 2:

Factored form: $(x + y)^2$

Unfactored form: $x^2 + 2xy + y^2$

Expression 3:

Factored form: $(x - y)^2$

Unfactored form: $x^2 - 2xy + y^2$

Can you factor these expressions quickly?

Here's an example of the form in which you might find Expression 1 on the GRE:

$$\frac{4x^2 - 4}{x - 1}$$

Here's how to crack it

What do you do with this expression? Factor it. Pull a 4 out of the numerator, to give you $4(x^2 - 1)$. Now notice that the expression $(x^2 - 1)$ follows the form $(x^2 - y^2)$, because it's the difference between squares, and can therefore be written in factored form as follows: $4(x + 1)(x - 1)$. Now go back and rewrite the original expression:

$$\frac{4x^2 - 4}{x - 1} = \frac{4(x+1)(x-1)}{(x-1)}$$

There's one more thing to do. You can simplify the factored form of our expression by canceling the common factor, $(x - 1)$, in the numerator and denominator. This means that our final, fully factored and simplified form of the original expression is simply $4(x + 1)$.

TRY PLUGGING IN

You will save yourself a lot of trouble if you just plug in numbers for the variables in complicated algebraic expressions. Here's an example of a complicated algebraic expression:

$$(4x^2 + 4x + 2) + (3 - 7x) - (5 - 3x) =$$

Let's plug in 2 for each x in the expression.

$$(4 \times 2^2 + 4 \times 2 + 2) + (3 - 7 \times 2) - (5 - 3 \times 2) =$$

$$16 + 8 + 2 + 3 - 14 - 5 + 6 = 16$$

Then you would plug in 2 for x in all the answer choices. Try this one.

19. If $m + n = p$, then $m^2 + 2mn + n^2 =$
   - (A) $4p$
   - (B) $np - m$
   - (C) p^2
   - (D) $p^2 + 4(m + p)$
   - (E) $p^2 + np + m^2$

Here's how to crack it

Let's use our favorite technique. Plug in 2 for m, 3 for n, and 5 for p in the equation given and in all the answer choices. Then plug those numbers into the question. You then get $2^2 + 2 \times 2 \times 3 + 3^2$, which equals 25. That's our target answer.

Always PLUG IN when you see variables in the answer choices!

(A) $4 \times 5 = 20$. Eliminate.
(B) $15 - 2 = 13$. Eliminate.
(C) 25. Bingo.
(D) 25 + something. Eliminate.
(E) 25 + something. Eliminate.
The ETS answer is C.

TRY BACKSOLVING

If there are numbers in the answer choices, it's often faster to backsolve than to FOIL or factor. Try this one.

Backsolve when there are numbers in the answer choices.

27. The roots of the equation $x^2 - x - 12 = 0$ are

(A) 2 and –6
(B) 3 and –4
(C) 4 and –3
(D) 6 and –2
(E) none of the above

Here's how to crack it

Although you could factor the equation, why bother? Try answer choice C. Plug in 4 for x. That works. Now try –3. $9 - (-3) - 12 = 0$.

So that's it! The ETS answer is C.

SIMULTANEOUS EQUATIONS

ETS will sometimes give you two equations and ask you to use them to find the value of a given expression. In such situations, you don't need any math class algebra; all you have to do to find ETS's answer is to add or subtract the two equations.

Here's an example:

If $5x + 4y = 6$ and $4x + 3y = 5$, then $x + y = ?$

Here's how to crack it

All you have to do is add the two equations together or subtract one from the other. Here's what we get when we add them:

$$\begin{array}{r} 5x + 4y = 6 \\ + \ 4x + 3y = 5 \\ \hline 9x + 7y = 11 \end{array}$$

A dead end. So let's try subtraction:

$$\begin{array}{r} 5x + 4y = 6 \\ - \ 4x + 3y = 5 \\ \hline x + y = 1 \end{array}$$

Eureka. The value of the expression $(x + y)$ is exactly what we're looking for.

On the GRE, you may see two equations written horizontally. Just rewrite the two equations, putting one on top of the other, then simply add or subtract them.

EQUATIONS SET TO ZERO

ETS loves 0, because it has so many unique properties. There are more than a few math problems on the GRE whose solutions turn on one of these properties.

One of the most important properties of 0 is its ability to annihilate other numbers. Any number multiplied by 0 equals 0. This fact gives you an important piece of information. For example, if you are told that $ab = 0$, then you know without a doubt that either a or b or both must be equal to 0. You can use this same fact to solve some equations on the GRE. Here's an example:

What are all the values of y for which $y(y + 5) = 0$?

Here's how to crack it

In order for $y(y + 5)$ to equal 0, either y or $(y + 5)$, or both of them, has to equal 0. All you need to do to solve this problem, therefore, is to determine what you need to do to each element in order to make it equal 0. What would y have to be for y to equal 0? Why, it would have to be 0, of course. What would y have to be for $(y + 5)$ to equal 0? Why, it would have to be –5, of course. To answer the question, here are all the values of y for which $y(y + 5) = 0$: 0 and –5.

SUMMARY

Exponents

Expand it out and you'll never be in doubt!

Square Roots

You can multiply and divide square roots, but you cannot add or subtract unless the roots are the same.

FOIL

- $(x + y)^2 = x^2 + 2xy + y^2$
- $(x - y)^2 = x^2 - 2xy + y^2$
- $(x + y)(x - y) = x^2 - y^2$

- PLUGGING IN NUMBERS MAKES THESE EASIER!

- If there are numbers in the answer choices, BACKSOLVE!

21

Geometry

WHAT YOU NEED TO KNOW

You don't need to know much about actual geometry on the GRE. We've boiled down the handful of bits and pieces that ETS actually tests. Don't forget to plug in and backsolve at every opportunity!

DEGREES AND ANGLES

You should know that:

1. A circle contains 360 degrees.

2. A line (which can be thought of as a perfectly flat angle) is a 180-degree angle.

3. When two lines intersect, four angles are formed, and the sum of the angles is 360 degrees.

4. When two lines are perpendicular to each other, their intersection forms four 90-degree angles. Here is the symbol ETS uses to indicate a perpendicular angle: $\perp$

5. Ninety-degree angles are also called right angles. A right angle on the GRE is identified by a little box at the intersection of the angle's arms:

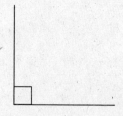

FRED'S THEOREM

Fred was one of our first teachers. Here's his theorem: When two parallel lines (the symbol for parallel is ∥) are cut by a third line, only two angles are formed, big angles and small angles. All the big angles are equal. All the small angles are equal. The sum of any big and any small angle is always 180 degrees. Here's an example of a diagram to which Fred's theorem applies:

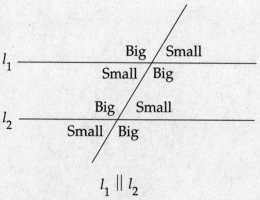

In this diagram, line 1 is parallel to line 2.

VERTICAL ANGLES

Vertical angles are the angles across from each other that are formed by the intersection of lines. Vertical angles are equal. In the drawing below, angle x is equal to angle y and angle a is equal to angle b.

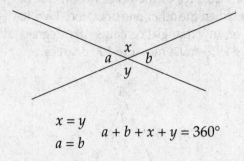

$$x = y$$
$$a = b$$
$$a + b + x + y = 360°$$

DEGREES AND TRIANGLES

Every triangle contains three interior angles, which add up to 180 degrees. You must know this. It applies to every triangle, no matter how skinny, fat, tall, or flat. **Every triangle contains 180 degrees.** Here are some examples:

We repeat: The three angles of every triangle add up to 180 degrees.

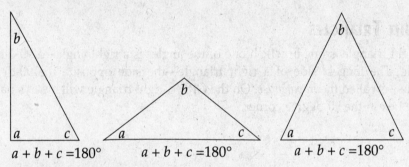

$a + b + c = 180°$ $a + b + c = 180°$ $a + b + c = 180°$

EQUILATERAL TRIANGLES

An equilateral triangle is one in which all three sides are equal in length. Because the sides are all equal, the angles are all equal, too. If they're all equal, how many degrees is each? We certainly hope you said, **"Each angle in an equilateral triangle contains 60 degrees."**

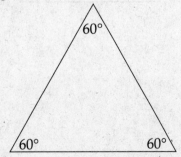

Isosceles Triangles

An isosceles triangle is one in which two of the three sides are equal in length. This means that two of the angles are also equal, and that the third angle is not.

If you know the degree measure of any angle in an isosceles triangle, you also know the degree of measures of the other two. If one of the two equal angles measures 40 degrees, then the other one does, too. Two 40-degree angles add up to 80 degrees. Since any triangle contains 180 degrees altogether, the third angle—the only one left—must measure 100 degrees.

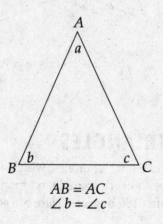

$$AB = AC$$
$$\angle b = \angle c$$

Right Triangles

There are no wrong triangles, but there are right ones.

A right triangle is one in which one of the angles is a right angle—a 90-degree angle. The longest side of a right triangle—the side opposite the 90-degree angle—is called the *hypotenuse*. On the GRE, a right triangle will always have a little box in the 90-degree corner.

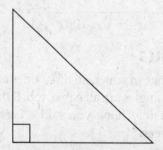

ANGLE/SIDE RELATIONSHIPS IN TRIANGLES

In any triangle, the longest side is opposite the largest interior angle; the shortest side is opposite the smallest interior angle. Furthermore, equal sides are opposite equal angles.

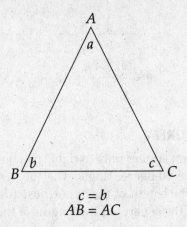

$$c = b$$
$$AB = AC$$

PERIMETER OF A TRIANGLE

The perimeter of a triangle is simply a measure of the distance around it. All you have to do to find the perimeter of a triangle is to add up the lengths of the sides.

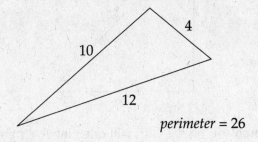

perimeter = 26

AREA OF A TRIANGLE

The area of any triangle is the height or altitude multiplied by the base, divided by 2. The altitude is defined as a line perpendicular to the base:

$$\text{area} = \frac{\text{altitude} \times \text{base}}{2}$$

This formula works on any triangle.

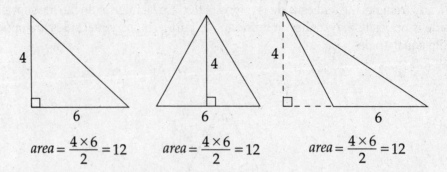

$$area = \frac{4 \times 6}{2} = 12 \qquad area = \frac{4 \times 6}{2} = 12 \qquad area = \frac{4 \times 6}{2} = 12$$

PYTHAGOREAN THEOREM

The Pythagorean theorem applies only to right triangles, which, as we said, are triangles containing one 90-degree angle. The theorem states that in a right triangle, the square of the length of the hypotenuse (the longest side—remember?) equals the sum of the squares of the lengths of the two other sides. In the right triangle below, in other words, $c^2 = a^2 + b^2$.

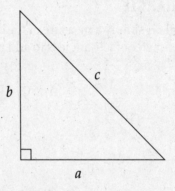

Pythagorean problems on the GRE will often involve right triangles whose sides measure 3, 4, and 5 or multiples of those numbers. Why is this? Because a 3-4-5 right triangle is the smallest one in which measures of the sides are all integers. Here are three examples of right triangles based on ETS's basic 3-4-5 right triangle:

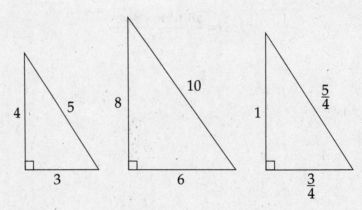

The Pythagorean theorem will sometimes be the key to solving problems where the theorem's application isn't obvious. For example, every rectangle or square contains two right triangles. This means that if you know the length and width of any rectangle or square, you also know the length of the diagonal—it's the shared hypotenuse of the hidden right triangles. Here's an example:

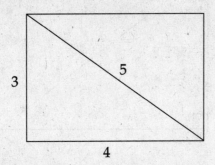

TWO SPECIAL RIGHT TRIANGLES

There are two special right triangles.

The first special right triangle is the 45:45:90. It's half of a square. In such a triangle, the two nonhypotenuse sides are equal. If you know one of the sides, you can use the Pythagorean theorem to find the other two sides. The ratio between the length of either of them and that of the hypotenuse is $1:\sqrt{2}$. That is, if the length of each short leg is x, then the length of the hypotenuse is $x\sqrt{2}$. Here are two examples:

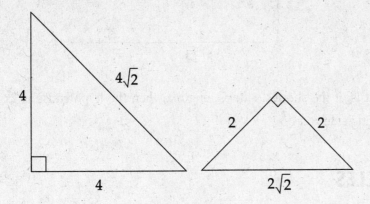

The other special right triangle is the so-called 30:60:90 right triangle. It's half of an equilateral triangle. Here's what it looks like:

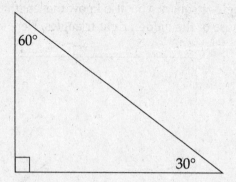

The ratio between the lengths of the sides in a 30:60:90 triangle is constant. Again, if you know the length of any of the sides, you can find the lengths of the others. The ratio of the sides is always the same:

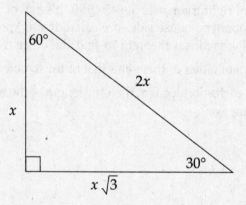

That is, if the shortest side is length x, then the hypotenuse is $2x$ and the remaining side is $x\sqrt{3}$:

CIRCLES

VALUE OF PI

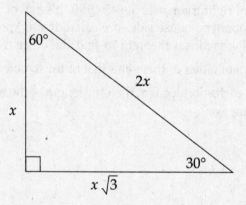

The value of pi (π) is taught in math class as being 3.14 or even 3.14159. On the GRE, $\pi = 3^+$ is a close enough approximation. You don't need to be any more precise than that in order to find ETS's answer, and 3^+ is much easier to work with than 3.14 or 3.14159. There will most likely be problems on your GRE that you can solve simply by plugging in 3 for each π among the answer choices and comparing the results. Just remember that π is a little bigger than 3.

Pi has been calculated to hundreds of decimal places; fortunately for you, you won't need to memorize it out that far.

Keep in mind the relationship that π expresses. Pi is the ratio between the circumference of a circle and its diameter. When we say that π is a little bigger than 3, therefore, we're saying that every circle is about three times as far around as it is across.

CIRCUMFERENCE OF A CIRCLE

The circumference of a circle is like the perimeter of a triangle: It's the measure of distance around the outside. The formula for finding the circumference of a circle is 2 times π times the radius, or π times the diameter:

circumference = $2\pi r$ or πd

If the diameter of a circle is 4, then its circumference is 4π, or about 12. If the circumference of a circle is 10, then its diameter is $\dfrac{10}{\pi}$, or a little more than 3.

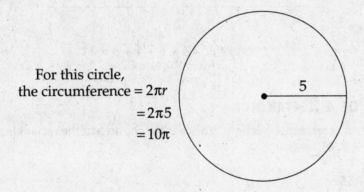

For this circle,
the circumference $= 2\pi r$
$= 2\pi 5$
$= 10\pi$

AREA OF A CIRCLE

The area of a circle is π times the square of the radius:

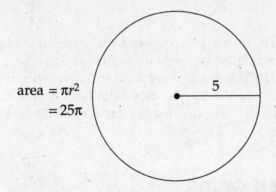

area $= \pi r^2$
$= 25\pi$

RECTANGLES

PERIMETER OF A RECTANGLE

The perimeter of a rectangle is just the sum of the lengths of the four sides.

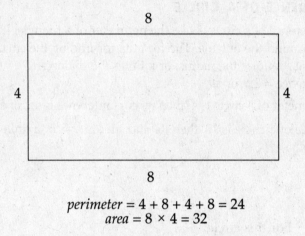

$$perimeter = 4 + 8 + 4 + 8 = 24$$
$$area = 8 \times 4 = 32$$

AREA OF A RECTANGLE

The area of a rectangle is length times width. The area of the rectangle above, for example, is 32.

SQUARES

A square is a rectangle with four equal sides. The perimeter of a square, therefore, is 4 times the length of any side. The area is the length of any side times itself, which is to say, the length of any side squared.

VOLUME

You can get the volume of a three-dimensional figure by multiplying the area of a two-dimensional figure by height (or depth). For example, to find the volume of a rectangular solid, you take the area of a rectangle and multiply by the depth. The formula is $l \times w \times d$ (length times width times depth). To find the volume of a circular cylinder, take the area of a circle and multiply by the height. The formula is $\pi r^2 \times h$.

CARTESIAN GRIDS

A Cartesian grid is shaped like a cross. The horizontal line is called the *x*-axis; the vertical line is called the *y*-axis. The four areas formed by the intersection of these axes are called *quadrants*. The point where the axes intersect is called the *origin*.

Here's an example:

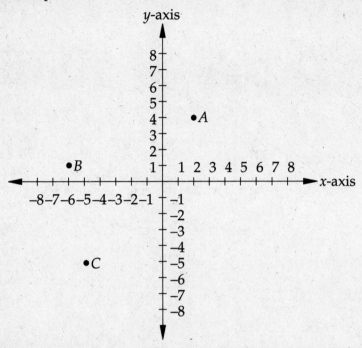

A Cartesian grid provides a method of describing the location of any point on the plane on which the Cartesian grid is inscribed. In the diagram above, the marked point above and to the right of the origin can be described by the coordinates (2, 4). That is, the point is two spaces to the right and four spaces above the origin. The point above and to the left of the origin can be described by the coordinates (–6, 1). That is, it is six spaces to the left and 1 space above the origin. What are the coordinates of the point to the left of and below the origin? (–5, –5).

DRILL 1
Check your answers on page 297.

1. In the figure below, if $l_1 \parallel l_2$, what is the measure of angle b?

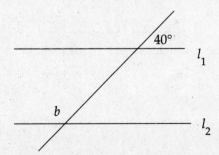

You do remember Fred's theorem, don't you? (If not, see the beginning of the chapter.)

2. In the triangle below, what is the measure of angle c?

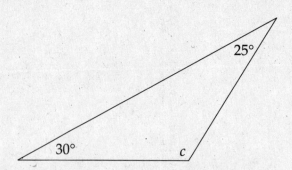

3. In the triangle below, what is the length of side AB?

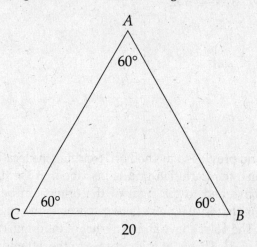

What type of triangle is the figure in question 3?

4. In the triangle below, what is the measure of angle c?

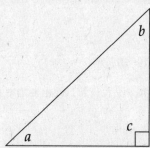

5. What are the perimeters of the triangle and rectangle below?

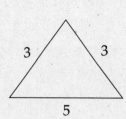 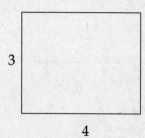

6. What are the areas of the triangle and rectangle below?

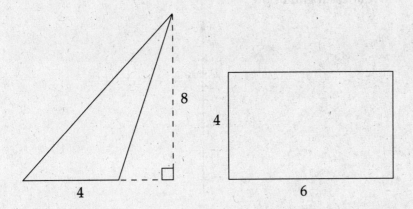

7. What is the length of the third side in the right triangle below?

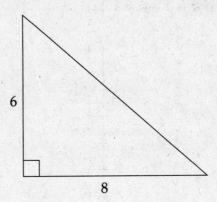

8. What is the approximate circumference of the circle below?

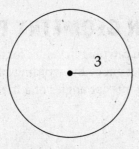

9. What is the approximate area of the circle in problem 8?

10. If a box is 5 inches wide, 10 inches long, and 4 inches deep, what is its volume in cubic inches?

11. Determine the coordinates of points *A*, *B*, *C*, and *D* in the Cartesian grid below:

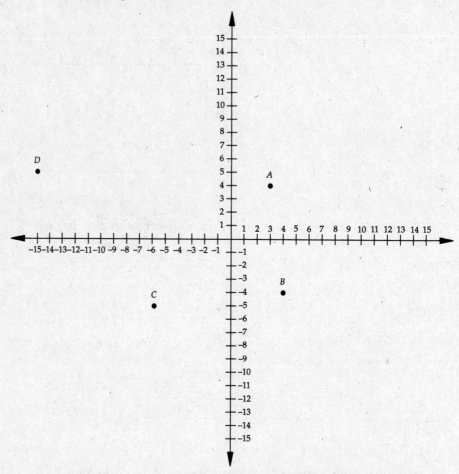

PLUGGING IN ON GEOMETRY PROBLEMS

On geometry problems, you can plug in values for angles or lengths if the values you plug in don't contradict either the wording of the problem or the laws of geometry (you can't let the interior angles of a triangle add up to anything but 180, for instance).

Here's an example:

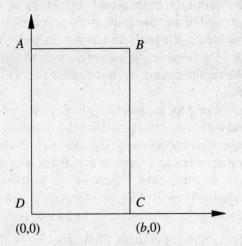

(0,0)   (b,0)

19. The area of the rectangle $ABCD$ is $3b^2$. The coordinates of C and D are given. In terms of b, $BD =$

(A) b
(B) $2b$
(C) $5\sqrt{5}$
(D) $3b$
(E) $b\sqrt{10}$

Don't forget to PLUG IN on geometry questions. Just plug in numbers according to the rules of geometry.

Here's how to crack it

The distance from D to C is b. Let's plug in a value for b. How about 2? Write "$b = 2$" in your test booklet. Put another 2 by side DC, to remind yourself of the length of that side of the rectangle.

With 2 plugged in for b, we see that the area of the rectangle ($3b^2$) is 12. That means that side BC is 6. Place a 6 on side BC, to remind yourself of the length of that side.

What the problem asks us for is the length of BD, which in addition to being one diagonal of the given rectangle is also the hypotenuse of right triangle BCD. We already know the lengths of the other two sides of right triangle BCD (2 and 6). From the Pythagorean theorem, we know that the square of the length of the hypotenuse is equal to the sum of the squares of 2 and 6. The squares of 2 and 6 are 4 and 36, which means that the square of the hypotenuse is 40. The length of BD therefore, is $\sqrt{40}$, or $2\sqrt{10}$. ($\sqrt{40} = \sqrt{4}\sqrt{10} = 2\sqrt{10}$.) That means that the length of BD is also $2\sqrt{10}$.

Now all we have to do is go to the answer choices, plug in our value for b, and see which one equals the answer we came up with. Choice E fits the bill. It is ETS's answer.

USE COMMON SENSE

You can very often work even more quickly by getting an approximate idea of what ETS's answer must be and then eliminating choices that are far wide of the mark. Take another look at the problem we just cracked. Once again, let's plug in 2 for b, giving us 2 for the rectangle's short dimension and 6 for the rectangle's long dimension. We're still looking for the length of BD, which is the hypotenuse of right triangle BCD.

Now, instead of looking for the exact length of BD, let's make a rough estimate based on something we know about right triangles. What do we know? We know that the length of the hypotenuse has to be greater than the length of either of the other sides. That means it has to be greater than 6. We also know that it has to be less than the sum of the other sides; otherwise, we wouldn't have a triangle. In other words, the number we're looking for is greater than 6 and less than 8.

Now go to the answer choices and plug in 2 for b:

(A) b is 2. This is much too small. Eliminate.

(B) $2b$ would be 4, which is less than 6. Eliminate.

(C) The square root of 5, as you should remember, is about 2.2. $2\sqrt{5}$ is therefore about 4.4. Eliminate.

(D) $3b$ is exactly 6. ETS's answer has to be greater than 6. Eliminate.

(E) You probably don't know the square root of 10 right off the top of your head, but you can easily see that it must be a bit more than 3 (which is the square root of 9). The value of $2\sqrt{10}$ must therefore be a little more than 6. This must be ETS's answer.

BACKSOLVING is also great for many geometry questions.

Here's another example of how you can use common sense to zero in on ETS's answer:

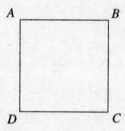

19. In square $ABCD$ above, what is the value of $\dfrac{(AD)(AB)}{(AC)(BD)}$?

(A) $\dfrac{1}{2}$

(B) $\dfrac{\sqrt{2}}{2}$

(C) 1

(D) $\sqrt{2}$

(E) 2

Here's how to crack it

This problem is similar to the previous one. Once again, we want to plug in some easy numbers to get a rough idea of what ETS's answer is. We can then try to eliminate some choices.

We can tell immediately that $(AD)(AB)$ is going to be smaller than $(AC)(BD)$. (Why? Because the diagonal of a square is larger than any of its sides, which means that the product of two sides has to be smaller than the product of two diagonals.) In other words, the numerator is going to be smaller than the denominator. That means we can eliminate choices C, D, and E.

We've narrowed it down to choices A and B. Plugging in 2 for the side of the square and using the side relationships of a 45:45:90 triangle, we get $(2)(2) \div (2\sqrt{2})(2\sqrt{2})$ or $\frac{1}{2}$. ETS's answer is A.

IF THERE'S NO DRAWING ON A GEOMETRY PROBLEM, MAKE ONE YOURSELF

When ETS doesn't include a drawing with a geometry problem, it usually means that the drawing, if supplied, would make ETS's answer obvious. On such problems, then, you should supply the drawing yourself. Here's an example:

Column A	Column B
10. The number of edges each face of a cube shares with other faces	The number of edges on one face of a cube

Here's how to crack it

There's no reason to visualize this problem in your head. Just make a quick sketch—something like this:

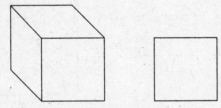

You should be able to see that each face shares an edge with four other faces. The value of Column A, therefore, is 4. And how about Column B? A square clearly has 4 sides. The values of the two columns are the same. ETS's answer is choice C.

REDRAW

On difficult quant comp geometry questions, you may need to draw the figure once, eliminate two answer choices, then redraw the figure to try to disprove your first answer. Be sure to ask yourself whether your first answer would be a Joe Bloggs choice. If so, you know it's wrong—even if you can't prove it.

13. The length of the diagonal of a rectangle with perimeter 16 | The length of the diagonal of a rectangle with perimeter 20

For quant comp geometry, draw, eliminate, REDRAW. It's like plugging in twice.

Here's how to crack it

Which choice looks good to Joe Bloggs? Choice B. So you know that choice is going to be wrong. Now let's draw a rectangle with perimeter 16 and one with perimeter 20. It's easiest to make them squares (a square is a rectangle with four equal sides).

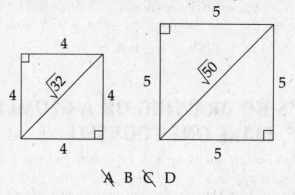

A B C D

Remember, in quant comp, it's not what it is in each column, but which is bigger. So just leave Column A as the square root of 32, and Column B as the square root of 50. Which is bigger? Column B. Eliminate choices A and C. But we know B can't be right, since it's the Joe Bloggs choice on this hard problem. So now try to disprove that answer.

Let's try to make the diagonal of the rectangle in Column A bigger. Think of "weird" numbers for the sides of the rectangle. How about sides of 1 and 7?

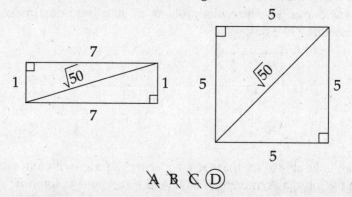

A B C D

What's the diagonal of this rectangle? It's the square root of 50! So we proved that answer choice B is wrong, and the ETS answer must be D.

Don't forget to redraw on quant comp geometry questions! It's the same as plugging in *more than once* on other quant comp problems with variables. Plug in one set of numbers to draw a figure to get your first answer. Eliminate two choices. Then plug in different numbers and redraw to try to disprove your first answer. For geometry questions, you can't plug in zero or negative numbers. Try using the number 1 or a fraction such as 1/2 as your "weird" numbers to disprove your first answer.

PART ◆ IV

How to Crack the
Analytical Sections

22

What Do the Analytical Sections Test?

WHAT ARE THE ANALYTICAL SECTIONS?

In addition to the math and verbal sections, there are two analytical sections that will count toward your score. They're scored the same way, on the 200–800 scale. Each section has two types of questions: what we call *games* questions (ETS claims these test "analytical reasoning") and *arguments* questions (which supposedly measure "logical reasoning").

SHOULD YOU CARE ABOUT YOUR ANALYTICAL SCORE?

Work slowly and carefully on the analytical sections. Write everything down on your test booklet.

Like your other GRE scores, your analytical score is used in different ways by different graduate programs. Some programs may not even consider your analytical scores; others may consider it very important. Even programs within the same discipline may differ in this regard. Don't guess—ask the programs to which you're applying whether they look at analytical scores. Keep in mind that admissions officers will see your analytical score, even if they claim not to consider it. Don't blow off this section completely.

HOW SHOULD YOU APPROACH THIS SECTION?

Analytical sections are organized, in **order of difficulty**, as follows:

Game 1	easy
3 arguments questions	2 easy, 1 medium
Game 2	easy/medium
Game 3	medium/difficult
Game 4 (sometimes)	difficult
3 arguments questions	1 medium, 2 difficult

or

3 arguments questions	easy
Game 1	easy
3 arguments questions	medium
Game 2	medium
Game 3	difficult
3 arguments questions	difficult

The section can have three or four games, each of which is followed by three to seven questions. There are always twenty-five questions in the section. The total number of games questions is either nineteen or sixteen; the total number of arguments questions is either six or nine.

Games and arguments are arranged in order of increasing difficulty. Although questions belonging to a particular game are often in a rough order of difficulty, this is not always the case.

Since the whole section is arranged in order of difficulty, to get the best score you should focus on getting the easiest questions right first, then concentrate on the medium questions. **Don't try to finish the section.** Remember that your score is based on the number of questions that you answer correctly, not on how many you attempt.

> **Worry about your accuracy, not about your speed!**

Spend enough time to get the easy and medium questions completely right.

SETTING YOUR GOAL

How many correct answers do you need on each section to get the score you want? On the chart below, we show you how many (or how few!) questions you need to work out correctly to get selected scores. Again, there's no "guessing penalty" on the GRE—be sure that you fill in a bubble for each question even if you don't work it out.

Score	Work out correctly	Fill in the bubbles for
400	questions 1–8	9–25
450	questions 1–10	11–25
500	questions 1–12	13–25
550	questions 1–14	15–25
600	questions 1–16	17–25
650	questions 1–18	19–25
700	questions 1–20	21–25
750	questions 1–23	24, 25
800	questions 1–24	25

Don't forget to fill in your guess "letter of the day" for all the questions you don't work on.

SCORE IMPROVEMENTS

As we've seen on the other sections of the test, the key to score improvements on the analytical section is to adopt a systematic approach to the problems. Look to the separate chapters on games and arguments to learn more about specific techniques. But begin by going slowly and carefully on the analytical sections. As you practice using the techniques, you will be able to use them more quickly.

23

Games

WHAT ARE GAMES?

This is beyond Monopoly, beyond Scrabble, beyond gin rummy.

Each analytical section of your GRE will contain three or four "analytical reasoning" sets, or games, accompanied by between three and seven questions. The games themselves will be presented in order of increasing difficulty.

THEORY VERSUS PRACTICE

Although games can be boiled down to a simple step-by-step procedure, improving your score on them will require practice. Our techniques should help you considerably, but you'll still need to work on games a little each day. The only way you will feel comfortable with games during the actual exam is by practicing them again and again. Our techniques are aimed at helping you become methodical and efficient in your approach.

Try to practice a game or two each day. Be sure to concentrate on using the step-by-step method, but have fun with games. Think of them as brainteasers—as challenges to your ingenuity.

ETS's DIRECTIONS

Here are the directions for the analytical section as they will appear on your GRE:

Welcome to the world of GRE Games.

> Directions: Each question or group of questions is based on a passage or set of conditions. In answering some of the questions, it may be useful to draw a rough diagram. For each question, select the best answer choice given.

OUR OWN DIRECTIONS

After reading those directions from ETS you may be thinking that in answering "some" questions it "may" *not* be useful to draw rough diagrams. Don't be fooled!

> Directions: Use diagrams to answer all games questions!

THE STRUCTURE OF A GAME

Games begin with a setup, followed by clues, which will apply to all of the questions with the game. The setup and clues are the *rules* of the game. They cannot be violated. Often a question will provide an additional clue, which will apply only to that particular question, but it doesn't break the original rules.

The best way to get a feel for GRE games is to look at a simple example.

> A radio station will schedule five programs—A, B, C, D, and E—to be aired Monday through Friday, one program each evening, in an order that conforms to the following restrictions:
>
> Program D must be aired before Program A.
> Programs C and D must be aired on consecutive evenings.
> Program E may not be the second program to be aired.

OUR GENERAL STEP-BY-STEP STRATEGY

We'll outline this strategy first. Then we'll discuss each step in it at greater length. Finally, we'll show you how the strategy applies to actual games. Here's the outline:

STEP 1: Read the whole setup and all the clues. Draw a model diagram that shows the structure of the game.

STEP 2: Symbolize the clues in a way that's consistent with your diagram for the game.

STEP 3: Double-check your diagram and symbols.

STEP 4: Size up the clues and draw deductions.

STEP 5: Attack the questions.

STEP 6: Keep your pencil moving.

STEP 1: READ THE SETUP AND CLUES AND DRAW A MODEL DIAGRAM

Students often begin to diagram a game before they've read all the setup clues.

Don't be in such a hurry.

The clues are in no particular order. Sometimes the most revealing clue—the one you'll want to use as the starting point for your diagram—is the last one given. **Read through *all* the clues before you begin to make your diagram.**

Make a model diagram that visually represents the information in the game. You'll use this model as a template, so you want it to include information that's **always** true for the game. Use this template to redraw the diagram as you answer the questions.

Most of the games on the GRE involve assigning the elements to places; we call them "assignment" games. For all of these games the best diagram to use is a simple grid. The places go on top of the grid, and you'll assign the elements to those places. So the first question to ask yourself is: What am I assigning to what? Let's look at our example.

> A radio station will schedule five programs—A, B, C, D, and E—to be aired Monday through Friday, one program each evening, in an order that conforms to the following restrictions:
>
> Program D must be aired before Program A.
> Programs C and D must be aired on consecutive evenings.
> Program E may not be the second program to be aired.

Put what doesn't change at the top of the diagram.

Here's how to crack it

M	T	W	R	F

Notice that the days of the week are the places, and the programs are the elements that will be assigned to those places (we'll deal with the clues shortly). Generally, put the things that don't change at the top of the grid. Often things that don't change have a natural order, such as days of the week, times of day, etc.

STEP 2: SYMBOLIZE THE CLUES

The most important skill in solving games, and in getting good at them, is the ability to translate the language of the clues into clear visual symbols. You want to be able to work through the questions with a game using your symbols—not the words! Symbolize the clues in a way that's consistent with your model diagram. For example, since the days of the week go from left to right, symbolize the clues so that the elements that have to be earlier are to the left of those that have to be later. Let's go back to our example.

> **Make a separate symbol for each element.**

> A radio station will schedule five programs—A, B, C, D, and E—to be aired Monday through Friday, one program each evening, in an order that conforms to the following restrictions:
>
> Program D must be aired before Program A.
> Programs C and D must be aired on consecutive evenings.
> Program E may not be the second program to be aired.

M	T	W	R	F
	~E			

D . . . A

| CD | / | DC |

Since Program D must be aired before Program A, we put it on the left. The ellipsis (. . .) shows that D must be sometime before A, but that other programs could be aired in between those two. However, we put a **block** around Programs C and D to show that no other programs can be aired in between those two. We also symbolized the block both ways, since the clue does not indicate that C must be aired before D or vice versa. Since Program E can never be the second program aired, we put that information in our model diagram to show that E can never be aired on Tuesday. The wavy negative sign (~) means "not."

Some Symbolizing Guidelines

- Make a separate symbol for each element: for example, WWWW, not 4W.

- When two elements are always next to each other, put a BLOCK around them. Blocks make games much easier.

- When two elements can never be next to each other, use an ANTIBLOCK symbol (◻⧄).

- For conditional clues (If . . . then . . .) use an ARROW. The element that depends on something goes on the left. The independent element goes on the right side of the arrow.

- In some cases it's just not possible to symbolize a clue. Be sure to write some shorthand summary of the clue, or circle it with your pencil, so that you don't forget to check that clue as you do each question.

> When two elements are always together, that's a BLOCK.

DRILL 1

Try symbolizing the clues below. Even though these clues are from different games, try to develop a simple system for symbolizing them. Check your symbols against ours on page 298.

Clue	Symbol

1. In a box of candies, four are brown, three are white, and two are red.

2. Bernie must enter before Erin.

3. Carol and Sue always sit together.

4. Dan and Mike cannot sit together.

5. If Fred participates, then Greg participates.

6. Barbara cannot perform before Warren performs.

7. David cannot attend unless Paula also attends.

8. Apples and pears are not adjacent.

9. Oranges and limes must be displayed on adjacent shelves.

10. If Doctor U is operating in Room 1, Doctor Z cannot operate there.

Step 3: Double-Check Your Diagram and Symbols

After you've symbolized the clues, take the time to double-check everything. Look at your symbols and then tell yourself what they mean. Then read the words of the clues to make sure you've symbolized correctly.

Double-checking saves time in the long run.

This may seem time-consuming, but it's crucial to success in solving games. If you go very slowly and carefully at the start of the game, you'll be much more familiar with the game, and the questions will be much easier to solve. On the other hand, if you go too quickly at the beginning of a game, you'll be much more likely to miss a crucial piece of information, or to misrepresent some of the clues. Then the questions will be impossible to solve!

The major cause of problems with games is misreading the clues.

Step 4: Size up the Clues and Draw Deductions

Before you go to the questions, ask yourself some questions about the game. Answering these questions will help you make deductions in the game.

- ♦ What are your most definite clues? What are your **most restricted elements**? Does any element always go in one place? If so, put that element in your model diagram. Are there certain places in the diagram where some elements could never go? If so, note that in those places in the model diagram.

- ♦ Do you have any blocks? Elements in blocks are very restricted.

- ♦ Do certain elements always have to be before other elements? If so, which places in the diagram would be closed to these elements? Make notes in your model diagram.

- ♦ Do you have clues about all the elements? If not, which elements have no restrictions? Make notes about any unrestricted elements. Always determine which elements are the **least restricted**.

Draw deductions. Add the deductions to your model diagram.

- ♦ Which places in the diagram are the most restricted? Which are the least restricted?

Always identify the most restricted elements in a game. If one of the elements always has to be in one of the places, you'll start every question by putting that element in place. If the most restricted elements can't go in certain places, then there are only a few places they can go. You'll start every question in the game by concentrating on the most restricted elements.

If you have elements in a block, you'll concentrate more on assigning that block than on assigning the individual elements.

If some elements have no restrictions, it's good to write that down so that when you are doing the questions you'll know that you didn't overlook any clues about those elements. You'll also know that unrestricted elements can be assigned to any place that's still open after you've assigned the more restricted elements.

STEP 5: ATTACK THE QUESTIONS

As usual on the GRE, you have to read the questions very carefully. Understanding exactly what the questions are asking is how to start solving them. First, make sure you understand the difference between a "COULD" question and a "MUST" question.

A COULD question asks which answer choice could be true, i.e., is possible once. Only one of the choices can be true. The wrong answers to a COULD question cannot be true. To answer a COULD question, try each answer choice. The right answer will lead to an assignment of elements that is possible according to the conditions. The wrong answers will lead to assignments of the elements that would violate the rules of the game.

A MUST question asks which answer choice is **always** true, not which choice could be true once. Several of the choices could be true, but only one choice cannot be false. The wrong answer choices could be false. To answer a MUST question, try to disprove the other four answer choices. Draw an assignment of the elements that fits the conditions of the game and eliminate the answer choices that this arrangement disproves. Then redraw your arrangement of the elements to disprove whatever choices remain. Never stop when one of the choices seems right; be sure to disprove the other choices.

STEP 6: KEEP YOUR PENCIL BUSY

Don't think, draw! Don't look for shortcuts, just get busy. Just try things. Try one arrangement, eliminate answer choices, then try another arrangement. You'll get the right answer faster by *trying something* than by sitting and staring at the question.

Keep your pencil moving!

PUTTING THE STRATEGY TO WORK

Here's a relatively simple game, followed by three questions. Read the game and try your hand at answering the questions. Don't worry about how much time it takes you. Refer to the strategy we've just outlined as you do the game. Concentrate on doing each step in the process correctly before you go on to the next step.

Then, when you've finished, carefully read our step-by-step implementation of the strategy, which follows the questions. If you picked ETS's answers all by yourself, terrific! If not, our analysis should help you learn from your mistakes. Try this sample game and its questions:

SAMPLE GAME 1

Six cars—P, Q, R, S, T, and U—are being placed in a parking lot. The parking lot has six spaces, numbered 1 through 6. Each car is placed in its own space, according to the following restrictions:

P can park anywhere except in 5 or 6.
Q can park in 4 or 5 only.
R can park in 3 or 6 only.
S can park in 2 or 6 only.
T can park in 1 or 3 only.
U can park anywhere except in 1 or 3.

1. If Q parks in 4, U must park in

   (A) 1
   (B) 2
   (C) 3
   (D) 5
   (E) 6

2. If P parks in 3, T must park in

   (A) 1
   (B) 2
   (C) 4
   (D) 5
   (E) 6

3. If S parks in 6, which of the following must be true?

   (A) T parks in 1.
   (B) P parks in 2.
   (C) Q parks in 4.
   (D) U parks in 4.
   (E) T parks in 3.

Cracking Sample Game 1: Step 1

We can tell that this game is relatively easy, because it has so many clues. Remember: The more clues you have, the easier the game.

What are you assigning to what? You're assigning cars to parking places. So draw a grid with the parking places on the top of the grid.

1	2	3	4	5	6

Each numbered column in the table represents a parking space.

Cracking Sample Game 1: Step 2

Symbolize the clues by adding the information right into your model diagram.

1	2	3	4	5	6
~Q	~Q	~Q	~R	~P	~P
~R	~R	~S	~S	~R	~Q
~S	~T	~U	~T	~S	~T
~U				~T	

Symbolize every clue.

We're showing the cars that *cannot* park in each space. The wavy minus sign (~) indicates where cars cannot be. For example, the ~P in the 5 slot indicates that P can't park there. In this diagram, a car can park anywhere it isn't prohibited. This type of diagram is very simple, and it has the advantage of showing at a glance that, for example, there are only two cars that can park in slot 1 and only two that can park in slot 5.

Cracking Sample Game 1: Steps 3 and 4

Double-check your symbols and make deductions. Which cars are more restricted? Which cars are less restricted? Which places are the most restricted?

Cars Q, R, S, and T are more restricted because they only have two places to park. Cars P and U are less restricted because they can park anywhere except in two places. Parking places 1 and 5 are more restricted because four of the six cars *can't* park in those places.

Cracking Sample Game 1: Step 5

Now that we're organized, let's go to the questions. Here's the first one:

1. If Q parks in 4, U must park in

   (A) 1
   (B) 2
   (C) 3
   (D) 5
   (E) 6

Here's how to crack it

Our first step is to cross out answer choices we can eliminate immediately. This question concerns where U can park. We already know from the set-up clues (as represented in the model diagram) that U cannot park in 1 or 3. This enables us to eliminate choices A and C.

First we draw a new grid diagram for all six places. Now add our new clue, provided in question 1. This new clue is that (for the purposes of this question) Q is parked in 4. Here's what the revised diagram looks like:

1	2	3	4	5	6
			Q		

Now, if Q is in 4, where are the other more restricted cars going to go? Remember that spaces 1 and 5 are the most restricted spaces. Put R, S, and T into your picture in one arrangement that conforms to the conditions.

1	2	3	4	5	6
T	S		Q		R

Now where can you put P? P can't go in space 5, so it must go in space 3. U must park in space 5.

Here's the second question:

2. If P parks in 3, T must park in

(A) 1
(B) 2
(C) 4
(D) 5
(E) 6

Don't even think about trying to do these in your head.

Here's how to crack it

This question is quite similar to the previous one. Before using the new clue, we consult our diagram, which tells us that T cannot park in 2, 4, 5, or 6. This lets us eliminate choices B, C, D, and E. ETS's answer is choice A.

Notice that we didn't even need to resort to the additional clue. Isn't POE great?

Here's the final question:

3. If S parks in 6, which of the following must be true?

(A) T parks in 1.
(B) P parks in 2.
(C) Q parks in 4.
(D) U parks in 4.
(E) T parks in 3.

Here's how to crack it

Rats! The diagram alone doesn't allow us to eliminate any choices immediately. We'll have to do some work. First, we add the new information to our diagram:

1	2	3	4	5	6
					S

If S parks in 6, neither U nor R can park there. That's not much help with U (which can still park in 2, 3, or 5), but it does tell us that R must park in 3. Add R to the diagram:

1	2	3	4	5	6
		R			S

Have we found ETS's answer? No. "R parks in 3" isn't one of the choices. But we can still eliminate a choice. If R is in 3, nothing else can be there, which means that choice E is impossible. Eliminate choice E.

Also look at what happens to T. If T can't be in 3 (as we've just proved), it can only be in 1. "T parks in 1" is choice A. Choice A is ETS's answer.

You can disprove the other choices with a diagram.

1	2	3	4	5	6
T	U	R	P	Q	S

You will find ETS's answer on problems like this by using POE to turn one piece of information into another. Every time you learn something new, every time you eliminate a choice, look for the consequences.

Draw everything.

SAMPLE GAME 2

Six books—on history, English, algebra, ceramics, Spanish, and philosophy—are arranged on a shelf, with a bookend at either end.

The history book is next to a bookend.
The English book is next to the algebra book.
At least one book separates the English and ceramics books, and the English and Spanish books.
The ceramics book and the Spanish book are next to each other.
At least two books separate the English and philosophy books.

1. Which of the following books can be next to a bookend?

    I. philosophy
    II. English
    III. ceramics

    (A) I only
    (B) II only
    (C) I and II only
    (D) II and III only
    (E) I, II, and III

2. The history book CANNOT be next to which of the following books?

    (A) algebra only
    (B) ceramics only
    (C) philosophy only
    (D) English or algebra only
    (E) ceramics, Spanish, and algebra

3. If the history book is next to the English book, which of the following must be true?

    (A) The philosophy book is next to a bookend.
    (B) The ceramics book is next to a bookend.
    (C) The Spanish book is next to the algebra book.
    (D) The philosophy book is next to the ceramics book.
    (E) The algebra book is next to the ceramics book.

Cracking Sample Game 2: Step 1

What's the diagram? How many elements are you assigning to how many places? Six books are going in six places. So the diagram would be similar to the one we used in the first game.

$$\text{Bookend} \quad \underline{1 \mid 2 \mid 3 \mid 4 \mid 5 \mid 6} \quad \text{Bookend}$$

The bookends would be next to places 1 and 6.

Cracking Sample Game 2: Step 2

Let's start to symbolize the clues. We can put the first clue right into our model diagram.

$$\text{Bookend} \quad \underline{\frac{1 \mid 2 \mid 3 \mid 4 \mid 5 \mid 6}{\sim H \sim H \sim H \sim H}} \quad \text{Bookend}$$

In other words, the table tells us that H (history) can't be in 2, 3, 4, or 5. The next clue is a good one—a block!

$$\text{Bookend} \quad \underline{\frac{1 \mid 2 \mid 3 \mid 4 \mid 5 \mid 6}{\sim H \sim H \sim H \sim H}} \quad \text{Bookend}$$

$$\boxed{\text{E A}} \quad \boxed{\text{A E}}$$

Notice that we symbolized both ways, because the clue doesn't tell us which book is to the left or right of the other.

Think carefully about the next clue. What does the clue tell you for sure? Neither the ceramics book nor the Spanish book can be next to the English book. Two antiblocks!

$$\text{Bookend} \quad \underline{\frac{1 \mid 2 \mid 3 \mid 4 \mid 5 \mid 6}{\sim H \sim H \sim H \sim H}} \quad \text{Bookend}$$

$$\boxed{\text{E A}} \quad \boxed{\text{A E}}$$

$$\boxed{\text{E}\!\!\!/\text{C}} \quad \boxed{\text{E}\!\!\!/\text{S}}$$

Does the next clue look familiar? How fabulous, another block!

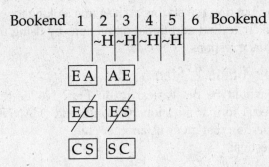

Be careful with clues that say "at least." You can symbolize clues like this in different ways. Try to adopt a consistent way of symbolizing them accurately that you can use from game to game. Here are a couple of different ways to symbolize the clue for this game.

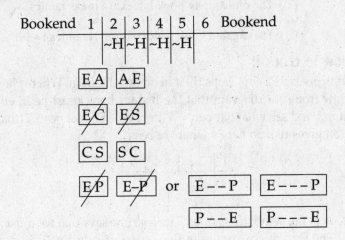

Cracking Sample Game 2: Step 3

Don't forget to double-check your symbols. This game has lots of clues (a good thing), but it would be easy to overlook one of them.

Cracking Sample Game 2: Step 4

The deductions in this game are important. What are the most restricted elements? Obviously H is very restricted, since it can go in only two of the six places. What other element has lots of restrictions? The English book is very restricted. We'll pay special attention to E as we do each question. Also notice that we have not one, but two blocks! In this game, we'll be more concerned with assigning these blocks than with assigning the individual elements. Lastly, be sure to notice that our least restricted element is P. P can be the last element we assign, and we just have to make sure that it's at least two books away from E.

You could go further and make further deductions on this game, and if you can do this quickly, by all means do so. Always make at least the deductions we've made so far, but don't sit staring at the game looking for other deductions. You'll be more likely to find additional deductions by using the ones we have made to answer the questions.

Cracking Sample Game 2: Step 5

Use all the clues. Which question would be the easiest to do first? Notice that the first two questions are special format questions (I, II, III; and "CANNOT"). Let's start with a regular question that gives us another clue.

Here's the question:

3. If the history book is next to the English book, which of the following must be true?

   (A) The philosophy book is next to a bookend.
   (B) The ceramics book is next to a bookend.
   (C) The Spanish book is next to the algebra book.
   (D) The philosophy book is next to the ceramics book.
   (E) The algebra book is next to the ceramics book.

Here's how to crack it

The question gives us a clue. Let's fill it in on our diagram. Where should we put it? We know from our diagram that the history book must be in either 1 or 6. Let's try it in 1 and see what happens. With H in 1, E must be in 2 (that's the clue the question gives us). So here's what we have:

1	2	3	4	5	6
H	E				

Now look at the symbolized rules. The first one says that we must have either EA or AE. The first choice applies in this case. Put A in slot 3:

1	2	3	4	5	6
H	E	A			

Now let's assign our other elements. Can we assign element P to space 4? If we did, there wouldn't be at least two books between E and P. So put the CS block in spaces 4 and 5. Don't worry about the order; we can flip the two elements later. Then where does P have to be assigned?

1	2	3	4	5	6
H	E	A	C	S	P

Now we use POE to go through the choices:

(A) Is the philosophy book next to a bookend? Yes. This is a possibility.

(B) Is the ceramics book next to a bookend? No, so eliminate this choice.

(C) Is the Spanish book next to the algebra book? Not in our first assignment. So it doesn't have to be. We've disproved this choice.

(D) Is the philosophy book next to the ceramics book? Not in the first assignment. Eliminate.

(E) Is the algebra book next to the ceramics book? It is in our first assignment. So keep this choice.

Don't forget that if A and B must be next to each other, they can be AB or BA.

When you're down to choices A and E, flip the CS block. That disproves choice E. ETS's answer is choice A.

Notice that for a MUST question, you draw an arrangement, eliminate all of the choices that this arrangement disproves, then redraw the assignment to disprove remaining choices. Also notice how important blocks can be. Assign the blocks first, then flip the elements in the block to disprove choices.

Now let's try another question.

Here's question 1:

1. Which of the following books can be next to a bookend?
   I. philosophy
   II. English
   III. ceramics

   (A) I only
   (B) II only
   (C) I and II only
   (D) II and III only
   (E) I, II, and III

Here's how to crack it

Our filled-in diagram from question 3 can help us on this question. It proves that the philosophy book can be next to a bookend. That means that statement I is true and that we can eliminate choices B and D.

Now let's test statement III. If we can figure out a way to get the ceramics book next to a bookend, choice E will be ETS's answer. If we can't, we'll have to test statement II as well. By testing statement III before statement II, there is at least a possibility that we won't have to test statement II.

Start a new line on the diagram, with H at one end and C at the other. We want to see if we can make this work. Here's what we start with:

1	2	3	4	5	6
H					C

Now look at the symbolized clues. We see quickly that S has to be next to C, so we put S in slot 5, like this:

1	2	3	4	5	6
H				S	C

The first half of the second symbolized clue tells us that slot 2 could be E. The second half of the second clue tells us that slot 3 could be E. Add a new line and show both possibilities, like this:

1	2	3	4	5	6
H	E	A		S	C
	A	E			

If E is in 2, then 3 must be A, according to the first clue. So put A in slot 3 on the first line. That means that P would have to be in 4, like this:

1	2	3	4	5	6
H	E	A	P	S	C
	A	E			

Is this arrangement possible? No, because the last clue says that P and E have to be at least two spaces apart. *Cross out the line.* (Be sure to cross out invalid lines. This will keep you from becoming confused later on.)

If E is in 3, then either 2 or 4 must be A (with P in the remaining slot). Add another line so that both these possibilities are represented:

1	2	3	4	5	6
H	E	A	P	S	C
	A	E			
H	P	E	A	S	C

Neither of these arrangements is possible, either, because P and E once again aren't far enough apart. In fact, with C and S together at one end, we're never going to have enough room in the middle, because we need at least four spaces for the English and philosophy books. Statement III is false. Cross out the lines and eliminate choice E.

Now we have to test statement II. Can we get the English book next to a bookend? Start a new line on the diagram with H at one end and E at the other:

1	2	3	4	5	6
H					E

With E in slot 6, we have to have A in slot 5 and either C or S in slot 4. We add a new line so that we can test both possibilities. That leaves P for the 2 slot. Here's what we end up with:

1	2	3	4	5	6
H	P	C	S	A	E
		S	C		

Are these valid arrangements? Yes, they are. Statement II is true, and ETS's answer is choice C.

Now we're ready for question 2:

2. The history book CANNOT be next to which of the following books?

(A) algebra only
(B) ceramics only
(C) philosophy only
(D) English or algebra only
(E) ceramics, Spanish, and algebra

Use POE in games.

Here's how to crack it

The first thing to do is check our old diagrams to see if we can eliminate any choices right off the bat. In previous, valid arrangements, we've had the history book next to the English book and the philosophy book. That means we can eliminate choices C and D.

Time for POE. Ceramics appears in two of the remaining three choices, so let's try it first. If this works (this is a CANNOT question, remember) we'll know that ETS's answer is A, because we'll be able to eliminate both choices B and E.

Start a new line on the diagram, with ceramics next to history. Then, following the clues, we put C in 3. This means that E would have to be in either 5 or 6. If this were the case, there would be no place for P. Cross out the line—E is the right answer.

1	2	3	4	5	6
H	C	S		E	

SAMPLE GAME 3

Seven passengers—J, K, L, M, N, O, and P—are riding on an elevator that makes four stops. Two passengers get off at every stop except the last, when the final passenger gets off. The following conditions apply:

Neither J nor N gets off with K.
L cannot get off with M.
O must get off with either M or P.

Don't forget to draw in your test booklet.

1. Which of the following is an acceptable list of passengers getting off the elevator, from the first stop to the last stop?

   (A) J and N, K and P, L and M, O
   (B) J and N, K and L, O and P, M
   (C) J and K, L and P, N and O, M
   (D) J and L, K and N, M and O, P
   (E) J and P, L and N, K and O, M

2. If L gets off with P, which of the following must be true?

   (A) K gets off with M.
   (B) K gets off with N.
   (C) J gets off with M.
   (D) K gets off last.
   (E) J gets off last.

3. If L gets off last, which of the following passengers must get off with J?

   (A) K
   (B) M
   (C) N
   (D) O
   (E) P

4. If K gets off with P, which of the following is a complete and accurate list of those passengers who could get off last?

   (A) J
   (B) L
   (C) J, L
   (D) L, N
   (E) J, L, N

5. If J gets off with M, which of the following must be true?

   (A) K gets off last.
   (B) L gets off last.
   (C) N gets off last.
   (D) L gets off with either K or N.
   (E) P gets off with either K or N.

6. If P gets off with N, all of the following could be true EXCEPT

    (A) O gets off with M
    (B) K gets off with L
    (C) J gets off last
    (D) K gets off last
    (E) L gets off last

Cracking Sample Game 3: Step 1

What does the diagram look like for this game? What doesn't change? The elevator makes four stops. So put the four stops at the top of the diagram. The first three floors have two slots, that last floor has only one.

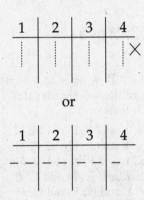

or

> The element that doesn't change goes at the top of the diagram. Floors don't change; put them at the top!

Cracking Sample Game 3: Step 2

We also need to symbolize the clues. Here's one way to do this:

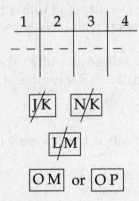

Cracking Sample Game 3: Steps 3 and 4

Double-check and make deductions. Which elements are the most restricted? O and K are the most restricted. If O always has to get off with either M or P, then O can never get off at the fourth stop. Be sure to put that in your model diagram. Notice that the fourth stop is the only place that is restricted. We don't have any other clues about the order of the four stops. The first three stops are all unrestricted, so whatever order we use to assign the elements to the first three places won't matter.

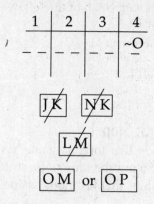

1	2	3	4
—	—	—	~O

J̶K̶   N̶K̶

L̶M̶

O M   or   O P

Cracking Sample Game 3: Step 5

Let's get busy with the questions.

1. Which of the following is an acceptable list of passengers getting off the elevator, from the first stop to the last stop?

   (A) J and N, K and P, L and M, O
   (B) J and N, K and L, O and P, M
   (C) J and K, L and P, N and O, M
   (D) J and L, K and N, M and O, P
   (E) J and P, L and N, K and O, M

Here's how to crack it

There's nothing to do here but use POE by applying the clues. Here goes:

Start by looking at element O. We can eliminate choice A right away, because it has O getting off last. Since O must get off with either M or P, we can eliminate any choices in which O gets off with other elements. This lets us eliminate choices C and E.

The first clue says that N can't get off with K. This lets us eliminate choice D. So, by process of elimination, the ETS answer must be choice B.

Here's question 2:

2. If L gets off with P, which of the following must be true?

   (A) K gets off with M.
   (B) K gets off with N.
   (C) J gets off with M.
   (D) K gets off last.
   (E) J gets off last.

Here's how to crack it

This question adds a clue. Let's start by drawing a new diagram incorporating the new clue. Since the first three stops have no restrictions, let's just put L and P in the first stop. Who's left to get off with O? Since P already got off with L, M must get off with O. Let's put them at the second stop.

2.

1	2	3	4
L P	O M	J N	K

Who's left? J, K, and N. The first clues says that neither J nor N gets off with K. So J and N have to get off together, and K has to get off last. Assign these elements and eliminate answer choices. The only choice that must be true is choice D, which states that K gets off last.

Here's the third question:

3. If L gets off last, which of the following passengers must get off with J?

(A) K
(B) M
(C) N
(D) O
(E) P

Remember: You'll be under time pressure on test day. Practice so you can do games quickly.

Here's how to crack it

Get your pencil busy. Put L in the last place. Then assign the rest of the elements according to the clues. Don't think, just draw.

3.

1	2	3	4
J N	P K	O M	L

This satisfies all the clues. What did you find out? The only element left to go with J is N. ETS's answer is choice C.

Here's the next question:

4. If K gets off with P, which of the following is a complete and accurate list of those passengers who could get off last?

(A) J
(B) L
(C) J, L
(D) L, N
(E) J, L, N

Here's how to crack it

Start with the clue in the question and get your pencil going. Since K gets off with P, let's just assign them to the first stop. What about O? The only element left to get off with O is M. Let's put them at the second stop:

4.

1	2	3	4
K P	O M	_ _	_

This leaves us with J, L, and N. We look back at our clues to see if we have any restrictions that apply to these letters. We don't. We can put them anywhere we like, which means that any of them could get off last. ETS's answer is choice E.

Here's question 5:

5. If J gets off with M, which of the following must be true?

(A) K gets off last.
(B) L gets off last.
(C) N gets off last.
(D) L gets off with either K or N.
(E) P gets off with either K or N.

Here's how to crack it

Draw, draw, and redraw.

Doesn't this seem easy now? Once again, start with the clue in the question. Assign J and M to the first stop. Who can get off with O? This time it has to be P. Put O and P in stop two:

5.

1	2	3	4
J M	O P	_ _	_

Who's left? N, L, and K. Don't think, just assign them.

5.

1	2	3	4
J M	O P	N L	K

Eliminate choices B, C, and E. Now redraw. Switch N and K to eliminate choice A.

ETS's answer is choice D. In our two valid examples, "L gets off with either K or N." It's faster to draw, eliminate, and redraw than to think it all through before you draw.

Here's the last question:

6. If P gets off with N, all of the following could be true EXCEPT

(A) O gets off with M.
(B) K gets off with L.
(C) J gets off last.
(D) K gets off last.
(E) L gets off last.

Here's how to crack it

This is an "EXCEPT" question, so we're looking for the choice that doesn't work.

Start by putting P and N at the first stop. Then M has to get off with O. Put them at the second stop. Who's left? J, K, and L. Just assign them according to the clues:

6.

1	2	3	4
P N	O M	J L	K

Eliminate the answer choices that could be true, based on your first picture. That gets rid of three choices. Then redraw the picture, switching J and K. There's no way you can put L last, because that would force J and K to get off together. So the ETS answer must be choice E. The other choices could be true.

CONDITIONAL GAMES

HOW TO SPOT A CONDITIONAL GAME

Conditional games are not that different from assignment games. The difference is that in a conditional game, the setup does not specify the exact number of places to which you must assign elements. In other words, you don't know how many elements you have to assign. You may assign a certain number of the elements for some questions and a different number of the elements for other questions. The number of elements you assign depends on the clues for the elements. These clues are all conditional ("if . . . then") in nature.

Conditional games are harder games because the setup doesn't tell you how many places there are.

THE CONTRAPOSITIVE

Symbolize conditional clues as you would other clues, using an arrow. Then draw secondary deductions by following the contrapositive rule:

Flip and negate.

For example:

If A is on the team, B must also be on the team.

First symbolize: $A \rightarrow B$

Then draw the contrapositive deduction: $\sim B \rightarrow \sim A$

If B is *not* on the team, then A *cannot* be on the team.

This is the *only* thing that *must* follow from the clue!

You may be tempted to say that if B is on the team, then A is on the team, but that's not necessarily true. B could be on the team without A. Remember, the restriction is on A, not on B. A cannot be on the team without B.

It works the same way even when the original clue includes a negative component. Just remember to flip and negate!

For example:

If C is selected, D cannot be selected.

You would symbolize: $C \rightarrow \sim D$

So the contrapositive deduction would be: $D \rightarrow \sim C$

If D *is* selected, then C *cannot* be selected.

Always draw the contrapositive deduction when you see "if . . . then" clues.

How to Approach Conditional Games

You should approach conditional games in pretty much the same way you approach assignment games. But with these games, you won't deduce any restrictions on places; all the restrictions will be on the elements. Be sure you symbolize the clues correctly (use arrows to symbolize "If . . . then"). The deductions always involve the contrapositives of the clues and linking the clues together.

Try this game.

Sample Game 4

Don't forget to symbolize every clue.

A track coach is deciding which and how many of her athletes—L, M, N, O, P, R, and S—will compete in an upcoming track meet. She will decide according to the following guidelines:

If L competes, M must compete.
If M and N both compete, O cannot compete.
If N and O both compete, R cannot compete.
If O competes, either P or S must compete.
Either P or R must compete, but they cannot both compete.
P and S cannot both compete.

10. If only three athletes can compete in the track meet, which of the following could be that group of athletes?

(A) L, M, and N
(B) M, P, and S
(C) M, P, and R
(D) N, O, and P
(E) N, O, and R

11. If O and S both compete in the track meet, which of the following must be true?

(A) N competes.
(B) P competes.
(C) R competes.
(D) L does not compete.
(E) M does not compete.

12. If O and R both compete in the track meet, which of the following CANNOT be true?

(A) M competes.
(B) N competes.
(C) S competes.
(D) L does not compete.
(E) P does not compete.

13. If L and N both compete in the track meet, what is the maximum number of athletes who can compete?

    (A) three
    (B) four
    (C) five
    (D) six
    (E) seven

14. If S competes in the track meet, which of the following combinations of three athletes can be among those who also compete?

    (A) L, M, and P
    (B) L, N, and O
    (C) L, O, and P
    (D) M, O, and R
    (E) N, O, and R

Cracking Sample Game 4: Step 1

What does the diagram look like for this game? What doesn't change? Some of the athletes compete, and some don't. Put these categories at the top of your grid.

> You can draw simpler diagrams for conditional games.

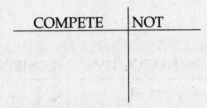

Cracking Sample Game 4: Step 2

Be very careful to symbolize the clues correctly. Here's the right way to do it:

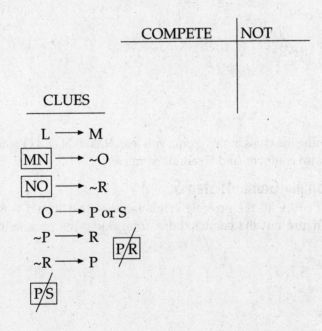

Notice the difference between a conditional clue and a clue that gives you a block. A block means that two elements are always together. A conditional clue restricts one of the elements more than the other one. In the first clue, for example, the element L is more restricted than M. If L competes, then M must compete. But M could compete without L. The element "with the problem," the one that requires another element, goes on the left of the arrow. For some of the clues you can use blocks and antiblocks, along with the symbols for conditional clues, where appropriate. An antiblock is the best way to symbolize the last clue in this game.

Cracking Sample Game 4: Steps 3 and 4

Double-check and make deductions. Make a separate column for the contrapositive for each clue. Go through the clues one by one, and write down the contrapositive next to each clue. Be sure to pay attention to elements that are in more than one clue. What happens when you combine those clues?

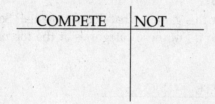

CLUES	CONTRAPOSITIVE	COMBINE
L ⟶ M	~M ⟶ ~L	NO ⟶ ~R ⟶ P ⟶ ~S
MN ⟶ ~O	O ⟶ ~MN	
NO ⟶ ~R	R ⟶ ~NO	
O ⟶ P or S	~P + ~S ⟶ ~O	
~P ⟶ R P̸R̸		
~R ⟶ P		
P̸S̸		

By combining the clues in this game, you learn that if N and O both compete, then P must also compete, and S cannot compete.

Cracking Sample Game 4: Step 5

Don't try to deduce all the possible combinations—that would waste a lot of time. You'll figure out the combinations from doing the questions. Let's get started.

10. If only three athletes can compete in the track meet, which of the following could be that group of athletes?

   (A) L, M, and N
   (B) M, P, and S
   (C) M, P, and R
   (D) N, O, and P
   (E) N, O, and R

Here's how to crack it

Just use Process of Elimination, as usual. Take each clue and eliminate the answer choices that violate it. It might be easiest to start with the antiblocks. P and R can't both compete. Eliminate choice C. P and S can't both compete. Eliminate choice B. But either P or R must compete, so eliminate choice A. If N and O both compete, then R cannot compete. Eliminate choice E. Using POE, we found the ETS answer, choice D.

11. If O and S both compete in the track meet, which of the following must be true?

   (A) N competes.
   (B) P competes.
   (C) R competes.
   (D) L does not compete.
   (E) M does not compete.

Here's how to crack it

Draw a diagram. Assign O and S to the "competing" place. Then go to the clues. What clues do we have about S? Since P and S cannot both compete, P cannot compete. Write that in the "not" column. What clues do we have about P? Either P or R must compete, so R must compete. Assign R to the "compete" place. Everything we've noted so far must be true. Do we have to use any of the other elements? We could, but we don't have to. The ETS answer is choice C.

	COMPETE	NOT
11.	O S R	P

12. If O and R both compete in the track meet, which of the following CANNOT be true?

   (A) M competes.
   (B) N competes.
   (C) S competes.
   (D) L does not compete.
   (E) P does not compete.

Here's how to crack it

Draw a diagram. Assign O and R to the "competing" place. Then go to the clues. What clues do we have about R? Since P and R cannot both compete, then P cannot compete. Write that in the "not" column. If R competes, then N and O cannot both compete (that's the contrapositive). So N cannot compete. Write N in the "not" column and go to the choices. That's it, choice B cannot be true.

	COMPETE	NOT
12.	O R	P N

Assign elements to places, then attack the questions.

13. If L and N both compete in the track meet, what is the maximum number of athletes who can compete?

    (A) three
    (B) four
    (C) five
    (D) six
    (E) seven

Here's how to crack it

Draw a diagram. Assign L and N to the "competing" place. Go to the clues, what clues do we have about L? If L competes, then M must compete. Write M in the "compete" column. What clues do we have about M and N? If M and N both compete, then O cannot compete. Write O in the "not" column. Who's left? P, R, and S. Since P can't compete with either R or S, let's assign P to the "not" column, and R and S to the "compete" column. How many athletes do we have? Five. So ETS's answer must be choice C.

	COMPETE	NOT
13.	L N M	O P
	R S	

14. If S competes in the track meet, which of the following combinations of three athletes can be among those who also compete?

    (A) L, M, and P
    (B) L, N, and O
    (C) L, O, and P
    (D) M, O, and R
    (E) N, O, and R

Here's how to crack it

Draw a diagram. Assign S to the "competing" place. Go to the clues. What clues do we have about S? P and S cannot both compete. Write P in the "not" column. Eliminate answer choices A and C. What clues do we have about P? Either P or R must compete, so R must compete. Write R in the "compete" column. Everything in our diagram so far must be true. Try the choices that remain.

	COMPETE	NOT
14.	S R	P

Eliminate choices B and E because if R competes, then N and O cannot both compete (it's the contrapositive again). By process of elimination, we've got the ETS answer, choice D.

Conditional games may look scary at first, but they're no problem if you keep your pencil busy.

MAP GAMES

HOW TO SPOT A MAP GAME

In an assignment game, you assign elements to places. In a map game, there are no places apart from the elements. Rather, the setup of the game describes *something moving* among the elements, or connections between pairs of elements.

> In map games, there are no places apart from the elements.

HOW TO APPROACH MAP GAMES

Take plenty of time to symbolize the clues carefully, then combine the clues into one diagram that incorporates all the information. Double-checking before you go to the questions is especially crucial. For map games, you'll refer to this one diagram to answer all of the questions.

SAMPLE GAME 5

In a message relay system there are exactly seven terminals—F, G, H, J, K, L, and M. A terminal can transmit any messages initiated by that terminal as well as any messages received from others, but only according to specific rules:

Messages can be transmitted in either direction between G and H, in either direction between J and M, and in either direction between K and L.

Messages can be transmitted from F to K, from H to J, from K to G, from M to F, and from M to H.

7. Which of the seven terminals can transmit messages directly to the greatest number of terminals?

(A) F
(B) H
(C) J
(D) K
(E) M

8. If a message initiated by G is to reach K, and is to be transmitted to no more terminals than necessary, it must be transmitted to a total of how many terminals other than G and K?

(A) 1
(B) 2
(C) 3
(D) 4
(E) 5

9. A message from H that eventually reaches L must have been transmitted to all of the following terminals EXCEPT

(A) F
(B) G
(C) J
(D) K
(E) M

10. If J is removed from the message relay system for a day, it is still possible for a message to be transmitted on that day all the way along a route from

(A) F to H
(B) G to K
(C) G to M
(D) H to K
(E) L to M

11. If K is removed from the message relay system for a day, which of the following terminals CANNOT receive any messages from any other terminal on that day?

(A) F
(B) G
(C) H
(D) J
(E) L

12. A message can travel along two alternative routes that have no terminal in common except the initiating terminal and the final recipient terminal if the initiating terminal and the final recipient terminal, respectively, are

(A) G and J
(B) G and L
(C) H and L
(D) K and M
(E) M and G

13. A message being transmitted along which of the following routes must reach each of the seven terminals at least once?

(A) F to G and then to M
(B) J to H and then to L
(C) L to H and then to M
(D) M to G and then to K
(E) M to L and then to F

Cracking Sample Game 5: Step 1

What does the diagram look like? There are no places, only connections among the elements.

Cracking Sample Game 5: Step 2

To symbolize the clues, use arrows to show the connections. Use two arrows for two-way connections, use one arrow for one-way connections. This makes it easier to see the difference.

$$G \rightleftarrows H$$
$$J \rightleftarrows M$$
$$K \rightleftarrows L$$
$$F \rightarrow K$$
$$H \rightarrow J$$
$$K \rightarrow G$$
$$M \rightarrow F$$
$$M \rightarrow H$$

Think about how the elements connect in map games.

Cracking Sample Game 5: Steps 3 and 4

Which elements do you have the most clues about? Start combining the clues into one diagram by putting those elements in the center of your new diagram. In this game, both K and M are in lots of the clues. Let's just use either K or M to get started. Make your new diagram large enough to refer to easily when you're doing the questions.

$$M \rightleftharpoons J$$
$$K \rightleftharpoons L$$

Now link these elements to the other elements that are connected to these elements in the clues.

When you've added a clue to your combined diagram, check it off, since you probably won't go through the clues in the order they were given. Take your time drawing your combined diagram. Make sure you've incorporated all the information. Be sure to double-check your final diagram against the words in the original clues. You won't be going back to those words again.

Cracking Sample Game 5: Step 5

Once you've drawn your map, you're ready to attack the questions.

7. Which of the seven terminals can transmit messages directly to the greatest number of terminals?

(A) F
(B) H
(C) J
(D) K
(E) M

Here's how to crack it

Use Process of Elimination. Using your map, you can see that F transmits directly to only one other terminal, K. Write numbers next to each answer choice. Put the number 1 next to choice A, and go to choice B. As soon as you see that H transmits to two other terminals, write 2 next to H and cross off choice A. Since J transmits directly only to M, cross off choice C. Be careful here. The question asks about transmitting, and K *transmits* only to 2 terminals, G and L. Since M transmits to F, H, and J, the ETS answer is E.

8. If a message initiated by G is to reach K, and is to be transmitted to no more terminals than necessary, it must be transmitted to a total of how many terminals other than G and K?

(A) 1
(B) 2
(C) 3
(D) 4
(E) 5

Here's how to crack it

Use your map carefully. Notice that K transmits directly to G, but not vice versa. So for G to transmit a message to K, the message from G has to be transmitted to H, then to J, then to M, then to F, and finally to K. The number of terminals other than G and K is 4, so the ETS answer is choice D.

9. A message from H that eventually reaches L must have been transmitted to all of the following terminals EXCEPT

(A) F
(B) G
(C) J
(D) K
(E) M

Here's how to crack it

To get to L, starting at H, the message has to go first to J, then to M, then to F, then to K, and finally to L. Eliminate the answer choices that contain J, M, F, and K. By using POE, the ETS answer must be choice B. Notice that if you've got the right map, these questions are really easy.

10. If J is removed from the message relay system for a day, it is still possible for a message to be transmitted on that day all the way along a route from

(A) F to H
(B) G to K
(C) G to M
(D) H to K
(E) L to M

> Doing games is like arranging tables at a wedding: Aunt Ida can't sit with Uncle Jack; Cousin Mary can't sit with Sister Sue; Tony and Tina must sit together.

Here's how to crack it

Either use your hand to cover up the connections to J in your original diagram, or redraw your map without J in it for this question. Then try each answer choice. Hey! A message can go from F to H! The message could go from F to K to G and then to H. We're done. The ETS answer is choice A.

Let's make sure that the other choices are wrong. To send a message from G to K, as we saw in question 8, the message would have to go to H and then to J, which would not be possible if J is removed from the system. To send a message from G to M, the same thing would be true. To send a message from H to K would be impossible without J, since the only other terminal that H can transmit to is G, and G can transmit only to H. A message could not be sent from L to M without J in the system, because it would again have to stop at H.

11. If K is removed from the message relay system for a day, which of the following terminals CANNOT receive any messages from any other terminal on that day?

    (A) F
    (B) G
    (C) H
    (D) J
    (E) L

Here's how to crack it

Either use your hand to cover up the connections to K in your original diagram, or redraw your map with out J in it for this question. Which terminal is no longer linked to the others when you remove K? Terminal L is gone, too. That's it. The ETS answer is choice E.

12. A message can travel along two alternative routes that have no terminal in common except the initiating terminal and the final recipient terminal if the initiating terminal and the final recipient terminal, respectively, are

    (A) G and J
    (B) G and L
    (C) H and L
    (D) K and M
    (E) M and G

Here's how to crack it

Use POE. Eliminate any answer choice for which there would only be one route for a message. Cross off choice A, since the only way to a message can go from G to J is to go from G to H to J. Also eliminate choice B, because the only way from G to L is to go from G to H to J to M to F to K to L. To get from H to L, the message has to go from H to J to M to F to K to L. So cross off C. There's only one way to get from K to M (from K to G to H to J to M). Eliminate D. Let's be sure that choice E works more than one way. A message could go from M to F to K to G. Or a message could be sent from M to H to G. The ETS answer is choice E.

Practice games every day.

13. A message being transmitted along which of the following routes must reach each of the seven terminals at least once?

(A) F to G and then to M
(B) J to H and then to L
(C) L to H and then to M
(D) M to G and then to K
(E) M to L and then to F

Here's how to crack it

Try each choice. If a message could travel on the route given in the choice without going through one of the terminals, then we can eliminate that choice. Eliminate choice A because a message can go from F to G and then to M without ever going to L. Eliminate choice B, since a message can go from J to H and then to L without ever going through G. Eliminate choice C because a message can be sent from L to H and then to M without ever going to F. And, finally, get rid of choice D, because a message can go from M to G and then to K without ever going to L. The ETS answer is E.

All map games are this easy if you take the time to get the right map before you go to the questions.

SUMMARY

Games appear in order of difficulty. Work slowly and carefully. Use this outline for all games:

STEP 1:   Read the whole setup and all the clues. Draw a model diagram that shows the structure of the game.

STEP 2:   Symbolize the clues in a way that's consistent with your diagram for the game.

STEP 3:   Double-check your diagram and symbols.

STEP 4:   Size up the clues and draw deductions.

STEP 5:   Attack the questions.

STEP 6:   Keep your pencil moving.

24

Arguments

WHAT ARE ARGUMENTS?

Each analytical section of your GRE will contain six or nine "logical reasoning" questions, or arguments. If you have six arguments, three will be located after the first game and three will be located after the last. The first group of arguments will be relatively easy, and the second group of arguments will be relatively difficult. If you have nine arguments, the section will begin with three easy arguments; the second set of three, after the first game, will be of medium difficulty; and the third set, after the last game, will be difficult.

GRE arguments aren't like the type you have with your sister.

Since the difficulty of an argument question depends on its placement in the analytical section, you can't just memorize the order of difficulty in terms of the question numbers (as you can for the verbal and math sections). Always pay attention to which *set* of arguments questions you're doing when you're doing each question. We'll use the real problem numbers for the questions in this chapter.

OUR APPROACH TO ARGUMENTS

Even the most difficult GRE arguments aren't terribly difficult. Most students don't have much trouble with them. If you study this chapter and practice our techniques, you should be able to use POE to eliminate incorrect choices and zero in on ETS's answer.

ETS'S DIRECTIONS

Here are the directions for the analytical section as they will appear on your GRE. ETS intends these directions to apply to both games and arguments. As you may have noticed already, they don't really apply to anything. At any rate, here they are:

> Directions: Each question or group of questions is based on a passage or set of conditions. In answering some of the questions, it may be useful to draw a rough diagram. For each question, select the best answer choice given.

OUR OWN DIRECTIONS

Naturally, you shouldn't even glance at ETS's directions when you take the GRE. They won't help you, anyway. Instead, make sure you understand our own directions. They'll give you a much clearer idea of what you're supposed to do on the test. Here they are:

> Directions: Each GRE argument consists of a brief argument followed by a question. The question following each argument is intended to test your ability to break down an argument into its parts, and determine how those parts are related to each other.

THE PARTS OF AN ARGUMENT

Although you don't need to know anything about logic, you do need to know a few simple terms to follow the rest of this chapter. Here's what you need to know:

Argument: An argument is a conclusion supported by premises and assumptions. It has three parts:

Conclusion: A conclusion is a claim, the main point of an argument.

Premise: A premise is a stated reason, a piece of evidence, that supports the conclusion.

Assumption: An assumption is an unstated premise that supports the conclusion.

OUR STEP-BY-STEP STRATEGY FOR ALL ARGUMENTS QUESTIONS

In solving most GRE argument problems, you'll be asked to find conclusions, draw inferences, identify assumptions, and strengthen or weaken arguments.

STEP 1: Read the question. The question tells you what to look for in the passage, and how to approach it.

STEP 2: Read the entire argument passage.

STEP 3: Find the conclusion and mark it (and, if necessary, the premises and any assumptions).

STEP 4: Answer the question in your own words (especially on conclusion, assumption, and strengthening/weakening questions).

STEP 5: Use Process of Elimination to eliminate wrong answer choices. Eliminate answer choices that are outside the scope.

READ THE QUESTION FIRST!

You need to read the question first to get an idea of what you're dealing with. You don't have to *study* the question. Since there are only a handful of different arguments questions, you just want to decide what the question's asking, before you read the argument. You shouldn't read the choices. Just read the question to see what you're looking for.

On arguments questions, always read the question first.

FINDING CONCLUSIONS

Unlike reading comprehension selections, you will have to read argument passages closely. As you read you should always look for the conclusion. Ask yourself, "What's the point?" The point of the argument is the conclusion. Let's try a simple example.

> "I like to watch television. My TV just broke down.
> Therefore, I should get a new TV."

Mark the CONCLUSION for every argument. Use the "Why Test" to make sure you've got the right conclusion.

What's the main point? "I should get a new TV." Did you notice that the conclusion was preceded by the indicator word *therefore*? Words like *therefore* are grammatical indications that a conclusion is about to be made.

The conclusion often comes after words like:

therefore

thus

hence

then

consequently

as a result

USE THE "WHY TEST"

Remember that the conclusion is *supported by* the other statements in the argument. The "Why Test" is a way to check that the statement you chose as the conclusion is supported by the other statements. State what you think is the conclusion, then ask, "Why?" The other statements should provide the reasons.

Try using the "Why Test" on the example already given above.

Conclusion: "I should get a new TV."

Why?   "I like to watch television. My TV just broke down."

You can see how the other statements support the conclusion. Notice that if we had mistakenly chosen the wrong statement as the conclusion, the other sentences would not have supported it.

Conclusion: "My TV just broke down."

Why?   "I like to watch television. I should get a new TV."

Huh? It just doesn't make sense this way. The other statements don't support this conclusion. So you would know that you chose the wrong statement as the conclusion.

PREMISES

Premises are the parts of the argument that support the conclusion. The premises answer the question, "Why?" They are the reasons that back up the claim made in the conclusion. Most of the time premises are facts, but they can also be assertions that are just given as evidence for the claim in the conclusion.

A conclusion gets support; premises provide it.

Certain words are used to introduce the premises of an argument:

because

since

if

given that

in view of

assume

suppose

CONCLUSION QUESTIONS

Conclusion questions ask you to identify the conclusion of an argument. Some questions simply ask you to *restate* the conclusion of the argument. Other questions ask you to *supply* a conclusion that wasn't ever stated explicitly in the passage. These questions can be worded in several different ways:

The main point of the passage is that . . .

Which of the following best states the author's conclusion in the passage above?

Which of the following statements about . . . is best supported by the statements above?

Which of the following best states the author's main point?

All of these questions are merely asking you to identify the conclusion of the argument.

HOW TO APPROACH CONCLUSION QUESTIONS

Always use the following step-by-step method:

1. Read the question.

2. Read the passage.

3. Find the conclusion and mark it. Use the "Why Test" to check.

4. Answer the question in your own words.

5. Use Process of Elimination (POE).

Eliminating Answer Choices on Conclusion Questions

Scope

Eliminate answers that are outside the scope of the argument.

Eliminate answer choices that are out of the scope of the argument!

Your most important consideration when using POE is whether an answer choice sticks to the scope of the argument. The scope of an argument is defined very narrowly. The scope is restricted by the conclusion and premises as stated in the passage.

If an answer choice goes beyond the issues of the argument, then it's *outside the scope*—eliminate it! If you have to make a case for the answer choice ("Well, if you look at it this way . . ."), it's outside the scope. Read arguments very naively. Remember that all you know about the topic is what you've been told in the passage! Don't consider whatever outside knowledge or opinions you may have of the issues in the argument.

Extreme Wording

Eliminate answer choices that use extreme language.

Stay away from extreme wording in answer choices to conclusion questions.

The best answer to a conclusion question will use indisputable, rather than extreme, language. Indisputable (soft) answer choices tend to use words like *can, may, might, often, some,* etc. Extreme answer choices tend to use words like *all, always, totally, must, no,* and *only,* or *the best* and *the first.* When two answer choices seem very similar, look for these differences in wording.

Use More than One Round of Elimination!

The first time you go through the answer choices, eliminate those answers that you know for sure are out of the scope. If you're not sure what an answer choice means, don't eliminate it at first. But when you're down to two or three choices, on the second round of elimination, you'll have to look more closely at the choices left. Focus on what makes an answer *wrong.* You don't have to understand why the best answer is right, only why the other four choices can't be right.

Not Sure?

If you don't understand an answer choice, don't eliminate it. Focus on what could be wrong with the answer choices that you do understand.

Sample Conclusion Argument

Try this example:

> Some people in the publishing business, concerned about the expense of publishing scholarly works and other esoteric titles, have suggested that research be done to determine in advance the probability of sales before such books are published. Opponents of this proposal argue that such books should be published in the name of education and enlightenment, and, in any case, that it is impossible to predict sales of any kind of literature in advance, because of unforeseen trends and changes in public tastes.

Remember: Read the question first!

> 9. Which of the following best states the opponents' main point?
>   - (A) Publishing scholarly works whose sales are indeterminable is morally superior to publishing books that will appeal to current public tastes.
>   - (B) In an ideal world, all books would be published, regardless of sales; however, this would not be possible economically.
>   - (C) Since there is no absolutely certain method for determining in advance the potential sales and public interest in a book, a publisher cannot and should not make publishing decisions as if there were such a method.
>   - (D) It is more vital to the public interest to publish books that are scholarly and esoteric than to publish books that sell well.
>   - (E) It is impossible to determine the popularity of some books.

Here's how to crack it

Read the question first. Then read the passage. From the question, you know to look for the opponents' conclusion. The opponents' conclusion is not really directly stated. It would be that the proposal to do sales research before deciding to publish books is not a good idea. Why? Because it is impossible to predict book sales in advance, and because books should be published in the name of education and enlightenment. Now that we've answered the question in our own words, let's use POE.

Use POE.

- (A) This choice may seem close to the opponents' conclusion, so keep it and consider the other choices.

- (B) This choice is pretty wild. There is nothing in the argument about what should happen in "an ideal world." The answer choice uses very extreme language. Eliminate.

- (C) Perhaps it's not entirely clear what the statement in this choice means. For that reason, keep this choice!

(D) Is there anything in the passage about what's "vital to the public interest?" This would be an entirely different issue. It's out of the scope of this argument. Eliminate.

(E) Although the opponents would agree with this statement, it is not their main point. It's a premise, not the conclusion. Eliminate.

Now we're down to choices A and C. Reread the question and go back to the passage. Look for something that makes one of the two choices worse. The easiest thing to consider would be whether there is anything in the opponents' argument to suggest that publishing scholarly works would be "morally superior" to publishing books that sell well. There's nothing in the passage that mentions morality. So choice A is out of scope, and the ETS answer is choice C.

Perhaps we wouldn't have phrased the conclusion in quite the way it is stated in choice C, but we can figure out that it's the best answer choice because the other four choices are clearly worse.

INFERENCE QUESTIONS

Arguments on the GRE often ask you to make inferences. **Inference questions ask you to find something that is *known* to be true from information presented in the argument.**

Here are some examples of the ways in which these questions can be worded:

> Which of the following inferences is best supported by the statement made above?

> If the statements above are true, which of the following must also be true?

> Which of the following is implied in the passage above?

> Which of the following conclusions can most properly be drawn if the statements above are true?

An inference is something KNOWN to be true.

Note that some of these questions appear to be conclusion questions, and may not even use the word *infer*. In general, to spot inference questions, look for words such as *infer, imply, implicit, most reasonably,* and *must also be true*.

WHAT'S THE DIFFERENCE BETWEEN A CONCLUSION AND AN INFERENCE?

Sometimes there is no difference. When the conclusion to an argument is not explicitly stated in the passage, it is something you could infer. In other cases, inferences have nothing to do with the main point of an argument. You can make inferences from the facts that are stated as premises.

INFERENCES IN REAL LIFE VERSUS INFERENCES ON THE GRE

Remember, don't approach these questions the same way you would in real life. We're talking only about the inferences that ETS credits on the GRE!

To see the difference between real life and the GRE, consider the following example.

> On the Connecticut Thruway, a driver was stopped by the State Police for exceeding the speed limit. In the process of checking the driver's license and car registration, the police officer decided to conduct a search of the driver and the car. The police officer discovered a handgun concealed in the driver's coat pocket, and the driver was immediately placed under arrest.

If this were *not* the GRE, what are some inferences you might make? You might say that the driver must have been acting in some way that aroused the police officer's suspicion. Perhaps there was a curious bulge in the driver's coat that tipped off the police officer. Maybe the driver had been speeding in the first place because he or she had just robbed a bank.

Since this is the GRE, what is a good inference to make? Although this won't sound terribly exciting, you can correctly infer that, in the state of Connecticut, it is illegal to carry a concealed handgun. On inference questions, an answer choice that appears to be very obvious is often correct.

HOW TO APPROACH INFERENCE QUESTIONS

1. Read the question.

2. Read the passage.

3. Find the conclusion and mark it. Use the "Why Test" to check.

4. Use Process of Elimination.

Don't forget to mark the conclusion.

ELIMINATING ANSWER CHOICES ON INFERENCE QUESTIONS

◆ As with conclusion questions, staying close to the scope of the passage is the key. You're looking for something that comes very close to what was stated in the passage. So immediately eliminate any answer choices that are obviously outside the scope of the argument.

◆ Then, as you consider the remaining choices, ask yourself, "Is this **known** to be true, according to the passage?" If you can't find the exact place in the passage that proves the answer choice is true, then eliminate that choice.

◆ Not sure? If you don't understand an answer choice, don't eliminate it! Focus on what could be wrong with the answer choices that you do understand.

SAMPLE INFERENCE QUESTIONS

Try this one.

10. Despite dramatically changing economic conditions at home and abroad, exports of Bilco Power Tools increased at an average annual rate of 2.1 percent between 1970 and 1979.

Which of the following conclusions can be validly drawn from the statement above?

(A) Changing economic conditions do not affect Bilco's exports.
(B) Exports of Bilco Power Tools increased at a constant rate between 1970 and 1979.
(C) The level of Bilco Power Tools exports was higher in 1979 than it was in 1970.
(D) Bilco Power Tools exports increased each year between 1970 and 1979.
(E) The level of Bilco's exports has not changed since 1979.

Here's how to crack it

Read the question. Then read the argument. Notice that there is no conclusion stated. The argument says (1) economic conditions changed, but (2) exports grew at an average annual rate of 2.1 percent in a particular decade. ETS's answer will be the one choice that is known to be true from these premises. Let's go to the choices:

(A) Do we know this? No, it contradicts the information in the passage. Eliminate.

(B) This could be true, but we don't know that exports increased "at a constant rate." Eliminate.

(C) This statement is known to be true according to the argument. If the average increase from 1970 to 1979 was 2.1 percent, then we know that the level was higher in 1979 than in 1970. This must be ETS's answer.

(D) Again, this could be true, but we don't know for sure. It could be that some of those years the exports decreased or stayed the same, but in other years the increases were above the average for the decade. Eliminate.

(E) We don't know anything about what happened after 1979; the passage deals only with the years from 1970 to 1979. Eliminate answer choices that are out of scope.

ETS's answer is indeed choice C.

Here's another:

10. A New York hospital recently performed a 10-week weight-loss experiment involving men and women. Participants lost an average of 25 pounds. Male participants lost an average of 40 pounds, while female participants lost an average of 20 pounds. Doctors connected with the study attributed the difference to the greater initial starting weights of the male participants.

Which of the following can be most reasonably concluded from the passage above?

(A) No female participant had a starting weight greater than that of any of the male participants.
(B) Everyone who participated in the study lost weight.
(C) The study included more female than male participants.
(D) Some of the participants did not lose weight.
(E) The average starting weight of the male participants was twice that of the female participants.

Here's how to crack it

Many inference questions involve some numbers. But don't let them intimidate you. In the math section of this book we've reviewed all the math you'll need to know. Besides, you don't have to *completely* understand what makes an answer choice right, you just have to figure out what's wrong with the other choices. Use the techniques we've discussed to eliminate choices.

(A) Do we know that "no" female participant had a starting weight greater than that of "any" male? The words *no* and *any* are too extreme. Eliminate.

(B) Do we know that "everyone" lost weight? No. We have only *average* weight-loss figures. Eliminate.

(C) You may think initially that we don't know this from the information we've been given. But we do. How? The males lost an average of 40 pounds; the females lost an average of 20 pounds. If there had been exactly as many males as females in the study, the average weight loss for the group would have been 30 pounds—not the 25 pounds given in the passage. To account for the 25-pound average, there had to be more females than males. The lower results for the females pulled down the group average. This is ETS's answer.

(D) Do we know this? It could be true, but we don't know. See choice B. Eliminate.

(E) Do we know that the males weighed exactly "twice" as much as the females? We don't know this. Eliminate.

ETS's answer is choice C. We didn't need to know much math—just a basic understanding of averages—but finding ETS's answer did turn on a mathematical concept.

Don't let numbers in inference questions intimidate you. You read the math section of this book, right?

ASSUMPTION QUESTIONS

An assumption is an unstated premise that supports the author's conclusion. It's something that the author's conclusion "depends on" or "relies on."

These questions can be worded in several ways:

> Which one of the following is an assumption that, if true, would support the conclusion in the passage above?

> Which of the following most accurately states an assumption that the author must make in order to advance the argument above?

> The author depends upon which of the following to draw his/her conclusion?

> In arguing his/her conclusion the author relies on . . .

Notice that some of these questions don't even use the word *assumption*. Let's consider a simple example.

> The mayor announced: "The crime problem has been solved. The city has hired 3,000 additional police officers."

What's the conclusion? "The crime problem has been solved." Why? Because "the city has hired 3,000 additional police officers." What's being assumed? The mayor is assuming that hiring 3,000 officers is sufficient to solve the crime problem. The assumption is the missing link in the argument. It's the connection between the explicit premises and the conclusion.

HOW TO APPROACH ASSUMPTION QUESTIONS

1. Read the question.

2. Read the passage.

3. Use the "Why Test" to find the conclusion and the premises.

Assumptions support the conclusion.

4. Look for a gap between the premises and conclusion. Before you go to the answer choices, try to get a sense of what assumption is necessary to fill that gap. Try to state that assumption in your own words.

5. Use Process of Elimination.

ELIMINATING ANSWER CHOICES ON ASSUMPTION QUESTIONS

- Since an assumption is merely an unstated connection between the stated premises and the conclusion, you can eliminate any answer choice that goes beyond the explicit scope of the passage.

- An assumption must support the conclusion that was stated in the argument. You can adapt the "Why Test" to check whether the answer choice supports the conclusion. Say the conclusion, then ask, "Why?" If an answer choice tells you why the conclusion is true, then it's an assumption that supports the conclusion.

- Beware of extreme language in the answer choices of assumption questions. If an answer choice is extreme, it would most likely lead to a different conclusion from the one stated in the argument. If a statement is so extreme it would have to be supported by other statements, it would not support the conclusion stated in the passage.

- Not sure? If you don't understand an answer choice, don't eliminate it! Focus on what could be wrong with the answer choices that you do understand.

THREE CLASSIC ARGUMENTS AND ASSUMPTIONS

There are some common forms of argument that make certain types of assumptions. Learn these classic arguments and their assumptions!

Sampling Arguments

Sampling arguments assume that the sample is representative—i.e., not biased. To spot a sampling argument, look for a conclusion that generalizes from a sample of evidence.

Here's an example:

> Recent polls taken in May indicate that the third-party candidate for president is already leading the two major-party candidates. Therefore, I'm sure that she will win the election in November.

Assumptions fill in gaps in the written argument.

Conclusion: _____

Why? (premises) _____

What is being assumed? _____

The conclusion is that the third party candidate for president will win the election in November. Why? Because she is leading the two major-party candidates in May. What's being assumed? The assumption is that the polls taken in May are representative of the voter's preferences in November.

Arguments by Analogy

Arguments by analogy assume that the things being compared are in fact similar. To spot them, look for comparisons.

Here's an example:

> I got good grades in my college courses. Therefore I will probably get good grades in my graduate school courses.

Conclusion: _____

Why? _____

Assumption: _____

What's the conclusion? "I will probably get good grades in my graduate school courses." Why? Because "I got good grades in my college courses." What's being assumed? The assumption is that the graduate school courses will be similar to the college courses.

Causal Arguments

To spot causal arguments, look for indicator words like *causes*, *responsible for*, and *due to*. Consider any argument that offers an explanation a causal argument. Causal arguments always assume that (1) if you remove the cause, that would remove the effect, and (2) there is no alternative cause.

Here's an example:

> Whenever I drink coffee after 10 p.m., I have trouble falling asleep. Therefore, drinking coffee after 10 p.m. causes my insomnia.

Conclusion: _____

Why? _____

Assumption: _____

What's the conclusion? "Drinking coffee after 10 p.m. causes my insomnia." Why? Because "whenever I drink coffee after 10 p.m., I have trouble falling asleep." What's being assumed? Causal arguments on the GRE take a strict view of causality. So if the argument is that coffee causes insomnia, one assumption is that if I *don't* drink coffee, I *won't* have trouble falling asleep. Also, strictly speaking, if the claim is that drinking coffee causes insomnia in this case, the assumption is that *nothing else* is causing the problem.

SAMPLE ASSUMPTION QUESTIONS

Now try this one.

8. Most scientists agree that life requires a planetary body. If so, the possibility of extraterrestrial life in our galaxy has increased dramatically. Astronomers have just discovered an enormous number of possible planetary systems in conjunction with nearby stars. There may be millions or even billions of planets in our galaxy alone.

Which of the following is an assumption of the argument above?

(A) There are an enormous number of planets in our galaxy.
(B) Life will soon be discovered in nearby planetary systems.
(C) Extraterrestrial life does not necessarily require earthlike conditions to exist.
(D) We will recognize extraterrestrial life when we encounter it.
(E) Nearby stars are representative of our galaxy as a whole.

Here's how to crack it

The question asks us to find an assumption, which is an unstated reason that strengthens the conclusion. What's the conclusion? "The possibility of extraterrestrial life in our galaxy has increased dramatically." Why? Because astronomers have just discovered an enormous number of possible planetary systems in conjunction with nearby stars. What's being assumed? Did you notice that the conclusion is a generalization made from a sample of evidence? So the assumption has to be that the sample is representative.

Eliminate out-of-scope answer choices.

(A) This is just another way of stating one of the premises. Eliminate.

(B) Any prediction of the future would itself have to be supported by additional evidence. In other words, it would be a conclusion, not an assumption. Eliminate.

(C) Other conditions for life to exist, aside from the requirement of a planetary body, are outside the scope of this argument. Eliminate.

(D) This is entirely irrelevant. Eliminate.

(E) The author's conclusion about the possibility of extraterrestrial life in our galaxy is based on observations of nearby stars. Did you notice that this is a sampling argument? If the author's conclusion is true, then what is true of nearby stars must be true of the galaxy as a whole. This is ETS's answer.

Here's another example:

23. The laws of economics do not always hold. The
Phillips Curve is an example. The Phillips Curve
depicts an inverse relationship between inflation
and unemployment. As unemployment goes down,
according to the curve, inflation goes up, and vice
versa. According to the Phillips Curve, we are
currently experiencing less inflation than we
should.

The argument above assumes that

(A) employment is relatively high
(B) the Phillips Curve was never valid
(C) inflation is actually good for the economy
(D) there is no relation between inflation and
    unemployment
(E) economics is not a true science

Here's how to crack it

What's the conclusion? It's in the last sentence: "According to the Phillips Curve,
we are currently experiencing less inflation than we should." Why? Because the
Phillips Curve suggests that as unemployment goes down, inflation goes up,
and vice versa. What has to be assumed? This argument is pretty complicated.
But by using POE, you still should be able to take a good guess. An assumption
must link the issues in the argument. The issues in this argument are unemployment and inflation. Go through the choices one at a time, eliminate choices that
are out of scope or too extreme, and be sure to keep any choice that you don't
understand.

(A) This choice is certainly within the scope of the argument. Keep
    it and check out the other choices.

(B) This choice doesn't say anything about inflation or unemploy-
    ment, and the word *never* is too extreme. This would be a
    totally different conclusion from the one in the argument. It
    doesn't support the conclusion given.

(C) This choice mentions inflation, but what's "good for the
    economy" is outside the scope of this passage. Eliminate.

(D) This choice goes *against* the conclusion in the passage. The
    word *no* is too extreme. Eliminate.

(E) Many people, including some economists, may believe this, but
    the issue of what constitutes "a true science" is far beyond the
    scope of the passage.

ETS's answer is choice A. If we are currently experiencing less inflation than
we should, then we have to assume that current unemployment must be lower
than the Phillips Curve predicts. Answer choice A tells us that employment is
relatively high. But you don't get points for understanding why the ETS answer
is best; you just have to figure out why the other choices are worse.

STRENGTHEN AND WEAKEN QUESTIONS

These questions come up frequently on the GRE. Strengthen questions ask you to look for the answer choice that provides the best evidence to make the argument stronger. More often, you'll be asked to weaken arguments. Weaken questions ask you to look for the answer choice that provides the best evidence to make the argument weaker.

Here are some examples of how these questions are worded:

Strengthening:

> Which of the following, if true, would most strengthen the conclusion drawn in the passage above?

> The argument as it is presented in the passage above would be most strengthened if which of the following were true?

> The conclusion would be more properly drawn if it were made clear that. . .

Weakening:

> Which of the following, if true, most seriously weakens the conclusion drawn above?

> Which of the following, if true, would provide the strongest evidence against the above?

> Which of the following, if true, casts the most serious doubt on the conclusion drawn above?

HOW TO APPROACH STRENGTHEN AND WEAKEN QUESTIONS

1. Read the question first.

2. Read the passage.

3. Find the conclusion and identify the premises. Use the "Why Test." Uncover assumptions specific to the argument. Ask yourself if the argument makes any of the causal, sampling, or analogical assumptions.

4. Answer the question in your own words. Look for an answer choice that, if true, would support or attack the assumptions of the argument.

5. Use Process of Elimination.
   - First eliminate answer choices that are way outside the scope of the argument.
   - If you're not sure about an answer choice, don't eliminate it.
   - For weakening and strengthening questions *don't eliminate answers that use extreme language.* Remember that you're looking for the choice that *most* weakens or strengthens the argument.

Think of a sentence that would strengthen the statement: "The GRE is not a measure of my intelligence."

- When you're down to two answer choices on strengthening and weakening questions, go with the answer choice that uses stronger language. Stronger wording makes that choice a better support for or a better attack on the argument.

STRENGTHENING ARGUMENTS

To strengthen an argument, don't simply restate the conclusion; support it by adding a missing premise or by making an assumption explicit.

To strengthen, find the assumption in the argument and support it.

Here's an example:

23. A cognitive psychologist studied a group of young children who regularly walk to school. The psychologist found that none of the children was able to draw a map indicating the route walked to school. The psychologist concluded that, since each child was able to walk to school each day without the assistance of an adult, knowing how to get from one place to another clearly does not depend on having the ability to draw a map of the route from the first place to the second.

    Which of the following statements, if true, provides the strongest support for the conclusion above?

    (A) The fact that an assignment can be completed by some people without a great deal of effort does not show that the assignment can be easily completed by other people.
    (B) Anyone who can accurately indicate a route by drawing the corresponding map has the ability to travel the route indicated.
    (C) Any map of a certain route will inevitably highlight some features of that route and deliberately neglect others.
    (D) If someone successfully reaches an intended destination, that person knows the route to that destination.
    (E) In order to draw an accurate map of a certain route, a person must be familiar with that route.

Here's how to crack it

What's the psychologist's conclusion? The conclusion is that "knowing how to get from one place to another clearly does not depend on having the ability to draw a map of the route from the first place to the second." Why? Because the children knew how to walk to school, but none of them was able to draw a map of the route he or she walked. What's being assumed? Obviously the argument assumes that if knowing how to get from one place to another depended on the ability to draw a map, then the children would not have been able to walk to school successfully. Let's use Process of Elimination.

(A) Huh? It's not entirely clear what this answer choice is about. But don't eliminate an answer choice just because you don't understand it. Let's check the other choices and come back to this one.

(B) This choice seems clearly related to the issues in the argument. But does it support the conclusion? No. This choice is about people who *can* draw maps. The conclusion is about people who *can't* draw maps, so this choice doesn't support the conclusion. Eliminate.

(C) Again, the argument is about lacking the ability to draw maps. This choice is about what maps would show. What would be featured on maps is a totally different issue, so it's out of the scope of the argument. Eliminate.

(D) This choice seems pretty obvious. Who even knew that this was an assumption in the argument? But if it's true, it would definitely strengthen the conclusion. Let's keep this.

(E) This choice seems within the scope. But would it strengthen the conclusion? Go back to the conclusion that you marked. The conclusion is that you can know the route and still not be able to draw a map. This choice is saying that if you can draw a map, then you must "be familiar" with the route. What does this mean, "be familiar?" That's different from "knowing" the route. This choice doesn't support the conclusion.

So we're left with choices A and D. After going through the other answer choices, we've got a much more precise idea of the scope of the argument and of what would support the conclusion. There's nothing in the argument at all about any "assignment" or about the issue of "effort." Those issues are out of the scope. So, by using POE, we found the ETS answer, choice D. It's not thrilling, but it's the best answer.

WEAKENING ARGUMENTS

To weaken an argument, **don't attack the conclusion** directly. Attack a premise or an assumption on which the conclusion is based.

To weaken, find the assumption in the argument and attack it.

10. The Federal Communications Commission (FCC) should not be permitted to regulate the content of television programs. If viewers don't like what they see, they can always change the channel or turn off the set. What offends one viewer may not offend another. People can decide for themselves whether a particular broadcast is offensive.

All of the following, if true, weaken the argument above, EXCEPT:

(A) Some people, such as children, are unable to decide matters of offensiveness for themselves.
(B) The FCC is fully capable of monitoring all the television stations in the country.
(C) A person encountering offensive broadcast material in a public place might not be able to change the channel.
(D) The ability to change channels is beside the point if the viewer has already been harmed by offensive material.
(E) Although standards of decency vary from region to region, there is general agreement on what is grossly offensive

> Down to two choices? Reread the question. Then go back to the conclusion of the argument. Which answer choice is WORSE?

The first step is to look at the question. It looks like a weaken question. But this is an EXCEPT question. That means that what we are really looking for is a choice that *doesn't* weaken the argument. But be careful! That *doesn't* necessarily mean that the ETS answer will strengthen the argument. It might not weaken the argument because it's out of the scope.

Because we need to find a choice that doesn't weaken the argument's conclusion, we need to make sure that we know what the argument's conclusion *is*. The author's conclusion is that the content of television programs should not be regulated.

Why? The content of television programs should not be regulated because (1) no one is forced to watch, (2) everyone has different standards, and (3) people can make up their own minds.

What is the argument assuming? It's assuming that if you see something you decide is offensive, you won't be harmed by it since you can change the channel, and that there is nothing that's offensive to everyone.

Remind yourself what you're looking for: a choice that doesn't make the argument less believable. That means that we can eliminate any choice that weakens the argument. Let's look at the choices one at a time:

(A) Does this weaken the argument? Yes, it does, by contradicting the premise that people can decide for themselves whether a broadcast is offensive. Eliminate.

(B) Does this weaken the argument? No. It is irrelevant to the argument. A possibility.

(C) Does this weaken the argument? Yes, it does, by undermining the premise that no one is forced to watch an offensive broadcast. Eliminate.

(D) Does this weaken the argument? Yes, it does, by undermining one of the assumptions. Eliminate.

(E) Does this weaken the argument? Yes, it does, by contradicting the assumption that there is nothing that is offensive to everyone. Eliminate.

ETS's answer is choice B.

SUMMARY

1. Read the question first. The question tells you what to look for in the passage, and how to approach it.

2. Read the passage.

3. Find the conclusion and mark it (and, if necessary, the premises and any assumptions).

4. Answer the question in your own words (especially on conclusion, assumption, and strengthening/weakening questions).

5. Use Process of Elimination (POE) to eliminate wrong answer choices.

   ◆ Eliminate answer choices that are outside the scope of the passage.

   ◆ On conclusion, assumption, and inference questions, eliminate answer choices that use extreme language.

FINAL THOUGHTS ON ARGUMENTS

Always do the first three arguments, if there are only six arguments in the section, or do the first six arguments if there are nine arguments in the section. Don't worry about the last three arguments at the end of the section. Games make up a much greater part of your analytic score.

PART ◆ V

The GRE Subject Tests

MORE BAD NEWS

In addition to the GRE General Test, many graduate school departments require or strongly recommend that you take a GRE Subject Test. Check with each of the departments at each of the graduate schools you are applying to for the names of the specific tests you have to take.

SIXTEEN SUBJECT TESTS

While the GRE purports to measure academic aptitude, the Subject Tests measure what you know. They're not much different from the Achievement or SAT II Tests you took back in high school—except that they're much more difficult.

Here is a list of the Subject Test areas:

1. Biochemistry, Cell and Molecular Biology
2. Biology
3. Chemistry
4. Computer Science
5. Economics
6. Education (discontinued after April 1998)
7. Engineering
8. Geology
9. History
10. Literature in English
11. Mathematics
12. Music
13. Physics
14. Political Science (discontinued after April 1998)
15. Psychology
16. Sociology

Each Subject Test is two hours and fifty minutes long, but the number of questions varies considerably. The Literature in English Test, for example, has 230 questions. That works out to less than a minute per question. The Engineering Test, however, has 144 questions. That works out to more than a minute a question. Of course, the engineering questions can take a lot longer to work out than the literature questions.

Just couldn't get enough standardized testing, eh?

PRACTICE MATERIALS

As with the General Test, the best way to prepare for the Subject Test is with actual tests. Fortunately, ETS currently offers full-length practice tests for most of the sixteen subjects. You can order any of these from ETS or look for them in a college bookstore. Each test is about $10, but prices vary. Here's the address:

> Graduate Record Examinations
> Educational Testing Service
> CN 6014
> Princeton, NJ 08541-6014

Free topic outlines and sample questions are available for the subject tests. If you're in a hurry, you can call the GRE publications office at 1-609-771-7243.

PREPARING FOR A SUBJECT TEST

Lack of practice material is a problem, so you'll have to make do with what's available.

Check out The Princeton Review's *Cracking the GRE Subject Test* series.

Send away for the Subject Test you'll be taking as soon as you can. If you need a lot of work in certain areas, you want to know this well in advance of the test. If there is no practice test for that particular subject, send away for the free sample questions.

Read the introductory material carefully, especially the outline of the test content. This will tell you the topics covered, and their relative importance. If there is no practice test, do the sample questions carefully. They're all you've got to go on.

If your subject offers a full-length practice test, use it as a diagnostic as soon as you get it.

STEP 1:   Take the test *timed*. Be sure to use the answer sheet.

STEP 2:   When the time limit is up, switch to a different-color pen or pencil and attempt any questions you didn't get to.

STEP 3:   Mark the test. When marking the questions, do *not* put down the correct answer. Simply "x" your errors for now.

STEP 4:   Score the questions you did during the time limit.

STEP 5:   Have another go at any questions you got wrong.

Once the test is over, tally your errors according to subject matter. For example, you may be fine in organic chemistry but need to review inorganic chemistry.

Scoring

For some esoteric reason known only to ETS psychometricians, the scaling on some Subject Tests is from 200 to 990. Don't ask us why. The important indicator is your percentile ranking. The scale for percentiles varies from test to test.

Some of the Subject Tests report subscore percentiles. For example, the Psychology Test reports percentiles for two categories: experimental psychology and social psychology. If you take this test, you'll receive an overall score, an overall percentile, and two subscore percentiles.

A more important difference is that unlike the General GRE, the Subject GREs subtract a quarter-point for errors. This means that random guessing probably won't affect your score much one way or the other.

To Guess or Not to Guess

If you lose a quarter-point for each error, when should you guess?

Some students have heard that they should never guess unless they can eliminate three choices and narrow down the selection to two choices. This is incorrect.

The best way to look at guessing is this: If you leave a question blank, you'll lose credit for a full question. If you guess, you have a chance to save that question, while if answering it incorrectly, you lose only another quarter of a point. **Here's the bottom line: If you can eliminate a single choice on a particular question, the odds favor guessing. Go for it!**

But Don't Try to Finish

The Subject Tests are much tougher than the General GRE. Unless you're scoring in the 99.9th percentile range, you won't have time to analyze every question. (Of course, if you do spend time on a question, you should be prepared to guess.)

Pacing is especially important on these exams. You'd be surprised how quickly 170 minutes can pass. Since you won't have time to analyze each question, where should you spend your time? In other words, which questions should you skip?

You'll have to be the judge. **The questions on the Subject Tests are not in order of difficulty.**

The fourth question on the Education Test might very well be the most difficult question on the test. You have no way of telling, other than by using general considerations. If a question looks longish, or covers a subject you're not familiar with, skip it for now. If you've got time at the end of the test—and you probably won't have much—return to the longer questions.

How many questions can you skip and still do well? It depends on how many questions you get right, but there's a rule of thumb for the Subject Tests: **If you answer two-thirds of the questions correctly, you'll be scoring better than 90 percent of the students taking the test.**

For example, on the Biology Test there are 210 questions. You could leave forty questions blank, get twenty-five questions wrong, and still score in the 90th percentile. Remember that when you're taking the test. Move quickly, but don't panic if you're not finishing.

PART VI

Answer Key to Drills

CHAPTER 7

DRILL 1
(pages 58–59)

1. A needle pulls thread.
2. Vernal means having to do with spring.
3. A breach is a rift in a dam.
4. Unrelated. Dogs and cats are both pets, but there is no relationship *between* them.
5. To be steadfast is not to vacillate.
6. A scintilla is a minuscule amount.
7. To calumniate is to ruin the reputation of.
8. Unrelated.
9. To be mordant is to be bitingly witty.
10. Mendacity is not telling the truth.
11. To be impertinent is not to be apposite.
12. A felony is a major infraction.
13. A door is an opening in a wall.
14. Unrelated.
15. A sanctuary provides protection.
16. To be flustered is to lack composure.
17. To malinger is not to work.
18. To have timorousness is not to be intrepid.
19. Unrelated.
20. Unrelated.
21. Filings are small pieces of metal.
22. A neophyte is characterized by inexperience.
23. A gaggle is a group of geese.
24. Unrelated.
25. Fervor is a lot of emotion.
26. To stultify is to make stupid.
27. Stratification is arrangement in layers.
28. What is ineluctable is impossible to avoid.
29. To be lethargic is to be impossible to stimulate.
30. Unrelated.
31. A log is a kind of fuel.
32. A carapace is the shell of a turtle.
33. To do something with stealth is to do it without detection.
34. Unrelated.
35. Something fortuitous happens without planning.
36. To ruminate is to engage in meditation.
37. To be vindictive is to seek revenge.
38. To be coltish is to lack discipline.
39. Vernacular is ordinary language.
40. Unrelated.
41. An arsenal is a store of weapons.
42. Obscurity is absence of light.
43. To be venal is to be corruptible by money.
44. To be tortuous means to have curves.
45. An illicit act is without legality.
46. To be histrionic is to be overly dramatic.
47. To glaze is to put glass in a window.
48. A voter is a participant in an election.
49. A manacle restrains freedom.
50. Something empirical is based on observations.

Chapter 8

DRILL 1
(page 74)

2. The clue is *dragged on for over a year*. The word "despite" is a trigger word that shows change in direction. More on this shortly. Anticipated words: *reasonableness, fairness, mildness*.

4. The clue is *excessively detailed and academic*. Here are some words you might have anticipated: *academic detail, pedantry, scholarship*.

DRILL 2
(page 74)

2. D

4. A

Chapter 12

DRILL 1
(page 134)

1. For example, –4, –3, –2

2. For example, 3, 5, 7

3. 11

4. –5

5. 3

6. 5,847

7. For example, 347

8. Two: 5 and 7

9. 4 (simply subtract 5 from the units digit)

10. 1

11. 21

12. odd

13. even

14. $2 \times 2 \times 3 \times 3$

15. positive

16. –2

17. 215

18. 52

19. 50

20. 16

Chapter 13

Drill 1
(page 141)

1. a. $\dfrac{1}{4}$

   b. $\dfrac{3}{4}$

   c. $\dfrac{1}{3}$

   d. $\dfrac{3}{2}$

   e. $\dfrac{13}{8}$

   f. $\dfrac{4}{9}$, can't be reduced

2. a $\dfrac{7}{15}$

   b. $-\dfrac{1}{8}$

   c. $\dfrac{1}{2}$

   d. $1\dfrac{1}{12}$

   e. $\dfrac{1}{12}$

   f. $\dfrac{3}{2}$

3. $\dfrac{8}{9}$

4. $\dfrac{22}{3}$

5. 12

Drill 2
(page 145)

1. 6.165
2. 5.28
3. 11.325
4. 45.3
5. 1.92
6. .304
7. .002
8. 6.5
9. $\dfrac{1}{8}$
10. approximately $\dfrac{1}{2}$

Chapter 14

Drill 1
(page 152)

1. $x=2$
2. $x=1$
3. $x=2$
4. $x=1/2$
5. $x=16$
6. $x=4/9$
7. $x=1/3$
8. $(2 \times 4)+(2 \times 20)$
9. $17(46-12-99)$
10. $xy-xz$
11. $a(b+c+d)$
12. $x(yz-vw)$

Chapter 17

DRILL 1
(page 176)

1. 60
2. 50%
3. 11
4. 12
5. 200

DRILL 2
(page 181)

1. 28.4
2. 100
3. 96
4. 27
5. 85

Chapter 20

DRILL 1
(page 200)

1. 3^6, or 729
2. 216
3. 16^3, or 4,096
4. 5 or –5
5. Approximately 3

Chapter 21

DRILL 1
(pages 217–220)

1. $b = 140°$
2. $c = 125°$
3. $AB = 20$
4. $c = 90°$
5. triangle = 11

   rectangle = 14
6. triangle = 16

   rectangle = 24
7. 10
8. approximately 18
9. approximately 27
10. volume = 200 cubic inches
11. $A = (3, 4)$

    $B = (4, –4)$

    $C = (–6, –5)$

    $D = (–15, 5)$

Chapter 23

DRILL 1
(page 235)

1. B B B B W W W R R

2. B...E

3. $\boxed{\text{CS}}\,/\,\boxed{\text{SC}}$

4. $\boxed{\text{DM}}$ (crossed out)

5. F→G

6. $\boxed{\text{B...W}}$ (crossed out)

7. D→P

8. $\boxed{\text{AP}}$ (crossed out)

9. $\boxed{\text{OL}}\,/\,\boxed{\text{LO}}$

10. $U_1 \rightarrow \sim Z_1$

PART ◆ VII

The Princeton Review
Diagnostic Test

SECTION 1
Time—30 minutes
30 Questions

Numbers: All numbers used are real numbers.

Figures: Position of points, angles, regions, etc. can be assumed to be in the order shown; and angle measures can be assumed to be positive.

Lines shown as straight can be assumed to be straight.

Figures can be assumed to lie in a plane unless otherwise indicated.

Figures that accompany questions are intended to provide information useful in answering the questions. However, unless a note states that a figure is drawn to scale, you should solve these problems NOT by estimating sizes by sight or by measurement, but by using your knowledge of mathematics (see Example 2 below).

Directions: Each of the Questions 1-15 consists of two quantities, one in Column A and one in Column B. You are to compare the two quantities and choose

- A   if the quantity in Column A is greater;
- B   if the quantity in Column B is greater;
- C   if the two quantities are equal;
- D   if the relationship cannot be determined from the information given.

Note: Since there are only four choices, NEVER MARK (E).

Common Information: In a question, information concerning one or both of the quantities to be compared is centered above the two columns. A symbol that appears in both columns represents the same thing in Column A as it does in Column B.

Column A	Column B	Sample Answers

Example 1: 2×6 $2 + 6$ ● Ⓑ Ⓒ Ⓓ Ⓔ

Examples 2-4 refer to $\triangle PQR$.

Example 2: PN NQ Ⓐ Ⓑ Ⓒ ● Ⓔ

(since equal measures cannot be assumed, even though PN and NQ appear equal)

Example 3: x y Ⓐ ● Ⓒ Ⓓ Ⓔ

(since N is between P and Q)

Example 4: $w + z$ 180 Ⓐ Ⓑ ● Ⓓ Ⓔ

(since PQ is a straight line)

GO ON TO THE NEXT PAGE.

A   if the quantity in Column A is greater;
B   if the quantity in Column B is greater;
C   if the two quantities are equal;
D   if the relationship cannot be determined from the information given.

Column A	Column B
1. $4[(3 + 3) + 4]$	45

a and *b* are each greater than 1.

Column A	Column B
2. $3ab$	$(3a)(3b)$

Column A	Column B
3. $\dfrac{5}{9}$	$\dfrac{4}{7}$

Column A	Column B
4. $4(2^6)$	$6(4^2)$

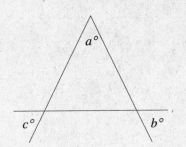

Column A	Column B
5. $b + c$	$180 - a$

Column A	Column B

Mr. Jones purchased a new bedroom set by using an extended payment plan. The regular price of the set was $900, but on the payment plan he paid $300 up front and 9 monthly payments of $69 each.

Column A	Column B
6. $23	The amount Mr. Jones paid in addition to the regular price of the bedroom set

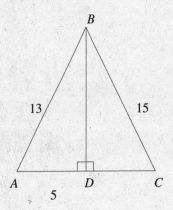

Column A	Column B
7. The perimeter of triangle *BCD*	42

Column A	Column B
8. $\dfrac{1}{5} + \dfrac{1}{7}$	$\dfrac{1}{9} + \dfrac{1}{4}$

GO ON TO THE NEXT PAGE.

A   if the quantity in Column A is greater;
B   if the quantity in Column B is greater;
C   if the two quantities are equal;
D   if the relationship cannot be determined from the information given.

Column A	Column B

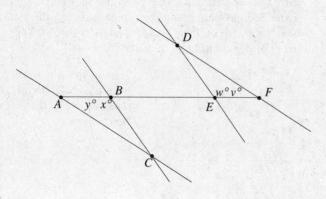

$BC \parallel DE$

9. $x + y$ $w + v$

10. The average (arith-   The average (arith-
    metic mean) of 7, 3,   metic mean) of $2a + 5$,
    4, and 2 $4a$, and $7 - 6a$

11. $\sqrt{7} + \sqrt{11}$ $\sqrt{3} + \sqrt{15}$

Column A	Column B

Questions 12-13 refer to the following number line.

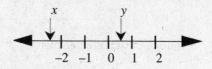

12. $-x$ $2y$

13. $x + 2y$ $2y - x$

$$\sqrt{4r} = 6 \text{ and } s^2 = 81$$

14. r s

15. $7^{15} - 7^{14}$ $7^{14}(6)$

GO ON TO THE NEXT PAGE.

Directions: Each of the Questions 16-30 has five answer choices. For each of these questions, select the best of the answer choices given.

16. What is the remainder when 117 is divided by 3?

(A) 3
(B) 2
(C) 1
(D) $\frac{1}{3}$
(E) 0

17. The price of a certain stock increased 8 points, then decreased 13 points, and then increased 9 points. If the stock price before the changes was x points, which of the following was the stock price, in points, after the changes?

(A) $x - 5$
(B) $x - 4$
(C) $x + 4$
(D) $x + 5$
(E) $x + 8$

18. If $x = 1$, then $\left(2 - \frac{1}{2-x}\right)\left(2 - \frac{1}{3-x}\right)\left(2 - \frac{1}{4-x}\right) =$

(A) $\frac{1}{6}$
(B) $\frac{5}{6}$
(C) $\frac{5}{2}$
(D) $\frac{10}{3}$
(E) $\frac{7}{2}$

19. If $s = 4r$ and $t = 2s$, then, in terms of r, $3r + 2s + t =$

(A) r
(B) $6r$
(C) $7r$
(D) $8r$
(E) $19r$

20. What is the least number r for which $(3r + 2)(r - 3) = 0$?

(A) -3
(B) -2
(C) $-\frac{2}{3}$
(D) $\frac{2}{3}$
(E) 3

GO ON TO THE NEXT PAGE.

Questions 21-25 refer to the following charts.

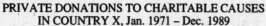

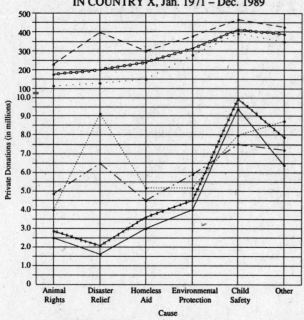

PRIVATE DONATIONS TO CHARITABLE CAUSES
IN COUNTRY X, Jan. 1971 – Dec. 1989

· · · · Jan. 1971 – April 1978
○-○-○-○ Feb. 1980 – Oct. 1984
– – – Sept. 1985 – Dec. 1989
——— Sept 1989
+ + + + Oct. 1989
· · · · · · Nov. 1989
– · – Dec. 1989

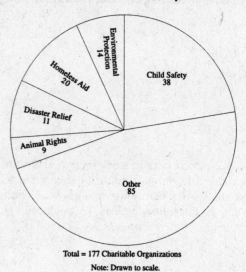

DISTRIBUTION OF CHARITABLE ORGANIZATIONS IN
COUNTRY X BY CAUSE, Sept. 1989

Total = 177 Charitable Organizations
Note: Drawn to scale.

21. Which of the following categories of charitable
causes received the third greatest amount in private
donations from January 1971 to April 1978?

(A) Disaster relief
(B) Homeless aid
(C) Environmental protection
(D) Child safety
(E) "Other" causes

GO ON TO THE NEXT PAGE.

22. If funds contributed to child safety organizations in September 1989 were distributed evenly to those organizations, approximately how much did each charity receive?

(A) $12,000,000
(B) $9,400,000
(C) $2,500,000
(D) $250,000
(E) $38,000

23. From February 1980 to October 1984, 13% of all private donations to disaster relief causes went to the Southeastern Hurricane Relief Organization. Approximately how many millions in private donations did the Southeastern Hurricane Relief Organization receive from February 1980 to October 1984?

(A) 9
(B) 13
(C) 18
(D) 26
(E) 200

24. From September 1985 to December 1989, what was the approximate ratio of private donations in millions to homeless aid to private donations in millions to animal rights?

(A) 20:9
(B) 3:2
(C) 4:3
(D) 9:7
(E) 6:5

25. Which of the following charitable causes received the smallest percent increase in private donations from September 1989 to October 1989?

(A) Animal rights
(B) Disaster relief
(C) Homeless aid
(D) Environmental protection
(E) Child safety

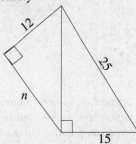

26. What is the value of n in the figure above?

(A) 9
(B) 15
(C) 16
(D) $12\sqrt{3}$
(E) 20

GO ON TO THE NEXT PAGE.

27. If $2 < r < 8$ and $1 < s < \frac{5}{2}$, which of the following expresses all possible values of rs?

    (A) $1 < rs < 5$

    (B) $2 < rs < 20$

    (C) $\frac{5}{2} < rs < 8$

    (D) $\frac{5}{2} < rs < 20$

    (E) $5 < rs < 10$

28. What is the perimeter, in centimeters, of a rectangular newspaper ad 14 centimeters wide that has the same area as a rectangular newspaper ad 52 centimeters long and 28 centimeters wide?

    (A) 80
    (B) 118
    (C) 160
    (D) 208
    (E) 236

29. A pipe of length x inches is cut into two segments so that the length of one segment is two inches more than three times the length of the other segment. Which of the following is the length, in inches, of the longer segment?

    (A) $\frac{x+4}{3}$

    (B) $\frac{3x+2}{3}$

    (C) $\frac{x-2}{4}$

    (D) $\frac{3x+5}{4}$

    (E) $\frac{3x+2}{4}$

30. For all real numbers x and y, if $x \star y = x(x - y)$, then $x \star (x \star y) =$

    (A) $x^2 - xy$
    (B) $x^2 - 2xy$
    (C) $x^3 - x^2 - xy$
    (D) $x^3 - (xy)^2$
    (E) $x^2 - x^3 + x^2y$

S T O P

IF YOU FINISH BEFORE TIME IS CALLED, YOU MAY CHECK YOUR WORK ON THIS SECTION ONLY.
DO NOT WORK ON ANY OTHER SECTION IN THE TEST.

NO TEST MATERIAL ON THIS PAGE

SECTION 2

Time—30 Minutes

38 Questions

Directions: Each sentence below has one or two blanks, each blank indicating that something has been omitted. Beneath the sentence are five lettered words or sets of words. Choose the word or set of words for each blank that best fits the meaning of the sentence as a whole.

1. It is the concern of many ecologists that the "greenhouse effect" is changing many of the Earth's ------ weather patterns into ------ systems, unable to be accurately forecast by those who study them.

   (A) predictable . . erratic
   (B) steady . . growing
   (C) uncertain . . uncanny
   (D) chaotic . . unforeseeable
   (E) weighty . . unbounded

2. Children, after more than a generation of television, have become "hasty viewers"; as a result, if the camera lags, the attention of these young viewers ------.

   (A) expands
   (B) starts
   (C) alternates
   (D) wanes
   (E) clarifies

3. Many of the troubles and deficiencies in otherwise thriving foreign enterprises are ------ ignored or diminished by the author of the article in order to ------ the ways in which other businesses might attempt to imitate them.

   (A) unintentionally . . overstate
   (B) deliberately . . stress
   (C) intermittently . . equalize
   (D) willfully . . confound
   (E) brilliantly . . illustrate

4. Frequently a copyright holder's property, published articles for example, is reproduced repeatedly in the absence of ------ for its reproduction, an action ----- by long-standing practice.

   (A) validation . . provoked
   (B) recognition . . forecast
   (C) payment . . licensed
   (D) accommodation . . instigated
   (E) allowance . . aggravated

5. The ------ of early metaphysicians' efforts to decipher the workings of the universe led some later thinkers to question the ------ of man's intellectual capabilities.

   (A) strain . . roots
   (B) intent . . superiority
   (C) intricacy . . realization
   (D) prevarications . . deceptiveness
   (E) failings . . adeptness

6. Being gracious should not be mistaken for a ------ characteristic of men's personalities; it is instead a fundamental virtue, one whose very state of being is increasingly ------ by the fashionable directive to "say what you feel."

   (A) trivial . . imperiled
   (B) pervading . . undermined
   (C) frivolous . . averted
   (D) superior . . renounced
   (E) immaterial . . influenced

7. While some individuals think that the purpose of sarcastic remarks is to disturb, by turning all communication into ------, other people see sarcastic remarks as a desire for supremacy in miniature over an environment that appears too ------.

   (A) chaos . . perplexed
   (B) equivalence . . confused
   (C) discord . . amiable
   (D) pandemonium . . disorderly
   (E) similarity . . upset

GO ON TO THE NEXT PAGE.

Directions: In each of the following questions, a related pair of words or phrases is followed by five lettered pairs of words or phrases. Select the lettered pair that best expresses a relationship similar to that expressed in the original pair.

8. CHOREOGRAPHER : DANCE ::

    (A) connoisseur : art
    (B) composer : music
    (C) acrobat : height
    (D) athlete : contest
    (E) virtuoso : skill

9. SCOWL : DISPLEASURE ::

    (A) sing : praise
    (B) kiss : affection
    (C) confess : crime
    (D) irritate : anger
    (E) hurl : disgust

10. GOGGLES : EYES ::

    (A) tie : neck
    (B) gloves : hands
    (C) elbow : arm
    (D) braid : hair
    (E) splint : leg

11. DRAWL : SPEAK ::

    (A) spurt : expel
    (B) foster : develop
    (C) scintillate : flash
    (D) pare : trim
    (E) saunter : walk

12. ARBORETUM : TREE ::

    (A) dam : water
    (B) planetarium : star
    (C) apiary : bee
    (D) museum : painting
    (E) forum : speech

13. SUBTERFUGE : DECEIVE ::

    (A) decanter : pour
    (B) interview : hire
    (C) account : save
    (D) outpost : protect
    (E) film : view

14. RATIFY : APPROVAL ::

    (A) mutate : change
    (B) pacify : conquest
    (C) duel : combat
    (D) appeal : authority
    (E) tribulate : opinion

15. SOPORIFIC : SLEEP ::

    (A) conductor : electricity
    (B) syncopation : beat
    (C) provocation : debate
    (D) coagulant : blood
    (E) astringent : pucker

16. METTLESOME : COURAGE ::

    (A) audacious : tenacity
    (B) mediocre : originality
    (C) ludicrous : inanity
    (D) dubious : suspiciousness
    (E) altruistic : donation

GO ON TO THE NEXT PAGE.

Directions: Each passage in this group is followed by questions based on its content. After reading a passage, choose the best answer to each question. Answer all questions following a passage on the basis of what is stated or implied in that passage.

Although the study of women's history has only been developed as an academic discipline in the last twenty years, it is not the case that the current wave
Line of feminist activity is the first in which interest in
(5) women's past was manifest. From its very beginnings, the nineteenth-century English women's movement sought to expand existing knowledge of the activities and achievements of women in the past. At the same time, like its American counterpart, the
(10) English women's movement had a powerful sense of its own historic importance and of its relationship to wider social and political change.

Nowhere is this sense of the historical importance—and of the historical connections between the
(15) women's movement and other social and political developments—more evident than in Ray Strachey's classic account of the movement, *The Cause*. "The true history of the Women's Movement," Strachey argues, "is the whole history of the nineteenth
(20) century." The women's movement was part of the broad sweep of liberal and progressive reform which was transforming society. Strachey emphasized this connection between the women's movement and the broader sweep of history by highlighting the impor-
(25) tance for it of the Enlightenment and the Industrial Revolution. The protest made by the women's movement at the confinement and injustices faced by women was, in Strachey's view, part of the liberal attack on traditional prejudices and injustice. This
(30) critique of women's confinement was supplemented by the demand for recognition of women's role in the public, particularly the philanthropic, realm. Indeed, it was the criticism of the limitations faced by women on the one hand, and their establishment of a new
(35) public role on the other hand, which provided the core of the movement, determining also its form: its organization around campaigns for legal, political and social reform.

Strachey's analysis was a very illuminating one,
(40) nowhere more so than in her insistence that, despite their differences and even antipathy to each other, both the radical Mary Wollstonecraft and evangelical Hannah More need to be seen as forerunners of the mid-Victorian feminism. At the same time, she
(45) omitted some issues which now seem crucial to any discussion of the context of Victorian feminism. Where Strachey pictured a relatively fixed image of domestic women throughout the first half of the nineteenth century, recent historical and literary
(50) works suggest that this image was both complex and unstable. The establishment of a separate domestic sphere for women was but one aspect of the enormous change in sexual and familial relationships which were occurring from the late eighteenth
(55) century through to the mid nineteenth. These changes were accompanied by both anxiety and by uncertainty and by the constant articulation of women's duty in a new social world.

17. The primary purpose of the passage is to

(A) present an overview of the economic changes that led to the English women's movement
(B) evaluate a view of the English women's movement as presented in a literary work
(C) describe the social and political context of the women's movement in England
(D) offer a novel analysis of England's reaction to the women's movement
(E) profile several of the women who were instrumental in the success of the English women's movement.

18. Which of the following is the best description of Ray Strachey's work, *The Cause*?

(A) A historical analysis of a social movement
(B) A critique of an important feminist text
(C) A feminist revision of accepted history
(D) A novel written as social commentary
(E) A treatise on women's issues in the 1900s

19. The passage contains information to answer all of the following questions EXCEPT

(A) In what respect were the goals of the women's movement in England similar to those of the women's movement in America?
(B) How were the emphases of the women's movement compatible with the liberal ideals of nineteenth-century England?
(C) In what way was the political orientation of Mary Wollstonecraft different from that of Ray Strachey?
(D) By what means did participants in the women's movement in England seek to achieve their goals?
(E) What historical movements were taking place at the same time as the women's movement in England?

GO ON TO THE NEXT PAGE.

20. The author includes Strachey's claim that "the true history of the Women's Movement . . . is the whole history of the nineteenth century" (lines 17-20) in order to emphasize

   (A) Strachey's belief that the advancement of women's rights was the most significant development of its century
   (B) the importance Strachey attributes to the women's movement in bringing about the Enlightenment
   (C) Strachey's awareness of the interconnection of the women's movement and other societal changes in the 1800s
   (D) Strachey's contention that the women's movement, unlike other social and political developments of the time, actually transformed society
   (E) Strachey's argument that the nineteenth century must play a role in any criticism of the limitations of women

21. While the author acknowledges Strachey's importance in the study of women's history, she faults Strachey for

   (A) focusing her study on the legal and political reform enacted by the women's movement
   (B) oversimplifying her conception of the social condition of women prior to the reforms of the women's movement
   (C) failing to eliminate the anachronistic idea of "women's duty" from her articulation of nineteenth-century feminism
   (D) omitting Mary Wollstonecraft and Hannah More from her discussion of important influences in feminism
   (E) recommending a static and domestic social role for women following the women's movement

22. Which of the following best describes the structure of the final paragraph?

   (A) The author acknowledges Strachey's accomplishment, indicates an oversight in Strachey's work and asserts her own view regarding that oversight.
   (B) The author offers an argument in favor of Strachey's position, presents an example to support that argument and concludes by discussing the theory's relevance to modern times.
   (C) The author presents a summary of Strachey's thesis, introduces a counterargument to that thesis and reconciles the difference between them.
   (D) The author contrasts the theories of two prominent feminists, places those theories in the context of Strachey's and posits an opinion about those theories as a whole.
   (E) The author introduces two forerunners of mid-Victorian feminism, describes their theories, and exposes the flaws inherent in their reasoning.

23. The author's attitude toward Strachey's analysis is one of

   (A) qualified admiration
   (B) optimistic enthusiasm
   (C) extreme criticism
   (D) studied impartiality
   (E) intellectual curiosity

24. Which of the following, if true, would most weaken the author's assertion about the similarity between the English and American women's movements?

   (A) The English and American women's movements took place in very different sociohistorical climates.
   (B) The English women's movement began almost a century before the American women's movement.
   (C) The English women's movement excluded men, while the American women's movement did not.
   (D) Few members of the English women's movement were aware of the impact it would have on society.
   (E) Many participants in the English women's movement continued to perform traditional domestic roles.

GO ON TO THE NEXT PAGE.

Following the discovery in 1895 that malaria is carried by *Anopheles* mosquitoes, governments around the world set out to eradicate those insect
Line vectors. In Europe the relation between the malarial
(5) agent, protozoan blood parasites of the genus *Plasmodium*, and the vector mosquito, *Anopheles maculipennis*, seemed at first inconsistent. In some localities the mosquito was abundant but malaria rare or absent, while in others the reverse was true. In
(10) 1934 the problem was solved. Entomologists discovered that *A. maculipennis* is not a single species but a group of at least seven.

In outward appearance the adult mosquitoes seem almost identical, but in fact they are marked by a host
(15) of distinctive biological traits, some of which prevent them from hybridizing. Some of the species distinguished by these traits were found to feed on human blood and thus to carry the malarial parasites. Once identified, the dangerous members of the *A.*
(20) *maculipennis* complex could be targeted and eradicated.

25. Which of the following best expresses the author's main point in the passage above?

(A) With the increasing density of the human population, it will become increasingly necessary to reduce populations of other species.

(B) Without an understanding of the seven groups of *A. maculipennis* mosquitos, eradication of malaria will be unlikely.

(C) Despite the eradication of large numbers of *Plasmodium*-carrying mosquitos, malaria is still a significant problem in certain localities.

(D) After establishing the relationship between *Plasmodium* and the vector mosquito, scientists discovered that *Anopheles* mosquitos carried malaria.

(E) To eradicate an insect disease vector, it was necessary to have a scientific understanding of that vector.

26. Which of the following best describes the reason that scientists were initially perplexed at the discovery that malaria was spread by *Anopheles* mosquitoes?

(A) Scientists had evidence that malaria was carried by the protozoan blood parasite *Plasmodium*.

(B) Scientists felt that because so many species of *Anopheles* existed they could not be carriers.

(C) Scientists were unable to find a direct correlation between *Anopheles* density and frequency of malaria occurrence.

(D) Scientists knew that many species of *Anopheles* mosquito did not feed on human blood.

(E) Scientists believed that the *Anopheles* mosquito could not be host to the parasite *Plasmodium*.

27. It can be inferred from the passage that a mosquito becomes a carrier of malaria when

(A) it ingests the blood of a human being infected with malaria

(B) it lives in regions where malaria is widespread

(C) it consumes blood from a protozoan malarial agent

(D) it has extended contact with other insect vectors

(E) it is spawned in *Plasmodium*-infested localities

GO ON TO THE NEXT PAGE.

Directions: Each question below consists of a word printed in capital letters, followed by five lettered words or phrases. Choose the lettered word or phrase that is most nearly opposite in meaning to the word in capital letters.

Since some of the questions require you to distinguish fine shades of meaning, be sure to consider all the choices before deciding which one is best.

28. SLUR:
   (A) honor agreements
   (B) settle disputes
   (C) pronounce clearly
   (D) criticize directly
   (E) exclude purposefully

29. MORATORIUM:
   (A) lack of emotion
   (B) discouragement
   (C) savings
   (D) brilliance
   (E) period of activity

30. DIFFUSE:
   (A) compare
   (B) chill
   (C) concentrate
   (D) blemish
   (E) oscillate

31. THWART:
   (A) aid
   (B) beseech
   (C) dislocate
   (D) assign
   (E) allege

32. AGITATE:
   (A) relieve
   (B) satisfy
   (C) reject
   (D) condense
   (E) confirm

33. AUTHENTICATE:
   (A) sentence
   (B) disseminate
   (C) scrutinize
   (D) theorize
   (E) discredit

34. ACCLIMATION:
   (A) alienation
   (B) adoration
   (C) facilitation
   (D) invigoration
   (E) exaltation

35. TENUOUSLY:
   (A) having a strong basis
   (B) following a formal procedure
   (C) having overall consensus
   (D) with evil intent
   (E) under loose supervision

36. FLORID:
   (A) pallid
   (B) vapid
   (C) lucid
   (D) rancid
   (E) candid

37. FACTIOUS:
   (A) totally generic
   (B) openly welcomed
   (C) closely observable
   (D) seriously rejected
   (E) given to agreement

38. MISCIBLE:
   (A) likely to agree
   (B) hard to please
   (C) generous
   (D) desirable
   (E) not capable of being mixed

STOP

IF YOU FINISH BEFORE TIME IS CALLED, YOU MAY CHECK YOUR WORK ON THIS SECTION ONLY.
DO NOT WORK ON ANY OTHER SECTION IN THE TEST.

SECTION 3

Time—30 Minutes

25 Questions

Directions: Each question or group of questions is based on a passage or set of conditions. In answering some of the questions, it may be useful to draw a rough diagram. For each question, select the best answer choice given.

Questions 1-5

A two-way messenger system exists between the following departments in a corporation:

F and G, F and H, H and K, K and M, K and N, M and J, and J and L.

There is also a one-way messenger system between department J and department G; the possible direction of transit is from J to G.

None of these messenger routes intersect each other except at the departments.

There are no other departments or messenger routes in the corporation.

Messengers must follow the direction established for transit between departments.

1. To send a message from L to G by messenger, it is necessary for the messenger to travel through department

(A) F
(B) J
(C) K
(D) M
(E) N

2. If a broken elevator temporarily makes the route between H and K unusable, then in order to send a message to F by messenger from N, a messenger would have to go through how many other departments besides F and N?

(A) 2
(B) 3
(C) 4
(D) 5
(E) 6

3. If the hallway between H and K is being resurfaced, making the route unusable, a messenger would NOT be able to travel from

(A) G to F
(B) G to L
(C) J to M
(D) J to L
(E) K to F

4. If a broken elevator affects the route from K to M, making it possible for a messenger to travel in only one direction from K to M, it will still be possible for a messenger to travel from J to

(A) G and/or L but not to F, H, K, M, or N
(B) G, L, and/or M but not to F, H, K, or N
(C) F, G, H, and/or M but not to L, K, or N
(D) F, H, K, L and/or M but not to G or N
(E) F, G, H, K, L, M, and/or N

5. Assume that building repairs make it possible for a messenger to travel from K to H, but not from H to K. It will then be possible for a messenger to travel between departments F, G, H, J, K, L, M, and N if which of the following temporary routes is erected?

(A) From F to N
(B) From J to K
(C) From L to K
(D) From L to N
(E) From M to N

GO ON TO THE NEXT PAGE.

6. For five years, while remodeling the town zoo, the Littleton parks commission has been transferring a large number of animals from the city of Littleton to both the Wambek and Starr King zoos in the city of Jefferson. It follows that when Littleton's zoo reopens next year, either Wambek or Starr King will have to be closed and their animal populations consolidated.

The author of the statements above assumes that

(A) The removal of the Littleton animals from the Wambek and Starr King zoos will leave one or both of these zoos considerably underpopulated.

(B) Littleton's remodeled zoo will not be large enough for the prospective animal population.

(C) The Littleton animals comprise only a small part of the total animal populations at both the Wambek and Starr King zoos.

(D) Incorporation of extra animals from Littleton has placed a tremendous burden on the resources of both the Wambek and Starr King zoos.

(E) Animals will not be sent between the Wambek and Starr King zoos in the next year.

7. A manmade plant hormone has been added to a section of a garden in order to ward off insect infestation. The designer of the hormone has asserted that the recent dearth of insects in that section of the garden demonstrates that the manmade plant hormone wards off insect infestation.

Which of the following, if true, would cast the greatest doubt on the designer's assertion?

(A) The recent dearth of insects in that section of the garden was not as complete as had been expected given the results derived in controlled experiments.

(B) Because the manmade plant hormone would ultimately be neutralized by soil erosion, more manmade plant hormones would need to be added to the garden every three months.

(C) A manmade plant hormone produced from different chemicals which had been developed by the designer at an earlier period was ineffective in warding off insect infestation.

(D) The recent dearth of insects in that section of the garden is the same as the recent dearth of insects in otherwise very similar sections of the garden without the manmade plant hormone.

(E) The recent dearth of insects in that section of the garden, even though substantial, is not yet sufficient to compensate for the plant loss in that section of the garden in the last year.

8. A higher level of safety in automotive braking mechanisms depends upon control by internal computer monitoring systems. Automotive braking mechanisms, to be safe, would have to pump in intervals, and determining that the brakes would compensate for all situations is impossible. Despite technological advances, every internal computer monitoring system has on use proved to have serious weaknesses which in certain circumstances would bring about significant failure.

Which of the following can be inferred from the statements above?

(A) If designers are diligent in planning the internal computer monitoring system to be used for automotive braking mechanisms, there is an exceptionally good chance that the braking mechanism will ensure a high level of safety if and when it is needed.

(B) Techniques for decreasing the number of errors in building internal computer monitoring systems will not be discovered.

(C) Automotive braking mechanisms will not function safely during pumping.

(D) Some method of control other than internal computer monitoring systems will have to be designed.

(E) The safety of automobile braking systems cannot be ensured during pumping.

GO ON TO THE NEXT PAGE.

Questions 9-15

A city planner is planning the layout of exactly six highway exits: Bainbridge, Crescent, Driscoll, Homer, Kimball, and Morrow. They are all to be placed on the same side of a highway, in positions numbered consecutively from 1 to 6. The arrangement of exits is subject to the following restrictions::

The Bainbridge exit must be placed before the Homer exit.
The Kimball exit must be placed before the Morrow exit.
The Crescent exit cannot be placed in position 1.
The Driscoll exit must be placed next to the Bainbridge exit.

9. Which of the following is an acceptable layout of exits, from positions 1 through 6, according to the restrictions above?

(A) Morrow, Bainbridge, Driscoll, Kimball, Homer, Crescent
(B) Crescent, Kimball, Morrow, Driscoll, Bainbridge, Homer
(C) Kimball, Crescent, Morrow, Homer, Driscoll, Bainbridge
(D) Bainbridge, Homer, Kimball, Morrow, Crescent, Driscoll
(E) Driscoll, Bainbridge, Kimball, Crescent, Homer, Morrow

10. If the Crescent exit is placed somewhere after the Homer exit, which of the following must be true?

(A) The Crescent exit is placed somewhere after the Bainbridge exit.
(B) The Crescent exit is placed somewhere after the Kimball exit.
(C) The Crescent exit is placed somewhere after the Morrow exit.
(D) The Homer exit is placed somewhere before the Kimball exit.
(E) The Homer exit is placed somewhere before the Driscoll exit.

11. If the Homer exit is placed somewhere before the Kimball exit, the Kimball exit could be placed in which of the following positions?

(A) 1
(B) 2
(C) 3
(D) 4
(E) 6

12. If the Morrow exit is placed somewhere before the Bainbridge exit, which of the following must be true?

(A) The Morrow exit is placed somewhere before the Crescent exit.
(B) The Morrow exit is placed somewhere before the Driscoll exit.
(C) The Bainbridge exit is placed somewhere before the Crescent exit.
(D) The Bainbridge exit is placed somewhere before the Driscoll exit.
(E) The Bainbridge exit is placed somewhere before the Kimball exit.

13. All of the following are possible orderings for the six exits EXCEPT

(A) Kimball, Morrow, Crescent, Driscoll, Bainbridge, Homer
(B) Kimball, Crescent, Morrow, Driscoll, Bainbridge, Homer
(C) Driscoll, Bainbridge, Kimball, Homer, Crescent, Morrow
(D) Kimball, Homer, Morrow, Driscoll, Bainbridge, Crescent
(E) Kimball, Driscoll, Bainbridge, Crescent, Homer, Morrow

14. If the Bainbridge exit is placed next to the Morrow exit, which of the following must be true?

(A) The Kimball exit is placed in position 1.
(B) The Crescent exit is placed in position 2.
(C) The Driscoll exit is placed in position 3.
(D) The Bainbridge exit is placed in position 4.
(E) The Morrow exit is placed in position 5.

15. If the Kimball exit is placed in position 5, how many logically possible orderings of all six exits are possible?

(A) 2
(B) 3
(C) 4
(D) 5
(E) 6

GO ON TO THE NEXT PAGE.

Questions 16-22

A catering company must schedule five different types of events within a seven-day period beginning on a Sunday and ending on the following Saturday. Exactly one event can be scheduled each day. The schedule must conform to the following conditions.

Two banquets are to be scheduled; the second banquet must be scheduled for the fourth day after the day of the first banquet.

Exactly one luncheon is to be scheduled.

Exactly one party is to be scheduled, and the party must be scheduled for either the day before or the day after the day of the first banquet.

Exactly one seminar is to be scheduled, and it must be scheduled on any day before the day of the second banquet.

Exactly one wedding is to be scheduled, and it must be scheduled for the third day after the day of the luncheon.

16. Any of the events could be scheduled for Sunday EXCEPT

(A) a banquet
(B) the luncheon
(C) the party
(D) the seminar
(E) the wedding

17. Which of the following is a possible schedule, including the day off, when no event is scheduled, for the six events from Sunday through Saturday?

(A) banquet, luncheon, party, seminar, banquet, wedding, day off
(B) luncheon, banquet, party, wedding, day off, banquet, seminar
(C) party, banquet, luncheon, seminar, wedding, banquet, day off
(D) party, banquet, seminar, luncheon, day off, banquet, wedding
(E) day off, banquet, luncheon, seminar, banquet, party, wedding

18. The day on which the luncheon is scheduled must be no more than how many days after the day scheduled for the first banquet?

(A) 1
(B) 2
(C) 3
(D) 4
(E) 5

19. The party could be scheduled for any of the following days EXCEPT

(A) Sunday
(B) Monday
(C) Tuesday
(D) Wednesday
(E) Thursday

20. If the luncheon is scheduled for Sunday, which of the following pairs of events CANNOT be scheduled for consecutive days?

(A) a banquet and the wedding
(B) the luncheon and a banquet
(C) the luncheon and the party
(D) the party and the seminar
(E) the party and the wedding

21. If no event is scheduled for Sunday, which of the following could be true?

(A) The luncheon is scheduled for the day before the day of the first banquet.
(B) The party is scheduled for the day before the day of the first banquet.
(C) The seminar is scheduled for the day before the day of the first banquet.
(D) The wedding is scheduled for the day before the day of the second banquet.
(E) The wedding is scheduled for the day after the day of the seminar.

22. If the party is scheduled for the day before the day of the first banquet, the days on which the luncheon can be scheduled include

(A) Sunday and Monday
(B) Sunday and Wednesday
(C) Monday and Tuesday
(D) Monday and Wednesday
(E) Tuesday and Wednesday

GO ON TO THE NEXT PAGE.

23. During the past fifteen years, 20 percent of the judges with sufficient experience to be considered for federal judgeships were women, and all of those deemed to have sufficient experience during those years received federal judgeships. Despite this fact, only 8 percent of federal judgeships are currently filled by women.

Which of the following, if true, could explain the discrepancy in the percentages cited in the passage above?

(A) Fifteen years ago, it required less experience to be considered for federal judgeships than it does today.

(B) The majority of those holding federal judgeships have held those positions for more than fifteen years, dating back to a time when practically everyone holding that position was male.

(C) The women with sufficient experience to be considered for federal judgeships have tended to specialize in different areas of law than the men considered for federal judgeships.

(D) Men and women holding federal judgeships have received equal financial compensation for the previous fifteen years.

(E) Although women currently hold eight percent of the federal judgeships, they hold only three percent of circuit judgeships.

24. It has been argued that medical researchers would make more impressive strides in their effort to develop cures for certain infectious diseases if they knew more about how cells replicate. This argument, however, could be challenged on the basis that a major advance in pest control has never come from any insight into the reproductive patterns of insects.

The argument above relies on an analogy that assumes that fighting infectious diseases is an endeavor similar to which of the following?

(A) Theories of cell replication
(B) Efforts at pest control
(C) Conclusions about how researchers make advances
(D) Patterns of infectious disease transmission in insects
(E) Research into the reproductive patterns of insects

25. Rita has more clients than Frank and more clients than Tom. Isabel has more clients than Rita. Sam has no fewer clients than Rita.

If all of the statements above are true, which of the following cannot be true?

(A) Tom has more clients than Sam.
(B) Tom has more clients than Frank.
(C) Isabel has more clients than Tom.
(D) Sam and Rita have the same number of clients.
(E) Frank has fewer clients than Sam.

STOP

IF YOU FINISH BEFORE TIME IS CALLED, YOU MAY CHECK YOUR WORK ON THIS SECTION ONLY.
DO NOT WORK ON ANY OTHER SECTION IN THE TEST.

NO TEST MATERIAL ON THIS PAGE

SECTION 4
Time—30 minutes
30 Questions

Numbers: All numbers used are real numbers.

Figures: Position of points, angles, regions, etc. can be assumed to be in the order shown; and angle measures can be assumed to be positive.

Lines shown as straight can be assumed to be straight.

Figures can be assumed to lie in a plane unless otherwise indicated.

Figures that accompany questions are intended to provide information useful in answering the questions. However, unless a note states that a figure is drawn to scale, you should solve these problems NOT by estimating sizes by sight or by measurement, but by using your knowledge of mathematics (see Example 2 below).

Directions: Each of the <u>Questions 1-15</u> consists of two quantities, one in Column A and one in Column B. You are to compare the two quantities and choose

A   if the quantity in Column A is greater;
B   if the quantity in Column B is greater;
C   if the two quantities are equal;
D   if the relationship cannot be determined from the information given.

Note: Since there are only four choices, NEVER MARK (E).

Common
Information: In a question, information concerning one or both of the quantities to be compared is centered above the two columns. A symbol that appears in both columns represents the same thing in Column A as it does in Column B.

Column A	Column B	Sample Answers

Example 1: 2×6 $2 + 6$ ● Ⓑ Ⓒ Ⓓ Ⓔ

Examples 2-4 refer to $\triangle PQR$.

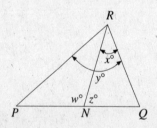

Example 2: PN NQ Ⓐ Ⓑ Ⓒ ● Ⓔ
(since equal measures cannot be assumed, even though PN and NQ appear equal)

Example 3: x y Ⓐ ● Ⓒ Ⓓ Ⓔ
(since N is between P and Q)

Example 4: $w + z$ 180 Ⓐ Ⓑ ● Ⓓ Ⓔ
(since PQ is a straight line)

GO ON TO THE NEXT PAGE.

A if the quantity in Column A is greater;
B if the quantity in Column B is greater;
C if the two quantities are equal;
D if the relationship cannot be determined from the information given.

Column A	Column B
1. The units digit in the number 1,743	The hundreds digit in the number 5,243

$$1.3 + .6 + .9 + x = 5$$

Column A	Column B
2. x	2.3
3. 4^3	3^4

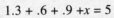

$x°$ 120°

$RSTU$ is a parallelogram.

Column A	Column B
4. x	45
5. 30 percent of $150	60 percent of $75
6. $\dfrac{n}{3}$	$\dfrac{m+n}{3}$

Column A	Column B
7. $\dfrac{\sqrt{27}}{\sqrt{3}}$	$\dfrac{\sqrt{45}}{\sqrt{5}}$
8. $5\left(\dfrac{x}{5} + \dfrac{y}{5} + \dfrac{7}{5}\right)$	$x + y + 7$

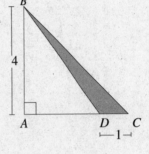

$\triangle ABC$ is isosceles.

Column A	Column B
9. $\dfrac{\text{Area of the shaded region in } \triangle ABC}{\text{Area of the unshaded region in } \triangle ABC}$	$\dfrac{1}{3}$

The average (arithmetic mean) of two positive integers is equal to 17. Each of the integers is greater than 12.

Column A	Column B
10. Twice the larger of the two integers	44

GO ON TO THE NEXT PAGE.

A   if the quantity in Column A is greater;
B   if the quantity in Column B is greater;
C   if the two quantities are equal;
D   if the relationship cannot be determined from the information given.

Column A	Column B

The circumference of a circle with a radius of $\frac{1}{2}$ meter is C meters.

11. C $\qquad\qquad\qquad$ 4

12. $\sqrt{\dfrac{7}{3}}$ $\qquad\qquad\qquad$ $\dfrac{1}{3}\sqrt{7}$

$$\frac{a}{b} = \frac{1}{3} \text{ and } \frac{b}{c} = \frac{15}{4}$$

13. a $\qquad\qquad\qquad$ c

Column A	Column B

14. The circumference of a circular region with radius r $\qquad$ The perimeter of a square with side r

15. $3^{17} + 3^{18}$ $\qquad\qquad$ $(4)3^{17}$

GO ON TO THE NEXT PAGE.

Directions: Each of the Questions 16-30 has five answer choices. For each of these questions, select the best of the answer choices given.

16. Which of the following numbers is greater than $-\frac{7}{3}$?

(A) -7

(B) -3

(C) -2

(D) $-\frac{8}{3}$

(E) $-\frac{5}{2}$

17. If the cost of a one-hour telephone call is $7.20, what would be the cost of a ten-minute telephone call at the same rate?

(A) $7.10
(B) $3.60
(C) $1.80
(D) $1.20
(E) $ .72

18. A pie is baked in a circular plate with a radius of 6 inches. If the pie is then cut into eight equal pieces, what would be the area, in square inches, of each slice of the pie?

(A) $\frac{1}{8}\pi$

(B) $\frac{2}{9}\pi$

(C) $\frac{9}{2}\pi$

(D) 6π

(E) 36π

19. If $s = 3r$ and $t = 7s$, then, in terms of r, $t - s - r =$

(A) $21r$
(B) $17r$
(C) $10r$
(D) $4r$
(E) r

20. $\sqrt{1.44} - .63 =$

(A) .9
(B) .81
(C) .12
(D) .09
(E) .03

GO ON TO THE NEXT PAGE.

Questions 21-25 refer to the following data.

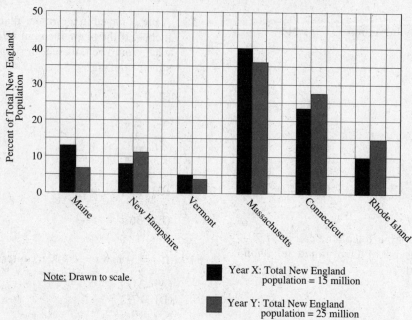

PERCENT OF POPULATION IN NEW ENGLAND BY STATE IN YEAR X AND YEAR Y

Note: Drawn to scale.

■ Year X: Total New England population = 15 million

■ Year Y: Total New England population = 25 million

21. Which of the following is the approximate average, in millions, of the populations of Maine and New Hampshire in Year X?

(A) 3.2
(B) 2.6
(C) 2.2
(D) 1.6
(E) 0.8

22. By approximately how much did the population of Rhode Island increase from Year X to Year Y?

(A)   750,000
(B)   1,250,000
(C)   1,500,000
(D)   2,250,000
(E)   3,750,000

23. In Year Y, the population of Massachusetts was approximately what percent of the population of Vermont?

(A)   50%
(B)   120%
(C)   300%
(D)   400%
(E)   900%

24. If the six New England states are ranked by population in Year X and in Year Y, how many states had a different ranking from Year X to Year Y?

(A) None
(B) Two
(C) Three
(D) Four
(E) Five

25. How many New England states decreased in population from Year X to Year Y?

(A) One
(B) Two
(C) Three
(D) Four
(E) Five

GO ON TO THE NEXT PAGE.

26. In a certain election, 60 percent of the voters were women. If 30 percent of the women and 20 percent of the men voted for candidate X, what percent of all the voters in that election voted for candidate X?

(A) 18%
(B) 25%
(C) 26%
(D) 30%
(E) 50%

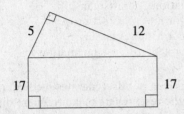

Note: Figure is not drawn to scale.

27. What is the perimeter of the figure above?

(A) 51
(B) 64
(C) 68
(D) 77
(E) 91

28. If a, b, and c are consecutive non-positive integers and $a < b < c$, which of the following must be true?

  I. $-a < -c$
  II. $abc < 0$
  III. abc is even

(A) None
(B) II only
(C) III only
(D) II and III only
(E) I, II, and III

29. If $5a - 3b = -9$ and $3a + b = 31$, then $a + b =$

(A) −7
(B) −3
(C) 6
(D) 13
(E) 19

30. 5×10^3 is what percent of $\frac{1}{5} \times 10^2$?

(A) 2,500%
(B) 4,900%
(C) 20,000%
(D) 24,900%
(E) 25,000%

STOP

IF YOU FINISH BEFORE TIME IS CALLED, YOU MAY CHECK YOUR WORK ON THIS SECTION ONLY.
DO NOT WORK ON ANY OTHER SECTION IN THE TEST.

SECTION 5

Time—30 Minutes

38 Questions

Directions: Each sentence below has one or two blanks, each blank indicating that something has been omitted. Beneath the sentence are five lettered words or sets of words. Choose the word or set of words for each blank that best fits the meaning of the sentence as a whole.

1. Many feature films are criticized for their ------- content, even though television news is more often the medium that depicts violent events in excessive detail.

(A) discretionary
(B) graphic
(C) dramatic
(D) artistic
(E) honest

2. The use of alcohol and other drugs, with the exception of tobacco, seems to increase and decrease -------; certain periods are marked by a social inclination toward abstinence, which after a time gives way to drug consumption by some part of society, and eventually to ------- acceptance.

(A) erratically . . partial
(B) cyclically . . widespread
(C) exponentially . . mitigated
(D) criminally . . absolute
(E) simultaneously . . conventional

3. After screenwriter Neil Jordan's most recent work opened in selected urban areas, many theatergoers were -------, but after pundits expressed their -------, appreciation of the film increased and distribution surged.

(A) skeptical . . approbation
(B) apathetic . . diffidence
(C) ebullient . . trepidation
(D) dubious . . disdain
(E) unimpressed . . antipathy

4. The pieces exhibited at many university galleries are chosen to reflect the diverse tastes of the academic communities they serve; the curators avoid ------- in favor of -------.

(A) continuity . . rigidity
(B) variation . . craftsmanship
(C) uniformity . . eclecticism
(D) modernism . . classics
(E) homogeneity . . segmentation

5. The American public venerates medical researchers because the researchers make frequent discoveries of tremendous humanitarian consequence; however, the daily routines of scientists are largely made up of result verification and statistical analysis, making their occupation seem -------.

(A) fascinating
(B) quotidian
(C) recalcitrant
(D) experimental
(E) amorphous

6. In a vitriolic message to his troops, General Patton insisted that he would ------- no further insubordination, no matter how barbarous the ensuing engagements might become.

(A) impede
(B) brief
(C) denote
(D) brook
(E) expose

7. Chang realized that she had been ------- in her duties; had she been more -------, the disaster may well have been avoided.

(A) unparalleled . . careful
(B) irreproachable . . aware
(C) derelict . . vigilant
(D) arbitrary . . interested
(E) neglectful . . insensible

GO ON TO THE NEXT PAGE.

Directions: In each of the following questions, a related pair of words or phrases is followed by five lettered pairs of words or phrases. Select the lettered pair that best expresses a relationship similar to that expressed in the original pair.

8. METEOROLOGY : WEATHER ::
(A) philology : love
(B) epistemology : disease
(C) physiology : mind
(D) demography : population
(E) astrology : planets

9. MAELSTROM : WATER ::
(A) downpour : rain
(B) wave : current
(C) cyclone : wind
(D) tornado : debris
(E) storm : snow

10. FIX : STABLE ::
(A) furrow : productive
(B) mend : torn
(C) fortify : strong
(D) deter : active
(E) captivate : attractive

11. GALL : IRRITATION ::
(A) accommodate : deception
(B) beleaguer : felicity
(C) awe : apathy
(D) discomfit : confusion
(E) inculcate : fear

12. PAPYRUS : PAPER ::
(A) manuscript : book
(B) hatchet : ax
(C) cart : wagon
(D) daguerreotype : photograph
(E) house : mansion

13. BLACKSMITH : FOUNDRY ::
(A) farmer : shed
(B) artist : studio
(C) physician : laboratory
(D) teacher : college
(E) reporter : television

14. ARIA : SONG ::
(A) covenant : agreement
(B) fable : story
(C) monument : sculpture
(D) prose : poem
(E) soliloquy : speech

15. LONGING : PINE ::
(A) remorse : rue
(B) anguish : seethe
(C) forbearance : dignify
(D) concern : intervene
(E) suffering : inflict

16. CHEVRON : BADGE ::
(A) caisson : cart
(B) calcium : bone
(C) wax : candle
(D) clothing : uniform
(E) oration : eulogy

GO ON TO THE NEXT PAGE.

Directions: Each passage in this group is followed by questions based on its content. After reading a passage, choose the best answer to each question. Answer all questions following a passage on the basis of what is <u>stated</u> or <u>implied</u> in that passage.

In *A Room of One's Own*, Virginia Woolf performs a typically stream-of-consciousness feat by beginning with a description of the view from her
Line window: a leaf falls from a tree, and a woman in
(5) leather boots and a man in a maroon overcoat climb into a taxi and glide away. Woolf uses this moment to discuss the unity of the mind, and the effortlessness with which she had invested this ordinary sight with a kind of rhythmic order. She ends with a
(10) consideration of Coleridge's remark that a great mind is androgynous. "What does one mean by 'the unity of the mind?'" Woolf asks.

One of Woolf's theses is that unity, and not repression, is the necessary state for creativity.
(15) Woolf describes men's sentences as having a particular shape, natural to men, but unnatural and clumsy to women. She rightly praises Austen for developing her own rhythm and her own sentence, which is expressive of her genius, her characters, and her
(20) history. Woolf suggests that the women's suffrage movement fomented a reaction of threatened male self-assertion that meant a decline in literary power. "It is fatal," she writes, "for any one who writes to think of their sex . . . it is fatal for a woman to lay the
(25) least stress on any grievance; to plead justice with any cause; in any way to speak consciously as a woman."

A Room of One's Own exhorts women to reach for a higher, almost religious approach to writing. "Do
(30) not dream of influencing other people;" she writes, "think of things in themselves."

17. Which of the following literary projects would Woolf most likely support?

(A) A narrative poem in which a heroine overcomes male challenges through intellectual superiority
(B) A fictional polemic asserting the importance of social equality of men and women
(C) A novel that expresses the unrepressed truth of the author's experience
(D) A short story that responds to the historical injustice in the treatment of women
(E) A critical essay on Coleridge which explains his remark about androgyny in terms of his psychological history

18. The author refers to Woolf's description of the man and woman climbing into the taxi in order to

(A) give an example of Woolf's mastery of stream-of-consciousness techniques
(B) show a typically feminine perspective of everyday life
(C) demonstrate how Woolf's writing was unconcerned with changing the social order
(D) refute the notion that Woolf's assertions are anti-female or anti-feminist
(E) begin the discussion of Woolf's conception of the ways in which the mind unifies the world

19. According to the passage, Woolf believes which of the following to be true about Jane Austen's work?

I. Austen's sentences are representative of an androgynous "unity of the mind."
II. Austen's syntax and literary form are products of her personal experience.
III. Austen's literary work exemplifies a particular form of well-realized female artistic expression.

(A) I only
(B) II only
(C) I and II only
(D) II and III only
(E) I, II, and III

20. It can be inferred from the passage that Woolf believes that

(A) women should not write about subjects that are specifically female
(B) the women's suffrage movement contributed to a decline in literary quality
(C) Austen created a narrative style that was appropriate for her gender and subject matter
(D) women's sentences should mimic the shape of men's sentences
(E) some readers could misinterpret her statements as being denigrating to women

GO ON TO THE NEXT PAGE.

NO TEST MATERIAL ON THIS PAGE

Because human anatomy does not change (except over long periods of time), knowledge acquired a century ago is still accurate today. Broad functions
Line of any part of the body, such as the skin, are dupli-
(5) cated in different ways by other organs. One can eventually understand the entire body as a larger system made up of smaller, interdependent systems.

A cross-section of the skin reveals a top layer of epidermis, or cuticle, followed by derma, and finally,
(10) subcutaneous cellular tissue. Sprouting through all three layers are hairs, with hair follicles and erector pili muscles embedded deep within the subcutaneous tissue. Sweat (sudoriferous glands), fat cells, and sebaceous glands are scattered throughout, while
(15) papillae, which are conical and extremely sensitive, can be found directly beneath the superficial layer.

The skin is the primary organ of the sense of touch. It can excrete substances as well as absorb them, and it plays a vital role in regulating body
(20) temperature and in protecting the tissues that lie beneath it.

The epidermis has no veins or arteries and varies considerably both in thickness and in the depth or fineness of its furrows. On the palm, for example,
(25) the skin is quite thick, or horny, and is marked by deep furrows or lines. On the back of the hand, however, the skin is less thick, and has only a faint network of lines crisscrossing it. The pigment found in the epidermis gives whatever color there is to the
(30) skin; this pigment is similar to that found in the retina of the eye. One layer down, in the derma, there is similar variation in thickness, mostly to protect underlying tissue.

In the derma lies the vascular system, which
(35) includes nerves, blood vessels, and lymphatics. The derma is divided into two sub-layers: the reticular layer and the papillary layer, which is closer to the epidermis. The less sensitive the skin, the fewer papillae reside there; in the most sensitive places,
(40) such as the fingertips and the nipples, the papillae are long, large, and grouped closely together to form parallel arcs with ducts to sweat glands lying in between. Under the papillary layer, and conforming to it, is the reticular layer, composed of fibrous bands
(45) and elastic tissue, and interlaced by fat and sudorifer- ous glands.

The basic functions of muscular contraction, vascular transport, nerve communication, and protec- tion all take place in the various layers of the skin, so
(50) that understanding the components of the skin and how they work together is a helpful step in under- standing the complex anatomy of the human body.

21. The author is primarily concerned with
(A) giving an overview of human anatomical functions
(B) describing the layers of the skin to show one example of an anatomical system
(C) concluding that the study of human anatomy must first begin with the skin
(D) discussing how the skin is only one system in a much larger and more complex system
(E) detailing the three layers of the skin: the epidermis, the derma, and the subcutaneous cellular tissue, each of which has its own separate functions

22. The passage suggests that the area of skin most closely associated with skin sensitivity is the
(A) reticular layer
(B) papillary layer
(C) sudoriferous gland
(D) subcutaneous tissue
(E) vascular system

23. The author would most likely agree with which of the following statements?
I. Extremely sensitive skin is characterized by a minute number of papillae.
II. Hair can be found in subcutaneous tissue.
III. Skin and the retina both rely on pigment to give them color.
(A) I only
(B) II only
(C) I and II only
(D) II and III only
(E) I, II, and III

24. The passage supplies information to answer which of the following questions?
(A) What causes the erector pili muscle to contract?
(B) Why is the epidermis covered with furrows?
(C) How quickly do papillae react to sensation?
(D) What do sudoriferous glands and sebaceous glands have in common?
(E) Where in the body can pigmentation be found?

GO ON TO THE NEXT PAGE.

25. The author implies that
    (A) there is a relationship between the thickness of the skin and the number and depth of the skin's furrows
    (B) the reticular layer is the only layer that contains fibrous bands
    (C) the skin is the only part of the body that has a sense of touch
    (D) areas of the skin with sudoriferous glands are extremely sensitive
    (E) both hair and the reticular layer are made up of the same kind of tissue

26. The passage suggests that if the skin were damaged in some way, and unable to perform some of its functions, which of the following might happen?
    (A) The pigmentation would no longer be similar to that found in the retina.
    (B) The deep furrows found on some parts of the skin would disappear.
    (C) The body would regulate its temperature less effectively.
    (D) The fingertips would no longer be characterized by an abundance of papillae.
    (E) The body would lose its sense of touch.

27. The passage states that all the following are found in the skin EXCEPT
    (A) fat cells
    (B) lymphatics
    (C) veins
    (D) pigmentation
    (E) ligaments

GO ON TO THE NEXT PAGE.

Directions: Each question below consists of a word printed in capital letters, followed by five lettered words or phrases. Choose the lettered word or phrase that is most nearly <u>opposite</u> in meaning to the word in capital letters.

Since some of the questions require you to distinguish fine shades of meaning, be sure to consider all the choices before deciding which one is best.

28. CHRONIC: (A) intermittent (B) healthy
    (C) tardy (D) consistently durable
    (E) suddenly available

29. FORK: (A) judge (B) praise
    (C) agitate (D) converge (E) impress

30. FANCY: (A) ornament (B) abhor
    (C) falsify (D) reclaim (E) stiffen

31. ANIMATE: (A) enervate (B) frustrate
    (C) regress (D) condemn (E) distort

32. CARDINAL: (A) wholesome (B) obscure
    (C) trivial (D) impious (E) lascivious

33. INCUBATE: (A) squelch (B) hatch
    (C) assemble (D) decide (E) sterilize

34. OBSTREPEROUS: (A) disciplined
    (B) insubordinate (C) predictable
    (D) well-formed (E) exhausted

35. CHECK: (A) assume (B) complete
    (C) disagree (D) emulate (E) unbridle

36. IMPRECATE: (A) evaluate carefully
    (B) uphold forcefully (C) bless
    (D) forgive (E) confine

37. BEREAVE: (A) tear (B) collaborate
    (C) solicit (D) radiate (E) furnish

38. HIE: (A) separate (B) dawdle
    (C) lower cautiously (D) comfort warmly
    (E) leave suddenly

STOP

IF YOU FINISH BEFORE TIME IS CALLED, YOU MAY CHECK YOUR WORK ON THIS SECTION ONLY.
DO NOT WORK ON ANY OTHER SECTION IN THE TEST.

NO TEST MATERIAL ON THIS PAGE

SECTION 6

Time—30 Minutes

25 Questions

Directions: Each question or group of questions is based on a passage or set of conditions. In answering some of the questions, it may be useful to draw a rough diagram. For each question, select the best answer choice given.

Questions 1-6

A strand of ten lights is to be hung in a store to decorate for the holidays. The bulbs to be used in the strand are three red bulbs, two blue bulbs, two green bulbs, two yellow bulbs, and a white bulb. The bulbs are located every three feet on the strand.

The strand has two different colored bulbs at either end.

The red bulbs must all be next to each other.

The white bulb must have a blue bulb immediately on either side of it.

A green bulb and a red bulb cannot be next to each other.

If a yellow bulb is at the end of the strand, then a blue bulb must be next to it.

1. Which of the following is a possible order for the bulbs on the strand?

   (A) Yellow, red, red, red, yellow, green, green, blue, white, blue
   (B) Green, blue, white, blue, red, red, red, yellow, yellow, green
   (C) Blue, white, blue, green, yellow, yellow, green, red, red, red
   (D) Yellow, blue, white, yellow, red, red, red, blue, green, green
   (E) Green, green, yellow, red, red, red, yellow, blue, white, blue

2. If a red bulb is at one end of the strand and a yellow bulb is at the other, which of the following statements must be true?

   (A) The two middle bulbs are both blue.
   (B) The two middle bulbs are both red.
   (C) The two middle bulbs are both green.
   (D) The two middle bulbs are green and blue.
   (E) The two middle bulbs are yellow and green.

3. If the two yellow bulbs are next to each other and the green bulbs are not next to each other, which of the following statements must be true?

   (A) A red bulb is next to a blue bulb.
   (B) A yellow bulb is next to a blue bulb.
   (C) A blue bulb is not next to a green bulb.
   (D) A white bulb is not next to a blue bulb.
   (E) A yellow bulb cannot be at either end of the strand.

4. If a yellow bulb is at the end of the strand, which of the following statements must be true?

   (A) A green bulb is next to a yellow bulb.
   (B) A white bulb is at the other end of the strand.
   (C) A blue bulb is at the other end of the strand.
   (D) A yellow bulb is at the other end of the strand.
   (E) A blue bulb is next to a red bulb.

5. If a white bulb is next to the bulb at the end of the strand and the two yellow bulbs are next to each other, which of the following statements could be true?

   (A) There is a yellow bulb at the end of the strand.
   (B) There is a red bulb next to a green bulb.
   (C) There is a blue bulb next to a green bulb.
   (D) There is not a yellow bulb next to a green bulb.
   (E) There is a blue bulb next to a yellow bulb.

6. Which of the following is NOT possible?

   (A) A yellow bulb is at one end of the strand, and a green bulb is at the other end.
   (B) A red bulb is at one end of the strand, and a green bulb is at the other end.
   (C) A yellow bulb is directly adjacent to a red bulb and a green bulb.
   (D) There are red bulbs next to a yellow bulb, a blue bulb, and a white bulb.
   (E) There are blue bulbs next to a red bulb, a white bulb, and a yellow bulb.

GO ON TO THE NEXT PAGE.

6 6 6 6 6 6 6 6 6 6 6

7. Over the past five years, Clean toothpaste has been advertised as the most effective means of preventing tooth decay. However, according to dentists' records, many patients experiencing severe tooth decay used Clean toothpaste. Clearly, Clean toothpaste is not an effective means of preventing tooth decay.

Which of the following statements, if true, would most seriously weaken the conclusion above?

(A) Of the patients experiencing tooth decay, two-thirds indicate that they would be willing to switch brands of toothpaste.
(B) The advertisements for Clean toothpaste advocate brushing twice a day.
(C) If Clean toothpaste were not available, more patients would experience severe tooth decay.
(D) Dentists continue to recommend Clean toothpaste more than any other brand.
(E) Of those who experienced severe tooth decay, only one-eighth also experienced gum disease.

8. A group of physicians wishing to explore the link between protein intake and high blood pressure performed a nutrition experiment on a selected group of ten vegetarians. Five of the people were given a high-protein, low-fat diet. The group given the high-protein, low-fat diet exhibited the same 5 percent increase in blood pressure as did the group given the low-protein, high-fat diet.

Which of the following conclusions can most properly be drawn if the statements above are true?

(A) The physicians did not establish a link between protein intake and high blood pressure.
(B) The sample chosen by the physicians was not representative of the general vegetarian population.
(C) Some physicians believe there is a link between protein intake and high blood pressure.
(D) Vegetarians are more likely to eat a high-protein, low-fat diet than a low-protein, high-fat diet.
(E) There is a link between protein intake and high blood pressure.

9. Whenever Joe does his laundry at the Main Street Laundromat, the loads turn out cleaner than they do when he does his laundry at the Elm Street Laundromat. Laundry done at the Main Street Laundromat is cleaner because the machines at the Main Street Laundromat use more water per load than do those at the Elm Street Laundromat.

Which of the following statements, if true, helps support the conclusion above?

(A) The clothes washed at the Elm Street Laundromat were, overall, less clean than those washed at the Main Street Laundromat.
(B) Joe uses the same detergent at both laundromats.
(C) The machines at the Oak Street Laundromat use twice as much water as do those at the Main Street Laundromat.
(D) Joe does three times as much laundry at the Main Street Laundromat as he does at the Elm Street Laundromat.
(E) Joe tends to do his dirtier laundry at the Elm Street Laundromat.

GO ON TO THE NEXT PAGE.

6 6 6 6 6 6 6 6 6 6 6 6

Questions 10-13

A clothing designer is presenting shows in five different cities in five days. The first four outfits of each show are either checkered, dotted, striped, or plaid. In every city the models wear these four outfits in a different order.

> In successive cities, the first outfits are never the same.
> In successive cities, the fourth outfits are never the same.
> The plaid outfit is never modeled directly after the striped outfit.
> The dotted outfit is never modeled first.

10. Which of the following could be an outfit order on the night following a night when the outfit order is plaid, striped, dotted, and checkered?

   (A) Checkered, dotted, striped, and plaid
   (B) Dotted, checkered, plaid, and striped
   (C) Plaid, dotted, checkered, and striped
   (D) Striped, plaid, checkered, and dotted
   (E) Striped, checkered, plaid, and dotted

11. All of the following could be an outfit order for the evening following an evening in which the outfit order has the checkered outfit fourth and the plaid outfit third EXCEPT

   (A) checkered, dotted, plaid, and striped
   (B) checkered, plaid, dotted, and striped
   (C) striped, dotted, plaid, and checkered
   (D) plaid, checkered, striped, and dotted
   (E) plaid, striped, checkered, and dotted

12. If the outfit order on one evening is checkered, plaid, dotted, and striped, and on the next evening the outfit order has the plaid outfit fourth, which of the following must be true of the outfit order on the second evening?

   (A) The checkered outfit is modeled first.
   (B) The striped outfit is modeled first.
   (C) The checkered outfit is modeled immediately before the striped outfit.
   (D) The dotted outfit is modeled immediately before the striped outfit.
   (E) The dotted outfit is modeled directly before the checkered outfit.

13. If on a Monday the outfit order is striped, dotted, plaid, and checkered, and on a Wednesday the outfit order is plaid, checkered, striped, and dotted, which of the following must be true about the outfit order for Tuesday?

   (A) The plaid outfit is modeled second.
   (B) The striped outfit is modeled second.
   (C) The dotted outfit is modeled third.
   (D) The striped outfit is modeled fourth.
   (E) The checkered outfit is modeled first.

GO ON TO THE NEXT PAGE.

Questions 14-18

There are three hiking paths at Miller's Farm Resort in Vermont. The paths are marked by signs on eight tall trees in the woods surrounding the Pine Lodge and the Old Barn: an ash, a birch, a cherry, an elm, a fir, a hemlock, a maple, and an oak.

> The Green Mountain Trail goes in a straight line from the Pine Lodge to the ash to the cherry to the maple to the birch and then to the Old Barn.
> The Cross Country Trail goes from the Pine Lodge to the cherry to the fir to the hemlock to the birch to the elm and back to the Pine Lodge.
> The Bethlehem Trail starts at the Pine Lodge and goes from the oak to the fir to the maple and back to the Pine Lodge.

There are no other routes available. Trails may be travelled in either direction.

14. Which of the following routes must be taken to go from the ash to the elm while passing the fewest trees?

(A) The Cross Country Trail
(B) The Green Mountain Trail, then the Cross Country Trail
(C) The Green Mountain Trail, then the Bethlehem Trail
(D) The Bethlehem Trail, then the Cross Country Trail
(E) The Green Mountain Trail, then the Bethlehem Trail, and then the Cross Country Trail

15. What is the maximum number of trees one can pass in order to get from the elm to the maple, without reusing any part of a path or passing the Pine Lodge?

(A) 1
(B) 2
(C) 3
(D) 4
(E) 5

16. Which sequence of trees is a possible route from the Old Barn to the Pine Lodge?

(A) Birch, maple, fir, oak
(B) Birch, elm, ash, cherry
(C) Birch, maple, fir, ash
(D) Birch, hemlock, cherry
(E) Birch, maple, cherry, elm, ash

17. How many different routes are there from the Pine Lodge to the birch which pass exactly three trees and do not reuse any part of a path?

(A) 2
(B) 3
(C) 4
(D) 5
(E) 6

18. If a new path is found that connects the fir tree to the Old Barn, what is the fewest number of trees that could be passed on a hike from the Pine Lodge to the Old Barn and back, taking a different route each way?

(A) 3
(B) 4
(C) 5
(D) 6
(E) 7

GO ON TO THE NEXT PAGE.

Questions 19-22

Five prints are being arranged in an artist's portfolio. The prints are to be chosen from among the artist's eight best works: M, N, O, P, Q, S, T, and W. The first print is to be on the right-hand side of the first two facing pages, opposite a blank page. The second and third prints are to be on the left- and right-hand sides, respectively, of the next two facing pages, with the fourth and fifth prints on the left- and right-hand sides, respectively, of the last two facing pages.

> If print O is selected for the portfolio, print W cannot be included.
> If either print P or Q is displayed, the other print must also be displayed, and they must be on facing pages.
> Print S must be displayed in the portfolio, but cannot be the first print displayed.
> Prints N and T must both be displayed, and can only be displayed on the front and back sides of the same page.
> Prints M and Q cannot both be displayed.

19. If N is the first print displayed in the portfolio, which of the following statements could be true?

(A) O is the second print displayed.
(B) P is the third print displayed.
(C) Q is the third print displayed.
(D) W is the fourth print displayed.
(E) T is the fifth print displayed.

20. If S is the second print displayed, all of the following statements could be true EXCEPT

(A) M is the first print displayed.
(B) W is the first print displayed.
(C) N is the third print displayed.
(D) N is the fourth print displayed.
(E) Q is the fifth print displayed.

21. All of the following prints could be displayed on the first page EXCEPT

(A) M
(B) O
(C) Q
(D) T
(E) W

22. If O is the first print displayed, which of the following statements must be true?

(A) P is the second print displayed.
(B) W is the third print displayed.
(C) N is the third print displayed.
(D) S is the fourth print displayed.
(E) S and M are both displayed.

GO ON TO THE NEXT PAGE.

23. Collies are the most frequently purchased dogs at dog breeding farms. Clearly, collies' superior performance in dog shows makes them popular dogs to buy as pets.

Which of the following, if true, would most seriously weaken the claim made above?

(A) Collies require less food and care than do most other dogs.
(B) It is because of their glossy fur that collies place well in dog shows.
(C) Public interest in dog shows has been surging in the recent past.
(D) Schnauzers generally place best in show and they are extremely popular dogs to buy as pets.
(E) Dogs that place well in shows invariably are the most popular dogs to buy as pets.

24. There are over fifty furniture stores in Middle Valley and not one of them charges less for furniture than does Green's Furniture Warehouse. It is clear that Green's Furniture Warehouse is the store that will provide the lowest price for furniture in all of Middle Valley.

Which of the following is an assumption on which the assertion made above is based?

(A) Customers do not have the option of shopping somewhere other than Middle Valley.
(B) The other furniture stores in Middle Valley charge more for furniture than does Green's Furniture Warehouse.
(C) The quality of the furniture at Green's Furniture Warehouse is equal to the quality of the furniture in other stores.
(D) Green's Furniture Warehouse is the most cost-effective store in Middle Valley.
(E) Other household items at Green's Furniture Warehouse are also well priced.

25. Unless there is an increase in federal spending, the national book program will fail.

Only if the national book program succeeds will the country escape recession.

There will be no increase in federal spending unless there is an increase in taxes.

If the statements above are true, which of the following must be true?

(A) If there is an increase in taxes, the country will definitely escape recession.
(B) Other programs will lose funding if the national book program succeeds.
(C) If the country escapes recession, the national book program must have succeeded.
(D) If the national book program succeeds, the country will escape recession.
(E) To escape recession, an alternate way of stimulating the economy must be found.

STOP

IF YOU FINISH BEFORE TIME IS CALLED, YOU MAY CHECK YOUR WORK ON THIS SECTION ONLY.
DO NOT WORK ON ANY OTHER SECTION IN THE TEST.

SAT DIAGNOSTIC TEST

PART

VIII

Answers and Explanations to the Diagnostic Test

CORRECT ANSWERS FOR THE PRINCETON REVIEW GRE DIAGNOSTIC TEST

Section 1	Section 2	Section 3	Section 4	Section 5	Section 6
1. B	1. A	1. B	1. A	1. B	1. E
2. B	2. D	2. C	2. B	2. B	2. C
3. B	3. B	3. B	3. B	3. A	3. E
4. A	4. C	4. E	4. A	4. C	4. A
5. C	5. E	5. A	5. C	5. B	5. C
6. A	6. A	6. A	6. D	6. D	6. D
7. B	7. D	7. D	7. C	7. C	7. C
8. B	8. B	8. E	8. C	8. D	8. A
9. D	9. B	9. E	9. C	9. C	9. B
10. C	10. B	10. A	10. B	10. C	10. E
11. A	11. E	11. D	11. B	11. D	11. C
12. A	12. C	12. B	12. A	12. D	12. B
13. B	13. A	13. D	13. D	13. B	13. E
14. D	14. C	14. A	14. A	14. E	14. B
15. C	15. E	15. C	15. C	15. A	15. D
16. E	16. C	16. E	16. C	16. A	16. A
17. C	17. C	17. D	17. D	17. C	17. D
18. C	18. A	18. C	18. C	18. E	18. B
19. E	19. C	19. E	19. B	19. D	19. D
20. C	20. C	20. D	20. A	20. C	20. E
21. C	21. B	21. A	21. D	21. B	21. C
22. D	22. A	22. B	22. D	22. B	22. E
23. D	23. A	23. B	23. E	23. D	23. A
24. C	24. D	24. B	24. C	24. E	24. B
25. E	25. E	25. A	25. A	25. A	25. C
26. C	26. C		26. C	26. C	
27. B	27. A		27. B	27. E	
28. E	28. C		28. C	28. A	
29. E	29. E		29. E	29. D	
30. E	30. C		30. E	30. B	
	31. A			31. A	
	32. A			32. C	
	33. E			33. A	
	34. A			34. A	
	35. A			35. E	
	36. A			36. C	
	37. E			37. E	
	38. E			38. B	

SCORE CONVERSION FOR THE PRINCETON REVIEW GRE DIAGNOSTIC TEST

Raw Score	VERBAL Scaled Score	VERBAL % Below	QUANTITATIVE Scaled Score	QUANTITATIVE % Below	ANALYTICAL Scaled Score	ANALYTICAL % Below	Raw Score	VERBAL Scaled Score	VERBAL % Below	QUANTITATIVE Scaled Score	QUANTITATIVE % Below	ANALYTICAL Scaled Score	ANALYTICAL % Below
74-76	800	99					39	430	36	540	45	680	87
73	790	99					38	420	33	530	43	660	84
72	780	99					37	420	33	520	40	650	82
71	770	99					36	410	30	500	35	630	77
70	750	98					35	400	26	490	33	620	75
							34	390	24	480	30	600	70
69	740	98					33	380	22	470	29	590	68
68	730	97					32	370	20	460	26	570	62
67	720	96					31	370	20	450	24	560	59
66	710	95					30	360	16	440	22	540	53
65	690	94											
64	680	93					29	350	14	430	20	530	51
63	670	92					28	340	12	420	18	510	44
62	660	90					27	340	12	400	15	500	42
61	650	89					26	330	10	390	13	490	39
60	640	87	800	98			25	320	9	380	12	470	33
							24	310	7	370	10	460	31
59	630	85	800	98			23	300	6	360	9	440	25
58	620	84	800	98			22	290	5	350	8	430	24
57	610	82	780	95			21	280	4	340	7	410	19
56	590	78	760	93			20	270	3	330	6	400	17
55	580	76	740	89									
54	570	74	730	87			19	260	2	320	5	390	15
53	560	72	710	83			18	250	1	310	4	370	12
52	550	69	700	81			17	240	1	290	3	360	10
51	540	67	680	77			16	230	1	280	2	340	8
50	530	64	670	75	800	99	15	220	1	270	2	330	6
							14	210	1	250	1	310	5
49	520	61	660	73	800	99	13	200	1	240	1	300	4
48	520	61	640	69	800	99	12	200	1	220	1	290	3
47	510	59	630	66	790	98	11	200	1	210	1	270	2
46	500	56	620	64	780	98							
45	490	54	610	62	760	96	10	200	1	200	1	250	1
44	480	51	590	57	750	96	9	200	1	200	1	230	1
43	470	48	580	55	730	94	8	200	1	200	1	220	1
42	460	44	570	52	720	93	0-7	200	1	200	1	200	1
41	450	41	560	50	710	91							
40	440	38	550	48	690	89							

What follows is a detailed explanation for each question in our diagnostic test. Although you will naturally be more curious about the questions you got wrong, don't forget to read the explanations for the questions you left blank. In fact, you should even read the explanation for the questions you got right! Our explanations present the safest, most direct solution to each question. Even though you may have gotten a question right does not mean you analyzed it in the most efficient way.

SECTION 1

1.   4[(3 + 3) + 4]   45

    1. The best answer is B. Use PEMDAS. (3 + 3) = 6. 6 + 4 = 10. 4(10) = 40.

    So Column A = 40 and Column B = 45.

a and *b* are each greater than 1.

2.   3*ab*   (3*a*)(3*b*)

    2. The best answer is B. Plug in numbers for *a* and *b*. Make *a* = 2 and *b* = 3. Then plug in to the two columns. Column A would be 3(2)(3) and Column B would be 3(2)3(3). So Column B is greater.

3. $\dfrac{5}{9}$ $\dfrac{4}{7}$

    3. The best answer is B. Use the Bowtie to compare fractions! In column A you would have 7(5) = 35 and in Column B you'd have 9(4) = 36.

4. $4(2^6)$ $6(4^2)$

    4. The best answer is A. For exponents, Expand It Out! In column A you have 4*2*2*2*2*2*2. In Column B you have 6*4*4. Then divide both sides by 4*4. In Column A that leaves 16. In Column B 6 is left.

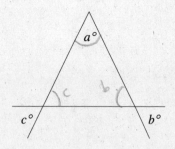

5.   *b* + *c*   180 − *a*

    5. The best answer is C. Plug in on geometry problems with variables. Plug in to the triangle according to the rule of 180. Let's make *a* = 50, and make the other two angles 60 and 70. Because *b* and *c* are vertical to the other angles in the triangle, *b* + *c* = 130 in column A. 180 − 50 = 130 in column B.

SECTION 1

QUESTIONS	EXPLANATIONS

Mr. Jones purchased a new bedroom set by using an extended payment plan. The regular price of the set was $900, but on the payment plan he paid $300 up front and 9 monthly payments of $69 each.

6. $23   The amount Mr. Jones paid in addition to the regular price of the bedroom set

6. The best answer is A. To find the amount Mr. Jones paid in addition to the regular price of the bedroom set, multiply $69 by the 9 months = $621. Then add the $300 payment. 621 + 300 = 921. So Mr. Jones paid an additional $21. $23 in Column A is larger than $21 in Column B.

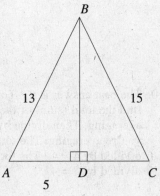

7.   The perimeter of   42
        triangle BCD

7. The best answer is B. To find the perimeter of triangle BCD, first find the length of BD using the Pythagorean Theorem. $5^2 + BD^2 = 13^2$. So $BD = 12$. Then you can find the third side of triangle BCD. $12^2 + DC^2 = 15^2$. Notice that this is a 3:4:5 right triangle. So DC is 9. Then add up the sides of triangle BCD. $9 + 12 + 15 = 36$. 42 in Column B is greater.

8. $\frac{1}{5} + \frac{1}{7}$ $\frac{1}{9} + \frac{1}{4}$

8. The best answer is B. Use the Bowtie to add fractions. $\frac{1}{5} + \frac{1}{7} = \frac{7+5}{35} = \frac{12}{35}$ in Column A. $\frac{1}{9} + \frac{1}{4} = \frac{4+9}{36} = \frac{13}{36}$ in Column B. Then use the Bowtie again to compare fractions. $(36)(12) = 432$ in Column A. $(35)(13) = 455$ in Column B.

SECTION 1

$BC \parallel DE$

9. $x + y$ $w + v$

10. The average (arithmetic mean) of 7, 3, 4, and 2.   The average (arithmetic mean) of $2a + 5$, $4a$, and $7 - 6a$

11. $\sqrt{7} + \sqrt{11}$ $\sqrt{3} + \sqrt{15}$

EXPLANATIONS

9. The best answer is D. We know that BC is parallel to DE. According to Fred's theorem, angle x must be equal to angle w. So the problem really depends on angle y and angle v. The diagram makes it look as if AC is parallel to DF, so Joe Bloggs would assume that they are parallel. That would make angle y equal to angle v. But we don't know that! Try redrawing the diagram, making AC not parallel to DF.

10. The best answer is C. To find the average, first find the total (sum) of the numbers you're averaging. Then divide by the number of elements you're averaging. The total in Column A is 16, divided by 4 = 4. The total in Column B is 12 divided by 3 = 4.

11. The best answer is A. First eliminate answer choice D, because there are no variables. Then eliminate the Joe Bloggs answer, which would be C, because the two columns "look" equal. But remember that you <u>cannot</u> add square roots! To help you estimate, you could use bigger numbers. Try comparing $\sqrt{70} + \sqrt{110}$ in Column A with $\sqrt{30} + \sqrt{150}$ in Column B. $\sqrt{70}$ would be a bit bigger than 8, and the $\sqrt{110}$ would be a bit bigger than 10. So Column A would be a bit bigger than 18. $\sqrt{30}$ would be a bit bigger than 5, and the $\sqrt{150}$ would be a bit bigger than 12. So Column B would be a bit bigger than 17. Column A is greater.

SECTION 1

QUESTIONS	EXPLANATIONS

Questions 12-13 refer to the following number line.

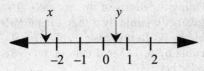

12. $-x$ $2y$

12. The best answer is A. Don't forget to eliminate the Joe Bloggs answers! Joe would say D is for this problem because there are no values for x and y. Another Joe Bloggs choice would be B, because $2y$ "looks" greater than $-x$. Now plug in! Make $x = -2.5$ and $y = .5$. Then Column A = 2.5 and Column B = 1.0.

13. $x + 2y$ $2y - x$

13. The best answer is B. Again Joe Bloggs would choose D because there are no values for x and y. Or Joe might choose Column A, because $x + 2y$ "looks" bigger than $2y - x$. Plug in the same values we used in #12. In Column A $-2.5 + 1 = -1.5$. In Column B $1-(-2.5) = 3.5$.

$$\sqrt{4r} = 6 \text{ and } s^2 = 81$$

14. r s

14. The best answer is D. $\sqrt{4r} = 6$ so $4r = 36$ and $r = 9$ in Column A. But if $s^2 = 81$, s could equal either $+9$ or -9. If $s = 9$, the two columns would be equal. If $s = -9$, then Column A is greater.

15. $7^{15} - 7^{14}$ $7^{14}(6)$

15. The best answer is C. Use process of elimination! Eliminate answer choice D because there are no variables. Then eliminate the Joe Bloggs answers. Joe would say that either Column A is greater, or that Column B is greater. So eliminate answer choices A and B! To see why C is the right choice, factor the expression in Column A.
$7^{15} - 7^{14} = 7^{14}(7-1) = 7^{14}(6)$

SECTION 1

QUESTIONS	EXPLANATIONS

16. What is the remainder when 117 is divided by 3?

   (A) 3
   (B) 2
   (C) 1
   (D) $\frac{1}{3}$
   (E) 0

16. The best answer is E. Without doing long division, you can determine whether a number is divisible by 3 by adding the digits of the number. If the sum of the digits is divisible by 3 then the number is divisible by 3. In this case $1 + 1 + 7 = 9$. Because 9 is divisible by 3, 117 is divisible by 3. So the remainder is 0.

17. The price of a certain stock increased 8 points, then decreased 13 points, and then increased 9 points. If the stock price before the changes was x points, which of the following was the stock price, in points, after the changes?

   (A) $x - 5$
   (B) $x - 4$
   (C) $x + 4$
   (D) $x + 5$
   (E) $x + 8$

17. The best answer is C. When you see variables in the answer choices, plug in! Let's make $x=10$. That's the starting point. So $10 + 8 = 18$. $18 - 13 = 5$. $5 + 9 = 14$. So 14 is the arithmetic answer we're looking for in the answer choices. Now plug in 10 for every x in the answer choices. $10 + 4 = 14$. Bingo!

18. If $x = 1$, then $\left(2 - \dfrac{1}{2-x}\right)\left(2 - \dfrac{1}{3-x}\right)\left(2 - \dfrac{1}{4-x}\right) =$

   (A) $\frac{1}{6}$
   (B) $\frac{5}{6}$
   (C) $\frac{5}{2}$
   (D) $\frac{10}{3}$
   (E) $\frac{7}{2}$

18. The best answer is C. If $x=1$ then the expression looks like this: $\left(2 - \dfrac{1}{1}\right)\left(2 - \dfrac{1}{2}\right)\left(2 - \dfrac{1}{3}\right)$. Use PEMDAS. Do what's in the parentheses first, then reduce. So you get: $(1)\left(\dfrac{3}{2}\right)\left(\dfrac{5}{3}\right) = \dfrac{5}{2}$

19. If $s = 4r$ and $t = 2s$, then, in terms of r, $3r + 2s + t =$

   (A) r
   (B) $6r$
   (C) $7r$
   (D) $8r$
   (E) $19r$

19. The best answer is E. Variables in the answer choices? PLUG IN! Let's make $r = 2$. Then $4r = 8$, so $s = 8$. If $s = 8$ then $t = 16$. So $3r + 2s + t = 6 + 16 + 16 = 38$. So the arithmetic answer is 38. Now plug in $r = 2$ in all the answer choices. $(19)(2) = 38$.

SECTION 1

QUESTIONS	EXPLANATIONS

20. What is the least number r for which $(3r + 2)(r - 3) = 0$?

   (A) −3

   (B) −2

   (C) $-\dfrac{2}{3}$

   (D) $\dfrac{2}{3}$

   (E) 3

20. The best answer is C. If $(3r + 2)(r - 3) = 0$, then either $(3r+2)=0$, or $(r–3)=0$, or both. If $r–3 = 0$ then $r = 3$. If $3r + 2 = 0$, then $3r = –2$ and $r = –2/3$. The "least number r" would be –2/3.

21. Which of the following categories of charitable causes received the third greatest amount in private donations from January 1971 to April 1978?

   (A) Disaster Relief
   (B) Homeless Aid
   (C) Environmental Protection
   (D) Child Safety
   (E) "Other" Causes

21. The best answer is C. Read the question carefully! Go to the graph for January 1971 to April 1978. Use process of elimination. The greatest amount of private donations to charitable causes for that period was to the category of Child Safety. Eliminate D. The second greatest was "Other." Eliminate choice E. The third greatest was Environmental Protection.

22. If funds contributed to child safety organizations in September 1989 were distributed evenly to those organizations, approximately how much did each charity receive?

   (A) $12,000,000
   (B) $9,400,000
   (C) $2,500,000
   (D) $250,000
   (E) $38,000

22. The best answer is D. This question requires you to find the amount of money received by Child Safety organizations in September 1989 from the left-hand chart. It was $9.4 million. Then divide that amount by the number of Child Safety organizations (from the right-hand chart). It's time to estimate! To make it as easy as possible, round both of those figures up. Pretend it's $10 million divided by 40. That's $250,000.

23. From February, 1980, to October, 1984, 13% of all private donations to disaster relief causes went to the Southeastern Hurricane Relief Organization. Approximately how many millions in private donations did the Southeastern Hurricane Relief Organization receive from February 1980 to October 1984?

   (A) 9
   (B) 13
   (C) 18
   (D) 26
   (E) 200

23. The best answer is D. Go to the graph for February 1980 to October 1984. The amount donated to Disaster Relief causes for that period was $200 million. Use translation. Forget about the millions. What is 13% of 200? Translate this as $x = 13/100 \cdot 200$. Reduce. $x = 26$.

SECTION 1

QUESTIONS	EXPLANATIONS

24. From September 1985 to December 1989, what was the approximate ratio of private donations in millions to homeless aid to private donations in millions to animal rights?

    (A) 20:9
    (B) 3:2
    (C) 4:3
    (D) 9:7
    (E) 6:5

24. The best answer is C. Go to the graph for September 1985 to December 1989. The amount donated to Homeless Aid causes for that period was about $300 million. The amount donated to Animal Rights causes for that period was about $225 million. You can reduce ratios! The ratio of 300:225 reduces to 12:9 or 4:3.

25. Which of the following charitable causes received the smallest percent increase in private donations from September 1989 to October 1989?

    (A) Animal rights
    (B) Disaster relief
    (C) Homeless aid
    (D) Environmental protection
    (E) Child safety

25. The best answer is E. Go to the two graphs for September 1989 and October 1989. All of the causes in the answer choices increased by about $\frac{1}{2}$ million, more or less. To find percent increase use the formula: change = x/100 • original number. The answer will be the cause for which $\frac{1}{2}$ is the smallest percentage of its September 1989 amount. So look for the cause with the greatest original amount in September 1989. It's Child safety.

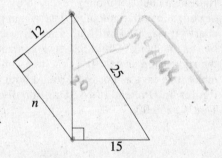

26. What is the value of n in the figure above?

    (A) 9
    (B) 15
    (C) 16
    (D) $12\sqrt{3}$
    (E) 20

26. The best answer is C. To find the value of n, start with the right triangle for which we're given two of the three sides. Use the Pythagorean theorem: $15^2 + b^2 = 25^2$. Notice that this is a 3:4:5 right triangle, since $15 = 3(5)$ and $25 = 5(5)$. So $b = 20$ or $4(5)$. Now we have two of the three sides of the triangle we're interested in: $12^2 + n^2 = 20$. Once again notice that we've got another 3:4:5 right triangle. $12 = 3(4)$ and $20 = 5(4)$. So $n = 4(4)$ or 16.

SECTION 1

QUESTIONS	EXPLANATIONS

27. If $2 < r < 8$ and $1 < s < \dfrac{5}{2}$, which of the following expresses all possible values of rs?

    (A) $1 < rs < 5$

    (B) $2 < rs < 20$

    (C) $\dfrac{5}{2} < rs < 8$

    (D) $\dfrac{5}{2} < rs < 20$

    (E) $5 < rs < 10$

27. The best answer is B. Break this problem into two parts, and use process of elimination. Which numbers are easier to work with? Since $r > 2$ and $s > 1$, the product of rs must be greater than the product of $(2)(1) = 2$. Now go to the answer choices and eliminate. The only answer choice in which $2 < rs$ is answer choice B. End of discussion!

28. What is the perimeter, in centimeters, of a rectangular newspaper ad 14 centimeters wide that has the same area as a rectangular newspaper ad 52 centimeters long and 28 centimeters wide?

    (A)   80
    (B) 118
    (C) 160
    (D) 208
    (E) 236

28. The best answer is E. To find the perimeter of a rectangle you need to know the length and the width. Of course you don't need to worry about the "centimeters." If the newspaper ad with a width of 14 has the same area as another ad 52 long and 28 wide, that means that 14(length) = 52(28). Divide both sides by 14, and you get length = 52(2) = 104. Now to find the perimeter, add up the sides of the rectangle. $104 + 104 + 14 + 14 = 236$.

29. A pipe of length x inches is cut into two segments so that the length of one segment is two inches more than three times the length of the other segment. Which of the following is the length, in inches, of the longer segment?

    (A) $\dfrac{x+4}{3}$

    (B) $\dfrac{3x+2}{3}$

    (C) $\dfrac{x-2}{4}$

    (D) $\dfrac{3x+5}{4}$

    (E) $\dfrac{3x+2}{4}$

29. The best answer is E. Variables in the answer choices? PLUG IN! In this problem start by plugging in a number for "the other segment." Let's make that 2. Then "three times the length of the other segment" would be 6. Two inches more than 6 is 8. If the longer segment is 8 and the shorter one is 2, then $x = 10$. Now plug in 10 for x in all the answer choices. Remember you're looking for the length of the longer segment, so you have to solve for 8. $\dfrac{3(10)+2}{4} = \dfrac{32}{4} = 8$.

SECTION 1

30. For all real numbers x and y, if $x \star y = x(x - y)$, then $x \star (x \star y) =$

    (A) $x^2 - xy$
    (B) $x^2 - 2xy$
    (C) $x^3 - x^2 - xy$
    (D) $x^3 - (xy)^2$
    (E) $x^2 - x^3 + x^2y$

30. The best answer is E. This function problem is obviously a huge waste of time, but it's not too difficult if you PLUG IN! To find $x \star (x \star y)$, we have to plug in to the parentheses first. If $x \star y = x(x-y)$, let's plug in $x = 3$ and $y = 2$. $3(3-2) = 3(1) = 3$. So if $x = 3$ and $(x \star y) = 3$, then the question really is $3 \star 3 = 3(3-3) = 3(0) = 0$. So by plugging in $x = 3$ and $y = 2$ in the answer choices, the right answer will be 0. Choice E works: $x^2 - x^3 + x^2y = 3^2 - 3^3 + 3^2(2) = 9 - 27 + 18 = 0$.

SECTION 2

QUESTIONS	EXPLANATIONS

1. It is the concern of many ecologists that the "greenhouse effect" is changing many of the Earth's ------- weather patterns into ------- systems, unable to be accurately forecast by those who study them.

   (A) predictable . . erratic
   (B) steady . . growing
   (C) uncertain . . uncanny
   (D) chaotic . . unforeseeable
   (E) weighty . . unbounded

1. The best answer is A. Focus on the second blank. The clue for the second blank is "unable to be accurately forecast." So a good word for the second blank would be "unpredictable." Looking at the second blank only, that eliminates answer choices B and E. The trigger word for the first blank is "changing" so the first blank must be a word that's the opposite of the one for the second blank. That eliminates answer choices C and D.

2. Children, after more than a generation of television, have become "hasty viewers"; as a result, if the camera lags, the attention of these young viewers -------.

   (A) expands
   (B) starts
   (C) alternates
   (D) wanes
   (E) clarifies

2. The best answer is D. The clue in the sentence is "Children . . . have become 'hasty viewers.'" The trigger words are "as a result." So a good word for the blank would be "wanders." In any case it must be one with negative connotations. The words in answer choices A, B, and E are positive. Answer choice C isn't really negative.

3. Many of the troubles and deficiencies in otherwise thriving foreign enterprises are ------- ignored or diminished by the author of the article in order to ------- the ways in which other businesses might attempt to imitate them.

   (A) unintentionally . . overstate
   (B) deliberately . . stress
   (C) intermittently . . equalize
   (D) willfully . . confound
   (E) brilliantly . . illustrate

3. The best answer is B. The clue for the second blank is "the ways in which other businesses might attempt to imitate them." The trigger words are "in order to." So a good word for the second blank would be "highlight." That eliminates answer choices A, C and D. The clue for the first blank is "the troubles and deficiencies . . . ignored or diminished by the author of the article." So a good word for the first blank would be "intentionally." That eliminates answer choice E.

SECTION 2

QUESTIONS	EXPLANATIONS

4. Frequently a copyright holder's property, published articles for example, is reproduced repeatedly in the absence of ------- for its reproduction, an action ------- by long-standing practice.

   (A) validation . . provoked
   (B) recognition . . forecast
   (C) payment . . licensed
   (D) accommodation . . instigated
   (E) allowance . . aggravated

4. The best answer is C. The clue for the second blank is "reproduced repeatedly ... by long-standing practice." A good word for the second blank would be "approved." Looking only at the word in the second blank, you can eliminate answer choices A, B, D and E.

5. The ------- of early metaphysicians' efforts to decipher the workings of the universe led some later thinkers to question the ------- of man's intellectual capabilities.

   (A) strain . . roots
   (B) intent . . superiority
   (C) intricacy . . realization
   (D) prevarications . . deceptiveness
   (E) failings . . adeptness

5. The best answer is E. The clue in the sentence is "led some later thinkers to question." That tells you that there was some problem with the "early metaphysicians efforts to decipher the workings of the universe." So a good word for the first blank would be "problems." That eliminates answer choices A, B, and C. The second blank must be a word such as "workings," or at least one with positive connotations. That eliminates answer choice D.

6. Being gracious should not be mistaken for a ------- characteristic of men's personalities; it is instead a fundamental virtue, one whose very state of being is increasingly ------- by the fashionable directive to "say what you feel."

   (A) trivial . . imperiled
   (B) pervading . . undermined
   (C) frivolous . . averted
   (D) superior . . renounced
   (E) immaterial . . influenced

6. The best answer is A. The clue in the sentence is "Being gracious ... is instead a fundamental virtue." This tells you that the word in the first blank means the opposite of "fundamental virtue," or at least is one with negative connotations. That eliminates answer choices B, C and D. The virtue of being gracious would be "threatened" by "the fashionable directive to 'say what you feel.'" That eliminates answer choice E.

QUESTIONS	EXPLANATIONS

7. While some individuals think that the purpose of sarcastic remarks is to disturb, by turning all communication into -------, other people see sarcastic remarks as a desire for supremacy in miniature over an environment that appears too -------.

   (A) chaos . . perplexed
   (B) equivalence . . confused
   (C) discord . . amiable
   (D) pandemonium . . disorderly
   (E) similarity . . upset

7. The best answer is D. The clue for the first blank is "the purpose of sarcastic remarks is to disturb." So a good word for the first blank would be "disturbances." That eliminates answer choices B and E. The clue for the second blank is "desire for supremacy in miniature over an environment." So a word for how that environment appears must have negative connotations. That eliminates answer choice C. Answer choice A would be a good guess, but remember to check both words. An "environment" can't really appear "perplexed."

8. CHOREOGRAPHER : DANCE ::

   (A) connoisseur : art
   (B) composer : music
   (C) acrobat : height
   (D) athlete : contest
   (E) virtuoso : skill

8. The best answer is B. A good sentence for the stem words would be "A choreographer creates a dance." Answer choices C and D don't fit that sentence for sure. Maybe you left answer choices A and E because you weren't sure what "connoisseur" or "virtuoso" meant. But remember the order of difficulty! Easy questions have easy answers, so choices A and E each would be too hard to be the answer to an easy question.

9. SCOWL : DISPLEASURE ::

   (A) sing : praise
   (B) kiss : affection
   (C) confess : crime
   (D) irritate : anger
   (E) hurl : disgust

9. The best answer is B. A good sentence for the stem words would be "To scowl shows displeasure." This is a very common relationship on the GRE. Some action shows or indicates some attitude. The only answer choice that fits this sentence is choice B.

10. GOGGLES : EYES ::

    (A) tie : neck
    (B) gloves : hands
    (C) elbow : arm
    (D) braid : hair
    (E) splint : leg

10. The best answer is B. A good sentence for the stem words would be "Goggles provide protection for the eyes." The only answer choice that fits this sentence is B.

SECTION 2

11. DRAWL : SPEAK ::

    (A) spurt : expel
    (B) foster : develop
    (C) scintillate : flash
    (D) pare : trim
    (E) saunter : walk

11. The best answer is E. A good sentence for the stem words would be "To drawl means to speak slowly." Answer choices A, B and D don't fit this sentence. If you weren't sure of the meaning of "scintillate," ask yourself "Could it mean to flash slowly?" Not likely. And "saunter" does mean to walk slowly.

12. ARBORETUM : TREE ::

    (A) dam : water
    (B) planetarium : star
    (C) apiary : bee
    (D) museum : painting
    (E) forum : speech

12. The best answer is C. If you're not exactly sure what "arboretum" means, work backwards! Make a sentence for each answer choice and see whether the stem words would fit that sentence. For answer choice A you could say "A dam holds back the flow of water." Could something hold back the flow of a tree? No way. For choice B you might say that "A planetarium is a room where the image of a star is projected." Could something be a room where the image of a tree is projected? Not likely. Perhaps you're not sure what an apiary is—never eliminate an answer choice when you don't know the meaning of one of the words. In choice D you could say "A museum is place to exhibit a painting." Could something be a place to exhibit a tree? Possibly. For E your sentence might be " A forum is a public place where a person makes a speech." Could something be a public place where a person makes a tree? No chance. #12 is right in the middle of the medium questions; doesn't answer choice D seem a bit too easy in comparison with the other choices? A good sentence for the stem words is "An arboretum is a man-made environment where a tree grows." This is another very common relationship on the GRE.

SECTION 2

13. SUBTERFUGE : DECEIVE ::

   (A) decanter : pour
   (B) interview : hire
   (C) account : save
   (D) outpost : protect
   (E) film : view

13. The best answer is A. If you're not sure what a "subterfuge" is, go right to the answer choices and eliminate answer choices that don't have a clear and necessary relationship. Answer choices B, C, and D aren't clear and necessary. #13 is the hardest medium question. Between answer choices A and E which is harder? The sentence for the stem words would be "The function of a subterfuge is to deceive." The function of a decanter is to pour.

14. RATIFY : APPROVAL ::

   (A) mutate : change
   (B) pacify : conquest
   (C) duel : combat
   (D) appeal : authority
   (E) tribulate : opinion

14. The best answer is C. First eliminate answer choices that don't have a clear and necessary relationship. That gets rid of choices B and D for sure. Work backwards on choices A and C. To "mutate is to make a change in nature or form." Could "ratify" mean to make an approval in nature or form? Not likely. For choice C, "to duel is to have a formal combat, according to rules." Could to "ratify" mean to have a formal approval, according to rules? Yes! Joe Bloggs likes answer choices D and E because "authority" and "opinion" remind him of "approval."

15. SOPORIFIC : SLEEP ::

   (A) conductor : electricity
   (B) syncopation : beat
   (C) provocation : debate
   (D) coagulant : blood
   (E) astringent : pucker

15. The best answer is E. "Soporific" is a word you need to know for the GRE. "A soporific causes sleep." Using that sentence you can eliminate answer choices A, B, C, and D. An astringent does cause a pucker. ETS loves this one.

SECTION 2

16. METTLESOME : COURAGE ::

    (A) audacious : tenacity
    (B) mediocre : originality
    (C) ludicrous : inanity
    (D) dubious : suspiciousness
    (E) altruistic : donation

16. The best answer is C. Go right to the answer choices and eliminate answer choices that do not have a clear and necessary relationship. Answer choices A, B and E are not clear and necessary relationships. Then make sentences for the remaining answer choices, and work backwards to the stem words. For answer choice C your sentence should be, "something ludicrous is characterized by inanity." Could something mettlesome be characterized by courage? Sure. For choice D your sentence would be, "something dubious causes suspiciousness." Could something mettlesome cause courage? Does <u>anything</u> cause courage? Not really.

SECTION 2

Although the study of women's history has only been developed as an academic discipline in the last twenty years, it is not the case that the current wave
(Line) of feminist activity is the first in which interest in
(5) women's past was manifest. From its very beginnings, the nineteenth-century English women's movement sought to expand existing knowledge of the activities and achievements of women in the past. At the same time, like its American counterpart, the
(10) English women's movement had a powerful sense of its own historic importance and of its relationship to wider social and political change.

Nowhere is this sense of the historical importance—and of the historical connections between the
(15) women's movement and other social and political developments—more evident than in Ray Strachey's classic account of the movement, *The Cause*. "The true history of the Women's Movement," Strachey argues, "is the whole history of the nineteenth
(20) century." The women's movement was part of the broad sweep of liberal and progressive reform which was transforming society. Strachey emphasized this connection between the women's movement and the broader sweep of history by highlighting the impor-
(25) tance for it of the Enlightenment and the Industrial Revolution. The protest made by the women's movement at the confinement and injustices faced by women was, in Strachey's view, part of the liberal attack on traditional prejudices and injustice. This
(30) critique of the women's confinement was supplemented by the demand for recognition of women's role in the public, particularly the philanthropic, realm. Indeed, it was the criticism of the limitations faced by women on the one hand, and their establish-
(35) ment of a new public role on the other hand, which provided the core of the movement, determining also its form: its organization around campaigns for legal, political and social reform.

Strachey's analysis was a very illuminating one,
(40) nowhere more so than in her insistence that, despite their differences and even antipathy to each other, both the radical Mary Wollstonecraft and evangelical Hannah More need to be seen as forerunners of the mid-Victorian feminism. At the same time, she
(45) omitted some issues which now seem crucial to any discussion of the context of Victorian feminism. Where Strachey pictured a relatively fixed image of domestic women throughout the first half of the nineteenth century, recent historical and literary
(50) works suggest that this image was both complex and unstable. The establishment of a separate domestic sphere for women was but one aspect of the enormous change in sexual and familial relationships which were occurring from the late eighteenth
(55) century through to the mid nineteenth. These changes were accompanied by both anxiety and uncertainty and by the constant articulation of women's duty in a new social world.

SECTION 2

QUESTIONS	EXPLANATIONS

17. The primary purpose of the passage is to

   (A) present an overview of the economic changes that led to the English women's movement

   (B) evaluate a view of the English women's movement as presented in a literary work

   (C) describe the social and political context of the women's movement in England

   (D) offer a novel analysis of England's reaction to the women's movement

   (E) profile several of the women who were instrumental in the success of the English women's movement.

17. The best answer is C. This is a main idea question, about the passage as a whole. You should do this question first. Answer the question in your own words, then use POE. The passage is basically discussing the way in which Strachey interprets the English women's movement. Eliminate B right away because it's not about a "literary" work. Eliminate D because it's not a "novel analysis." Eliminate A and E because they are too specific.

18. Which of the following is the best description of Ray Strachey's work, *The Cause*?

   (A) A historical analysis of a social movement

   (B) A critique of an important feminist text

   (C) A feminist revision of accepted history

   (D) A novel written as social commentary

   (E) A treatise on women's issues in the 1900s

18. The best answer is A. Go back to the second paragraph, where the book is described. From the first sentence you know it's about "the historical connections between the women's movement and other social and political developments."

19. The passage contains information to answer all of the following questions EXCEPT

   (A) In what respect were the goals of the women's movement in England similar to those of the women's movement in America?

   (B) How were the emphases of the women's movement compatible with the liberal ideals of nineteenth-century England?

   (C) In what way was the political orientation of Mary Wollstonecraft different from that of Ray Strachey?

   (D) By what means did participants in the women's movement in England seek to achieve their goals?

   (E) What historical movements were taking place at the same time as the women's movement in England?

19. The best answer is C. Since this is an EXCEPT question, you should have saved it for last. Remember, you're looking for the choice that the passage does not answer. The passage discussed how Wollstonecraft's political orientation differed from More's, but not how it differed from Strachey's.

SECTION 2

20. The author includes Strachey's claim that "the true history of the Women's Movement . . . is the whole history of the nineteenth century" (lines 16-18) in order to emphasize

   (A) Strachey's belief that the advancement of women's rights was the most significant development of its century

   (B) the importance Strachey attributes to the women's movement in bringing about the Enlightenment

   (C) Strachey's awareness of the interconnection of the women's movement and other societal changes in the 1800s

   (D) Strachey's contention that the women's movement, unlike other social and political developments of the time, actually transformed society

   (E) Strachey's argument that the nineteenth century must play a role in any criticism of the limitations of women

20. The best answer is C. For line reference questions, go back to the lines cited, and read about five lines before and after those lines. You can find the answer in either place for this question. As we've already learned, the first sentence of the paragraph tells us Strachey is writing about "the historical connections between the women's movement and other social and political developments." Choice C is just a paraphrase of this.

21. While the author acknowledges Strachey's importance in the study of women's history, she faults Strachey for

   (A) focusing her study on the legal and political reform enacted by the women's movement

   (B) oversimplifying her conception of the social condition of women prior to the reforms of the women's movement

   (C) failing to eliminate the anachronistic idea of "women's duty" from her articulation of nineteenth-century feminism

   (D) omitting Mary Wollstonecraft and Hannah More from her discussion of important influences in feminism

   (E) recommending a static and domestic social role for women following the women's movement

21. The best answer is B. Look back in the passage for the place where the author "faults" Strachey. It's in the last paragraph, beginning in line 47. The author states, "Where Strachey pictured a relatively fixed image of domestic women throughout the first half of the nineteenth century, recent historical and literary works suggest that this image was both complex and unstable."

SECTION 2

QUESTIONS	EXPLANATIONS

22. Which of the following best describes the structure of the final paragraph?

(A) The author acknowledges Strachey's accomplishment, indicates an oversight in Strachey's work and asserts her own view regarding that oversight.

(B) The author offers an argument in favor of Strachey's position, presents an example to support that argument and concludes by discussing the theory's relevance to modern times.

(C) The author presents a summary of Strachey's thesis, introduces a counterargument to that thesis and reconciles the difference between them.

(D) The author contrasts the theories of two prominent feminists, places those theories in the context of Strachey's and posits an opinion about those theories as a whole.

(E) The author introduces two forerunners of mid-Victorian feminism, describes their theories, and exposes the flaws inherent in their reasoning.

22. The best answer is A. Answer the question in your own words first. You know from question 21 that the author likes Strachey's book, but points out something that Strachey omitted. Eliminate C, D, and E, because they don't say that the author likes the book. Eliminate B because the author is not making an "argument."

23. The author's attitude toward Strachey's analysis is one of

(A) qualified admiration
(B) optimistic enthusiasm
(C) extreme criticism
(D) studied impartiality
(E) intellectual curiosity

23. The best answer is A. This question is almost the same as the last one. You know from question 21 that the author likes Strachey's book, but points out something that Strachey omitted. Same question, same answer. Make sure you know the meaning of the word "qualified" as it's used in this context.

24. Which of the following, if true, would most weaken the author's assertion about the similarity between the English and American women's movements?

(A) The English and American women's movements took place in very different sociohistorical climates.

(B) The English women's movement began almost a century before the American women's movement.

(C) The English women's movement excluded men, while the American women's movement did not.

(D) Few members of the English women's movement were aware of the impact it would have on society.

(E) Many participants in the English women's movement continued to perform traditional domestic roles.

24. The best answer is D. First, go back to the passage to find out what the author said about "the similarity between the English and American women's movements." It's at the end of the first paragraph. The author says that "like its American counterpart, the English women's movement had a powerful sense of its own historic importance and of its relationship to wider social and political change." So you're looking for an answer choice that would indicate that that was not true. Choice D directly contradicts the author's assertion.

SECTION 2

QUESTIONS	EXPLANATIONS

Following the discovery in 1895 that malaria is carried by *Anopheles* mosquitoes, governments around the world set out to eradicate those insect
Line vectors. In Europe the relation between the malarial
(5) agent, protozoan blood parasites of the genus *Plasmodium*, and the vector mosquito, *Anopheles maculipennis*, seemed at first inconsistent. In some localities the mosquito was abundant but malaria rare or absent, while in others the reverse was true. In
(10) 1934 the problem was solved. Entomologists discovered that *A. maculipennis* is not a single species but a group of at least seven.

In outward appearance the adult mosquitoes seem almost identical, but in fact they are marked by a host
(15) of distinctive biological traits, some of which prevent them from hybridizing. Some of the species distinguished by these traits were found to feed on human blood and thus to carry the malarial parasites. Once identified, the dangerous members of the *A.*
(20) *maculipennis* complex could be targeted and eradicated.

25. Which of the following best expresses the author's main point in the passage above?

(A) With the increasing density of the human population, it will become increasingly necessary to reduce populations of other species.

(B) Without an understanding of the seven groups of *A. maculipennis* mosquitos, eradication of malaria will be unlikely.

(C) Despite the eradication of large numbers of *Plasmodium*-carrying mosquitos, malaria is still a significant problem in certain localities.

(D) After establishing the relationship between *Plasmodium* and the vector mosquito, scientists discovered that *Anopheles* mosquitos carried malaria.

(E) To eradicate an insect disease vector, it was necessary to have a scientific understanding of that vector.

25. The best answer is E. This is a main idea question, about the passage as a whole. You should do this question first. Answer the question in your own words first, then use process of elimination. The passage is about how scientists study insects that carry malaria so that those insects could be eradicated. A is ridiculous and doesn't mention insects. C doesn't mention how scientists study the bugs. D doesn't mention eradicating the insects. Since there's no prediction of the future, you can eliminate B.

SECTION 2

QUESTIONS	EXPLANATIONS

26. Which of the following best describes the reason that scientists were initially perplexed at the discovery that malaria was spread by *Anopheles* mosquitoes?

   (A) Scientists had evidence that malaria was carried by the protozoan blood parasite *Plasmodium*.
   (B) Scientists felt that because so many species of *Anopheles* existed they could not be carriers.
   (C) Scientists were unable to find a direct correlation between *Anopheles* density and frequency of malaria occurrence.
   (D) Scientists knew that many species of *Anopheles* mosquito did not feed on human blood.
   (E) Scientists believed that the *Anopheles* mosquito could not be host to the parasite *Plasmodium*.

26. The best answer is C. Go back to the first paragraph. In lines 7-9 the passage states "In some localities the mosquito was abundant but malaria rare or absent."

27. It can be inferred from the passage that a mosquito becomes a carrier of malaria when

   (A) it ingests the blood of a human being infected with malaria
   (B) it lives in regions where malaria is widespread
   (C) it consumes blood from a protozoan malarial agent
   (D) it has extended contact with other insect vectors
   (E) it is spawned in *Plasmodium*-infested localities

27. The best answer is A. Go back to the second sentence of the second paragraph. It says that the mosquito becomes a carrier when it feeds on human blood.

SECTION 2

QUESTIONS	EXPLANATIONS
28. SLUR: (A) honor agreements (B) settle disputes (C) pronounce clearly (D) criticize directly (E) exclude purposefully	28. The best answer is C. To "slur" means to pronounce indistinctly.
29. MORATORIUM: (A) lack of emotion (B) discouragement (C) savings (D) brilliance (E) period of activity	29. The best answer is E. A "moratorium" is a period of inactivity.
30. DIFFUSE: (A) compare (B) chill (C) concentrate (D) blemish (E) oscillate	30. The best answer is C. To "diffuse" means to spread out, or disperse.
31. THWART: (A) aid (B) beseech (C) dislocate (D) assign (E) allege	31. The best answer is A. To "thwart" means to prevent from taking place, or to frustrate.
32. AGITATE: (A) relieve (B) satisfy (C) reject (D) condense (E) confirm	32. The best answer is A. To "agitate" means to upset or disturb.
33. AUTHENTICATE: (A) sentence (B) disseminate (C) scrutinize (D) theorize (E) discredit	33. The best answer is E. To "authenticate" means to establish as being genuine.

SECTION 2

QUESTIONS	EXPLANATIONS

34. ACCLIMATION:

    (A) alienation
    (B) adoration
    (C) facilitation
    (D) invigoration
    (E) exaltation

34. The best answer is A. "Acclimation" means an adjustment to a new environment or situation. It's a word with positive connotations. So you can eliminate answer choices that have positive connotations, because the opposite of "acclimation" must be a negative word. Answer choices B, C, D and E are all positive words.

35. TENUOUSLY:

    (A) having a strong basis
    (B) following a formal procedure
    (C) having overall consensus
    (D) with evil intent
    (E) under loose supervision

35. The best answer is A. "Tenuous" means insubstantial or flimsy. So you can eliminate answer choices with negative connotations. That eliminates answer choices D and E for sure. Answer choice B isn't really very positive.

36. FLORID:

    (A) pallid
    (B) vapid
    (C) lucid
    (D) rancid
    (E) candid

36. The best answer is A. "Florid" means flushed, or ruddy. So you could say that it has positive connotations, or at least not negative ones. So you could eliminate answer choices C and E, which are positive words. Answer choices B and D would be good guesses.

37. FACTIOUS:

    (A) totally generic
    (B) openly welcomed
    (C) closely observable
    (D) seriously rejected
    (E) given to agreement

37. The best answer is E. "Factious" means tending to cause conflict or discord. If you knew that "factious" has negative connotations, you could eliminate answer choices A and D. And you could eliminate answer choices A and C because they don't have clear, direct opposites. Answer choice B is a good guess.

38. MISCIBLE:

    (A) likely to agree
    (B) hard to please
    (C) generous
    (D) desirable
    (E) not capable of being mixed

38. The best answer is E. "Miscible" means able to be mixed. Yeah, right. Who's ever heard of this one? Don't worry about it. You can get a few questions wrong and still get an 800 on the Verbal section of the GRE.

SECTION 3

QUESTIONS	EXPLANATIONS

1. To send a message from L to G by messenger, it is necessary for the messenger to travel through department

   (A) F
   (B) J
   (C) K
   (D) M
   (E) N

1. The best answer is B. Combine the clues into one diagram. Your diagram might look like this:

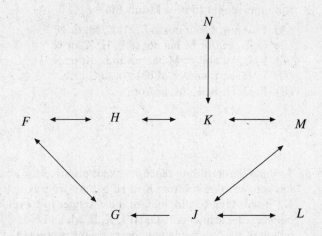

You can see that, to get from L to G, you have to go through J.

2. If a broken elevator temporarily makes the route between H and K unusable, then in order to send a message to F by messenger from N, a messenger would have to go through how many other departments besides F and N?

   (A) 2
   (B) 3
   (C) 4
   (D) 5
   (E) 6

2. The best answer is C. You could use the same diagram, and just cover up the connection between H and K. To get to F from N you'd have to go through K, M, J, and G.

3. If the hallway between H and K is being resurfaced, making the route unusable, a messenger would NOT be able to travel from

   (A) G to F
   (B) G to L
   (C) J to M
   (D) J to L
   (E) K to F

3. The best answer is B. As in the previous question, cover up the connection between H and K. Notice that you can only go from J to G, not from G to J. So you can't go from G to L.

QUESTIONS	EXPLANATIONS

4. If a broken elevator affects the route from K to M, making it possible for a messenger to travel in only one direction from K to M, it will still be possible for a messenger to travel from J to

   (A) G and/or L but not to F, H, K, M, or N
   (B) G, L, and/or M but not to F, H, K, or N
   (C) F, G, H, and/or M but not to L, K, or N
   (D) F, H, K, L and/or M but not to G or N
   (E) F, G, H, K, L, M, and/or N

4. The best answer is E. This time, cover up the connection between K and M. Then use process of elimination. You can go from J to all of the other departments.

5. Assume that building repairs make it possible for a messenger to travel from K to H, but not from H to K. It will then be possible for a messenger to travel between departments F, G, H, J, K, L, M, and N if which of the following temporary routes is erected?

   (A) From F to N
   (B) From J to K
   (C) From L to K
   (D) From L to N
   (E) From M to N

5. The best answer is A. You might want to redraw the diagram according to the changed conditions.

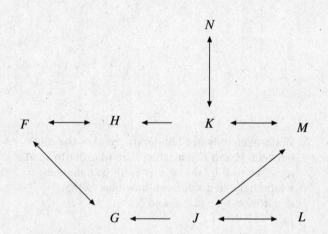

Notice that you need some way to get from the departments on the left side of the diagram (F, G and H) to the departments on the right side of the diagram. The only answer choice that makes a connection between the left side and the right side is A.

QUESTIONS	EXPLANATIONS

6. For five years, while remodeling the town zoo, the Littleton parks commission has been transferring a large number of animals from the city of Littleton to both the Wambek and Starr King zoos in the city of Jefferson. It follows that when Littleton's zoo reopens next year, either Wambek or Starr King will have to be closed and their animal populations consolidated.

The author of the statements above assumes that

(A) The removal of the Littleton animals from the Wambek and Starr King zoos will leave one or both of these zoos considerably underpopulated.
(B) Littleton's remodeled zoo will not be large enough for the prospective animal population.
(C) The Littleton animals comprise only a small part of the total animal populations at both the Wambek and Starr King zoos.
(D) Incorporation of extra animals from Littleton has placed a tremendous burden on the resources of both the Wambek and Starr King zoos.
(E) Animals will not be sent between the Wambek and Starr King zoos in the next year.

6. The best answer is A. The last sentence of the argument is the conclusion. An assumption must support the conclusion. Answer choice A does support it. Answer choice B, C, and E go against the conclusion. Answer choice D is out of the scope of the argument.

7. A manmade plant hormone has been added to a section of a garden in order to ward off insect infestation. The designer of the hormone has asserted that the recent dearth of insects in that section of the garden demonstrates that the manmade plant hormone wards off insect infestation.

Which of the following, if true, would cast the greatest doubt on the designer's assertion?

(A) The recent dearth of insects in that section of the garden was not as complete as had been expected given the results derived in controlled experiments.
(B) Because the manmade plant hormone would ultimately be neutralized by soil erosion, more manmade plant hormones would need to be added to the garden every three months.
(C) A manmade plant hormone produced from different chemicals which had been developed by the designer at an earlier period was ineffective in warding off insect infestation.
(D) The recent dearth of insects in that section of the garden is the same as the recent dearth of insects in otherwise very similar sections of the garden without the manmade plant hormone.
(E) The recent dearth of insects in that section of the garden, even though substantial, is not yet sufficient to compensate for the plant loss in that section of the garden in the last year.

7. The best answer is D. The conclusion is that the manmade hormone wards off insect infestation. This assumes that without the manmade hormone, there wouldn't have been a "dearth of insects" in that section of the garden. If it were true that there would be a dearth of insects without the hormone, that undermines the argument.

SECTION 3

QUESTIONS	EXPLANATIONS

8. A higher level of safety in automotive braking mechanisms depends upon control by internal computer monitoring systems.

   Automotive braking mechanisms, to be safe, would have to pump in intervals, and determining that the brakes would compensate for all situations is impossible.

   Despite technological advances, every internal computer monitoring system has on use proved to have serious weaknesses which in certain circumstances would bring about significant failure.

   Which of the following can be inferred from the statements above?

   (A) If designers are diligent in planning the internal computer monitoring system to be used for automotive braking mechanisms, there is an exceptionally good chance that the braking mechanism will ensure a high level of safety if and when it is needed.
   (B) Techniques for decreasing the number of errors in building internal computer monitoring systems will not be discovered.
   (C) Automotive braking mechanisms will not function safely during pumping.
   (D) Some method of control other than internal computer monitoring systems will have to be designed.
   (E) The safety of automobile braking systems cannot be ensured during pumping.

8. The best answer is E. Remember that an inference is something that is known to be true, based on what you're told in the argument. For inference questions, go with the safest, least disputable, answer choice that supports the argument. Answer choice A goes against the argument. Answer choices B, C, and D are all too disputable.

9. Which of the following is an acceptable layout of exits, from positions 1 through 6, according to the restrictions above?

   (A) Morrow, Bainbridge, Driscoll, Kimball, Homer, Crescent
   (B) Crescent, Kimball, Morrow, Driscoll, Bainbridge, Homer
   (C) Kimball, Crescent, Morrow, Homer, Driscoll, Bainbridge
   (D) Bainbridge, Homer, Kimball, Morrow, Crescent, Driscoll
   (E) Driscoll, Bainbridge, Kimball, Crescent, Homer, Morrow

9. The best answer is E. Your original diagram should look like this:

```
1   2   3   4   5   6
H                   B
C                   K
M

B ... H

K ... M
```

BD DB

Then, eliminate answer choices that violate the clues.
(A) M cannot be in 1.
(B) C cannot be in 1.
(C) B cannot be after H.
(D) B and D cannot be separated.

SECTION 3

QUESTIONS	EXPLANATIONS

10. If the Crescent exit is placed somewhere after the Homer exit, which of the following must be true?

(A) The Crescent exit is placed somewhere after the Bainbridge exit.
(B) The Crescent exit is placed somewhere after the Kimball exit.
(C) The Crescent exit is placed somewhere after the Morrow exit.
(D) The Homer exit is placed somewhere before the Kimball exit.
(E) The Homer exit is placed somewhere before the Driscoll exit.

10. The best answer is A. If C is placed after H, and B must be before H, then C must be after B.

11. If the Homer exit is placed somewhere before the Kimball exit, the Kimball exit could be placed in which of the following positions?

(A) 1
(B) 2
(C) 3
(D) 4
(E) 6

11. The best answer is D. Draw a new picture.

1	2	3	4	5	6
B	D	H	K		

12. If the Morrow exit is placed somewhere before the Bainbridge exit, which of the following must be true?

(A) The Morrow exit is placed somewhere before the Crescent exit.
(B) The Morrow exit is placed somewhere before the Driscoll exit.
(C) The Bainbridge exit is placed somewhere before the Crescent exit.
(D) The Bainbridge exit is placed somewhere before the Driscoll exit.
(E) The Bainbridge exit is placed somewhere before the Kimball exit.

12. The best answer is B. Draw a picture that fits the question, then eliminate answer choices that aren't in it.

1	2	3	4	5	6
K	M	D	B	H	C

Eliminate choices D and E.
Then redraw the picture to eliminate any remaining answer choices.

1	2	3	4	5	6
K	C	M	B	D	H

Eliminate choices A and C.

SECTION 3

QUESTIONS	EXPLANATIONS

13. All of the following are possible orderings for the six exits EXCEPT

    (A) Kimball, Morrow, Crescent, Driscoll, Bainbridge, Homer

    (B) Kimball, Crescent, Morrow, Driscoll, Bainbridge, Homer

    (C) Driscoll, Bainbridge, Kimball, Homer, Crescent, Morrow

    (D) Kimball, Homer, Morrow, Driscoll, Bainbridge, Crescent

    (E) Kimball, Driscoll, Bainbridge, Crescent, Homer, Morrow

13. The best answer is D. On an EXCEPT question, four of the answer choices are okay, so look for the violation of the clues. In choice D, *H* cannot be before *B*.

14. If the Bainbridge exit is placed next to the Morrow exit, which of the following must be true?

    (A) The Kimball exit is placed in position 1.

    (B) The Crescent exit is placed in position 2.

    (C) The Driscoll exit is placed in position 3.

    (D) The Bainbridge exit is placed in position 4.

    (E) The Morrow exit is placed in position 5.

14. The best answer is A. Draw a picture that fits the question, then eliminate answer choices that aren't in it.

1	2	3	4	5	6
K	M	B	D	C	H

That eliminates choices B, C, D and E.

15. If the Kimball exit is placed in position 5, how many logically possible orderings of all six exits are possible?

    (A) 2

    (B) 3

    (C) 4

    (D) 5

    (E) 6

15. The best answer is C. Just do it. Draw out the possibilities. If *K* is in position 5, then *M* must be in position 6.

1	2	3	4	5	6
D	B	H	C	K	M
D	B	C	H	K	M
B	D	H	C	K	M
B	D	C	H	K	M

SECTION 3

QUESTIONS	EXPLANATIONS

16. Any of the events could be scheduled for Sunday EXCEPT

(A) a banquet
(B) the luncheon
(C) the party
(D) the seminar
(E) the wedding

16. The best answer is E. Your original diagram should look like this:

S	M	T	W	Th	F	S
~W	~W	~W		~L	~L	~L/~S

$$\boxed{B1 - - - B2}$$

$$\boxed{PB1}\ \boxed{B1P}$$

$$S\ldots B2$$

$$\boxed{L - - W}$$

If the wedding is always the third day after the luncheon, the wedding can never be on Sunday, Monday, or Tuesday.

17. Which of the following is a possible schedule, including the day off, when no event is scheduled, for the six events from Sunday through Saturday?

(A) banquet, luncheon, party, seminar, banquet, wedding, day off
(B) luncheon, banquet, party, wedding, day off, banquet, seminar
(C) party, banquet, luncheon, seminar, wedding, banquet, day off
(D) party, banquet, seminar, luncheon, day off, banquet, wedding
(E) day off, banquet, luncheon, seminar, banquet, party, wedding

17. The best answer is D. Use process of elimination to eliminate choices.

(A) The party must be the day before or the day after the first banquet.
(B) The seminar can never be Saturday.
(C) The wedding must be the third day after the luncheon.
(E) The wedding must be the third day after the luncheon.

18. The day on which the luncheon is scheduled must be no more than how many days after the day scheduled for the first banquet?

(A) 1
(B) 2
(C) 3
(D) 4
(E) 5

18. The best answer is C. Draw a picture, trying to make the luncheon as many days after the first banquet as you can.

S	M	T	W	Th	F	S
B1	P	S	L	B2	O	W

QUESTIONS	EXPLANATIONS

19. The party could be scheduled for any of the following days EXCEPT

    (A) Sunday
    (B) Monday
    (C) Tuesday
    (D) Wednesday
    (E) Thursday

19. The best answer is E. Draw a picture using your B1 - - - B2 block.

S	M	T	W	Th	F	S
	B1	P	–	–	B2	

Notice that the latest the first Banquet can be is Tuesday. Therefore, the latest that the Party could be is Wednesday.

20. If the luncheon is scheduled for Sunday, which of the following pairs of events CANNOT be scheduled for consecutive days?

    (A) a banquet and the wedding
    (B) the luncheon and a banquet
    (C) the luncheon and the party
    (D) the party and the seminar
    (E) the party and the wedding

20. The best answer is D. Draw a picture, trying the answer choices. If the answer choice could be true, eliminate that choice.

S	M	T	W	Th	F	S
L	P	B1	W			B2

Eliminate choices (A) and (C).

L	B1	P	W		B2	

Eliminate choices (B) and (E).

21. If no event is scheduled for Sunday, which of the following could be true?

    (A) The luncheon is scheduled for the day before the day of the first banquet.
    (B) The party is scheduled for the day before the day of the first banquet.
    (C) The seminar is scheduled for the day before the day of the first banquet.
    (D) The wedding is scheduled for the day before the day of the second banquet.
    (E) The wedding is scheduled for the day after the day of the seminar.

21. The best answer is A. Draw a picture, trying the answer choices. If the answer choice could be true, that's it!

S	M	T	W	Th	F	S
O	L	B1	P	W	S	B2

That works.

22. If the party is scheduled for the day before the day of the first banquet, the days on which the luncheon can be scheduled include

    (A) Sunday and Monday
    (B) Sunday and Wednesday
    (C) Monday and Tuesday
    (D) Monday and Wednesday
    (E) Tuesday and Wednesday

22. The best answer is B. Draw a picture, eliminate answer choices, then redraw the picture to eliminate remaining choices.

S	M	T	W	Th	F	S
L	P	B1	W	S	O	B2

Eliminate choices C, D and E.

P	B1	O	L	S	B2	W

Eliminate choice A.

SECTION 3

QUESTIONS	EXPLANATIONS

23. During the past fifteen years, 20 percent of the judges with sufficient experience to be considered for federal judgeships were women, and all of those deemed to have sufficient experience during those years received federal judgeships. Despite this fact, only 8 percent of federal judgeships are currently filled by women.

Which of the following, if true, could explain the discrepancy in the percentages cited in the passage above?

(A) Fifteen years ago, it required less experience to be considered for federal judgeships than it does today.

(B) The majority of those holding federal judgeships have held those positions for more than fifteen years, dating back to a time when practically everyone holding that position was male.

(C) The women with sufficient experience to be considered for federal judgeships have tended to specialize in different areas of law than the men considered for federal judgeships.

(D) Men and women holding federal judgeships have received equal financial compensation for the previous fifteen years.

(E) Although women currently hold eight percent of the federal judgeships, they hold only three percent of circuit judgeships.

23. The best answer is B. Use process of elimination. Answer choices C, D, and E are out of scope. Answer choice A doesn't say anything about women or men.

24. It has been argued that medical researchers would make more impressive strides in their effort to develop cures for certain infectious diseases if they knew more about how cells replicate. This argument, however, could be challenged on the basis that a major advance in pest control has never come from any insight into the reproductive patterns of insects.

The argument above relies on an analogy that assumes that fighting infectious diseases is an endeavor similar to which of the following?

(A) Theories of cell-replication
(B) Efforts at pest control
(C) Conclusions about how researchers make advances
(D) Patterns of infectious disease transmission in insects
(E) Research into the reproductive patterns of insects

24. The best answer is B. The analogy is between fighting infectious diseases and attempts at pest control.

SECTION 3

25. Rita has more clients than Frank and more clients than Tom. Isabel has more clients than Rita. Sam has no fewer clients than Rita.

    If all of the statements above are true, which of the following cannot be true?

    (A) Tom has more clients than Sam.
    (B) Tom has more clients than Frank.
    (C) Isabel has more clients than Tom.
    (D) Sam and Rita have the same number of clients.
    (E) Frank has fewer clients than Sam.

25. The best answer is A. This is a game disguised as an argument. You should symbolize the clues, then combine them into one diagram:

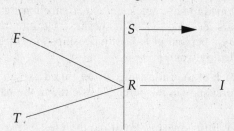

    (B) Could be true.
    (C) Must be true.
    (D) Could be true.
    (E) Must be true.

SECTION 4

QUESTIONS	EXPLANATIONS

1. The units digit in   The hundreds digit in
    the number 1,743   the number 5,243

1. The best answer is A. The units digit in 1,743 is 3. The hundreds digit in 5243 is 2.

$$1.3 + .6 + .9 + x = 5$$

2. x 2.3

2. The best answer is B. $1.3 + .6 + .9 = 2.8$ So $x = 5 - 2.8 = 2.2$ in Column A.

3. 4^3 3^4

3. The best answer is B. In Column A, $4^3 = 64$. In Column B, $3^4 = 81$.

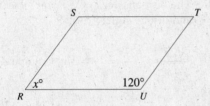

RSTU is a parallelogram

4. x 45

4. The best answer is A. Use Fred's theorem on parallelograms! Opposite angles are equal, and the big angle plus the small angle add up to 180 degrees. So $x + 120 = 180$. $x = 60$ in Column A.

5. 30 percent of \$150   60 percent of \$75

5. The best answer is C. Translate percentages into fractions. $\left(\dfrac{30}{100}\right)150 = 45$ in Column A. $\left(\dfrac{60}{100}\right)75 = 45$ in Column B.

QUESTIONS	EXPLANATIONS

6.

$$\frac{n}{3} \qquad\qquad \frac{m+n}{3}$$

6. The best answer is D. Plug in numbers for variables in Quant Comp. Let's make $n = 3$ and $m = 2$. In Column A $\frac{3}{3} = 1$. In Column B $\frac{2+3}{3} = \frac{5}{3}$.

So you can eliminate answer choices A and C, because Column B is greater when you use those numbers. Now plug in again. Keep $n = 3$, but let's make $m = 0$. If $m = 0$, the two columns are equal. That eliminates answer choice B. So, by process of elimination, D is the answer.

7.

$$\frac{\sqrt{27}}{\sqrt{3}} \qquad\qquad \frac{\sqrt{45}}{\sqrt{5}}$$

7. The best answer is C. Remember, you _can_ multiply and divide square roots!

$$\frac{\sqrt{27}}{\sqrt{3}} = \sqrt{\frac{27}{3}} = \sqrt{9} = 3 \text{ in Column A}$$

$$\frac{\sqrt{45}}{\sqrt{5}} = \sqrt{\frac{45}{5}} = \sqrt{9} = 3 \text{ in Column B.}$$

8.

$$5\left(\frac{x}{5} + \frac{y}{5} + \frac{7}{5}\right) \qquad\qquad x + y + 7$$

8. The best answer is C. You should distribute the product in Column A.

$$5\left(\frac{x}{5} + \frac{y}{5} + \frac{7}{5}\right) = 5\left(\frac{x}{5}\right) + 5\left(\frac{y}{5}\right) + 5\left(\frac{7}{5}\right) = x + y + 7.$$

SECTION 4

QUESTIONS	EXPLANATIONS

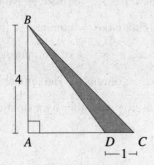

$\triangle ABC$ is isosceles

9. $\dfrac{\text{Area of the shaded region of } \triangle ABC}{\text{Area of the unshaded region of } \triangle ABC}$ $\qquad$ $\dfrac{1}{3}$

9. The best answer is C. Joe Bloggs puts answer choice D. But did you notice that triangle ABC is isosceles? That means that the base and the height are each equal to 4. So the base of the unshaded region is 3, and the base of the shaded region is 1. Then use the formula for area of a triangle

$\dfrac{1}{2}$(base)(height) and you get

$$\dfrac{\frac{1}{2}(1)(4)}{\frac{1}{2}(3)(4)} = \dfrac{2}{6} = \dfrac{1}{3} \text{ in Column A.}$$

The average (arithmetic mean) of two positive integers is equal to 17. Each of the integers is greater than 12.

10. Twice the larger of $\qquad$ 44
the two integers.

10. The best answer is B. Joe Bloggs says D, because you could have different values for Column A. But if the average of two positive integers is 17, then the total of the two numbers = 34. Since the smallest one of the numbers could be is 13, the largest the other number could be is 21. Twice 21 = 42. That's the largest possible value for Column A. So Column B is <u>always</u> greater.

The circumference of a circle with a radius of $\dfrac{1}{2}$ meter is C meters.

11. C $\qquad$ 4

11. The best answer is B. If a circle has a radius of $\dfrac{1}{2}$, then its diameter = 1. To find the circumference of a circle, use the formula $2\pi r$ or πd. So the circumference would be $(1)(\pi) = \pi$ in Column A. Remember π is only slightly greater than 3. So 4 in Column B is greater.

SECTION 4

12. $$\sqrt{\frac{7}{3}} \qquad\qquad \frac{1}{3}\sqrt{7}$$

12. The best answer is A. Joe Bloggs would say C. But if you manipulate the two quantities it's easier to see the difference. $\sqrt{\frac{7}{3}} = \frac{\sqrt{7}}{\sqrt{3}}$ in Column A and $\frac{1}{3}\sqrt{7} = \frac{\sqrt{7}}{3}$ in Column B. Remember that $\sqrt{3} \approx 1.7$. When you divide a number by a smaller number you get a bigger result.

$$\frac{a}{b} = \frac{1}{3} \text{ and } \frac{b}{c} = \frac{15}{4}$$

13. $\qquad a \qquad\qquad\qquad c$

13. The best answer is D. Joe Bloggs looks at it too quickly and picks B. Try to make b the same for both ratios. Let's use 15. Then $\frac{a}{b} = \frac{1}{3} = \frac{5}{15}$. Now that b is the same for both ratios, you can compare a and c. $a = 5$ in Column A, and $c = 4$ in Column B. Eliminate choices B and C. But we're not done! What if $b = -15$, $a = -5$ and $c = -4$. Now which column is bigger? Column B is greater if the numbers are negative. Now eliminate choice A.

14. The circumference of a circular region with radius r The perimeter of a square with side r

14. The best answer is A. Joe Bloggs chooses D, because he says, "We don't know what r is." But let's plug in some numbers and see what happens. To start with, make $r = 2$.
Then you get $2\pi r = 4\pi$ in Column A and $4(2) = 8$ in Column B.
So Column A is greater if $r = 2$. So you can eliminate choices B and C.
Now let's plug in a weird number; make $r = 1$.
Then you get 2π in Column A and 4 in Column B. Column A wins again.
Plug in once more, to be sure. Make $r = \frac{1}{2}$.
Then you get π in Column A and 2 in Column B. Column A wins again.
You can't plug in 0 or a negative number, because r is the radius of the circle and the side of the square.

SECTION 4

QUESTIONS	EXPLANATIONS

15. $3^{17} + 3^{18}$ $(4)3^{17}$

15. The best answer is C. Use process of elimination. Answer choice D is impossible, because there are no variables in the problem. Joe Bloggs would choose either A or B because either one or the other "looks" greater. So the right answer must be C. To see why, factor the quantity in Column A.
$$3^{17} + 3^{18} = 3^{17}(1+3) = 3^{17}(4)$$

16. Which of the following numbers is greater than $-\dfrac{7}{3}$?

(A) -7

(B) -3

(C) -2

(D) $-\dfrac{8}{3}$

(E) $-\dfrac{5}{2}$

16. The best answer is C. Use the Bowtie to compare fractions, or change $-\dfrac{7}{3}$ into $-2\dfrac{1}{3}$.

17. If the cost of a one-hour telephone call is $7.20, what would be the cost of a ten-minute telephone call at the same rate?

(A) $7.10

(B) $3.60

(C) $1.80

(D) $1.20

(E) $ .72

17. The best answer is D. If the cost of a one-hour telephone call is $7.20, divide that by 6 to find the cost for a ten-minute call, because ten minutes is one-sixth of an hour. $7.20 ÷ 6 = $1.20.

18. A pie is baked in a circular plate with a radius of 6 inches. If the pie is then cut into eight equal pieces, what would be the area, in square inches, of each slice of the pie?

(A) $\dfrac{1}{8}\pi$

(B) $\dfrac{2}{9}\pi$

(C) $\dfrac{9}{2}\pi$

(D) 6π

(E) 36π

18. The best answer is C. To find the area of a slice of the pie, first you need to find the area of the whole pie, then divide the area of the whole pie by 8 to find the area of each slice. If the radius of the pie is 6, then the area of the whole pie would be $\pi r^2 = \pi 6^2 = 36\pi$. Then divide by 8. $\dfrac{36\pi}{8} = \dfrac{9\pi}{2}$.

SECTION 4

QUESTIONS	EXPLANATIONS

19. If $s=3r$ and $t=7s$, then, in terms of r, $t-s-r=$

   (A) $21r$
   (B) $17r$
   (C) $10r$
   (D) $4r$
   (E) r

19. The best answer is B. Variables in the answer choices? Plug in! Start with r, because r is the variable in all the answer choices.
Let's make $r=2$. Then $s=6$ and $t=42$. So the question really would be: $42-6-2=34$. Plug in $r=2$ in all the answer choices, to see which one equals 34.

20. $\sqrt{1.44-.63}=$

   (A) .9
   (B) .81
   (C) .12
   (D) .09
   (E) .03

20. The best answer is A. Remember that you can't subtract square roots. So you have to do the subtraction under the square root sign first.
$\sqrt{1.44-.63}=\sqrt{.81}$ Then, change the decimal to a fraction to make it easier to find the square root.
$\sqrt{\dfrac{81}{100}}=\dfrac{\sqrt{81}}{\sqrt{100}}=\dfrac{9}{10}=.9$.

SECTION 4

QUESTIONS	EXPLANATIONS

Questions 21-25 refer to the following data.

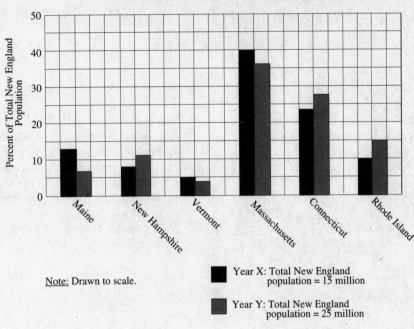

PERCENT OF POPULATION IN NEW ENGLAND
BY STATE IN YEAR X AND YEAR Y

Note: Drawn to scale.

■ Year X: Total New England
population = 15 million

■ Year Y: Total New England
population = 25 million

21. Which of the following is the approximate average, in millions, of the populations of Maine and New Hampshire in Year X?

(A) 3.2
(B) 2.6
(C) 2.2
(D) 1.6
(E) 0.8

21. The best answer is D. According to the chart, in Year X Maine's population was 13% of 15 million and New Hampshire's was 8%. Since these percentages are of the same total, you can just average the two percentages, APPROXIMATELY. The average of the two is about 10%. 10% of 15 is 1.5. Which choice is closest to 1.5?

22. By approximately how much did the population of Rhode Island increase from Year X to Year Y?

(A)   750,000
(B) 1,250,000
(C) 1,500,000
(D) 2,250,000
(E) 3,750,000

22. The best answer is D. For this question you do have to find the numbers for Rhode Island for each year. Use translation. In Year X Rhode Island's population was 10% of 15, or 1.5 million. Eliminate choice C, because we're not done yet. In Year Y it was 15% of 25 million, or 3. 75 million. Eliminate choice E, because we're still not done. The difference between the two figures was a little more than 2 million.

SECTION 4

23. In Year Y, the population of Massachusetts was approximately what percent of the population of Vermont?

   (A) 50%
   (B) 120%
   (C) 300%
   (D) 400%
   (E) 900%

23. The best answer is E. Again, since these are percentages of the same total, you don't need to find the actual numbers. The question is really asking 36 is what percent of 4? Use translation. $36 = x/100 \cdot 4$? Solve for x. $3600 = 4x$. $900 = x$.

24. If the six New England states are ranked by population in Year X and in Year Y, how many states had a different ranking from Year X to Year Y?

   (A) None
   (B) Two
   (C) Three
   (D) Four
   (E) Five

24. The best answer is C. The fastest way to do this question is to just write down the rankings for Year X, then the rankings for Year Y. Then count the number of states whose rankings changed. The rankings for Year X were (1) MA, (2) CT, (3) ME, (4) RI, (5) NH, (6) VT. The rankings for Year Y were (1) MA, (2) CT, (3) RI, (4) NH, (5) ME, (6) VT. Which changed? ME, RI, and NH. So the answer is three.

25. How many New England states decreased in population from Year X to Year Y?

   (A) One
   (B) Two
   (C) Three
   (D) Four
   (E) Five

25. The best answer is A. Don't waste lots of time on Question 25! Since the total population for all the New England states increased from Year X to Year Y, any state that increased in its percentage of the total must have increased in population. That eliminates three of the states. Eliminate choices D and E. To calculate the exact answer you have to find the population for both Year X and Year Y for the three states we have left. Only Maine's went down. In Year X Maine's population was $13/100 \cdot 15$ million or about 1.95 million. In Year Y Maine's population was $7/100 \cdot 25$ million or about 1.75 million.

SECTION 4

QUESTIONS	EXPLANATIONS

26. In a certain election, 60 percent of the voters were women. If 30 percent of the women and 20 percent of the men voted for candidate X, what percent of all the voters in that election voted for candidate X?

(A) 18%
(B) 25%
(C) 26%
(D) 30%
(E) 50%

26. The best answer is C. What's missing? How many voters there were. Let's say there were 100 voters. Then if 60% were women, 60 were women and 40 were men. If 30% of the 60 women voted for candidate X, then $\frac{30}{100}(60) = 18$ women voted for candidate X. And if 20% of the 40 men voted for candidate X, then $\frac{20}{100}(40) = 8$ men voted for candidate X. So out of the 100 voters, $18 + 8 = 26$ voted for candidate X, or 26%.

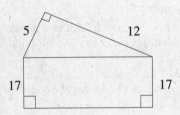

27. What is the perimeter of the figure above?

(A) 51
(B) 64
(C) 68
(D) 77
(E) 91

27. The best answer is B. To find the perimeter of the figure, you need to add up all the sides. To find the missing side of the rectangle, solve for the opposite side of the rectangle, using the Pythagorean Theorem: $a^2 + b^2 = c^2$. You may remember that $5^2 + 12^2 = 13^2$. So the missing sides of the rectangle are each 13. Now add up the sides of the figure: $5 + 12 + 17 + 13 + 17 = 64$.

28. If a, b, and c are consecutive non-positive integers and $a < b < c$, which of the following must be true?

   I. $-a < -c$
  II. $abc < 0$
 III. abc is even

(A) None
(B) II only
(C) III only
(D) II and III only
(E) I, II, and III

28. The best answer is C. Plug in numbers! You have to plug in consecutive non-positive integers. Let's make $a = -2$, $b = -1$ and $c = 0$. Using these numbers, you can see right away that II is false: $(-2)(-1)(0) = 0$. So you can eliminate every answer choice that includes II. That eliminates answer choices (B), (D), and (E). Now you only have to check III. Using these numbers, the product is even, because 0 is even, but let's plug in different numbers to be sure. Now make $a = -3$, $b = -2$, and $c = -1$. $(-3)(-2)(-1) = -6$. That's also even, so III must be true.

SECTION 4

QUESTIONS	EXPLANATIONS

29. If $5a - 3b = -9$ and $3a + b = 31$, then $a + b =$

   (A) -7
   (B) -3
   (C) 6
   (D) 13
   (E) 19

29. The best answer is E. When you have two equations with two variables, usually you can either add or subtract the two equations to solve for one of the variables. When you try that with these two equations, however, it doesn't work with the two equations in their original forms. So you have to manipulate one of the equations to get it into a form that will be useful.

Let's multiply both sides of the second equation by 3, so that we get $+3b$.

$3(3a + b) = 3(31)$ Remember to distribute! You get:
$9a + 3b = 93$. Now we can add the two equations to solve for a.

$$9a + 3b = 93$$
$$5a - 3b = -9$$
$$14a + 0 = 84$$

so $a = 6$. Now plug $a = 6$ back into the second equation we started with, in order to solve for b most easily.

$3(6) + b = 31$
$18 + b = 31$
$b = 13$. Finally, we can answer the question. $6 + 13 = 19$. Whew!

30. 5×10^3 is what percent of $\frac{1}{5} \times 10^2$?

   (A) $2,500\%$
   (B) $4,900\%$
   (C) $20,000\%$
   (D) $24,900\%$
   (E) $5,000\%$

30. The best answer is E. Translate into a math equation and expand out the exponents.

$$5 \times 10^3 = \left(\frac{x}{100}\right)\frac{1}{5} \times 10^2 \text{ or}$$

$$5 \times 10 \times 10 \times 10 = \left(\frac{x}{100}\right)\frac{1}{5} \times 10 \times 10$$

When you reduce and solve for x you get:

$5 \times 5 \times 10 \times 10 \times 10 = x$ or $25,000 = x$. So the answer is $25,000\%$.

SECTION 5

QUESTIONS	EXPLANATIONS
1. Many feature films are criticized for their ------- content, even though television news is more often the medium that depicts violent events in excessive detail. (A) discretionary (B) graphic (C) dramatic (D) artistic (E) honest	1. The best answer is B. The clue in the sentence is "that depicts violent events in excessive detail." So the word in the blank must mean "depicting in excessive detail." Also, feature films are criticized for some reason, so the word in the blank must have negative connotations.
2. The use of alcohol and other drugs, with the exception of tobacco, seems to increase and decrease -------; certain periods are marked by a social inclination toward abstinence, which after a time gives way to drug consumption by some part of society, and eventually to ------- acceptance. (A) erratically . . partial (B) cyclically . . widespread (C) exponentially . . mitigated (D) criminally . . absolute (E) simultaneously . . conventional	2. The best answer is B. The clue for the first blank is "certain periods are marked by a social inclination toward abstinence, which after a time gives way to drug consumption." So a good word for the first blank would be "periodically." The only answer choice with a first word meaning "periodically" is B.
3. After screenwriter Neil Jordan's most recent work opened in selected urban areas, many theatergoers were -------, but after pundits expressed their -------, appreciation of the film increased and distribution surged. (A) skeptical . . approbation (B) apathetic . . diffidence (C) ebullient . . trepidation (D) dubious . . disdain (E) unimpressed . . antipathy	3. The best answer is A. The clue for the second blank is "appreciation of the film increased. . . ." So the word in the second blank must have positive connotations. Looking only at the second word, you can eliminate answer choices B, C, D and E, because the second words in all these choices have negative connotations.

SECTION 5

4. The pieces exhibited at many university galleries are chosen to reflect the diverse tastes of the academic communities they serve; the curators avoid ------- in favor of -------.

   (A) continuity . . rigidity
   (B) variation . . craftsmanship
   (C) uniformity . . eclecticism
   (D) modernism . . classics
   (E) homogeneity . . segmentation

4. The best answer is C. The clue in the sentence is "chosen to reflect the diverse tastes of the academic communities they serve." So the word in the second blank must mean "diversity" and the word in the first blank must mean the opposite of "diversity."

5. The American public venerates medical researchers because the researchers make frequent discoveries of tremendous humanitarian consequence; however, the daily routines of scientists are largely made up of result verification and statistical analysis, making their occupation seem -------.

   (A) fascinating
   (B) quotidian
   (C) recalcitrant
   (D) experimental
   (E) amorphous

5. The best answer is B. The clue for the blank is "the daily routines of scientists are largely made up of result verification. . . ." So the word in the blank must be one meaning "characterized by daily routine." That's what "quotidian" means. Also, since the first part of the sentence is positive, and the trigger word is "however," you know that the word in the blank must be negative. Choice C would be a good guess.

6. In a vitriolic message to his troops, General Patton insisted that he would ------- no further insubordination, no matter how barbarous the ensuing engagements might become.

   (A) impede
   (B) brief
   (C) denote
   (D) brook
   (E) expose

6. The best answer is D. The clue for the blank is "no further insubordination. . . ." So the word in the blank must mean "tolerate." That's what "brook" means.

SECTION 5

QUESTIONS	EXPLANATIONS

7. Chang realized that she had been ------- in her duties; had she been more -------, the disaster may well have been avoided.

   (A) unparalleled . . careful
   (B) irreproachable . . aware
   (C) derelict . . vigilant
   (D) arbitrary . . interested
   (E) neglectful . . insensible

7. The best answer is C. The clue in the sentence is "the disaster may well have been avoided." So you know that the first word must be negative, and the second word must be positive. Eliminate positive words for the first blank [choices A and B]. Eliminate negative words for the second blank, choice E. Then choose the most difficult answer you have left.

8. METEOROLOGY : WEATHER ::

   (A) philology : love
   (B) epistemology : disease
   (C) physiology : mind
   (D) demography : population
   (E) astrology : planets

8. The best answer is D. A good sentence would be, "Meteorology is the study of weather."

9. MAELSTROM : WATER ::

   (A) downpour : rain
   (B) wave : current
   (C) cyclone : wind
   (D) tornado : debris
   (E) storm : snow

9. The best answer is C. If you weren't sure what a "maelstrom" is, eliminate answer choices that don't have clear and necessary relationships. Answer choices B, D and E aren't clear and necessary relationships.

10. FIX : STABLE ::

   (A) furrow : productive
   (B) mend : torn
   (C) fortify : strong
   (D) deter : active
   (E) captivate : attractive

10. The best answer is C. A good sentence for the stem words would be, "To fix means to make stable."

11. GALL : IRRITATION ::

   (A) accommodate : deception
   (B) beleaguer : felicity
   (C) awe : apathy
   (D) discomfit : confusion
   (E) inculcate : fear

11. The best answer is D. Eliminate answer choices A, C, and E because they don't have clear and necessary relationships. D: "discomfit" means to cause "confusion," and "gall" means to cause "irritation."

SECTION 5

QUESTIONS	EXPLANATIONS

12. PAPYRUS : PAPER ::

    (A) manuscript : book
    (B) hatchet : ax
    (C) cart : wagon
    (D) daguerreotype : photograph
    (E) house : mansion

12. The best answer is D. A good sentence would be "Papyrus is a primitive form of paper." If you didn't know "daguerreotype" you could use process of elimination. A hatchet is not a primitive ax, it's just a small one. A cart is not a primitive wagon; it's a two-wheeled vehicle, and a wagon is a four-wheeled vehicle.

13. BLACKSMITH : FOUNDRY ::

    (A) farmer : shed
    (B) artist : studio
    (C) physician : laboratory
    (D) teacher : college
    (E) reporter : television

13. The best answer is B. If you weren't sure what a "foundry" is, go right to the answer choices and eliminate answer choices that don't have clear and necessary relationships. That eliminates A, C, D, and E. Work backwards from answer choice B: "A studio is a place where an artist works." Could a "foundry" be a place where a blacksmith works? You bet. If you thought a college is where a teacher works, make a more specific sentence. You could say that a studio is where an artist <u>makes things</u>.

14. ARIA : SONG ::

    (A) covenant : agreement
    (B) fable : story
    (C) monument : sculpture
    (D) prose : poem
    (E) soliloquy : speech

14. The best answer is E. You might start with the sentence, "An aria a type of song." Then eliminate answer choice D. Then make your original sentence more specific, "An aria is a song performed by one person." Now you can eliminate A, B, and C.

15. LONGING : PINE ::

    (A) remorse : rue
    (B) anguish : seethe
    (C) forbearance : dignify
    (D) concern : intervene
    (E) suffering : inflict

15. The best answer is A. Eliminate answer choices B, C, D, and E. They don't have clear and necessary relationships. Hard questions have hard answers, and answer choice A is the hardest answer.

16. CHEVRON : BADGE ::

    (A) caisson : cart
    (B) calcium : bone
    (C) wax : candle
    (D) clothing : uniform
    (E) oration : eulogy

16. The best answer is A. Don't waste too much time on the hardest problem! Answer choices B, C, and D are awfully easy, don't you think? Choice D is a Joe Bloggs trap. Choice E would be a good guess, but isn't A more difficult?

SECTION 5

Each passage in this group is followed by questions based on its content. After reading a passage, choose the best answer to each question. Answer all questions following a passage on the basis of what is stated or implied in that passage.

In *A Room of One's Own*, Virginia Woolf performs a typically stream-of-consciousness feat by beginning with a description of the view from her window: a leaf falls

Line from a tree, and a woman in leather boots and a man in a
(5) maroon overcoat climb into a taxi and glide away. Woolf uses this moment to discuss the unity of the mind, and the effortlessness with which she had invested this ordinary sight with a kind of rhythmic order. She ends with a consideration of Coleridge's remark that a great

(10) mind is androgynous. "What does one mean by 'the unity of the mind?'" Woolf asks.

One of Woolf's theses is that unity, and not repression, is the necessary state for creativity. Woolf describes men's sentences as having a particular shape, natural to

(15) men, but unnatural and clumsy to women. She rightly praises Austen for developing her own rhythm and her own sentence, which is expressive of her genius, her characters, and her history. Woolf suggests that the women's suffrage movement fomented a reaction of

(20) threatened male self-assertion that meant a decline in literary power. "It is fatal," she writes, "for any one who writes to think of their sex. . . it is fatal for a woman to lay the least stress on any grievance; to plead justice with any cause; in any way to speak consciously as a

(25) woman."

A Room of One's Own exhorts women to reach for a higher, almost religious approach to writing. "Do not dream of influencing other people;" she writes, "think of things in themselves."

SECTION 5

QUESTIONS	EXPLANATIONS
17. Which of the following literary projects would Woolf most likely support?	17. The best answer is C. The passage tells you that Woolf said not to "dream of influencing other people." So she wouldn't like the literary projects described in choices A, B, and D. The first sentence of the second paragraph stresses "unity, and not repression, is the necessary state for creativity."

17. Which of the following literary projects would Woolf most likely support?

(A) A narrative poem in which a heroine overcomes male challenges through intellectual superiority

(B) A fictional polemic asserting the importance of social equality of men and women

(C) A novel that expresses the unrepressed truth of the author's experience

(D) A short story that responds to the historical injustice in the treatment of women

(E) A critical essay on Coleridge which explains his remark about androgyny in terms of his psychological history

17. The best answer is C. The passage tells you that Woolf said not to "dream of influencing other people." So she wouldn't like the literary projects described in choices A, B, and D. The first sentence of the second paragraph stresses "unity, and not repression, is the necessary state for creativity."

18. The author refers to Woolf's description of the man and woman climbing into the taxi in order to

(A) give an example of Woolf's mastery of stream-of-consciousness techniques

(B) show a typically feminine perspective of everyday life

(C) demonstrate how Woolf's writing was unconcerned with changing the social order

(D) refute the notion that Woolf's assertions are anti-female or anti-feminist

(E) begin the discussion of Woolf's conception of the ways in which the mind unifies the world

18. The best answer is E. See the sentence following the one referred to in the question. The passage states, "Woolf uses this moment to discuss the unity of the mind. . . ."

19. According to the passage, Woolf believes which of the following to be true about Jane Austen's work?

I. Austen's sentences are representative of an androgynous 'unity of the mind.'

II. Austen's syntax and literary form are products of her personal experience.

III. Austen's literary work exemplifies a particular form of well-realized female artistic expression.

(A) I only
(B) II only
(C) I and II only
(D) II and III only
(E) I, II, and III

19. The best answer is D. Beware of direct repetitions of words from the passage! It was Coleridge, not Woolf, who said that a great mind is androgynous. Eliminate answer choices A, C, and E. You don't have to check II, because it's in both remaining choices. III is true, because in the middle of the second paragraph the author tells you that Woolf praised Austen.

SECTION 5

QUESTIONS	EXPLANATIONS
20. It can be inferred from the passage that Woolf believes that (A) women should not write about subjects that are specifically female (B) the women's suffrage movement contributed to a decline in literary quality (C) Austen created a narrative style that was appropriate for her gender and subject matter (D) women's sentences should mimic the shape of men's sentences (E) some readers could misinterpret her statements as being denigrating to women	20. The best answer is C. Use common sense to eliminate answer choices B, D and E. Answer choice A is close, but it's worded in a way that's too disputable.

Because human anatomy does not change (except over long periods of time), knowledge acquired a century ago is still accurate today. Broad functions
Line of any part of the body, such as the skin, are dupli-
(5) cated in different ways by other organs. One can eventually understand the entire body as a larger system made up of smaller, interdependent systems.

A cross-section of the skin reveals a top layer of epidermis, or cuticle, followed by derma, and finally,
(10) subcutaneous cellular tissue. Sprouting through all three layers are hairs, with hair follicles and erector pili muscles embedded deep within the subcutaneous tissue. Sweat (sudoriferous glands), fat cells, and sebaceous glands are scattered throughout, while
(15) papillae, which are conical and extremely sensitive, can be found directly beneath the superficial layer.

The skin is the primary organ of the sense of touch. It can excrete substances as well as absorb them, and it plays a vital role in regulating body
(20) temperature and in protecting the tissues that lie beneath it.

The epidermis has no veins or arteries and varies considerably both in thickness and in the depth or fineness of its furrows. On the palm, for example,
(25) the skin is quite thick, or horny, and is marked by deep furrows or lines. On the back of the hand, however, the skin is less thick, and has only a faint network of lines crisscrossing it. The pigment found in the epidermis gives whatever color there is to the
(30) skin; this pigment is similar to that found in the retina of the eye. One layer down, in the derma, there is similar variation in thickness, mostly to protect underlying tissue.

In the derma lies the vascular system, which
(35) includes nerves, blood vessels, and lymphatics. The derma is divided into two sub-layers: the reticular layer and the papillary layer, which is closer to the epidermis. The less sensitive the skin, the fewer papillae reside there; in the most sensitive places,
(40) such as the fingertips and the nipples, the papillae are long, large, and grouped closely together to form parallel arcs with ducts to sweat glands lying in between. Under the papillary layer, and conforming to it, is the reticular layer, composed of fibrous bands
(45) and elastic tissue, and interlaced by fat and sudorifer-ous glands.

The basic functions of muscular contraction, vascular transport, nerve communication, and protec-tion all take place in the various layers of the skin, so
(50) that understanding the components of the skin and how they work together is a helpful step in under-standing the complex anatomy of the human body.

SECTION 5

QUESTIONS	EXPLANATIONS

21. The author is primarily concerned with

    (A) giving an overview of human anatomical functions
    (B) describing the layers of the skin to show one example of an anatomical system
    (C) concluding that the study of human anatomy must first begin with the skin
    (D) discussing how the skin is only one system in a much larger and more complex system
    (E) detailing the three layers of the skin: the epidermis, the derma, and the subcutaneous cellular tissue, each of which has its own separate functions

21. The best answer is B. The main idea of the passage could be expressed: "The skin is an example of one of the systems that work together in the body." Then use process of elimination.

    (A) Nothing about the skin.
    (C) "Must first begin with" is too disputable.
    (D) Close, but there really isn't much about the "complex system".
    (E) What about the context? See the first paragraph and last sentence.

22. The passage suggests that the area of skin most closely associated with skin sensitivity is the

    (A) reticular layer
    (B) papillary layer
    (C) sudoriferous gland
    (D) subcutaneous tissue
    (E) vascular system

22. The best answer is B. See lines 17–18 and 43–45.

23. The author would most likely agree with which of the following statements?

    I.   Extremely sensitive skin is characterized by a minute number of papillae.
    II. Hair can be found in subcutaneous tissue.
    III. Skin and the retina both rely on pigment to give them color.
    (A) I only
    (B) II only
    (C) I and II only
    (D) II and III only
    (E) I, II, and III

23. The best answer is D. If you took the time to get Question 22 right, it pays off here, because you know that I is false. Eliminate answer choices A, B, and E. Don't check II because it's in both remaining choices. To see why III is true go back to lines 28–31.

24. The passage supplies information to answer which of the following questions?

    (A) What causes the erector pili muscle to contract?
    (B) Why is the epidermis covered with furrows?
    (C) How quickly do papillae react to sensation?
    (D) What do sudoriferous glands and sebaceous glands have in common?
    (E) Where in the body can pigmentation be found?

24. The best answer is E. A repeat of III in Question 23! See lines 28–31.

SECTION 5

QUESTIONS	EXPLANATIONS

25. The author implies that

    (A) there is a relationship between the thickness of the skin and the number and depth of the skin's furrows

    (B) the reticular layer is the only layer that contains fibrous bands

    (C) the skin is the only part of the body that has a sense of touch

    (D) areas of the skin with sudoriferous glands are extremely sensitive

    (E) both hair and the reticular layer are made up of the same kind of tissue

25. The best answer is A. See lines 25–26. Answer choices B and C are too disputable ("the only"), as is choice E ("the same kind").

26. The passage suggests that if the skin were damaged in some way, and unable to perform some of its functions, which of the following might happen?

    (A) The pigmentation would no longer be similar to that found in the retina.

    (B) The deep furrows found on some parts of the skin would disappear.

    (C) The body would regulate its temperature less effectively.

    (D) The fingertips would no longer be characterized by an abundance of papillae.

    (E) The body would lose its sense of touch.

26. The best answer is C. To answer this question, look for the place in the passage which describes some of the normal functions of undamaged skin. See the third paragraph, lines 18–21. Answer choices B and E go against common sense.

27. The passage states that all the following are found in the skin EXCEPT

    (A) fat cells
    (B) lymphatics
    (C) veins
    (D) pigmentation
    (E) ligaments

27. The best answer is E. Use Process of Elimination! Eliminate D based on what you learned in the previous questions. Common sense tells you the skin has veins, so eliminate C. Fat cells are mentioned in line 13, as are lymphatics in line 35.

28. CHRONIC: (A) intermittent (B) healthy
    (C) tardy (D) consistently durable
    (E) suddenly available

28. The best answer is A. "Chronic" means continuing, or of long duration.

29. FORK: (A) judge (B) praise
    (C) agitate (D) converge (E) impress

29. The best answer is D. "Fork" means to divide into branches.

SECTION 5

QUESTIONS	EXPLANATIONS
30. FANCY: (A) ornament (B) abhor (C) falsify (D) reclaim (E) stiffen	30. The best answer is B. To "fancy" means to be fond of. To "abhor" means to detest.
31. ANIMATE: (A) enervate (B) frustrate (C) regress (D) condemn (E) distort	31. The best answer is A. "Animate" means to give life to. "Enervate" means to deprive of vitality.
32. CARDINAL: (A) wholesome (B) obscure (C) trivial (D) impious (E) lascivious	32. The best answer is C. "Cardinal" means of foremost importance.
33. INCUBATE: (A) squelch (B) hatch (C) assemble (D) decide (E) sterilize	33. The best answer is A. To "incubate" means to maintain in favorable environmental conditions for development. You know that "incubate has positive connotations, so eliminate positive answer choices (C), (D), and (E). Answer choice (B) is a Joe Bloggs trap. To "squelch" means to crush completely.
34. OBSTREPEROUS: (A) disciplined (B) insubordinate (C) predictable (D) well-formed (E) exhausted	34. The best answer is A. If you knew that "obstreperous" is a negative word, eliminate answer choices (B) and (E). "Obstreperous" means unruly.
35. CHECK: (A) assume (B) complete (C) disagree (D) emulate (E) unbridle	35. The best answer is E. To "check" means to hold in restraint. To "unbridle" means to remove restraint.
36. IMPRECATE: (A) evaluate carefully (B) uphold forcefully (C) bless (D) forgive (E) confine	36. The best answer is C. If you knew that "imprecate" has negative connotations, eliminate choice (E), because it's negative. Choices (A) and (B) aren't as positive as choices (C) and (D). "Imprecate" means to curse.
37. BEREAVE: (A) tear (B) collaborate (C) solicit (D) radiate (E) furnish	37. The best answer is E. You know that "bereave" is a negative word. Eliminate answer choices (A), because it's negative, and choices (B) and (C), because they aren't really very positive. Choice (D) has no direct opposite. "Bereave" means to deprive of, as by death, but not always.
38. HIE: (A) separate (B) dawdle (C) lower cautiously (D) comfort warmly (E) leave suddenly	38. The best answer is B. Who knew "hie"? Shakespeare did, and he used it a lot. "Hie" means to go quickly.

SECTION 6

QUESTIONS	EXPLANATIONS

1. Which of the following is a possible order for the bulbs on the strand?

    (A) Yellow, red, red, red, yellow, green, green, blue, white, blue

    (B) Green, blue, white, blue, red, red, red, yellow, yellow, green

    (C) Blue, white, blue, green, yellow, yellow, green, red, red, red

    (D) Yellow, blue, white, yellow, red, red, red, blue, green, green

    (E) Green, green, yellow, red, red, red, yellow, blue, white, blue

---

1. The best answer is E. Your diagram for the set-up might look like this:

1 2 3 4 5 6 7 8 9 10

1/10 different

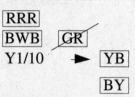

Use process of elimination .

(A) If Y is first, it must be next to B.
(B) 1 and 10 must be different colors.
(C) G can't be next to R.
(D) W must have B on either side of it.

---

2. If a red bulb is at one end of the strand and a yellow bulb is at the other, which of the following statements must be true?

    (A) The two middle bulbs are both blue.

    (B) The two middle bulbs are both red.

    (C) The two middle bulbs are both green.

    (D) The two middle bulbs are green and blue.

    (E) The two middle bulbs are yellow and green.

---

2. The best answer is C. Draw a picture. The two middle bulbs are in places 5 and 6.

1	2	3	4	5	6	7	8	9	10
R	R	R	Y	G	G	B	W	B	Y

---

3. If the two yellow bulbs are next to each other and the green bulbs are not next to each other, which of the following statements must be true?

    (A) A red bulb is next to a blue bulb.

    (B) A yellow bulb is next to a blue bulb.

    (C) A blue bulb is not next to a green bulb.

    (D) A white bulb is not next to a blue bulb.

    (E) A yellow bulb cannot be at either end of the strand.

---

3. The best answer is E. If the two yellow bulbs are next to each other, then a yellow bulb cannot be at either end of the strand, because if a yellow bulb is at either end, it must be next to a blue bulb. You could draw a picture.

1	2	3	4	5	6	7	8	9	10
R	R	R	Y	Y	G	B	W	B	G

SECTION 6

QUESTIONS

4. If a yellow bulb is at the end of the strand, which of the following statements must be true?

   (A) A green bulb is next to a yellow bulb.
   (B) A white bulb is at the other end of the strand.
   (C) A blue bulb is at the other end of the strand.
   (D) A yellow bulb is at the other end of the strand.
   (E) A blue bulb is next to a red bulb.

5. If a white bulb is next to the bulb at the end of the strand and the two yellow bulbs are next to each other, which of the following statements could be true?

   (A) There is a yellow bulb at the end of the strand.
   (B) There is a red bulb next to a green bulb.
   (C) There is a blue bulb next to a green bulb.
   (D) There is not a yellow bulb next to a green bulb.
   (E) There is a blue bulb next to a yellow bulb.

6. Which of the following is NOT possible?

   (A) A yellow bulb is at one end of the strand, and a green bulb is at the other end.
   (B) A red bulb is at one end of the strand, and a green bulb is at the other end.
   (C) A yellow bulb is directly adjacent to a red bulb and a green bulb.
   (D) There are red bulbs next to a yellow bulb, a blue bulb, and a white bulb.
   (E) There are blue bulbs next to a red bulb, a white bulb, and a yellow bulb.

EXPLANATIONS

4. The best answer is A. Draw a picture.

1	2	3	4	5	6	7	8	9	10
R	R	R	Y	G	G	B	W	B	Y

5. The best answer is C. Again, draw a picture.

1	2	3	4	5	6	7	8	9	10
B	W	B	G	G	Y	Y	R	R	R

6. The best answer is D. Look back to the pictures you drew for earlier questions to eliminate answers. The picture for Question 3 eliminates C. Then draw pictures to eliminate other choices.

1	2	3	4	5	6	7	8	9	10
Y	B	W	B	R	R	R	Y	G	G

eliminate choice (A).

R	R	R	B	W	B	Y	Y	G	G

eliminate choices (B) and (E).

SECTION 6

7. Over the past five years, Clean toothpaste has been advertised as the most effective means of preventing tooth decay. However, according to dentists' records, many patients experiencing severe tooth decay used Clean toothpaste. Clearly, Clean toothpaste is not an effective means of preventing tooth decay

Which of the following statements, if true, would most seriously weaken the conclusion above?

(A) Of the patients experiencing tooth decay, two-thirds indicate that they would be willing to switch brands of toothpaste.
(B) The advertisements for Clean toothpaste advocate brushing twice a day.
(C) If Clean toothpaste were not available, more patients would experience severe tooth decay.
(D) Dentists continue to recommend Clean toothpaste more than any other brand.
(E) Of those who experienced severe tooth decay, only one-eighth also experienced gum disease.

7. The best answer is C. Use process of elimination. Answer choices A, B, D, and E are out of the scope of the argument.

8. A group of physicians wishing to explore the link between protein intake and high blood pressure performed a nutrition experiment on a selected group of ten vegetarians. Five of the people were given a high-protein, low-fat diet. The group given the high-protein, low-fat diet exhibited the same five-percent increase in blood pressure as did the group given the low-protein, high-fat diet.

Which of the following conclusions can most properly be drawn if the statements above are true?

(A) The physicians did not establish a link between protein and high blood pressure.
(B) The sample chosen by the physicians was not representative of the general vegetarian population.
(C) Some physicians believe there is a link between protein and high blood pressure.
(D) Vegetarians are more likely to eat a high protein, low fat diet than a low protein, high fat diet.
(E) There is a link between protein and high blood pressure.

8. The best answer is A. Answer choices B, C, and D are out of the scope of the argument. Choice E goes against the argument.

SECTION 6

QUESTIONS	EXPLANATIONS

9. Whenever Joe does his laundry at the Main Street Laundromat, the loads turn out cleaner than they do when he does his laundry at the Elm Street Laundromat. Laundry done at the Main Street Laundromat is cleaner because the machines at the Main Street Laundromat use more water per load than do those at the Elm Street Laundromat.

Which of the following statements, if true, helps support the conclusion above?

(A) The clothes washed at the Elm Street Laundromat were, overall, less clean than those washed at the Main Street Laundromat.

(B) Joe uses the same detergent at both laundromats.

(C) The machines at the Oak Street Laundromat use twice as much water as do those at the Main Street Laundromat.

(D) Joe does three times as much laundry at the Main Street Laundromat as he does at the Elm Street Laundromat.

(E) Joe tends to do his dirtier laundry at the Elm Street Laundromat.

9. The best answer is B. Answer choices C and D are out of scope. Choices A and E go against the argument.

10. Which of the following could be an outfit order on the night following a night when the outfit order is plaid, striped, dotted, and checkered?

(A) Checkered, dotted, striped, and plaid
(B) Dotted, checkered, plaid, and striped
(C) Plaid, dotted, checkered, and striped
(D) Striped, plaid, checkered, and dotted
(E) Striped, checkered, plaid, and dotted

10. The best answer is E. Since the first order is: P–S–D–C, use process of elimination.

(A) P can never be directly after S.

(B) D can never be first.

(C) P can't be first because it was first in the previous order.

(D) P can never be directly after S.

11. All of the following could be an outfit order for the evening following an evening in which the outfit order has the checkered outfit fourth and the plaid outfit third EXCEPT

(A) Checkered, dotted, plaid, and striped
(B) Checkered, plaid, dotted, and striped
(C) Striped, dotted, plaid, and checkered
(D) Plaid, checkered, striped, and dotted
(E) Plaid, striped, checkered, and dotted

11. The best answer is C. The previous order would be: S–D–P–C.

Now look for the violation of the clues. Choice C has S first, and that violates the clue that the first outfits can never be the same.

SECTION 6

QUESTIONS	EXPLANATIONS

12. If the outfit order on one evening is checkered, plaid, dotted, and striped, and on the next evening the outfit order has the plaid outfit fourth, which of the following must be true of the outfit order on the second evening?

   (A) The checkered outfit is modeled first.
   (B) The striped outfit is modeled first.
   (C) The checkered outfit is modeled immediately before the striped outfit.
   (D) The dotted outfit is modeled immediately before the striped outfit.
   (E) The dotted outfit is modeled directly before the checkered outfit.

12. The best answer is B. If the order on the first evening is C–P–D–S, and on the next evening P is fourth, C can't be first, and D can never be first, so S must be first. The order would have to be S–C–D–P or S–D–C–P.

13. If on a Monday the outfit order is striped, dotted, plaid, and checkered, and on a Wednesday the outfit order is plaid, checkered, striped, and dotted, which of the following must be true about the outfit order for Tuesday?

   (A) The plaid outfit is modeled second.
   (B) The striped outfit is modeled second.
   (C) The dotted outfit is modeled third.
   (D) The striped outfit is modeled fourth.
   (E) The checkered outfit is modeled first.

13. The best answer is E. If on Monday the order is S–D–P–C, and on Wednesday is P–C–S–D, then which outfit can be first on Tuesday? S can't be first, because it was first Monday. P can't be first on Tuesday, because it is first on Wednesday. D can never be the first outfit. So, by process of elimination, C must be the first outfit on Tuesday.

14. Which of the following routes must be taken to go from the ash to the elm while passing the fewest trees?

   (A) The Cross Country Trail
   (B) The Green Mountain Trail, then the Cross Country Trail
   (C) The Green Mountain Trail, then the Bethlehem Trail
   (D) The Bethlehem Trail, then the Cross Country Trail
   (E) The Green Mountain Trail, then the Bethlehem Trail, and then the Cross Country Trail

14. The best answer is B. For a map game, work off of one diagram.

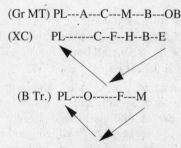

(Gr MT) PL---A---C---M---B---OB

(XC)   PL-------C--F--H--B--E

(B Tr.) PL---O------F---M

The A is on the Green Mountain Trail, then, at B, switch to the Cross Country Trail.

SECTION 6

QUESTIONS	EXPLANATIONS
15. What is the maximum number of trees one can pass in order to get from the elm to the maple, without reusing any part of a path or passing the Pine Lodge? (A) 1 (B) 2 (C) 3 (D) 4 (E) 5	**15.** The best answer is D. From the elm, use the Cross Country Trail go past B, H, F to C. Switch at C to the Green Mt. Trail and go to M.
16. Which sequence of trees is a possible route from the Old Barn to the Pine Lodge? (A) Birch, maple, fir, oak (B) Birch, elm, ash, cherry (C) Birch, maple, fir, ash (D) Birch, hemlock, cherry (E) Birch, maple, cherry, elm, ash	**16.** The best answer is A. You can go on the Green Mt. Trail to B and to M. Switch at M for the Bethlehem Trail and go past F and O.
17. How many different routes are there from the Pine Lodge to the birch which pass exactly three trees and do not reuse any part of a path? (A) 2 (B) 3 (C) 4 (D) 5 (E) 6	**17.** The best answer is D. 1. Green Mt. Trail from PL past A, C and M. 2. Cross Country Trail from PL past C, F and H. 3. Bethlehem Trail from PL past O and F to M. Switch at M to Green Mt. Trail to B. 4. Cross Country Trail from PL past C to F. Switch to Bethlehem Trail at F and go to M. Switch at M to Green Mt. Trail to B. 5. Bethlehem Trail from PL past O to F. At F switch to Cross Country Trail past H to B.
18. If a new path is found that connects the fir tree to the Old Barn, what is the fewest number of trees that could be passed on a hike from the Pine Lodge to the Old Barn and back, taking a different route each way? (A) 3 (B) 4 (C) 5 (D) 6 (E) 7	**18.** The best answer is B. With the new connection between F and the OB, you could start at the PL and pass C and F on the way to the OB. That's two trees so far. From the OB go past B and E on your way back to the PL. That's four all together.

QUESTIONS	EXPLANATIONS

19. If N is the first print displayed in the portfolio, which of the following statements could be true?

    (A) O is the second print displayed.
    (B) P is the third print displayed.
    (C) Q is the third print displayed.
    (D) W is the fourth print displayed.
    (E) T is the fifth print displayed.

19. The best answer is D. Your set up for the game should look like this:

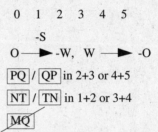

Then draw a diagram for this question

   0   1   2   3   4   5
       N   T

Eliminate choices A and E. Now the only places to put P and Q would be on pages 4 and 5. So eliminate choices B and C.

20. If S is the second print displayed, all of the following statements could be true EXCEPT

    (A) M is the first print displayed
    (B) W is the first print displayed
    (C) N is the third print displayed
    (D) N is the fourth print displayed
    (E) Q is the fifth print displayed

20. The best answer is E. Draw a new picture. If S is the second print, prints N and T must be on pages 3 and 4.

   0   1   2   3   4   5
          S   N   T
          S   T   N

So you have no room to put both P and Q.

21. All of the following prints could be displayed on the first page EXCEPT

    (A) M
    (B) O
    (C) Q
    (D) T
    (E) W

21. The best answer is C. This should have been one of your original deductions. If P and Q must be on facing pages, neither P nor Q can ever be on the first page, because the first page faces the blank page 0.

SECTION 6

22. If O is the first print displayed, which of the following statements must be true?

    (A) P is the second print displayed.
    (B) W is the third print displayed.
    (C) N is the third print displayed.
    (D) S is the fourth print displayed.
    (E) S and M are both displayed.

22. The best answer is E. Again, draw a new picture. If O is the first print, W cannot be displayed. Eliminate choice B. N and T must be displayed on pages 3 and 4.

0	1	2	3	4	5
	O		N	T	
			T	N	

Eliminate choices C and D. And there's no room for P and Q. Eliminate choice A.

23. Collies are the most frequently purchased dogs at dog breeding farms. Clearly, collies' superior performance in dog shows makes them popular dogs to buy as pets.

    Which of the following, if true, would most seriously weaken the claim made above?

    (A) Collies require less food and care than do most other dogs.
    (B) It is because of their glossy fur that collies place well in dog shows.
    (C) Public interest in dog shows has been surging in the recent past.
    (D) Schnauzers generally place best in show and they are extremely popular dogs to buy as pets.
    (E) Dogs that place well in shows invariably are the most popular dogs to buy as pets.

23. The best answer is A. Use process of elimination. Answer choices B and E strengthen the argument. Choice C is out of scope, as is choice D—the argument is about collies, not schnauzers.

SECTION 6

24. There are over fifty furniture stores in Middle Valley and not one of them charges less for furniture than does Green's Furniture Warehouse. It is clear that Green's Furniture Warehouse is the store that will provide the lowest price for furniture in all of Middle Valley.

Which of the following is an assumption on which the assertion made above is based?

(A) Customers do not have the option of shopping somewhere other than Middle Valley.

(B) The other furniture stores in Middle Valley charge more for furniture than does Green's Furniture Warehouse.

(C) The quality of the furniture at Green's Furniture Warehouse is equal to the quality of the furniture in other stores.

(D) Green's Furniture Warehouse is the most cost-effective store in Middle Valley.

(E) Other household items at Green's Furniture Warehouse are also well priced.

24. The best answer is B. Choice B fills the gap between the premise and the conclusion. The other answer choices are beyond the scope of the argument.

25. Unless there is an increase in federal spending, the national book program will fail.

Only if the national book program succeeds will the country escape recession.

There will be no increase in federal spending unless there is an increase in taxes.

If the statements above are true, which of the following must be true?

(A) If there is an increase in taxes, the country will definitely escape recession.

(B) Other programs will lose funding if the national book program succeeds.

(C) If the country escapes recession, the national book program must have succeeded.

(D) If the national book program succeeds, the country will escape recession.

(E) To escape recession, an alternate way of stimulating the economy must be found.

25. The best answer is C. This is merely a restatement of the second premise. Answer choices A and D could be true, but also could be false. Choices B and E are out of scope.

Afterword

ABOUT THE PRINCETON REVIEW COURSE

The Princeton Review GRE Course is a six-week course to prepare students for the GRE.

Students are assigned to small classes (no more than twelve to fifteen students), grouped by ability. Everyone in your math class is scoring at the same math level; everyone in your verbal class is scoring at the same verbal level; everyone in your analytical class is scoring at the same logic level. This enables your teacher to focus each lesson on your problems because everybody else in your class has precisely the same problems.

Each week you will cover one math area and one verbal area. Some weeks also include preparation for the analytical sections. If you don't understand a particular topic thoroughly, we won't ask you to listen to audiocassettes, as some other companies do. If you need more work on a particular topic, you can come to an extra help session later in the week. And if after coming to an extra help session, you want still more practice, you can request free private tutoring with your instructor.

Four times during the course you will take a computer-evaluated diagnostic test. Each diagnostic test is constructed according to the statistical design of actual GREs. The computer evaluation of your diagnostic tests is used to assign you to your class, as well as to measure your progress. The computer evaluation tells you what specific areas you need to concentrate on. We know how busy you are. We don't ask you to spend time on topics you already understand.

Princeton Review instructors undergo a strict selection process and a rigorous training period. All of them have done exceedingly well on standardized tests like the GRE, and most of them have gone to highly competitive colleges. All Princeton Review instructors are chosen because we believe they can make the course enjoyable as well as instructive.

Our materials are updated each year to reflect changes in the test design and improved techniques.

ARE YOUR BOOKS JUST LIKE YOUR COURSES?

Since our SAT book first came out in 1986, many students and teachers have asked us, "Are your books just like your courses?"

No.

We like to think that this book is fun, informative, and well-written, but no book can capture the rigor and advantages of our course structure, or the magic of our instructors. It isn't easy to raise GRE scores. Our course is spread over six weeks and requires class participation, diagnostic exams, and some homework.

Moreover, this book cannot contain all of the techniques we teach in our course for a number of reasons. Some of our techniques are too difficult to explain without a trained Princeton Review teacher to explain and demonstrate them. Also, this book is written for the average student. Classes in our course are grouped by ability so that we can gear our techniques to each student's level. A 500-level Princeton Review student learns different techniques from those learned by a 400- or 600-level Princeton Review student.

IF YOU'D LIKE MORE INFORMATION

The Princeton Review offers courses in hundreds of cities around the country and around the world. For the office nearest you, call 1-800-2 REVIEW.

The Princeton Review
Diagnostic Test Form ○ Side 1

1.

YOUR NAME: _____
(Print)   Last   First   M.I.

SIGNATURE: _____ DATE: ___ / ___ / ___

HOME ADDRESS: _____
(Print)   Number and Street

_____
City   State   Zip Code

PHONE NO.: _____
(Print)

IMPORTANT: Please fill in these boxes exactly as shown on the back cover of your test book.

2. TEST FORM
_____

3. TEST CODE

4. REGISTRATION NUMBER

5. YOUR NAME

First 4 letters of last name				FIRST INIT	MID INIT

(Bubble columns A–Z)

6. DATE OF BIRTH

MONTH	DAY	YEAR
○ JAN		
○ FEB		
○ MAR		
○ APR		
○ MAY		
○ JUN		
○ JUL		
○ AUG		
○ SEP		
○ OCT		
○ NOV		
○ DEC		

7. SEX
○ MALE
○ FEMALE

SCANTRON® FORM NO. F-592-KIN
© SCANTRON CORPORATION 1989 3289-C553-5
ALL RIGHTS RESERVED.

Begin with number 1 for each new section of the test. Leave blank any extra answer spaces.

SECTION 1

1 Ⓐ Ⓑ Ⓒ Ⓓ Ⓔ
2 Ⓐ Ⓑ Ⓒ Ⓓ Ⓔ
3 Ⓐ Ⓑ Ⓒ Ⓓ Ⓔ
4 Ⓐ Ⓑ Ⓒ Ⓓ Ⓔ
5 Ⓐ Ⓑ Ⓒ Ⓓ Ⓔ
6 Ⓐ Ⓑ Ⓒ Ⓓ Ⓔ
7 Ⓐ Ⓑ Ⓒ Ⓓ Ⓔ
8 Ⓐ Ⓑ Ⓒ Ⓓ Ⓔ
9 Ⓐ Ⓑ Ⓒ Ⓓ Ⓔ
10 Ⓐ Ⓑ Ⓒ Ⓓ Ⓔ
11 Ⓐ Ⓑ Ⓒ Ⓓ Ⓔ
12 Ⓐ Ⓑ Ⓒ Ⓓ Ⓔ
13 Ⓐ Ⓑ Ⓒ Ⓓ Ⓔ
14 Ⓐ Ⓑ Ⓒ Ⓓ Ⓔ
15 Ⓐ Ⓑ Ⓒ Ⓓ Ⓔ
16 Ⓐ Ⓑ Ⓒ Ⓓ Ⓔ
17 Ⓐ Ⓑ Ⓒ Ⓓ Ⓔ
18 Ⓐ Ⓑ Ⓒ Ⓓ Ⓔ
19 Ⓐ Ⓑ Ⓒ Ⓓ Ⓔ
20 Ⓐ Ⓑ Ⓒ Ⓓ Ⓔ
21 Ⓐ Ⓑ Ⓒ Ⓓ Ⓔ
22 Ⓐ Ⓑ Ⓒ Ⓓ Ⓔ
23 Ⓐ Ⓑ Ⓒ Ⓓ Ⓔ
24 Ⓐ Ⓑ Ⓒ Ⓓ Ⓔ
25 Ⓐ Ⓑ Ⓒ Ⓓ Ⓔ
26 Ⓐ Ⓑ Ⓒ Ⓓ Ⓔ
27 Ⓐ Ⓑ Ⓒ Ⓓ Ⓔ
28 Ⓐ Ⓑ Ⓒ Ⓓ Ⓔ
29 Ⓐ Ⓑ Ⓒ Ⓓ Ⓔ
30 Ⓐ Ⓑ Ⓒ Ⓓ Ⓔ
31 Ⓐ Ⓑ Ⓒ Ⓓ Ⓔ
32 Ⓐ Ⓑ Ⓒ Ⓓ Ⓔ
33 Ⓐ Ⓑ Ⓒ Ⓓ Ⓔ
34 Ⓐ Ⓑ Ⓒ Ⓓ Ⓔ
35 Ⓐ Ⓑ Ⓒ Ⓓ Ⓔ
36 Ⓐ Ⓑ Ⓒ Ⓓ Ⓔ
37 Ⓐ Ⓑ Ⓒ Ⓓ Ⓔ
38 Ⓐ Ⓑ Ⓒ Ⓓ Ⓔ
39 Ⓐ Ⓑ Ⓒ Ⓓ Ⓔ
40 Ⓐ Ⓑ Ⓒ Ⓓ Ⓔ
41 Ⓐ Ⓑ Ⓒ Ⓓ Ⓔ
42 Ⓐ Ⓑ Ⓒ Ⓓ Ⓔ
43 Ⓐ Ⓑ Ⓒ Ⓓ Ⓔ
44 Ⓐ Ⓑ Ⓒ Ⓓ Ⓔ
45 Ⓐ Ⓑ Ⓒ Ⓓ Ⓔ
46 Ⓐ Ⓑ Ⓒ Ⓓ Ⓔ
47 Ⓐ Ⓑ Ⓒ Ⓓ Ⓔ
48 Ⓐ Ⓑ Ⓒ Ⓓ Ⓔ
49 Ⓐ Ⓑ Ⓒ Ⓓ Ⓔ
50 Ⓐ Ⓑ Ⓒ Ⓓ Ⓔ
51 Ⓐ Ⓑ Ⓒ Ⓓ Ⓔ
52 Ⓐ Ⓑ Ⓒ Ⓓ Ⓔ
53 Ⓐ Ⓑ Ⓒ Ⓓ Ⓔ
54 Ⓐ Ⓑ Ⓒ Ⓓ Ⓔ
55 Ⓐ Ⓑ Ⓒ Ⓓ Ⓔ
56 Ⓐ Ⓑ Ⓒ Ⓓ Ⓔ
57 Ⓐ Ⓑ Ⓒ Ⓓ Ⓔ
58 Ⓐ Ⓑ Ⓒ Ⓓ Ⓔ
59 Ⓐ Ⓑ Ⓒ Ⓓ Ⓔ
60 Ⓐ Ⓑ Ⓒ Ⓓ Ⓔ
61 Ⓐ Ⓑ Ⓒ Ⓓ Ⓔ
62 Ⓐ Ⓑ Ⓒ Ⓓ Ⓔ
63 Ⓐ Ⓑ Ⓒ Ⓓ Ⓔ
64 Ⓐ Ⓑ Ⓒ Ⓓ Ⓔ
65 Ⓐ Ⓑ Ⓒ Ⓓ Ⓔ
66 Ⓐ Ⓑ Ⓒ Ⓓ Ⓔ
67 Ⓐ Ⓑ Ⓒ Ⓓ Ⓔ
68 Ⓐ Ⓑ Ⓒ Ⓓ Ⓔ
69 Ⓐ Ⓑ Ⓒ Ⓓ Ⓔ
70 Ⓐ Ⓑ Ⓒ Ⓓ Ⓔ
71 Ⓐ Ⓑ Ⓒ Ⓓ Ⓔ
72 Ⓐ Ⓑ Ⓒ Ⓓ Ⓔ
73 Ⓐ Ⓑ Ⓒ Ⓓ Ⓔ
74 Ⓐ Ⓑ Ⓒ Ⓓ Ⓔ
75 Ⓐ Ⓑ Ⓒ Ⓓ Ⓔ
76 Ⓐ Ⓑ Ⓒ Ⓓ Ⓔ
77 Ⓐ Ⓑ Ⓒ Ⓓ Ⓔ
78 Ⓐ Ⓑ Ⓒ Ⓓ Ⓔ
79 Ⓐ Ⓑ Ⓒ Ⓓ Ⓔ
80 Ⓐ Ⓑ Ⓒ Ⓓ Ⓔ
81 Ⓐ Ⓑ Ⓒ Ⓓ Ⓔ
82 Ⓐ Ⓑ Ⓒ Ⓓ Ⓔ
83 Ⓐ Ⓑ Ⓒ Ⓓ Ⓔ
84 Ⓐ Ⓑ Ⓒ Ⓓ Ⓔ
85 Ⓐ Ⓑ Ⓒ Ⓓ Ⓔ
86 Ⓐ Ⓑ Ⓒ Ⓓ Ⓔ
87 Ⓐ Ⓑ Ⓒ Ⓓ Ⓔ
88 Ⓐ Ⓑ Ⓒ Ⓓ Ⓔ
89 Ⓐ Ⓑ Ⓒ Ⓓ Ⓔ
90 Ⓐ Ⓑ Ⓒ Ⓓ Ⓔ
91 Ⓐ Ⓑ Ⓒ Ⓓ Ⓔ
92 Ⓐ Ⓑ Ⓒ Ⓓ Ⓔ
93 Ⓐ Ⓑ Ⓒ Ⓓ Ⓔ
94 Ⓐ Ⓑ Ⓒ Ⓓ Ⓔ
95 Ⓐ Ⓑ Ⓒ Ⓓ Ⓔ
96 Ⓐ Ⓑ Ⓒ Ⓓ Ⓔ
97 Ⓐ Ⓑ Ⓒ Ⓓ Ⓔ
98 Ⓐ Ⓑ Ⓒ Ⓓ Ⓔ
99 Ⓐ Ⓑ Ⓒ Ⓓ Ⓔ
100 Ⓐ Ⓑ Ⓒ Ⓓ Ⓔ

The Princeton Review
Diagnostic Test Form ○ Side 2

Completely darken bubbles with a No. 2 pencil. If you make a mistake, be sure to erase mark completely. Erase all stray marks.

Begin with number 1 for each new section of the test. Leave blank any extra answer spaces.

SECTION 2

1	A	B	C	D	E	26	A	B	C	D	E	51	A	B	C	D	E	76	A	B	C	D	E
2	A	B	C	D	E	27	A	B	C	D	E	52	A	B	C	D	E	77	A	B	C	D	E
3	A	B	C	D	E	28	A	B	C	D	E	53	A	B	C	D	E	78	A	B	C	D	E
4	A	B	C	D	E	29	A	B	C	D	E	54	A	B	C	D	E	79	A	B	C	D	E
5	A	B	C	D	E	30	A	B	C	D	E	55	A	B	C	D	E	80	A	B	C	D	E
6	A	B	C	D	E	31	A	B	C	D	E	56	A	B	C	D	E	81	A	B	C	D	E
7	A	B	C	D	E	32	A	B	C	D	E	57	A	B	C	D	E	82	A	B	C	D	E
8	A	B	C	D	E	33	A	B	C	D	E	58	A	B	C	D	E	83	A	B	C	D	E
9	A	B	C	D	E	34	A	B	C	D	E	59	A	B	C	D	E	84	A	B	C	D	E
10	A	B	C	D	E	35	A	B	C	D	E	60	A	B	C	D	E	85	A	B	C	D	E
11	A	B	C	D	E	36	A	B	C	D	E	61	A	B	C	D	E	86	A	B	C	D	E
12	A	B	C	D	E	37	A	B	C	D	E	62	A	B	C	D	E	87	A	B	C	D	E
13	A	B	C	D	E	38	A	B	C	D	E	63	A	B	C	D	E	88	A	B	C	D	E
14	A	B	C	D	E	39	A	B	C	D	E	64	A	B	C	D	E	89	A	B	C	D	E
15	A	B	C	D	E	40	A	B	C	D	E	65	A	B	C	D	E	90	A	B	C	D	E
16	A	B	C	D	E	41	A	B	C	D	E	66	A	B	C	D	E	91	A	B	C	D	E
17	A	B	C	D	E	42	A	B	C	D	E	67	A	B	C	D	E	92	A	B	C	D	E
18	A	B	C	D	E	43	A	B	C	D	E	68	A	B	C	D	E	93	A	B	C	D	E
19	A	B	C	D	E	44	A	B	C	D	E	69	A	B	C	D	E	94	A	B	C	D	E
20	A	B	C	D	E	45	A	B	C	D	E	70	A	B	C	D	E	95	A	B	C	D	E
21	A	B	C	D	E	46	A	B	C	D	E	71	A	B	C	D	E	96	A	B	C	D	E
22	A	B	C	D	E	47	A	B	C	D	E	72	A	B	C	D	E	97	A	B	C	D	E
23	A	B	C	D	E	48	A	B	C	D	E	73	A	B	C	D	E	98	A	B	C	D	E
24	A	B	C	D	E	49	A	B	C	D	E	74	A	B	C	D	E	99	A	B	C	D	E
25	A	B	C	D	E	50	A	B	C	D	E	75	A	B	C	D	E	100	A	B	C	D	E

SECTION 3

1	A	B	C	D	E	26	A	B	C	D	E	51	A	B	C	D	E	76	A	B	C	D	E
2	A	B	C	D	E	27	A	B	C	D	E	52	A	B	C	D	E	77	A	B	C	D	E
3	A	B	C	D	E	28	A	B	C	D	E	53	A	B	C	D	E	78	A	B	C	D	E
4	A	B	C	D	E	29	A	B	C	D	E	54	A	B	C	D	E	79	A	B	C	D	E
5	A	B	C	D	E	30	A	B	C	D	E	55	A	B	C	D	E	80	A	B	C	D	E
6	A	B	C	D	E	31	A	B	C	D	E	56	A	B	C	D	E	81	A	B	C	D	E
7	A	B	C	D	E	32	A	B	C	D	E	57	A	B	C	D	E	82	A	B	C	D	E
8	A	B	C	D	E	33	A	B	C	D	E	58	A	B	C	D	E	83	A	B	C	D	E
9	A	B	C	D	E	34	A	B	C	D	E	59	A	B	C	D	E	84	A	B	C	D	E
10	A	B	C	D	E	35	A	B	C	D	E	60	A	B	C	D	E	85	A	B	C	D	E
11	A	B	C	D	E	36	A	B	C	D	E	61	A	B	C	D	E	86	A	B	C	D	E
12	A	B	C	D	E	37	A	B	C	D	E	62	A	B	C	D	E	87	A	B	C	D	E
13	A	B	C	D	E	38	A	B	C	D	E	63	A	B	C	D	E	88	A	B	C	D	E
14	A	B	C	D	E	39	A	B	C	D	E	64	A	B	C	D	E	89	A	B	C	D	E
15	A	B	C	D	E	40	A	B	C	D	E	65	A	B	C	D	E	90	A	B	C	D	E
16	A	B	C	D	E	41	A	B	C	D	E	66	A	B	C	D	E	91	A	B	C	D	E
17	A	B	C	D	E	42	A	B	C	D	E	67	A	B	C	D	E	92	A	B	C	D	E
18	A	B	C	D	E	43	A	B	C	D	E	68	A	B	C	D	E	93	A	B	C	D	E
19	A	B	C	D	E	44	A	B	C	D	E	69	A	B	C	D	E	94	A	B	C	D	E
20	A	B	C	D	E	45	A	B	C	D	E	70	A	B	C	D	E	95	A	B	C	D	E
21	A	B	C	D	E	46	A	B	C	D	E	71	A	B	C	D	E	96	A	B	C	D	E
22	A	B	C	D	E	47	A	B	C	D	E	72	A	B	C	D	E	97	A	B	C	D	E
23	A	B	C	D	E	48	A	B	C	D	E	73	A	B	C	D	E	98	A	B	C	D	E
24	A	B	C	D	E	49	A	B	C	D	E	74	A	B	C	D	E	99	A	B	C	D	E
25	A	B	C	D	E	50	A	B	C	D	E	75	A	B	C	D	E	100	A	B	C	D	E

FOR TPR USE ONLY	V1	V2	V3	V4	M1	M2	M3	M4	M5	M6	M7	M8

ABOUT THE AUTHORS

Adam Robinson was born in 1955. He graduated from Wharton before earning a law degree at Oxford University in England. Robinson, a rated chess master, devised and perfected the now-famous "Joe Bloggs" approach to beating standardized tests in 1980, as well as numerous other core Princeton Review techniques. A freelance author of many books, Robinson has collaborated with The Princeton Review to develop a number of its courses.

John Katzman was born in 1959. He graduated from Princeton University in 1980. After working briefly on Wall Street, he founded The Princeton Review in 1981. Having begun with nineteen high school students in his parents' apartment, Katzman now oversees courses that prepare tens of thousands of high school and college students annually for tests, including the SAT, GRE, GMAT, and LSAT.

Both authors live in New York City.

NOTES

NOTES